D1112166

Advance praise for
Ashley Bristowe's *My Own Blood*

"I was completely swept away by Ashley Bristowe's book. For three days I could do nothing but read it. I felt totally immersed in her life, her struggles, and her thoughts. She writes about her son's early years, not retrospectively, but in the midst of the experience, ongoingly, from that high-stakes perspective where nothing is resolved. I don't think I will ever forget my encounter with her frankness, her devotion, her lostness, her immersion in the extremes of life, or her propulsive and urgent writing."

—Sheila Heti, author of *Motherhood*

"Most books about raising children with serious disabilities aim for optimism, and sound exactly alike. But once in a while, a gifted writer produces a brutally honest and utterly readable account of that dark, detailed, furious, unseen world, after which you can't see ordinary life the same way again. It's a rare gift, but Ashley Bristowe's *My Own Blood* is that kind of book. You need to read it, as soon as possible."

—Ian Brown, author of *The Boy in the Moon*

"This memoir is as unputdownable as the best thriller. Really, I was awake until 3 a.m. reading this true story of a sharp-witted, foul-mouthed mother losing her mind as she saves (and utterly transforms) her severely disabled son's life. Ashley Bristowe meets our collective silence about disability head-on and speaks, cries, sings and laughs in its (our) face. This is not a tidy depiction of singular heroism. It's shockingly real, painful, hilarious, and, at times, terrifying. Over and over again, she shows how we, too, each of us, can and must summon the political will and the moral courage to respect, to love and to share our power with the most vulnerable people among us. An extraordinary testament to human connection. And swearing."

—Karen Connelly, author of *Burmese Lessons* and *The Lizard Cage*

"*My Own Blood* is a look-you-in-the-eye conversation about motherhood—the glory and the wretchedness. Ashley Bristowe tells her remarkable story with ferocious candour and hard-won insights into how we regard disability and parents who grapple with its challenges. A wonderful book, just bursting at the seams with bravery, honesty and heart. My own heart beat faster as I read it."

—Gillian Deacon, broadcaster and author

"Written with spare, feisty, sparkling prose, *My Own Blood* places the reader squarely inside a human experience few could imagine but many must endure—raising a special-needs child amidst a society far less caring than we pretend to ourselves. A gripping and defiant memoir of parental commitment, distress, struggle and vindication."

—Gabor Maté, MD, author of *When the Body Says No*

"*My Own Blood* is like the clearest window pane, through which we have the privilege to observe, absorb, the extraordinary journey of love between a mother and her very special child, and also view the price she, and all of us, pay for freedom, perseverance, hope and fulfillment. A stunner of a memoir in which each sentence either sings or stings."

—Deepa Mehta, filmmaker

MY OWN BLOOD

ASHLEY BRISTOWE

A MEMOIR OF MADNESS
AND SPECIAL-NEEDS PARENTING

my own blood

RANDOM HOUSE CANADA

PUBLISHED BY RANDOM HOUSE CANADA

Copyright © 2021 Ashley Bristowe

www.penguinrandomhouse.ca

Random House Canada and colophon are registered trademarks.

Library and Archives Canada Cataloguing in Publication

Title: My own blood : a memoir of madness and
special-needs parenting / Ashley Bristowe.
Names: Bristowe, Ashley, author.
Identifiers: Canadiana (print) 20190159294 | Canadiana (ebook)
20190159367 | ISBN 9780735278165 (hardcover) |
ISBN 9780735278172 (EPUB)
Subjects: LCSH: Bristowe, Ashley. | LCSH: Bristowe, Ashley—Family. |
LCSH: Mothers of children with disabilities—Canada—Biography. | LCSH:
Parents of children with disabilities—Canada—Biography. | LCSH: Children
with disabilities—Services for—Canada. | LCSH: Children with disabilities—
Services for—United States. | LCSH: Children with disabilities—Family. |
LCSH: Children with disabilities—Care.
Classification: LCC HQ759.913 .B75 2021 | DDC 362.4/043—dc23

Text design: Kelly Hill
Jacket design: Kelly Hill
Image credits: (paint) © mustafahacalaki / DigitalVision Vectors / Getty Images

Printed and bound in Canada

2 4 6 8 9 7 5 3 1

Penguin
Random House
RANDOM HOUSE CANADA

*For the Ashley who walked into the January darkness
with nowhere to go but the river
For mothers fresh out of the genetics appointment,
headed the same way*

*And for Turner, Sloane, and Alexander
You're my favourites*

You have my blood in you.
My blood is *in you*.
      — ALEC HORBOW (OCTOBER 3, 1919—
                        JANUARY 11, 2009)

BEFORE THE START

This is the story I told myself about what happened. Not because it is a good or inspiring story, although in some ways it is. And not because it is a true story, even though it's mostly true.

This is the involuntary story—less grateful, hard-won wisdom than wounded, cornered bird-think. I scuttled through the years described here down a thin straw of windpipe. Nobody wants to nearly lose their mind, for months and months and years. It was unbearable at the time, and if I've written it right, it will be achy to read. This time wasn't fun, but we made parts of it funny, because without dark humour and authentic laughter we never could have kept on.

Anyone who claims that our society cares about people with special needs, families in crisis, mothers in general, or the exigencies of working parents can suck my strap-on. Individuals care, when there's an inescapable or financial reason that makes it impossible not to. But society at large cares not a lick. I didn't really know this before 2009. Call Past-Me an optimist. Current me isn't as naive.

I didn't come through this experience better or stronger or grateful for it (though maybe I did). I used everything I had in me, and I couldn't do it again (though maybe I could). Every moment I wasn't doing something pointed and specific and physical, I had fantasies of escape. Or was wracked with self-pity. Or fell into suicidal ideation.

I don't remember everything perfectly (who does?), and I've described some events here in a different order than they unfolded in real life, for clarity and flow. However, many of the conversations were transcribed verbatim soon after they happened (I am a journaller, and a fast typer). So everything in the story is basically true, except the parts I imagined, which felt true when I was in their grip.

If you're the sort who gets itchy when women swear or threaten casual violence for emphasis, parts of this story will make you uncomfortable. If, at those moments, you pretend I'm the *father* of this disabled boy, a man at the end of his rope, it'll all seem way more reasonable. Then ask yourself why *that's* necessary, and you'll get to some idea of the societal bullshit mothers of special-needs kids put up with when we have actual, honest reactions to sincerely fucked-up situations.

Good for you, you're growing.

PART
ONE

"nothing"
the unjust man complained
"is just" ("or un-" the just rejoined.

E.E. CUMMINGS

1.

In May 2009 I was nine months pregnant with my second child. In those last days before I delivered, our family was three: me, my husband and our four-year-old daughter. We lived in a little green house in Ramsay, a Calgary community close to the Stampede grounds. I was an editorial and portrait photographer, and a media project manager. I loved my work; I was building a solid reputation as a book runner, and was never idle. My husband, Chris Turner—whom I call Turner, in this book and in real life—was (and remains) an award-winning writer on sustainability and climate change, though earlier in his career he'd written an international bestseller about the TV show *The Simpsons*. We worked together on projects—him writing, me shooting photos, researching together—across Canada and abroad, bringing our daughter, Sloane, with us when we travelled (which was often).

Our lives were unusual in Calgary. We were some of the only full-time freelance culture workers we knew of in the city. We'd head to Toronto a few times a year to see our Ontario friends and keep our professional circles alive, but lived in the West, where being a full-time writer seemed so unlikely that for the first year after Turner arrived, people didn't believe he was working on a book. He got, "Uh, but what do you *really* do?"

I was known locally as a photographer, but my business card still had "chase producer" on it too, from my earlier work in radio, which I'd loved. Albertans' eyes would go wide, and many asked if I organized car chases for movies. I don't know why this seemed more possible to people than Turner being a full-time writer.

We lived in Calgary because my father, Bruce, is here, and my brother, John, was here, and I had other relatives in town and nearby. I'd grown up here. And the city has an international airport. We didn't see ourselves in Alberta forever, and we threw around vague plans about moving back to Asia (where we'd been for a long stint before children), or maybe buying a summer shack near Antigonish, Nova Scotia (where Turner's people are from). But by 2009 we were settled in our bungalow on Spiller Road, and Calgary tempered by lots of travel did us fine. We had a trampoline, and a cat named Loki, and we threw a big annual Christmas party. We had friends, solid neighbours, and a car that worked (this last is mandatory for survival in Calgary). It was a periodically-fancy-always-interesting life.

When I was pregnant with the second baby, we had lots of cool plans for the coming year. We'd spend three months of that summer and fall doing work and research in Europe, with the kids in tow. Turner and I each had new book projects starting later on in the year, and I had grant money for travel to Dubai in early 2010 to explore a different direction with my photography: large-scale collage.

Then, just after midnight on May 11, 2009, I went into labour. You know what I'm going to say next, because the story is clearly about to go sideways. We'd gone to bed with ten thousand ideas for the future, all of which were doable, achievable, or in progress. Less than twenty-four hours later our lives had changed totally—and forever. We now had a son, and we chose to name him Alexander.

That was the last independent, unrushed, unpanicked decision we made for years to come.

Now I have a special-needs child.

In real life I say, *He was unexpectedly born disabled. Not unexpectedly born—we totally knew he was coming. But we didn't know he'd be disabled.*

There's an edge to the "not unexpectedly born" part that strikes people as funny. Helps them relax, before I gut-punch them with the bit nobody wants to hear.

Did it work for you?

———

Here we go:

The pregnancy was normal, fine, even easy in comparison to my first. But soon after our boy arrived, it was clear there was something wrong. First "they" said it was a blood sugar problem, but then they noticed the other things—flared nostrils, a heart murmur, a forehead birthmark, strange ear folds. He couldn't breathe on his own and needed to be in NICU, in a box, on oxygen. We met with Genetics on day three, a rush referral. The doctor came right to Alexander's bedside and looked him over carefully. Dr. Innes was smart and reserved and funny, a type of man I enjoy. We might have been friends, had we met out in the regular world.

"This is a syndrome of some kind," he said, tracing two fingers down Alexander's body, like half the sign of the cross. "See the midline markers? All these things on the midline of his body, like the hernia . . . or they repeat on both sides, like the folds on his ears." He paused, and looked up. "We'll run his DNA."

They didn't find anything, that first time. We wanted to believe there was nothing to find. The nurses in NICU kept saying, "Don't worry, it's likely just routine to test him." Later, the pediatrician said, "He'll catch up."

But Genetics kept at it. Months went by. Two more DNA tests, more specific, showed nothing.

Then they found it.

Our son has a chromosomal deletion. He's missing a tiny piece off the bottom of one of his chromosomal pairs; these pairs are called alleles. Humans have twenty-three pairs of chromosomes, and they're numbered. At the bottom of one of the alleles, in Alexander's ninth pair, there's a little piece missing. It was just never made.

When this child was conceived, something went wrong, for no reason other than sometimes, something goes wrong. A tiny bit of data wasn't there in the sperm when it arrived, or in the egg when it exited my ovary, or the RNA sequence was copied incorrectly as Alexander's cells divided in those first days after conception. Then the omission replicated over and over as the little fertilized bunch went from 2 cells to 4 to 16 to 256, and exponentially forth from there, onward and expanding for nine months.

A newborn baby has about 26 billion cells. And all of those cells in our son are missing one copy of a specific gene, called EHMT-1. The other allele in his ninth pair *does* contain this gene, so our son has what's called "haploid expression": half the expression of this one gene. The role of EHMT-1 is not conclusively determined. But missing one copy of that gene on the ninth pair of chromosomes earns Alexander a diagnosis of Kleefstra syndrome.

But that came later. When he was first diagnosed, it was still called "9q34.3 telomeric deletion syndrome." Really rolls off the tongue. Fewer than seventy-five cases had been identified worldwide when Alexander joined their ranks and our whole world changed.

Turner and I got tested, and we don't have this deletion, and we're not carriers. So our son's deletion is considered *de novo*, Latin for "something spontaneous," something that's happened for the first time in our genetic line. Translation: it's not my fault and it's not Turner's fault. You might think this doesn't matter, but it matters. Being blameless is huge. When something like this goes wrong, fingers begin to point.

And as I say, we didn't know it was coming. I'd had the nuchal translucency test that checks the thickness of the fluid at the back of the embryo's neck, which was deemed normal. The related blood-work came back kind of funny, but without actual red flags. The doctors just looked at the results and said, "Huh."

When I said, *"Huh" what? Does "huh" mean anything?*, they said, "No, no, it's fine, just not what we usually see, but everything else is good. We don't need to run it again."

At about the twelve-week mark, I had an amniocentesis, mandated by the Alberta health-care system because I was thirty-five. I was the youngest woman in the waiting room and considered the amnio a formality. The procedure itself was gross and handled badly by the clinic, but the results came back "normal."

Did you know that amnios test for only the most common abnormalities? Down syndrome, cystic fibrosis, Trisomy 18—that stuff. I didn't. They can test for other things if requested, and if they'd been looking for Kleefstra syndrome, in theory they could've detected it. But there's such a low possibility of anything "going wrong" other than the handful of the most common going-wrong things that they don't test for anything else. Kleefstra syndrome itself is an impossibly rare diagnosis, one in probably tens of millions. I was a believer in statistical probability. Ruling out just the common genetic problems made sense to pre-second-baby me.

We were on holiday at my father's holiday house in Costa Rica when I called back to Calgary for the results. The nurse said, "Everything's fine, all clear. Do you want to know the sex of the baby?"

I said no, and hung up.

Done and done, back to the pool.

And five months later, Alexander was born.

2.

My water broke on the floor of our bedroom while I was on the phone with Peggy, my dad's partner. She had called to tell me that my father is proud of me, that he thinks I am an exceptional mother. It was perfect timing. If she'd phoned even ten minutes later, I would have missed that simple and generous call.

Turner hustled us out of the house and down to the car. My cousin Jana, who'd come to doula the birth, crammed in beside me and closed the passenger door as the next contraction came on. After it released, I glanced at the house as Turner struggled with the gear shift. Sloane was at the living-room window, with one hand on the glass, standing up on the back of the couch, watching us leave. Jay, Jana's husband, was behind her. I could see him speaking to Sloane, explaining what was happening. Uncle Jay, now the adult in charge, was rolling out their plan for the day. Probably something about the zoo. But Sloane didn't move, just stood at the window, big eyes looking out at me, as Turner swore and finally jiggled the vehicle into gear.

I waved hard at Sloane: *Bye-bye! Bye-bye! We're going*!—smiling big on purpose, pretending away the meconium on the floor when my water broke, ignoring the hurry. My girl and I looked at each other through two sheets of glass and across fence and grass. I saw myself there, in her, as she looked right back at me.

Everything is going to change today, yes, I wanted to tell her. *But this is our golden life. This will be good.* To her and to myself, a prayer, a susurration of wings trying to take flight, a gear belt trying to catch: *This will be good.*

We drove the back way, out the old road, and inside another

contraction I could hear myself moaning. Then my leg was cramping at the hip but there was no room to stretch. Turner went through a light on Blackfoot so red that everyone at the intersection knew our car contained a woman in labour. "I would've done that, too. Good job, Turner," Jana said. They kept reassuring each other over the din of my moos and the flaps of my hands, *Shut up shut up jesus christ you two, fucking shuddup*.

When we arrived at the hospital, Jana helped me to the elevators while Turner parked the car. Then the ride up, and standing at the desk in the intake room, the nurse going slow and making sure, because that's triage. Another woman behind a curtain off the hallway was calling out, "Allahhhh, Allahhhh." Between contractions I put my palm down hard on the counter and said to the nurse through my hair, *Let's talk about pain management right now*.

Then a delivery room, big and surgical, no windows or wallpaper. No time for an epidural to kick in, they said. This baby was coming fast and now, and I hollered loud loud very loud. A nurse told me to shush because it wouldn't help to yell. She stepped back quick and got busy in another spot because I was about to jut my soccer knee into her jaw. Nurses know these things, somehow. But Jana was perfect, Teflon, knew all the staff's names immediately, her gift alight, my beloved cousin keeping the room awake to me, this animal on the bed being torn in half.

Turner held my hand, putting his head down during the contractions, petting my hair while I clutched the bed like it was a crashing plane. Jana said my vagina opened then, like a sea creature unfurling. The baby emerged, head coming slowly as the foldy bits of me went wider and wider, and then one shoulder emerged and the rest of the baby came all at once, *plop*.

3.

The room, full of what happened, tilts back-forth as I hitch across the floor. There are three rolling laundry baskets of sheets and towels, bloody edges flung over the sides, and even dripping below. *How can there be that much blood there, and still some in me?*

There's garbage all over the floor, plastic wrappers for medical supplies—they'd used a lot of whatever those were—a few cups. Oh right, I had ice, those crushed bits from the machine. I hold my stomach up, a wobbly bag in front of me, heading for the shower. I walk barefoot, leaving bloody footprints after I step on a drip from myself when I pause to look at the wreckage.

Fuck. I can't bend down right now. *Can you wipe that, Jana, please?*

We're the only ones left in the room. As soon as I was sewn up, the staff scattered, and Turner accompanied the baby to the NICU to get his sugars checked. Jana rolls her eyes and gestures at the bloody sheets and the wrappers and the mayhem of the room.

I know, I know. But please, could you. Just the footprints. There shouldn't be bloody footprints.

"Yes, of course."

I carry earplugs everywhere. Now I put them in and the sound of my steps fades away. I can hear my bones moving from the inside as I head for the bathroom.

It is done. Wow. Proud this time. Good job, me. But why does delivering the placenta hurt like such a fucking fucker? Just when it's supposed to be over, they have to force this last thing out like something that's supposed to stay in. Jana said there was so much goo, lots of it, as they shoved at my stomach—c'mon, placenta, c'mon. The goo just came and came.

They gave me something, in the IV, so I wouldn't hemorrhage afterward. I look up at the ceiling, check the floor edges to test my visual perception. Yep, whatever's in my system isn't wonking my balance. That's good.

But hey, that morphine never hit! Jesus christ. Do nurses actually pocket ampules of morphine? That's an actual thing? Woulda been that asshole who told me not to moan. Shoulda punched her in the mouth. . . . Can you be charged with assault when you're in labour? Probably a grey zone. Still, those nurses seem to sense when you're about to come at them.

Turning on the shower, I am suddenly shuddering, frozen. I'm waiting for the water to go warm, staring at the stained curtain, hard-water yellow all along the bottom, brown flecks across. So gross. People endow wings at hospitals. I'm going to endow shower curtains. I stand there holding the IV pole, my shivers making it clatter.

The big door swings and a nurse pokes her head into the bathroom. "You done?"

Ha. *No, I am not done. I'm not even wet yet.*

"The baby has low blood sugar."

That kid is fine. I held him. He waved his arm. *Did he swallow meconium? They should suck him out.*

"I don't know. His blood sugars are low. You need to come."

Give him a bottle if it's urgent. This is my verbal consent. My milk isn't in yet, anyway. They can give him an IV if they need to. I'm giving my permission right now.

"You need to wrap it up in here."

Oh, I see. I'm being hurried along. *Is this about my son's blood sugars? Give him a bottle.*

She's standing there like she's going to wait for me, so I roll the IV pole away and part my legs to show the insides of my thighs. I'm naked except for a necklace. *I smell all like blood. I need to get washed.*

She says, "We need the room," and leaves. I put the earplugs back in.

I see in the mirror that my lips are blue, but this is just the post-birth crash. The shower is finally warming, and I stand in the fabulous blast, stretching, ticking down from the labour, gathering up the calm, the post-birth fugue. My body mine again now, finally unsticky. My fingertips start to *pew-pew* with little zings, vestibular antennae waking, a different wash of hormones starting.

And looking down, I smile at my thick flipper feet, those sausage toes. I know what's happening this time. I've done this before. *I'll pee all that fluid out over the next few days.*

I've been in the shower for three minutes when the door pushes open. It's the nurse again: "We need the room. You need to get out."

After Sloane's birth I had a nurse roll her eyes at me when I couldn't pee fast enough, my legs still frozen from the epidural. She was holding me over the toilet, saying, "You're done. You're done." (I was not.)

If flipping the room for the next labouring mother is important, cleaning up the general carnage out in the labour area will need to happen before me being in the shower is the problem. Over her shoulder I don't see anyone picking up the place. I pull the curtain back and stare right at her, hard. *I just got in here. I'm freezing.*

I just gave birth without drugs and I'm still pulling black clots out of my pubic hair, feeling gloriously empty and human for the first time in three-quarters of a year. So she can just fucking wait. *It's important I don't get hypothermic. Give me a second to warm up.*

She doesn't move, so I make my voice pointy: <u>Please</u>.

She leaves.

As the door is slowly falling closed, Jana pokes her head in, then steps into the room. "I'm going to get coffee and call Jay. They took your stuff to the ward. They'll tell you where. You good?"

Yeah.

"She really wants you out of here. I think her shift is over. Were you mean to make her go away?"

Yeah.

"Well, they still need to clear it and nobody's come to do that, yet. If you don't need me, I'm going downstairs. I'll come back later."

Yes. I'm good. Thank you for everything, Jana—thank you. And when you call, ask about Sloane. Let Jay tell her it's a boy.

"Okay. . . . Good job, Mama!" She leaves. Fucking superstar.

After another minute I turn off the shower. I'm finally warmed, glowing. My teeth are chattering from the after-birth shock, but it's okay. Time to start this new phase, this new era, this two-child world.

I wrap myself in towels and rub hard, drying off. Jana left some warmer-drawer blankets on the counter, so I put on a hospital wrap and then layer four of the blankets over my shoulders. I am a post-natal hunchback walking barefoot again through the birthing room (wrappers still on the floor, but Jana has gathered them into one area and pushed the drippy bloody laundry over to the door).

I should probably be wearing shoes. . . . I wonder where my shoes ended up.

Across the hall in NICU I find Turner sitting in a rocking chair, lightly patting the wrapped boy's bum. Everything seems fine. The baby seems fine. He is tiny, as new babies are. I take him and sit in Turner's place.

He good?

Turner stretches, his voice stretches. "Yeah, he seems good. They say his blood sugars are low, but he's not crying or anything." Turner has been up since early-early and had to endure fifteen minutes of close-range needle phobia as nursing students tried and failed to find a vein on me mid-labour. And now he's got a son. It's been a big day.

I look at my new baby. There is a huge red birthmark on his forehead that continues between his brows and all the way down to the tip of his nose. *Look at that stork bite. Wow. Remember Sloane's at the base of her hair?*

Turner nods. "Is that permanent?"

It'll go down after a few days. Just the stress of the birth canal on his head. I stroke the baby's hair, pull away the blankets and put him to breast. My little boy lightly flails one arm, delicately brushing at my nipple underhand with his fingertips. Then he starts bonk-nuzzling back and forth across my boob, and latches softly. Easy. I don't have any milk yet, but he should get some colostrum.

That's a lot of hair, hey? And look at his ear, all folded. That's neat.

Turner is rubbing his head with both hands, scratching at his beard, exhausted. "Yeah, they're both like that."

Both ears? Wait a minute. I pull the baby off and shift him to look at the other side of his head. *They match. Weird.*

Turner: "Yeah, well, who knows? He's got a hernia, too."

What?

"They said it was no problem, just a little hernia on his belly. Like, above his belly button."

I unwrap the baby more. The hernia is a little bubble poking out above his umbilical cord (itself still blue and soft, newly clamped). It looks like his abdomen wall is split. Like the muscle didn't form properly, didn't come all the way together. *But they said it was okay? Will it need surgery?*

"The guy was only here for a minute. The one nurse said it isn't urgent, that it could be fixed later. Like, when he's older." Turner seems unworried. I wrap up the baby again and put him back on my breast. He latches again. What a champ. I look up at Turner. *God, so much easier than Sloane, eh?*

"Maybe it's true what they say about second babies."

Speaking of—let's take some pictures. I don't want this kid to say Sloane has all the pictures.

And here is the pivot point, the start of our car accident, the slow-motion slide off the road. As we are getting out the camera, a nurse is coming toward us. Looking back, I know it starts here.

Soon, doctors are coming and going, each pushing a computer on a trolley, trailing teams of students, not saying much within earshot. The baby is quiet and floppy, doesn't seem quite awake. The nurses come check on him every fifteen minutes. They say, "He's just a bit preemie, you probably got your dates wrong."

But I know my dates aren't wrong. This baby is full term and more.

Night comes to the NICU and they send me to the ward down the hall. The boy will stay here, in his isolette. They'll let me know if they need me. "Go get some sleep. You've earned it."

Jana and Turner settle me into my part of the shared room just as the day hits me full in the chest. Suddenly I'm so tired I catch myself falling asleep perched on the edge of the bed. A minute later my cousin is literally tucking me in, pushing the sheets under my shoulders and legs, and Turner getting the lights, when a nurse comes running in: "You need to go to NICU now. NOW. There's an emergency. HURRY."

What is it? What's wrong with the baby?

She looks very worried. "I can't say. Just go now. Go right now."

I tell Turner to run. Jana helps me into a wheelchair and pushes me fast fast down the hall, through the doors, down the unit, into the room where our baby is lying unattended at his station. He is bright red in the face, but crying so quietly we can't hear him. We push the call button and a voice comes on. "Hello?"

Me: *What? What is the emergency? They told us to hurry. No one is here.*

"I'll check."

Eventually a nurse comes in and shuts the door behind her. We are braced, waiting. I have one hand on the baby, protecting him. The nurse says, "Okay. So we need to get your permission to bottle-feed him. He's bringing up the milk you gave him earlier."

Wait, what? I look at her, confused and ready to be blazing mad. *We already gave consent. Verbally, several times, and plus, I signed the form. I initialled it before we went to the ward.*

She pulls up his file, riffles through some screens. "Oh—yes. There it is. Okay, got it. Okay, we'll feed him now."

I look at Turner and Jana. It's only a bit of a relief that we came for nearly nothing. Now anger blooms in my chest. I say, *Didn't you check his chart? At the ward they ran in and said it was an emergency.*

She shifts back on her hip. "Your son is hungry, he's a newborn, he needs to eat. It's very urgent."

And we gave permission. Go ahead and feed him any way you want.

"Yes, okay. We will."

From now on.

"Yes. It's in his file now."

It was in his file before.

"Yes. It's no problem."

Jana puts her hand on my shoulder. "We were just scared," she says. "It's okay now. Now everyone's on the same page. We got it. Thank you for everything." This is why you bring your diplomatic cousin to the hospital. So you don't end up going for people's throats over "small" oversights.

The nurse smiles at Jana and moves to push buttons on the machine tracking the baby's heart rate and blood oxygen. She's pretending everything is fine. We look at each other. Turner says, "Let's go."

When we get back to the post-birth ward, they tuck me back in and leave. But even though I'm exhausted like you can only be after childbirth, I can't fall asleep. I spend all night trying to breathe off the adrenaline. Finally I get up and go to the NICU to check on the baby, hunching along the hallway in my hospital gown. I sit with the baby for fifteen minutes, then return to bed. In another hour, I'm back at the boy's isolette. And again another hour later. When Turner comes in the morning, he looks punch-drunk but rested. I haven't slept at all.

My father, Bruce, comes to the NICU wearing his hospital ID so he can enter without questions. This morning there's been different doctors coming in and out, looking at the baby's birthmark and hernia. They've found a heart murmur, too. I tell Dad about the new referrals to various departments, including Genetics. He says it's good that things are happening, that things are moving along, that I'm "accepting" them. I don't know what that means. He's being a doctor and a dad now, holding my shoulder, looking away from the baby.

Then Bruce says suddenly, "We'll get him the best. We'll take him to the States."

It feels like a non sequitur. I'm still awash in postnatal optimism. *Oh, Dad. We won't need to take him down there. Look at everything we have here.* We are surrounded by first-world health care, nurses puttering on all sides, specialists. It seems unnecessary, preposterous, to do anything other than what they tell us to do, here. *He'll be fine. I'm sure he'll be fine.*

(We will take him to the States.)

We have to leave the baby behind in NICU when I'm discharged.

This child isn't able to keep his feeds down. He regurgitates everything. I'm sure he swallowed some meconium during the birth and I've asked repeatedly for his stomach to be sucked out. Finally, at three o'clock one morning, with a sympathetic nurse to back me up, I convince the exhausted on-call resident to approve a stomach flush. Afterward, the baby's blood sugars rebound immediately. The nurse and I catch each other's eyes and nearly high-five.

She says, "Go home and get some rest. He's going to be fine." I get my things and drive back to our house under a navy pre-dawn sky.

I crawl into bed with Turner and doze-wake-doze for a few hours, never falling into full sleep. I haven't slept since the birth. Something is keeping me wary, watching, ready.

When I get back to the hospital mid-morning, I'm met in the hall by another nurse. She tells me that after I went home, Alexander's oxygen levels collapsed. I go to his incubator. On his bedside chart I see they had to revive him—that his heart stopped. As I'm sitting there, holding the baby, he desats again, with alarms ringing and nurses and doctors rushing in, and again. They arrange to put him on oxygen, little tubes bunched into his nose. What is going on?

Alexander, I can feel you loving me from where you're lying in that NICU incubator. The box has a little door, and when I put my hand in, when I gather the tubes and lift you, so light, mostly blanket, to my chest, my hand patting pat-pat against the flannel, there is a wave from you, a wash, sloshing over us both. There is a pure note in the air, unmistakable. It is your gratitude.

I tell the baby, *Turner is Dada. He's calling you the little green mango. Just not ripe yet.*

Let that be it. Let that be it.

(I know that's not it.)

The nighttime collapse and continuing problems make the NICU doctors look more and more closely at the baby. They make more referrals, more urgent calls for the other physiological problems and issues Alexander is presenting.

Then people start to ask us, "Who does he look like?" They suspect something big, but they want me to be the one to say it.

I say he looks like his sister, which is true. Alexander is very like us, except small and reddish, and with ever-half-closed eyes. Under the bleach smell of the isolette and the stink of Pampers, he smells like mine. The back of my throat and my chest say he is mine. I made this one, we made him, he's ours.

The boy is dozing on the tray inside the box, floppy flat, and I'm in the chair alongside. *He sucks but won't turn to sound. He cries but there's no noise to it.* The worry catches up with me, reaches up under my scalp for real.

There is something wrong.

Then I notice at last that we're not even in the regular NICU. For days we've been in a special room with a sliding glass door, right beside the doctors' station. We are separate from the rest of the unit. . . . *Why are we in a special room?*

There's a huge sticker on the wall in here: BELIEVE. In a stupid scrapbooking font.

Oh no. Believe in what? Children die in the NICU.

This boy, my boy, died right here and they brought him back, and they still don't know why his oxygen levels are low. I am suddenly clutched with hate for the sticker. *Fuck you, sticker.* I want to rip it off the wall.

Believe what? Believe that this is okay? This is not okay.

As a teenager, one Christmas I saw an elderly mother in a dirty winter jacket leading her past-middle-age daughter with Down syndrome down the escalator at Southcentre Mall. The woman was resigned, broken, needing care herself; her daughter was vacant, grey-haired, submissive. The younger woman had her head back, looking at the oversized decorations hanging from the roof high above, gaping, mouth open.

Now from this hospital rocker, inside the mesh netting walling us off from the other plastic boxes and machines, I'm remembering spectres I've seen out in the world. A boy in the back seat of a car in the community association parking lot, rhythmically hitting his head, yelling. The monster brother in chains in the movie *Goonies*. I see a drooling, slack-necked child with a flat-tray wheelchair coming toward us, moaning his way through our days. . . . Are we spooling toward that? *What is going on?*

This boy is just a tiny thing, with peeling waffle tape holding the feeding tube onto his cheek, all maroon veins against blotchy skin. But is he actually an engine, blasting sideways silently in the vacuum of this special room, shoving us off our planned trajectory? Acceleration G-forces are pinning me harder and harder to the seat. Nobody will say it, but they are hinting.

My breath smells like something's burning. *No. . . no. . .* I've been awake since three days ago. This was already very not-how-it-was-going-to-be.

And now fate pounds at the portal: *Are you. . . disabled, boy?*

I need out of this room, away from the sticker. Cut the engine. I don't BELIEVE.

The last moment I remember being Ashley-before-all-this is at the hospital elevator.

Turner and I have left Alexander in the NICU and are waiting in the hallway. The unit nurses are sombre with us, now. The doctors are telling us less and less each time they visit the special room. The baby's been needing more and more oxygen to keep his levels up. They're watching his heart closely. He's scheduled for a special kind of echocardiogram. They tell us things are much more complicated than they initially thought. Their faces say that it's bad.

I push the down button. Turner and I are silent. We aren't holding hands, but we're standing close, our upper arms and shoulders touching. We are orbiting each other as our son lies probably-dying fifteen metres away, beyond the elevator shaft and past the hallway where they keep tubs of tiny clothing.

There is something wrong with the child I pushed out in that room just down the hall. We can't talk to anyone about it, because we don't know what to say. There is a clench of the unspoken about these unexplained problems, staff whirling by, tutting, not explaining. Every hour of these two days and three days and four days is a prayer of *please* and *please*.

But in this moment, at the elevator, I feel a sudden lift in my chest. I turn and grab Turner's arm. And I say the thing bubbling up in me, so inappropriate: *Our wonderful life is still here.*

Everything in Turner's face is, "How can you say that? We just left our probably-dying son. . . . We both know he's probably-dying now." All that in his face.

But I have the radiance of a true believer. I feel the heat of it in my face as I smile. I have only the one thing to say, and I know it is true. I tell him: *Whatever happens, we will be okay. Our wonderful lives are still there. Even if . . .* [I wave my hand back toward the door of the NICU]. *We are okay.*

Turner softens. Is Ashley seeing a way through? He shakes his head, not in a negative. "But, holy shit."

I leap on it. *Yes, holy shit! Right? And my milk is going to come in any second now and then REALLY holy shit!* (We both remember how, last time, my breasts seemed to grow ten sizes in an hour.)

Turner lets himself chuckle. We know how to do irreverence. He takes a step away from the holy-shittedness for a second. Enough for a breath. Enough to put some space between us and everything that's been happening the last few days.

This is us, still. We are still here, our wonderful lives are still here, in this. I am saying breathe. We are so fucking lucky to have found each other, yes. And we've made amazing interwoven careers, yes. We have this articulate, maddening four-year-old who is half of each of us, a being we *made*. She is at playschool right now, and we have to be there to pick her up in forty-five minutes or they'll give us crap for being late again. Yes.

This next thing? What the fuck. But—we can do it. We can handle it. Because our amazing life is still with us, still in us. Who we are won't change. We will be okay. We will be okay, we will be okay.

I'm looking right at him, into him. I see Turner wanting to believe me.

The elevator arrives. *Our wonderful life is still here.*

. . . And what I mean, of course, is . . . *if he dies.* I don't say that, but that's what I mean. The hand wave toward the NICU doors: our wonderful life is still here, if that baby dies. Turner knows that's what I mean, and you know it too.

Our new son has been wavering between pale and limp, limp and pale, with cords coming out of his blankets at all angles. The machines all ping slower than the doctors say they should be pinging. His chart reads: *Blood sugar unstable. Low O2, HR lapse. Resuscitated, 4:10am.* It is twenty, fifty, seventy-five hours, and things are getting worse and they don't know why. "Start preparing yourself," the nurses' faces say.

Our son, born blue, with his folded ears and oxygen problems and heart defect, is probably not coming home. That reality is getting bigger. The gift, through that horror: He *will* die.

I let myself think it, without letting myself feel it. It is the natural end to this guttering limbo. We wanted another child, but we got a dying boy. We have him now, and he will live for as long as he lives, and then he will be gone.

When he dies, we'll still be here. And we will be okay, eventually, because there will only have been a truncated beginning. We can get pregnant again. Or Sloane will be an only child with a delicious solo childhood full of cousins and dogs and trips and friends. We'll focus on her, and our work, and our house. Our projects. Our garden. Our families.

We'll grieve, and we will always think of him, our son, who'd been hypotonic at birth and then went hypoxic for no reason, really, and then descended from there. And we will stare into the middle distance for a long time, and over the years it will become family-mythologized, the birth of our little boy, who died.

A part of us will always be sad. But we'll get on with our amazing life, together.

We go into the elevator. I hold Turner's hand now, calm, looking up at the numbers. Believing—*knowing*—we'll be okay.

It is sad, very, very sad, but there is a way out.

(I had no plan if he lived.)

4.

I can't breathe. I can't sleep, and I can't dream, and I can't breathe.

I think, *I should be fine*, because nothing here at home has changed. The walls are the same colour they were, the lilacs still grow beside the house, the stovetop is still smooth under my hand.

But I lie in bed (same duvet cover, same cheap sheets) and can't bring in enough air. Pushing my neck back, craning it—I finally understand this term. My chin is the top of a gooseneck bend as I reach for breath from the window. In the night, I sit up, cross-legged, next to sleeping Turner, and push my face into the screen, my nose and lips, my tongue. *Come into me, air. Come on, I need you.* My moments of unconsciousness now are stuffed with hallucinatory scenes that jolt me awake, and I feel like I'm choking. Really, I don't sleep for five days after the birth. (Five days is too long to not sleep.)

The public-health nurse comes for the postpartum checkup. I am on the verge of asking her about psychiatric resources when she takes my blood pressure. "You're going to Emerg," she says. Apparently 140/90 is not okay when you've just had a baby.

I sit in Emergency for hours and hours. I make it inside the unit doors, to a bed, and am up next to be seen. But my boobs are rocks. I need to go upstairs to nurse the baby. I know he is hungry four floors away. I tell them, twice, *I'll only be gone fifteen minutes, just to* NICU, *just to nurse my baby. I've-been-here-seven-hours-and-my-baby-in-*NICU-*needs-to-eat. I'll be <u>right back</u>.*

And they say, "Oh, god, yes! Go, go! We'll hold your spot, don't worry, you can come right back."

Fifteen minutes later, I return. Some dude holding his arm is in my bed. The shift has changed. When I go to the desk, a male nurse I've never seen says, "You left. We took you out of the system. You can't just stand up and leave. You have to go back to the waiting room and start again."

I could have flipped a gurney. Are you kidding me? Instead, I say, *I was up in the* NICU. *I cleared it with two nurses. Everyone said I could come back.*

He counters with a hard no.

I call Bruce. My dad is working just down the hall, in radiology, and he arrives in sixty seconds. I sit in a chair in the not-in-not-out Emerg hallway while Dr. Bristowe walks back and forth, talking to the staff. They still want me to go to the waiting room outside and get back in line.

My father has worked in this hospital for thirty years, done favours, moved dates and expedited cases and taken special care of anyone colleagues have asked him to. But everyone working in Emerg today is newer, younger, and they don't know him or owe him. He is hurt and mad. "Stay put," he says and shoulders through the exit. Five minutes later he is back, and grabs my chart from under the nose of a nurse. I leap up and run along behind him, down the long hospital corridors to Internal Medicine. A doctor checks me over, a friend of a friend of a friend of my dad's. As a clinic nurse takes my blood pressure, the doc says, "Your dad really wants you seen." Good ol' Brucie.

The internal medicine guy puts me on blood pressure medication and hands me four Ativan to help with sleep. My father says, "Thankyou-thankyouBenthankyou," shaking his hand hard, holding his arm. (Later, Bruce will send him wine.) They both tell me to go home.

I start for the parking garage, but I watch and after my dad and the internal medicine guy walk away, I double back to the elevators and return to NICU. There's no just "going home" in the midst of this.

After two weeks in intensive care, Alexander is released from the hospital. He's breathing on his own, his stats just-high-enough without supplemental oxygen. He's not going to die. So now we're in the what-now phase of whatever is next.

When I bring the baby home, Turner is in the basement, at his desk, scrabbling among his papers, reorienting. Sloane is at play-school up the street, safe for the rest of the day. Now Alexander is on the living-room floor in the Moses basket, shifting under old blankets, soundless. And I am on the couch with Bruce.

My dad and I are just sitting together in the quiet of the house, the Friday sun at our backs through the big picture window. There's been no baby here for two weeks and nothing much for the helper I'd hired (before Alexander was born) to do, so she's been cleaning. Piles of folded laundry line the kitchen island, the carpet in here is vacuumed, the windows have been washed. This is definitely the cleanest this house has ever been.

When we brought Sloane home, we had a huge sushi party. Ours was a house of high delight that night, a homecoming celebration for the first grandchild, the first niece and great-niece, the first little baby in our Calgary circle.

In attendance:

• My mom, Valerie, a nurse and psychiatric counsellor, who'd come from British Columbia to attend the birth,

• My brother, John, who'd bought the house three doors down from us so we could raise our children together,

• My uncle Leo, an itinerant old hippie who lived with my dad,

• My aunt Jacqueline, a teacher and theatre director in nearby Canmore,

• My cousin Tanya, at the time a snowboard bum living in Lake Louise,

• My cousin Jana and her husband, Jay, Sloane's guardians, who lived in Calgary,

• And my father, Bruce.

Now it is four years later and we have come home again. Same scene, different baby. This tiny boy's arrival isn't a party. The worry and mystery around this child has sucked up the new-baby momentum. Over the last few weeks, people have left flowers at our back door and dropped off lasagna for the freezer. But all the air has leaked out of the welcome-home balloons. The house is empty.

I look around at the chairs and places on the floor where my family and my loves sat four years ago:

- My mother, Valerie, mostly gone from our lives,
- My brother, John, partnered up and moved to the far-south suburbs,
- My uncle Leo had a stroke a few years back, and now lives at a rehab facility north of the city,
- My aunt Jacqueline, at home in Canmore, readying for a move to the West Coast,
- My cousin Tanya, at university in Vancouver, studying engineering physics,
- My cousin Jana and her husband, Jay, who you met, who were here for the birth, but are now back at their lake house in Ontario, where they'd moved a few years ago,
- And my father, Bruce, sitting on the couch here with me.

Everyone else has straightforward reasons for their change in circumstances. But that my mother isn't here is a whole other story, like all parent-child troubles are. Her absence—her flat refusal to even try to be what I needed at this time—is an ache that I will carry throughout the years to come.

The first morning Alexander is home, I wake in a panic. *I slept all night. He didn't wake me up.* I lunge over the side of the bed: the baby is full-asleep in the Moses basket. I hurry to gather him up, jostle him awake. As soon as the nipple is in his mouth, he comes to and sucks so hard he chokes. . . . He's starving, but couldn't wake himself? My heart is bonking around in my chest. What two-week-old sleeps through the night?

The NICU has assigned us a pediatrician and, when the boy continues to sleep through unless I wake him, I ask what's going on. "He's too weak yet," she says. "Set alarms and wake him on a schedule to feed. He needs more calories."

Alexander is only half-conscious even when he's not sleeping. But he'll suck. So I rouse him before I go to bed, and at midnight, and at 3 a.m., and at 5 a.m. He'll sleep through to when Sloane is awake and the house is awake, and all the way until I wake him up on purpose: *Get up, kid.*

The days start to pass. I spend them carrying this half-conscious baby through the house, pumping extra milk, doing dishes, and sweeping the walk with the boy strapped to my front. Turner and I are finding a new routine, balancing the one-more-child care and our ongoing work projects. The moon was full the day before Alexander was born, bright in the sky as Jana and I walked the stairs on Scotsman's Hill, trying to bring on labour. By the June strawberry moon, Alexander is four weeks old.

Today I carry him around town, doing errands, getting ready for our departure for Europe. The staff at The Camera Store let me feed him in a storeroom, a big room jumbled full of broken equipment and photographic sales stands, all nice and shadowy and dark. The outside world falls away, leaving just me and this wee squirming child. There's such peace in some motherhood moments. I'm here, breathing in time with my boy, stroking his cheek as he eats.

But someone has pushed the mute button on this kid. Sometimes I peek into the folds of his blankets and find him all squished-faced, struggling with almost no sound, no breath, and I pull him out, stabbed in the throat with worry: *What? What, Baby? What's going on?* The change in position and fresh air on his legs is enough to soothe him, and he relaxes. The half-mast eyelids sink. He's gone again.

This happens while I'm clearing weeds from the garden one day. I stand there in the yard, holding the baby in front of me. We live on a commuter artery, and this old community is just starting to gentrify. Cars zoom past our house, people flooring it home, or looking to score, or perusing the real estate. If I'd been driving down Spiller Road today, I would've seen a woman with a crazy bun, in Crocs and a stretched-out shirt, holding the tiniest baby you've ever seen—*God, could that kid be more than a few days old?*—at arm's length, turning him around and over, checking his back and staring at his face, examining him like some unexpected artifact she'd just yanked out of the garden. *What . . . are you? What do I do with you?*

—

Alexander at ten weeks is little. Really, really little. I am walking through Eau Claire Market and a woman asks how old he is.

Two months, I say.

"He's really little," she says.

Yes, I know.

She puts her hand on my arm. "No. He's *really little*."

I step back, pulling my arm away. *YES. I KNOW.*

Then I punch her in the boob.

No, I don't. But I stalk away, thinking for a long time about all the things I should have said.

See? Even now, years later, I'm still thinking about it.

The pediatrician is being a shithead about Al's weight. When she weighs him at checkups, she sighs and tells me to feed him more. Finally, she suggests we begin adding human growth supplement to Alexander's bottle feeds.

I'm all ears. *Where do we get that?*

The doctor waves her hand around. "Just the drugstore. At the pharmacy."

We go to four pharmacies on the way home and none have heard of human growth supplement.

So Turner calls around Calgary, to four more pharmacies, then ten, then twenty-five; he calls every chain, all the little independents, and the pharmacy in the lobby of the Children's Hospital. None of them carry human growth supplement. None of the pharmacists have even heard of it. Twenty-five is a lot of phone calls to make for a guy who hates the phone.

Turner calls the pediatrician's office, and they won't let him speak to the doctor over the phone. So we head back in for another appointment the next day.

What's this growth thing called exactly? Like, specifically. We need a specific brand name or manufacturer. None of the pharmacies have heard of it.

The pediatrician says, "You're probably not using the right term. Ask for human growth supplement."

Yes. We did, exactly. They don't know what we're talking about. Turner found something online, in the US. Should we be bringing it in from the States?

She starts to look uncomfortable. "Oh, no. Don't go to all that trouble."

What trouble? She said he isn't growing, so we're trying to do what she told us.

Well, wait a minute, does our kid need this growth supplement in his feeds or not?

Pediatrician: "Yes." She reaches up and clutches the lanyard around her neck: her ID and a dangling plastic Woody from *Toy Story*.

There's nothing like what you're recommending available in Calgary, and presumably Shoppers Drug Mart carries the same stuff across the country. Right? But if we need it, we should be bringing it in. Right?

"Oh, no. You should be able to find it here."

Something's going weird here. *But it's not available. Where have your other patients found it? Where do you source it?*

Now she's backpedalling. "I don't have any in the office. I don't know specifically where parents get it. It's your responsibility to buy it. I don't have samples."

What? *We're happy to buy it, but we can't find it. Could you ask your other patients? Let us know where they got it?*

"I'm not sure if any of my other patients are on this supplement."

What? I stop. Then start again. *Have you ever seen it in real life? Is it a powder? Can we use something else? Is it basically formula? Should we add more formula to pumped breast milk, make it even thicker?*

The doctor tips her head, and then begins anew, in a talking-to-the-desperate-mother voice. "We're trying to help your baby gain weight, right? You should be supplementing his feeds. Does that make sense?" She's officious, even.

In an I'm-the-actual-mother-of-this-kid, you-can't-bully-me voice, I say, *Yes, of course, we're trying to help him gain weight. I'm breastfeeding him everything I've got and also giving him formula.*

She sighs. (She SIGHS!)

I square my body toward her. *Doctor, you suggested we put a specific supplement in his bottle feeds. YOU said it was available at any drugstore. You waved your hand* [waving my hand, like she'd waved hers] *like it was easy to find. We called everywhere and can't find it.* I stop myself and say this next bit slowly: *So we are here to figure out where to obtain the supplement you suggested we give him. The question is: Should we bring it in from the States? That's the question. It's not available here. What do you recommend?*

"Well, do you want your son to gain weight?"

I want to wave my arms semaphore-style now. *Yes. Of course!*

The pediatrician turns to speak to Turner, as though he may be more reasonable. "You should be able to find it here. A supplement will be available here. Don't bring in something from the US. You don't even know if it's the same product. But you need to be feeding him more. He needs the calories. Are you waking him in the night to feed him? He should be gaining weight on a regular feed schedule."

Holy hell. This is our second child. I'm waking with rock-solid breasts three times a night and forcing them on this tiny, half-conscious kid. On top of that, I'm pumping and we mix formula with my breast milk. Of course we are feeding him regularly.

Turner knows this. He stays quiet, holding the baby, not answering her.

She reaches for the chart, ending the appointment. I want to open-palm punch her, leave a Woody-shaped dent in her sternum. (I don't.)

Doctor, you're trying to make me seem difficult, implying I am not feeding my son as often as I should or could.

I don't say this. Over her shoulder, there is a sign on the wall that reads: ABUSE OF OUR STAFF WILL RESULT IN PATIENTS BEING DIS-MISSED IMMEDIATELY FROM CLINIC CARE. These signs have appeared over the last few years at every clinic across the city. The poster is fair warning that we must swallow this gaslighting. She'll never say, "I don't like you because you caught me in a lie and I don't understand what's wrong with your son. I have other complicated patients that I do understand. I'm making you the failure here, because you have to take the blame. He's your problem." But that's what she means.

This silent kid who barely moves and we forget is in the room will need referrals and consults and whoknowswhatelse going for-ward. That storm is coming; I can smell it, electric, nearly in the room. And this pediatrician—the one assigned to us by the hospital, in this city and at a time when finding a pediatrician is impossible—is the key master and gatekeeper. We need her.

She looks at her watch. (For real.) It's silent in the exam room, and we can hear each other breathing.

So into the silence I finally say: *Okay. Well. Thanks for your time today. We'll try to find the supplement in Calgary.*

She audibly exhales.

Holy shit. Turner puts his hand on my hip, pulls me toward him. I turn and take the baby. I'm shaking.

The doctor pulls the door open. "Yes. Well, let me know. Good luck with everything."

It's midday in July, but the parking tower is dark. I sob, leaning against the car, while Turner holds me. Alexander is on my chest, mashed between us in the sling, ten pounds of barely-there and all-questions-no-answers.

We stand there, sweating and adrift and hating our kid's doctor. No rudder or recourse.

The next day I am at my desk, again holding Alexander out in front of me, looking at his body falling long and floppy from my hands. I don't know how to feed him more. Could we thread a tube up his nose, like in the hospital? Nobody has suggested that. I'll ask Bruce. But why is he so small? Why won't he look at us? I hear someone suddenly bellow, *GROW!*

It is me, screaming into his face. That tiny, passive face. I scare us both.

My yell is so loud, so unexpected and violent, that Alexander finally howls. It is the first time.

5.

Alexander is three months old.

And yesterday, the pediatrician finally said the words: "There's something wrong." But she wouldn't say what.

When we get home, I call our friend Moonira. *The doctor is not telling us the whole story. I hate her and I can't get any information out of her. I don't think this kid can see. He might be deaf. I need you to come.*

Moonira is an occupational therapist and a specialist in pediatric feeding difficulties. She works with special-needs children every day, has done for years. I've been avoiding asking for her help because she's our friend, and she does this stuff all day. But now I need to know, and Moonira will know and she will tell me what she knows. She will tell me if it is very very bad.

Six months pregnant and radiant, Moonira arrives at our house straight from work. Alexander is on the floor, under an "activity gym" that has crinkly animals and colourful rattles he doesn't reach for hanging from plastic arches. Moonira gets down on the floor to assess him, right at his level, her face just above the carpet, looking at him, listening. She snaps her fingers at his ears, rolls him from side to side. I'm standing, then sitting, then lying on the floor beside them. Watching, watching, I'm trying to see what she sees.

Finally, she pulls up on both of Alexander's hands slowly, letting his head fall back as his shoulders lift off the floor. I know this one.

That. What is that? The doctor does that to him every time, and I've asked what it means. She says it's nothing.

Moonira: "Oh, no—no, it's not nothing. I'm testing his *tone*. His head should come up when I pull on his hands." She lifts Alexander's arms again, to show me. "See how his head is lagging, falling back? At his age we would expect that he start trying to hold it up, even a little bit, when I do this."

My stomach drops. *Ah fuck.*

She puts her hand on my arm. "It's okay, though. It's just testing where he is right now, this second. We can address his tone. He can totally get stronger. I'm just getting a baseline." This is already more information than the pediatrician has given me in three months of appointments. We need a new doctor.

Moonira has me feed Alexander so she can watch him eat. She listens to his chest. "He's not aspirating the milk—that means he's not breathing it in. That's good." She checks the formula we are using for supplementation and the nipples on the bottles we're using, and suggests I cut the holes a little bigger so he can get more per suck.

She grabs a bit of Alexander's underarm, showing me. "See this? That's nice fat. Sure, he's not a chunky baby. But he's got an okay base layer. He has an actual bum. He's small, but he's just growing at his own rate. Don't worry about that weight percentile chart. Just keep feeding him super-regularly."

I say, *But the pediatrician . . .*

She waves a hand. "*Don't* stress too much about what the pediatrician is saying. She doesn't sound very supportive. Not all doctors are ideal fits."

Moonira sits back on her heels and smiles. "Okay. Ashley, overall, this is what I'm seeing: he *is* delayed. I think you already know this and it's scary."

My heart stops altogether. Here we go.

She goes on. "*But* I am absolutely seeing evidence that he can see and that he can hear. Hearing in little kiddos is hard to assess, though, so you should get a referral to the hearing clinic at the hospital. But I am certain he is not deaf. So that's good!" She beams at me. . . . Okay, I believe her.

"The thing that's making you feel like he can't see is actually his *attention.* He isn't *attending* to sounds and movement in the way we would expect." She grabs both my hands. "But there is a *lot* of *hope.*"

She shakes my hands together, up and down: Pay attention. "Ash, he is *lovely*. *Really* lovely. You may not feel lucky right now, but you are *lucky*. You wouldn't believe how many kiddos I see every day who don't have even one one-hundredth of his capacity."

She puts one hand on Al's belly, holding my gaze. "He's hypotonic, which means that he's floppy, but it's not affecting his eating, which can be a big problem for floppy kids. In Alexander, this [air quotes] 'hypotonia' is mainly affecting his extremities, and it can be dealt with. He may catch up. I know you will get through this and he will thrive." She points right at me. "I *know* you. I know you can handle this."

Turner has been standing at the counter, listening, for the last few minutes. I look up at him. He points at me, wiggling the finger: ["Youuuuu."]

Moonira gives us a binder that has places for Alexander's information and ways to organize his hospital visits and referrals to come. She gives us the number of a youth physiotherapy clinic and the name of a friend who works there. "Take him to physio. They'll give you stuff to do. An early start is the best thing."

After an hour with us, Moon heads out. I stand in the doorway, holding Alexander, watching her walk to her car. When she turns to wave, she sees my worried look, my resting face these days. She yells: "Stop it! You are awesome! Everything is okay!"

A cyclist going by happens to hear her, and lifts his fist as he zooms past: "Aw yeah!"

I smile, finally.

Bruce comes over two weeks before we leave for Europe. As he walks through the door, he says, "I need to talk to you about something." It sounds serious. I call Turner up from the basement. We all sit down in the living room.

My dad says, "So, ah . . . you kids need to move."

Turner and I look at each other. He knows I'm always stalking the real estate listings to see if we can trade up to an inner-city neighbourhood with some kids (or fewer crackheads), or back to Toronto.

"Lookit, this kid is going to be a trial for you." Bruce is staring into the middle distance, not at us. "You need to get somewhere that's safe, and settled, and where you can walk to get groceries. My granddaughter should be able to go up the street to play with friends on her own. That's just not possible here. This street is too busy. You need to live in a house that's going to make life with a kid like Al possible."

I think he's about to tell us to move to the suburbs, and I'm gearing up to yell, *Never!*

He pulls a paper out of his pocket. "Have you seen this place?"

I take the sheet and unfold it. It's a real estate listing in an area just northwest of downtown, far more gentrified than where we are, full of stylish infills and refurbished century homes, and bordered by shops and a huge park. I look at the price and laugh with relief at the impossibility of such a move.

Dad—no. Of course I haven't looked at this house. We love that area, but this is way more than we can afford. Our Ramsay house has doubled in value since we bought it, but with our up-down freelance incomes, the modest mortgage here is all we can carry.

"I want you to go see it," Bruce says. "I've arranged a viewing tomorrow. I think you can afford it. . . . I want to help."

So we go see the house. We step out of the car with the kids and face an actual white picket fence. It's an old two-storey with decorative stained glass windows and a huge porch. Gigantic trees line the street.

As we're waiting for the realtor to arrive, a woman stops on the sidewalk. "Oh! Are you going to buy this house? This is the best neighbourhood in the city! Do you have kids? I'm Mary! We've got lots of families on this block. You should totally buy this house!"

Inside, the place is a wreck. The electrical, plumbing, floors, doors, windows and insulation all need redoing. It will take years of work to make it a proper, functioning, finished home. But it reminds us of our old rentals in Ontario, and the location is unbeatable. And Bruce will help us make it work. It's so tempting. . . . How can we say no?

A week later we close the sale. We'll take possession in the fall, after we get back from Europe. Because we're still going. Oh, you bet your boots we are. Alexander is a bit delayed but, Turner says, "There's a spectrum of ability, right? Not every kid is going to roll and talk and walk early like Sloane. Be patient, Ash. There'll be lots of stimulation for both kids along the way. And"—he ruffles Alexander's wee head of brown hair—"at least he'll be easy to travel with!"

Groan, Turner.

Anyway, fine, we now have a new house a block from groceries and transit, two blocks from a park, three blocks from playgrounds and the drugstore. We'll ride our bikes on the river pathways, maybe we'll even get a dog. There will be paint colours to choose, new people to meet, shops to become regulars at, future trees to plant in the yard. And if we ever need the Children's Hospital, we'll be way closer . . . but let's hope it doesn't come to that. (It will.)

We head to Europe, feeling like things are moving upward and outward in our world.

6.

Europe, that summer and fall, is glorious. Far away from doctor appointments and worried faces, we dig in like well-funded big shots in Copenhagen, Berlin, Freiburg, Seville, Gibraltar. It's fabulous, the opportunity a huge privilege.

When I think back on walking Europe's cobbled streets with four-year-old Sloane, I can't find Al in those scenes. In those weeks, as he was four months and then five months and then six months old, Alexander was mostly a fuzzy-gazed ball who periodically squirmed from hunger. But that was it. Dogs licked his face and he wouldn't blink—literally wouldn't blink. I'd be wiping goober out of his eyelashes and off his eyeball, and he wouldn't flinch then, either. I just remember carrying a warm bundle all the time, with little eyes peering out of the folds of the fabric.

Copenhagen in the summertime: I'm jet-lagging, fried and awake. The futon is musty, undergrad-y under the thin sheets. Low clouds out the window are moving across the early-morning city sky. I'd dreamed of Asia, running in the rain down the nighttime Delhi street. I try to hold on to the dream, press it into my waking day: *The world is big. Remember, the world is big.*

I roll to tap Turner on the arm and he bolts up: "HUH!"

Just seeing if you were awake.

"No." He flops back, turns away from the curtain-less window, pulls the cotton sheet up over his shoulder and tucks it under his chin. He's out again.

We've been together in Copenhagen for two days. Sloane is in the living room, sleeping like a champ on a single bed out there. She came here early with Dada and spent her first days at Legoland, while Alexander and I went to Thunder Bay for the interring of my grandparents' ashes. She's already fully on Danish time, while I'm still getting into gear here.

I turn to Alexander, on the floor, tucked in a blanket bed we made for him, his eyes half-open. He's in a gentle fugue state, his early-morning normal. I pull him into the bed and snuggle around him. As he starts to eat, my milk lets down, *whoosh*. Whether he puts on weight or not, this kid's a good eater.

On a table beside the bed I've put the only book I brought to Europe with me. After Al's birth I was speaking with a friend about the medical suspicions, my frustration and fears. She connected me with her neighbour in Toronto, a woman named Gillian, whose son was born with a portion of his brain missing due to a rare infection in the womb.

Gillian had taken her son to a clinic in Philadelphia called The Institutes for the Achievement of Human Potential. There, she and her husband learned a whole training program she then ran for their son at home. On the phone Gillian told me more: a hard-core therapy schedule, essentially a structured battle plan for disabled children to catch up with (and sometimes surpass) their neurotypical peers. For a week she attended lectures on the brain with other parents from all over the world. They gave her binders full of notes and clear instructions on how to target and hit goals for her son, and then she went home and ran the program herself.

Doctors in Toronto thought that Gillian's son would never walk or speak or communicate at all. Now, after four years of full-time Institutes therapy, he is entering the regular kindergarten at their local school in September, just a few weeks away. It sounded like a miracle.

Gillian said, "This program is absolutely *not* for everyone. It's hard and you have to recruit everyone you know to help. It's every single day. No weekends. You have to change everything about your life and just give yourself over to it. But it worked for us. Something like this might work for you."

A light went on in my chest. The recognition of a destiny. One I didn't want.

Gillian suggested I order the introductory Institutes book to get a sense of the program's philosophy and history. The cover is colourful and full of text, lying spine-out on the table beside my bed in Copenhagen: *What To Do About Your Brain-Injured Child: Or Your Brain-Damaged, Mentally Retarded, Mentally Deficient, Cerebral-palsied, Epileptic, Autistic, Athetoid, Hyperactive, Attention Deficit Disordered, Developmentally Delayed, Down's Child.* Quite the title.

As Alexander and I lie on the futon beside sleeping Turner, I glance at the book. I opened it on the plane, read the first few pages. . . . But I just want to enjoy Europe, not worry about Alexander every single second of my waking life. Do I have to make myself read this thing?

Not today. Maybe tomorrow.

As Alexander finishes up, I hear Sloane stirring down the hall. Then her voice comes: "MAAAAAM?" She runs thumpity-thump into the room, dragging her yellow baba blanket and leaps onto Turner: "Ooooff."

We're all awake now.

Our girl asks, "What are we doing today?"

August in Denmark is chilly in the morning and windy in the afternoon, so we stop often for coffee to get out of the weather. While we're standing in lines, the people around me notice Alexander's face in the folds of my jacket. The Europeans just see a wee baby snuggled against my chest. "Hello, ohhh, he is lovely," they say. Sloane materializes in these moments to rub the baby's cheeks and make *moogoo-moogoo* sounds, asserting ownership over this tiny, brown-eyed focus of strangers' attention.

Being here, away and far away from home, is good for me. Good for us. We are working, trading off the kids as Turner interviews people and I do location shoots. The Danes have a way of making discipline and cheer and blankets at sidewalk cafés feel everyday-extraordinary. They step aside with bicycles to make space for me and Sloane on the sidewalk. We meet other parents in restaurants and have simple, friendly conversations of the sort that seem never to happen in Canada anymore. We rent cargo bikes and trundle out with the children to a wind farm south of the city to shoot photos.

The Fear still nibbles at my edges. This baby moved more in the womb than he does out in the world. When I pull him out of the sling, he slowly uncurls like a lamb pulled from a warming drawer. All the walking I'm doing in Europe lulls him, ambient sounds cooing him into all-day stupors. But I wake up each day and look out at the grey Danish summer sky and make sure my first thought is, *The world is big. Remember, the world is big.*

It's a down day, with no interviews. We dress the kids in matching dinosaur pyjamas and plop them on the red leather couch. Alexander is four months old today. It's our first attempt at a sibling photo shoot.

Okay, Sloaner, be good, and smile, and look at the camera. Al doesn't really look, only super-sometimes, so we have to catch it when it happens. You just keep looking at the camera, okay?

Turner: "Sloane, please just look at the camera. . . . Don't grab him. Just hug him."

Nicely, please! Okay—okay, yes. Like that. Stay like that.

"Just hold him, Sloane."

Okay—no! Sloane, please don't bunch his face like that—no. Stoppit. Stop!

". . . Okay, good." Turner is waving, up-down on tiptoe. "Hello! Mister! Hello! Can you look at the camera? Sloane and you both. Both just look." He makes kissing noises, breathy-whistling, trying to get Al to look up.

Ooh, can you be dinosaurs? Like on the pyjamas. Raaaah—dinosaurs! Both of you are dinosaurs.

"Right, Sloane? Gramma sent those PJs months ago and now they fit! So cute!"

Cute dinosaurs!

Alexander puts his hand up in a claw. Makes a face like *Raaaah.* Turner and I are both shocked.

Did you see that!?

"Yeah."

Wow.

"Yeah!"

[Looking through the digital playback on the camera] *Oh, I got it! —oh, Sloaner, no, we are not done. Sit down. Prop your brother— wait . . .*

"Just prop him up like you had him."

Sloane, hug him. Hold him! . . . No!

Sloane lets go and Alexander tips and rolls onto his face, lies unmoving on the couch.

I yank Alexander up with my non-camera hand. *Okay, okay, you're fine, it's fine. . . . Turner, if we can get a nice one of him looking, I can photoshop his face onto a good Sloane one. Sloane, can you just—*

Sloane begins to leave. Turner says, "There's an expiry date rapidly approaching here."

Sloane, no, you just . . . jesus christ Sloane, please just fucking SIT DOWN and hold your brother. Please! [Quieter:] *Sloane, we need your help. We need him to look. Just be a big girl and <u>sit there</u>.*

"Take it easy, they're kids."

Yes, but fuck's sake.

Sloane: "Oh, Mamaaaa!"

I know. You shut up. Everybody just shut up. Just sit, Sloane, hold him nice. Let us get him looking at us. <u>Don't do anything</u>, just hold him. <u>Please</u>.

Turner is tapping on the top of the flash, "Hello, Alex-AAANNNderrrr!"

Okay, yes. . . . Yes! Good boy. And good girl. . . . Let me check that one. . . . I got it! Okay, we are good. I can put this face on one of the other ones. Thank you, Sloane. . . . No, don't just drop him!

Turner: "Okay, I have him. Okay, yes, you can go."

The photoshopped version of the photo is perfect.

We have been in Berlin for a week. I don't usually like Germany, but Berlin is very tolerable. I fall off a months-long no-carbs wagon when faced with the Wiener Feinbäcker bakery display soon after our arrival. Our work here is split between talking to policy wonks and going back and forth to an area of the former East Germany where the government has helped establish an industrial solar industry.

Today Turner and I are meeting Hermann Scheer, a German MP and the architect of the German Energiewende—the country's full-scale transition to a sustainable energy model. We left Sloane with her

Berlin nanny and have set up with Alexander in a restaurant beside the Bundestag to wait. We run back and forth to the government complex, talk through the glass to the security guys. Eight hours after his scheduled time, Turner is finally admitted. My appointment, during which I'm to take Hermann Scheer's portrait, will follow.

We'd arranged a fifteen-minute break between Turner's session and mine so I could hand the baby over to him and maintain the illusion of professionalism. But Turner and Scheer hit it off so well that, when their interview ends, Scheer decides to walk Turner back and escort me into the building himself.

Turner and I are not yet adept texters, and are using numeric keypads on cheap phones. After he has been gone forty minutes, I get a ping: *Coming to restaurant 2 min out HS w/ me.*

Oh fuck. What am I going to do with Alexander?

Café Einstein, the restaurant we've used as a base, is large but quiet, with white table linens and neatly refolded newspapers for the parliamentarians and other stern men who are regulars here. We were only stopping in for pre-appointment coffees at 8 a.m., but then came the delays. We did scout the neighbourhood for another place to wait, but it is drizzling and windy, so outside isn't an option.

Another ping from Turner: *1 min.* I can feel his anxiety bubbling. We don't want to be caught looking like we schlep around an infant on work stuff. The staff here are already prickly that we've only ordered soup and coffees all day and probably changed the baby in their bathroom. I can't exactly ask a waiter to hold Alexander in the kitchen while Turner and I swap places.

This wouldn't have worked with any other four-month-old but Al: with thirty seconds left, I put him on the seat pad of the booth, bolstered on one side with a backpack. As a sweating Turner and slouchy Scheer step through the side door, I casually lay my cardigan on top of the baby and stand up to greet the men. (*Everything is fine, situation normal. How are you?*)

Half a step behind Scheer, Turner's eyes sweep the restaurant, looking at the waiters and at other patrons: ("Where is the baby? Who has the baby?")

To focus him, I say, *Hey, Turner, it was good?* He hears my calm tone: (*We're okay, we're good, proceed.*)

"Oh? –Yes. Really good." [Turning.] "Sir, let me introduce Ashley Bristowe. She's the photographer I'm working with on this project."

I shake Hermann Scheer's hand, firmly. *Hello, good to meet you.* Below, on the bench, Alexander is quiet. This is working. We are working, it is working. But oh my god, I swear next time we'll have child care for Al, too. (There is no next time.)

Turner again: "Thank you, sir. Thank you for everything. I'll send you a copy of the book. And I'll let you know when other stuff comes out of it—I'm talking to a few magazines."

Hermann Scheer has beautiful eyes, young eyes, set into the folds of his face. He's a pro, a busy and important politician, called the "solar pope." Scheer made his career about playing the long game for renewable energy in Germany over decades. He has affected energy policy worldwide. Once we're in his office, I will have to work him hard for almost an hour to get the lovely, natural shot of him at his desk that will have pride of place in my useless portfolio, a souvenir of 2009's broken trajectory. Just over a year from now he will die suddenly of a heart attack. My portrait will become the definitive photo of his later years, used now by the foundation that serves his legacy of environmental activism.

Right now, that's ahead. In this moment the only thing that could go wrong is Hermann Scheer deciding to join us at the table. I grab my camera bag and swing it hard over my shoulder. *Okay! Shall we go?*

Scheer nods. "Yes. Okay, goodbye Chris, see you."

He steps to the side to let me pass. I point behind me at the bench so only Turner will see: (*There. Al is there, under the sweater.*) Turner sits quickly and puts a hand over the pile.

As we are walking away, Alexander says "Mm!" quietly and clearly.

I hear it, Turner hears it.

Tomorrow, when the Café Einstein staff tell Scheer we had a baby with us, he will remember this sound. But he doesn't pay attention to it today.

Scheer and I walk out the door and onto the cobblestones of the grey Berlin afternoon.

—

Later, proud of the shot I got, I prance down the parliamentary stairs and out a double security courtyard door. I jog to a stop at finding Turner, with Alexander in the sling, standing in front of the café, swinging from foot to foot.

"They got sick of us in there. I don't blame them," he says.

I take the baby and put the sling over my shoulders. We have to hurry. After a whole morning on trolleys and the entire afternoon at the Berlin zoo, the nanny has been with Sloane hours and hours longer than we planned, and has called to say our girl is on strike. They are waiting for us outside the zoo gates.

Turner and I run the U-Bahn steps, and when we come into view, the nineteen-year-old nanny has a veteran's look of exhausted relief. We've made her late for a weekly dinner at her grandparents' house in the western suburbs, and she leaves immediately.

Sloane yells, "Mamaaaa!" and flings herself at my neck, bashing into Al. He's bumped awake and starts to cry. He cries so seldom it's like a terrible bell in my head.

Sloane! DOOOOON'T-ahh!

She does not care. "Mama, I want you to hold *me*. I don't want the baby here. Give him to Dada."

Sloane, he's hungry. You woke him, so now I need to feed him. Come sit with us over here. I start to move toward a bench nearby.

"No. I want you to tickle me. Tickle me, Mama!"

I sit down, latch Alexander on and drape the nursing blanket around my neck and over his face. *Sloaner—tell me about the zoo. There was a polar bear?*

"No. I don't want to. Anne wouldn't let me climb on the fence. Where *were* you?"

We went to the Bundestag again. We met a man who wrote the feed-in tariff legislation for Germany. Dad interviewed him and I took his photo. Sloane, Anne said the zoo was awesome, that you saw a baby polar bear named Knut? She said you loved it. And you flattened a coin in a machine? Then she said you did a drawing and a necklace.

"It was only colouring, and they put it on a string. No! I don't want to tell you about it."

Where's the coin? Do you have it, lovey?

"Anne took it. I didn't want it. Tickle me, Mama!"

What? Why didn't you want it?

"I have one already. At home. When are we going home, Mama?"

It's not the same as a German coin, love. The one you have at home is Canadian. You should have kept it for your box of treasures.

"I didn't want to keep it. Anne liked it. I gave it to her. When are we going *home*?"

We're going back in October. Now it's the beginning of September. We have weeks and weeks left. More time here, then we're in Freiburg, near where Gramma and Grampa John lived when they were posted here—we'll take a train across the country to get there. Then we'll fly to Spain. Grampa Bruce will meet us in Spain, and Auntie Jana. Where's the necklace you made at the zoo?

"And Uncle Jay? I didn't want the necklace. It was paper."

Yes. And Peggy. We're renting a holiday house in Spain.

"Do they speak Danish in Spain?"

Ha! No! Spanish!

Sloane pulls at my arm, looks especially plaintive. "Please, Mama. Please tickle me."

I'm feeding Al. Lookit him. She doesn't look. She wants me to herself.

This snack has taken the edge off Al's hunger, soothed him. I point at the wall of the zoo: *Sloane, is that the fence Anne wouldn't let you climb?* She looks over, and while she's turned away, I slip the sling over my head and nicker to Turner to come take the baby from me.

"No. It was a little fence in the zoo. It was low, I could've climbed it safely, Mama." She's mad about it all over again.

I gesture at the fence with my chin. *Well, run over there for a sec, take a quick look, see if that one's climbable.*

Turner sidles up and quietly takes Alexander as Sloane glances at the fence again. "No, Mama, it's too high—"

I jump up and *RAAAAH!* toward her. Sloane leaps, all spinny glee, YES YES YES. She flees, screeching, dodging two young men coming up the sidewalk.

I chase after her, and as I pass the boys, I see my left breast is flopping free. I didn't put it away after feeding Al. The two boys change trajectory, pivoting away from our absurdity. Not even a chuckle for my ridiculous thirty-six-year-old boob. Just derisive exhales.

I tuck it in and sprint at my kid, grabbing a handful of the back of her jacket: *Gotcha.* I gather her up: *Delicious armpits! Give me the armpits! I love them! Delicioso!*

Sloane is squirming, laughing. I tickle her for a minute and then pretend to be done, grab her again and tickle some more, waggling my tongue.

When I let her go, she dances out of reach. She wants more. "CHASE ME, MAMA! CHASE ME!" The sun is still up but we are in the early-evening shadow of a building, the air is chilly. It's good to move, shaking off the day of sitting at the restaurant. I feel still-young-enough: I can still run, can still swing my girl high. We have about five minutes before everyone but Al begins to melt down from hunger . . . but we've got the five minutes.

I chase Sloane around the planters, making loud monster eating noises. We're right by Kaiser Wilhelm Memorial Church, being way too loud. We are tourists now for sure. A group of deaf teens shambles by and Sloane slows down, then stops, and watches them.

Sloane: "What are they doing?"

That's sign language—probably German sign language. Those kids are deaf—they're talking to each other.

"It looks like they're flapping and waving."

They can't hear, so that's how they're getting each other's attention, interrupting with what they want to say.

"Mama, if it weren't for us, they'd *all* be speaking German!" I've been repeating this line from *A Fish Called Wanda* since we got to Berlin.

Exactly.

She leans into my hip, my lovely funny moody articulate girl. She puts her thumb in her mouth, then pulls it out. "I love you, Mama." Thumb back in. Contented sigh.

I super-dooooper love you, love. We sit for a sec as the deaf teens walk up the block and away.

Now Turner calls, "Okay, gang, let's wrap this up! Gotta go eat!" Al, in the sling, is looking down at his clasped hands.

Sloane pats my leg. "Can I sit next to you on the subway, Mama?"

We're going to get a cab, love.

"Can I sit next to you in the cab, Mama?

Of course, lovey.

"Can we sit alone? Just us."

No —Dad has to go in the front, and Al has to be with us. Babies can't go in the front seat. Airbag.

"We can all be in the back. Dad can hold Al."

We can't all sit in the back. Too squooshy.

"We can take two different taxis. Dad can go with Al."

This girl, so persistent. I love her. Oh, lovey. No no. We'll take one cab home. Then we'll get dinner at that Thai place in our building.

Sloane gives a big sigh against my leg, and steps away. "Chase me, Mama."

I've got one more left in me. Okay. She brightens up.

But head for the elephant gate, k? [To Turner:] *Okay, let's go!* [To Sloane:] *Ready? . . . RAAAAH!*

We've driven around Gibraltar all day, and up the Rock, where Sloane shrieked at the apes jumping on the roadside and reaching into car windows, Alexander curled mute in the car seat.

For seemingly no reason the baby sometimes perks up and says, "Ah." I tilt the rear-view mirror so I can watch him. This kid. What is going on in there?

I find an opera radio station and we drive out to see the mosque at Gibraltar's southern tip. As we emerge from the Keightley Way Tunnel into the autumn sunshine again, the song goes into a big crescendo and Alexander starts crying. I turn the radio off.

Sloane says, "That lady was singing too loud for him."

I take the kids to the grocery store, where we roam the aisles and finally sit on the floor in the cards and magazine section near the front. I buy Gibraltar postage stamps and we sit sticking them into the front cover of my journal. The staff smile at me and the kids as they pass. We are content today to float in this English-speaking bubble on the edge of Spain.

Sloane: "Do they have Halloween here?"

Well, they're selling the candy and decorations, but I don't know if there's much actual trick-or-treating. I don't think Britain actually does Halloween.

"I can ask those girls," she says.

Which ones?

"The ones on the merry-go-round. When I see them again."

Oh, love. We won't see them again. We leave tomorrow.

"To home?"

Tomorrow we drive to a hotel near the airport, then we fly to London and meet up with Dada. We'll spend another night near the airport, and <u>then</u> we fly home. It's days and days, a long journey with stops along the way. So tomorrow we leave, but we won't be home-home for awhile yet.

"I want to go home now. I like it here, but if we can't stay, I want to go home straight."

Yeah . . .

"Do you want to go home, Mama?"

This kid doesn't miss anything. No, lovey.

"Why? Don't you miss Loki?" (Our cat.)

I love Loki, but it will be cold when we get home. Calgary in October is heading into winter already. I like our rooms here and eating dinner on our rooftop. I like doing different things every day, and having to work hard to get things really right because we only have a short time in each place. I like how much you've grown and learned while we've been travelling around. I like the things that Dada and I talk about and think about when we're working overseas. The world seems large and wonderful.

"Home isn't wonderful?"

Calgary is not wonderful, lovey. It's just where we live.

"I think Calgary is wonderful."

I know you do! And you should! But I grew up there, in years when the city was lucky but angry and trying to be something in the world and not quite managing it. So it's different for me. Calgary is fine for us right now, but the world is big. I want to see all of it.

"I like to be at home."

Of course you do! You're a homebody. I know you like a place you remember. But we have to share how we live our lives. Sometimes we go and sometimes we stay. That way we are together and learning and everyone gets a bit of what they need.

Sloane is holding a giant golden chocolate coin she admired in one of the aisles. "Thank you for buying me the coin, Mama."

You're welcome, my love. It's like the world!

—

Heathrow. On the plane I'm seated across and up from a woman and her child, who are stuck in that middle section of big-plane seats. Turner and I have a little side row to ourselves with the kids, but even before takeoff I'm ready to strangle Sloane with my free hand. This other woman is calm and kind with her child, and in the general sitting-down-getting-oriented-for-the-eight-hour-flight process, I notice something about her little girl that makes me pause. She's not Down syndrome, but . . . there's something.

I glance over my shoulder slightly, put one ear out to listen. The mother is giving no obvious sign that she notices me, but I think she does. Her daughter is quiet and happy, not dexterous enough to open the tray table, wants a book younger than her years, speaks slowly, but too low for me to hear. I carry on watching them, covertly. The mother is self-contained, and connected, and seems . . . content.

We take off and hours pass. The plane lights are turned down, even though it is daytime outside. Alexander sleeps in my lap, and even Sloane dozes.

Now the woman has the reading light on and is helping the girl with colouring, talking with her, showing her things. I've never seen a mother like this in a circumstance like this. I am calmly focused with Sloane when we're on our own, yes. But Sloane is alert and articulate, has books she will look at on her own and snacks she can feed herself, can pull up the window shade without help, and notices things I haven't yet—stewardesses helping straighten each other's scarves, older men whose comb-overs are falling down in the back.

What if there's something really wrong with Alexander? *The universe placed this woman across the aisle from me, and I should talk to her,* I think. *I should . . . get her email address.* She may be British and going to Toronto on holiday. Or she may be Canadian, going home. Either way, she's travelling with her little girl, solo. I want to ask, *What are you doing for her at home? Does she go to school? How do you . . . do it?*

But now Sloane is awake, chewing on bread and drawing alongside me. I don't want her to hear me talking to this other woman. I don't want my girl to see my fear. I don't want Sloane to hear me say that her brother might have a problem that scares me.

Alexander is purse-lipped in the wrap on Turner's chest. He's hasn't made a noise for hours. European church bells were clanging away these last few months, trolleys banging by, and he'd barely shift in the carrier. You want an easy second baby, but not this easy.

In my bag is the book from The Institutes for the Achievement of Human Potential that I have carried across Europe, flipping through it every few weeks. With this mother and child in mind, I pull it out. I start in on the third chapter. I don't want to need it, but . . .

I look over at the woman's hair, tousled and cut in simple layers. Like mine. *God, leave her alone, Ashley. Alexander is going to be fine.* I'll probably just remember her in passing as a good mother, if I remember her at all. But I keep reading all the way across the Atlantic. Just in case.

That mother on the plane does not fade or go hazy. I'll recall her in detail all at once, standing at my kitchen counter, doing Alexander's therapy program, nine months later. Her grey sweater, the thin green scarf. Her long fingers, curled around the girl's shoulder, leaning in for a squeeze. The mother's own book on the tray, left upside down, as she reads from the storybook in the girl's lap. Easing the girl along, keeping her quietly engaged, herself undisappointed. She embodies an unbeaten but stormless acceptance.

I'll realize later that I've been moving toward that one calm stranger. I'm taking my fleeting impressions from those over-shoulder glances and gluing them hard onto a frame, shoving what I can fit of myself inside. Slicing away everything else. The edges'll bleed a bit, because I'm not made like that. But I can be her, I *will* be her.

I will.

(I won't.)

7.

<u>INT. DIMLY-LIT CHILD'S BEDROOM—NIGHT</u>

ASHLEY and four-year-old SLOANE lie together in an IKEA canopy bed in Sloane's room in the old house. It's the night before the big move. Ashley is nursing six-month-old ALEXANDER. His eyes are closed, face half covered by a blue BLANKET.

Ashley and Sloane are talking about *The Empire Strikes Back.*

> SLOANE
> Howcome they didn't know it was a worm?

> ASHLEY
> It was hidden, in the asteroid cave. They thought it was just a regular cave. It was just a hole they flew into to escape the Imperial fighters. They didn't know.

> SLOANE
> Then howcome they were in such a big hurry to get back in the Minnellium . . .

> ASHLEY
> (slowly)
> Mill-enn-ium.

SLOANE
Minnemmim . . .

ASHLEY
MILL-ENN-ium

SLOANE
MINN-ELL-ium

ASHLEY
MILL—

SLOANE
Just let me say it how I want to say it!
(resettles and continues)
Howcome they were in such a hurry to get back in?

ASHLEY
Well, Han Solo shot the ground and the ground was suddenly
shaking, right?

SLOANE
It was the worm?

ASHLEY
Yes.

SLOANE
How did they know?

ASHLEY
(aside)
Bit of a giveaway with the teeth. . . .
(to Sloane)
Han Solo shot the ground because he started to suspect
something was amiss.

SLOANE
What's "suspect"?

ASHLEY
When you think something but you don't know for sure.
There are things happening, and it's making you think,
Something's not right . . . Like—it was humid in the cave
and Leia said the ground didn't feel like rock. Those were
clues. If you suspect something, you may think something's
wrong, and even though you don't want something to be
wrong, you might feel the truth in your gut.

SLOANE
Han Solo knew they'd get eaten?

ASHLEY
Not for sure. And they didn't get eaten, did they? The worm
only tried to eat them, like a monster, right?

SLOANE
Han Solo knew it was a worm and he knew it was trying to
eat them?

ASHLEY
Eventually, yes, of course.

SLOANE
What would have happened if they got swallowed?

ASHLEY
Down the hatch. Down to the worm stomach. Juices.

SLOANE
. . . Would Boba Fett be down there?

ASHLEY
(guffaw)
No! Different worm! Next movie!

TURNER comes to the bedroom door.

TURNER
Time for bed, Sloane. Big day tomorrow! Auntie Jackie is
coming er-er-early to take you to Canmore! We'll be moving all
the stuff to the new house while you get to play with Auntie!

SLOANE
But after my sleepover there, I come back and we sleep in the
new house?

TURNER
Yes. This is your last night in the oooooold house.
(to Ashley)
Her teeth are brushed?

ASHLEY
Yes.

SLOANE
Okay, okay, Dada.
(makes air quotes)
"I get it." Bedtime.

ASHLEY gets up carefully, holding Alexander in place with
the blanket. He is asleep, unlatches, mouth open, breathes in
deep and sighs.

ASHLEY
(going to door, turning off the light)
Good night, lovey-love.

SLOANE
Mama, do you suspect something is wrong?

ASHLEY
(starting)
What?

SLOANE
I mean, have you ever suspected?

ASHLEY
. . . Like, in my life? Are you asking if that has happened to
me, where I suspected something, but didn't know for sure?

SLOANE
Yes.

ASHLEY
Yes, I have.
(beat)
. . . Good night, love.

SLOANE
'Night, Mama.

Suspicions. They keep growing. This last month, stuck between packing up the old house and fixing up the new one enough that we can
move in, has been rough. I went down with pneumonia as soon as we
got back from Europe, and was out for two weeks. My lungs are
damaged from radiation I had at eighteen to treat Hodgkin's lymphoma, so any little cough I get moves from my throat to my chest in a
day, and within forty-eight hours I'm in bed, doped up on antibiotics
and prescription cough syrup.

Increasingly panicky about managing the move, we send up the
bat signal and Turner's mom, Margo, swoops in from Nova Scotia.
She runs Halloween at our door, with Alexander in a bouncy chair in

front of the empty and echoing house, as Turner and I take Sloane around the new block to meet our future neighbours.

Once I stop gagging from this year's first ferocious cough, we find a new pediatrician and get Alexander into a special early intervention team at the Children's Hospital, called Infant Team, which treats severely delayed children. All this means going to the hospital every week. Multiple times every week.

Earlier today I was packing boxes and handed Alexander a huge white square of wrapping paper. He slowly crumpled it, tearing off bits and letting them flutter to the floor, delighted. Turner and I watched him through the first two sheets, near-breathless at his sudden coming-to-life faced with this paper. Alexander then spent the whole day crumpling wrapping paper.

Now I'm in bed, looking at the ceiling. I say to Turner in the dark, *What if he can only ever crumple paper? What if that's his whole life?*

Turner puts his hand in mine. "We know he is capable of joy. It's our job to give him every opportunity to find that joy. He's going to do so much more. But if he only ever crumples paper . . . we can buy him lots of paper."

8.

We move during the first snowfall of the year (a huge crazy storm, of course). Now we are surrounded by packed boxes, half-unpacked boxes, piles of belongings removed from boxes with nowhere to actually be yet, and tiny areas where we've marshalled order: a part of the kitchen counter is deliberately empty for food prep. The front hall has the jackets and boots. The floor of the master bedroom is clutter-free. But everything else is chaos. Have you ever moved house? Well, then. You know.

Day three in the new house is a dark day, a cold day, a Thursday. It begins with a late-morning phone call from Genetics at the hospital. "We see you have an appointment with the hearing clinic this afternoon. We're hoping we can fit you in just afterward. Just come up and check in at the desk."

I put the phone down. Turner and I are standing in the kitchen.

They've found something, I say.

Turner: "Now don't get freaked out. They probably need to see us and the dates just worked out."

No. *They've figured out what it is. This is the appointment where they'll tell us.*

Four hours later, we are leaving the hospital. As Turner navigates the damp turns through the parking garage, I say into the quiet, *Can we agree we won't drink for at least a month?*

"Huh? A month?"

We like to drink. A month is a long time.

I am smoothing down a clutch of papers in my lap. The cover

shows children who look like Alexander. *We need to get a handle on this. There's so much to grapple with here. We need clear heads.*

Turner glances at my lap. Looks in the rear-view mirror at Al in his car seat. Then back at the road. "Okay. Except for Christmas. My parents and brother will be here."

Keep it to a very dull roar. I won't be drinking at all. I could drink until I was gone over this.

We drive from the hospital to the Lycée and pick up Sloane. Turner and I are badly rattled but pretending hard for our girl that it is a day like any day. We've got the music on loud to keep from having to talk to her. All three of us reach up to bonk the ceiling of the car in unison for the start of "Lookin' Out My Back Door." I glance back and Al is slumped to one side in his car seat, tongue stuck out. I don't ask Sloane to push him upright like I usually would. By Memorial Drive, I am slumped against the passenger window myself, the glass pushing cold into my forehead.

We pull up to the new house and park, enveloped in sudden silence as the music stops and the car clicks off. All those unpacked boxes in there and now the new baggage we're dragging. My god, just a few weeks ago I was looking across the Strait of Gibraltar at Africa. Why the fuck did we come back to Canada? It's cold and clinical and they do genetic tests on your quiet baby that prove he's incomplete.

Then I hear my Mama voice punch into the void, all love and business: *Okay, c'mon love. Grab your backpack. Don't forget your mitts.*

Keep going. Keep going for Sloane. For the quiet baby, too.

I notice Turner reach to touch the fence's white pickets as we enter the yard, all unconscious irony. Up the wide steps to our new door we go, Sloane dragging her jacket over one arm. How is this kid not cold, ever?

The front door of this house is warped. It'll have to be replaced, but not yet. Turner twists the key and shoves the door open with his shoulder. It's all we can do to take off our boots, pick up the mail and throw it at the hall table. We've lived here not even a week— none of those envelopes or bills are ours. I want to just lie down on the floor. Turner is standing halfway to the kitchen, turning slowly in half circles like he's trying to remember something. As I'm unzipping Alexander from his snowsuit on the floor, Sloane sees her chance: "I'm tired. It would be a good day to sit on the couch. Can I watch *Cars?*"

(Fuck, yes.) . . .*Again, lovey?* I say it softly, so she can push back.

Sloane rushes into the space: "Yes, yes! I haven't seen it in the new house. It's time to watch it here." She flings herself over the back of the couch, landing on Loki, who howls and runs.

Turner and I need to process everything that just happened at the hospital. The movie will immobilize her. But we have to play it out; the long game of parenthood never sleeps. *Sloanerrrrr,* I say, *are you suuuuure you want to watch* Cars? *Haven't you seen it a hundred zillion times?*

"Yes, yes, I want to! I'll get Shinga George and Sylvester!" She makes her stuffed animals into the pit crew when she watches *Cars.* She flips over the couch arm and starts for the stairs, then turns. "Where's the headset, Mama?"

I'd hoped in this new place she'd forget that thing she puts on the stuffed puma for *Cars* viewings (Sylvester is her pit crew captain). I sweep my hand over the mess of the main floor: it's anyone's guess where that broken dictation headset could be (99 percent sure it landed in the trash during the move, but now's not the time to break that news). *Dunno, kid. Maybe in a box somewhere . . .*

After a few minutes Sloane is set up on the couch, and the movie is starting. We get her some orange sections in a bowl and tuck a blanket around her legs. I lean in and look her in the face: *You good?*

She moves her head so she can see around me and nods big, eyes locked on the TV. She stuffs a piece of orange into her mouth and sighs. As the DVD title music comes on, she leans forward to push Play on the remote. She's set. We have almost ninety minutes, if she doesn't skip through too many of the movie's "boring" parts.

I lean toward Turner and say very quietly, barely breathing out: *Let's go upstairs. We need to just lie the fuck down and deal with this for a bit. She's settled. We don't have to talk.*

"Alright."

Upstairs, I put a new diaper on Alexander and put him in the Moses basket in Sloane's room. He slept in the car and probably isn't tired, but we just can't deal with him right now. I close the curtains and put two blankets on the baby. Nice and toasty, he might doze again. I walk out and shut the door without looking back. Turner is in bed, under the covers and fully clothed, and I crawl in beside him. I feel a hundred years old.

We lock our elbows, wrap our socked feet together under the duvet. Then we just lean in a shocked cocoon, awake and silent, as the light moves across the room. It gradually dims, goes grey, then departs. Musical bits from the movie float upstairs, and eventually we hear the guitar riff from the credits. We exhale in unison. Here it comes.

"Maaaaaaamaaaa! It's done!"

We heave up and move toward the door. I go fetch Alexander and carry him downstairs. There's dinner or something next. Someday we'll go to sleep tonight and someday we'll wake up tomorrow. Someday it finally won't be the day we sat in the genetics appointment being told that our son is broken.

As we'd walked into the clinic, both Dr. Innes, the geneticist assigned to Alexander in the NICU, and the departmental counsellor, Mary, greeted us at the desk. Doctors never greet you at the desk.

This is going to be bad.

They lead us to a room with a low table and a whiteboard. In a corner there is a television with old Disney tapes piled below an aging VCR. *Kids come to this room*, I realize. *Parents with kids who need to be distracted come to this room.* I put Alexander down on the floor, in his car seat bucket.

We all sit, and Dr. Innes gets right to it: "We have news for you, as you may have guessed. The last test identified a chromosomal error. Alexander has something called 9q34.3 telomeric deletion syndrome. He's missing a gene on his ninth chromosomal pair."

I remember my undergrad biology, high-school Mendelian genetics, meiosis, RNA sequencing. I know some of what a missing gene means. Holy fuck. There is a hole down down down into which my stomach falls.

I look over at Turner. He's wearing old, worn jeans, and he's looking confused, surprised. He really did think we were just schlepping to the hospital for another appointment. My dear love.

The doctor goes on. "This explains Alexander's hypotonia—his floppiness—the weight gain difficulties, the heart murmur, and other things you've identified."

I breathe and breathe and deliberately keep breathing. There's a whole new world coming at us inside this announcement. I need to know everything they know. They need to see that they can tell me everything. I make sure my face remains calm.

So *what does this mean? What does it* mean *for him?*

Mary, the counsellor, sitting alongside Dr. Innes, speaks gently from across the table. "This syndrome is very, very rare. But, from what we know, these kiddos seem to develop at about half speed." I notice she has a new file in front of her, with a TURNER, ALEXANDER sticker on the tab.

I say, So *he'll be small? Is it a kind of dwarfism?* Alexander has always been tiny, below a recordable percentile on the standard growth charts. Dwarfism could be fine. I can parent dwarfism.

Dr. Innes: "Perhaps slightly smaller than other kids his age in stature, but the slow development is primarily cognitive." Being a geneticist suddenly strikes me as a dangerous job. Every day Dr. Innes looks human parents in the eye and tells us our kids aren't normal. He has probably seen the complete range of human emotion unpack in this room.

So . . . *Alexander will develop at half speed—you mean that, psychologically, when he's ten he'll seem like he's five, when he's twenty he'll seem like he's ten?*

"Well . . . not quite that. Their development seems to plateau at a certain point."

Plateau? Forever? Oh god. *At what point do they plateau?*

"There's no way to say for sure. How Alexander will develop is a very individual thing." This is vague and highly unsatisfactory.

They explain that Alexander is only the seventy-second person diagnosed with this specific condition, worldwide. They say there are probably many more people who have it than are identified, so far. They predict that as years pass and testing improves, thousands more will be discovered.

But for now, it's so, so rare. Hard to pinpoint in the testing. They had to look specifically at the ninth pair of chromosomes, and request a precise test to do so.

How did you know to look for it? How did you think to request the test for this syndrome?

The doctor says, "I've seen one other case."

Nearby? Are there other kids with this syndrome in Calgary? Is this a cluster point for this condition? Are we part of a larger community here?

"No. Out of town."

But that one child you've seen—that kid is your patient.

"Yes."

And none of the other genetics docs have one of these kids in their caseload.

"Right."

So if we'd been assigned a different doctor in the NICU, *Alexander's condition might not have been diagnosed. You requested the test because you had seen this syndrome before. But it's rare, so the other doctors wouldn't have known to ask for that test.*

"Yes."

Okay. This seems like a ray of luck? Nothing else about this is lucky, though. This whole situation is the very definition of bad luck.

Dr. Innes and Mary look calmly across at us. They are obviously in no rush. This is unusual in Canadian health care.

Then I realize they're waiting for the next question, the one they've heard a hundred thousand times at this point in the conversation. So I go ahead and ask: *Is this syndrome hereditary?*

"It's possible, but very unlikely. We can do tests to rule you out as carriers, but this is generally a spontaneous error in chromosomal replication just after conception. It's one of those things that can just happen."

Just one of those things that happen, like frogs in your bed or three days of darkness, whatevs.

Me: *Okay, yes, of course we'd like the tests.*

Mary pulls requisitions out of the file folder and hands them across the table. Our names are already at the top of the pages, our health-care numbers inserted, the doctor's signature in place. Wow.

Turner, looking at the papers: "Um, is this a blood test?" (He really hates needles.)

I keep going, gesturing at Alexander in his car seat on the floor. *Will he be able to learn to drive, eventually?* Growing up, I knew someone whose older brother was called "retarded." He was able to drive the tractor, mow the lawn, make himself food.

Dr. Innes folds his hands together on the tabletop. "To my knowledge, no individual with this syndrome is able to drive."

But he will walk, right?

"They walk late, if they walk. Around age six or eight or so. But about half have very limited mobility and require a wheelchair."

I flash to a view of the stairs in our new house.

. . . Focus, Ashley. *Okay. How about talking? They learn to talk?*

Dr. Innes: "The ones we know of so far don't talk. There's some evidence for progress with sign language, but individuals with this condition have a very limited capacity to communicate."

A faraway scream is starting inside my skull. If I was standing, now is when I would fall. Turner and I reach for each other's hands under the table. We make meaning of our world with words. This boy will not be able to keep up with us. He won't be able to interrupt, he won't throw verbal barbs at dinner or sling double entendres into conversation. He will not make ironic air quotes around phrases to make them mean exactly what he wants to say. (The joy of Sloane's words these last four years, oh, our eloquent girl . . .)

Mary, the counsellor, breaks in. "Your child is an individual. What we know right now—these things are just generalizations from a small set of examples. This syndrome is still *very* rarely diagnosed, so there's not much to know about it yet. Your son will be his own person. He will be like you in a lot of ways." She gives a small and encouraging smile.

I get it. Move on. *Okay, understood. Speech is an issue for these kids. But please clarify: Will he be able to follow what we say? Will he understand knock-knock jokes? Can we even make him laugh?*

Dr. Innes: "He is learning and growing just like other babies, and we don't know how much he'll understand, because every child is going to be different."

I make a "sure, I get it, BUT" two-palms-up gesture. *But . . . he can learn basic things, surely? Will he be able to go to school?*

"There are special-needs programs in the school system that can accommodate even very severely disabled children."

So—that means there's a range of severity of disability? Where does Alexander fall, having this syndrome? How disabled will he be?

The doctor doesn't hesitate. "Kids with this syndrome are considered severely disabled. Physically, cognitively, they are severely delayed in all areas."

Now I'm picturing a Handi-Bus double-parked in front of our house, mechanical lift attachments in our stairwell, a nurse who comes at night . . .

"What I *will* say is it's good you've got a diagnosis for him. It shouldn't matter, but in truth it helps a lot with getting services." Dr. Innes waits for the next inevitable question, which of course is:

Services? What kind of services?

"FSCD, PUF, and later on, PDD." These initialisms might be in that fistful of papers I got from the NICU. They're probably also at the back of that binder Moonira gave us. I make a note to google this shit. Need to get a handle on all these things ASAP.

Mary says, "You should apply to FSCD right away. It's a provincial government department, and you just call them. They can help with getting an aide to work with him." She pushes another pamphlet across the table, a pink one from the province. It has a cute disabled toddler on the front. Always with the pamphlets.

My breath is starting to feel hot and weird. I am lightheaded. But a part of me is keeping on, can keep going. I need to find the edges of this new territory. I say, *Alexander is almost silent, like he's too weak to make noise.* I think of the journalist Ian Brown's son, Walker, who also has a rare genetic abnormality, which Ian wrote about in *The Boy in the Moon.* So I ask: *Is he in pain?*

"These kids seem to have a high pain tolerance, so no, he's probably not in any pain because of this condition."

We all sit there for a few seconds. It's quiet in the room. We can hear the tick of the clock. They're patient. They're waiting.

Now I ask the big one. *What is his life expectancy?*

Turner starts in his chair. I can feel his shock that I would verbalize such a thing. But it sounds like we are in for a world of hell with this kid. Will the hell be forever? I can't be the first or even the forty thousandth parent of a disabled child to want to know.

And Dr. Innes is unfazed. "Same as any neurotypical person. These kids have a normal lifespan."

Ah.

Our baby is broken, but he will not be lifted from us by his brokenness. I notice my disappointment in a detached way. I mentally note it for later, for when this is an old, old story I'll be remembering.

Now Turner and I both glance at the ticking clock and suddenly realize we must leave to pick up Sloane. Our lives have just caved in, but the world outside carries on. Being late is not an option at the Lycée. I have lots more to ask, but we have to go, and right now.

As we rise, Mary slides a collection of pages, stapled at the corner, across the table. She says, "This is a study of kids with Alexander's syndrome. It's the only collected information we have about this condition. It's a limited study, but it tells you what you can expect in the years to come."

I pick it up. On the title page are eight pixelated photos of children who look like Alexander. Unmistakably like him.

I fold this newest, most dangerous pamphlet and put it deep in my bag. Turner and I will read it later—later. Today we have to keep going. We can't think about what this is in real life yet. Not yet.

That night I dream I am at a ruined farm, the big wood-beamed barn falling down around me. I run outside, and in the sky there is an eclipse.

9.

You bargain. You bargain with the universe.

In the birth preparation class before Sloane was born, we did an exercise where we wrote down all the things we wanted from the birth experience. We, first-time parents all, wanted drugs or no drugs, we all wanted the baby to breastfeed exclusively (so no giving water or formula), we wanted day labours so our families could be there, we wanted private rooms, we didn't want C-sections.

When we'd written the big, long lists of all the things we all wanted, the facilitator told us to cross off one thing we could do without.

Nooooo . . . we all said. But we did it.

Then she told us to cross off two more things.

Then two more.

We balked—*Wait, wait, some of these items are mandatory!*

But the facilitator kept going. Cross off one more thing. And again. Again. Until everyone had only one thing left.

All of us, every parent in that room, had the same final item at the end: "A healthy baby."

The facilitator said, "Isn't that what we want? That's the only thing that matters, right? That the baby is born healthy."

Fabulous exercise.

Five years later my second child is not a "healthy" baby in the way any of us meant with our last-item-on-the-list. He is a child not strong enough to sneeze or cough, who doesn't turn when you call his name, who doesn't lean in or hold on to your clothing when you're carrying him. And now we know why, this 9q-something-something syndrome.

So I'm remembering the exercise, working it, bargaining myself down. I'm taking things off my list for this baby. But it's a whole-life list now.

I want him to ~~go to university, scuba dive, be a safe driver~~.

I want him to ~~back flip on the trampoline~~ *and* ~~be bilingual~~.

I want him to ~~ride a bicycle~~. *I want him to* ~~go to school~~. God, that one.

I want him to ~~walk~~. . . . Okay. Yes. I'll let that one go. Metaphorical hand across the forehead, wiping.

Then: *I want him to read.*

. . . *I want him to read.*

The pen, hovering.

I want him to read.

I can't cross it off. I need him to be able to read.

I think, *He's not blind; they've tested him. He can see, even if he doesn't look at us. If he can see, surely he can learn to read? If I put in years and years on it? Gradually, gradually? Right?*

There's a flicker in my chest.

I don't cross it off.

Our dining table is a Formica thing, with a design of gold ovals across the top and chrome along the sides. Bruce and I are sitting at it in silence. I've just told my dad the diagnosis. He exhales finally and says, "What are we gonna do?"

The dining-room lights are off, and the illuminated kitchen is reflected in the picture window: another kitchen over there, backward. No curtains on that big window yet. Any day now, though. (It will be another five years.) Outside, dark winter, blue moonlight. Squeaky December snow.

". . . What are we gonna do?"

I say aloud the biggest reach I can make: *I want him to read.*

And Bruce is suddenly sick at heart—he can't hide it.

I follow on, *If he can read, he can have an inner life.*

"Ashley . . ." My father thinks I don't understand the big picture here, so he levels with me. He's being brave, hurting as he says, slowly, "He's never going to read."

He will, I say.

(*He won't*, I think.)

He can, I say.

(*He can't*, I think.)

"Oh, dear. No." My dad is so sorry to say it.

The diagnosis is swallowing us. We are falling and I am flailing. But there has to be a light. I am saying *He will* to hear something defiant, a hypnic jerk, a flickering flashlight in my hand.

He will. He can learn. He can.

At that table, that night, I say *He will read* out loud for the first time. Even though I know he won't ever read. Never.

(He will.)

10.

The kids and I are on the bed in my room. It's bedtime and we're getting into pyjamas. Sloane is moody, refusing to play with me. I try to
tickle her while holding Alexander under my arm.

Sloane, rolling away: "Mama, maybe I don't want a little brother."

Oh my god. . . . *What? Why would you say that?*

Sloane tilts her head, says quietly, "Maybe we shouldn't keep him."

Goddamn, little kids and their ESP. She's been hearing me screaming it on the inside.

No, Sloane. He's ours. We're his. He's our blood. Forever.

At this, she softens. "Are you mad at me?"

Oh my heart.

*No, no, lovey. I'm an older sister too. Of course you think like
that sometimes. It's okay. But it's also my job to tell you no.*

She nods.

I put Al down beside her and deliberately hold our world to the light.
For her, and for me. *Who're the most important people in your life?*

Sloane blinks and looks away, likely thinking through her friends
at school, Grampa Bruce and Gramma, trying to settle on an order
of preference.

I interrupt. *You don't have to think about it, love. I'll tell you. It's
me, Dada and Al: we are the most important people in your life.
That's it. Everyone else is after us.*

She's surprised. So I go on.

Who're the most important people in <u>my</u> life?

"Dada. And . . . me and Al?" She's hopeful.

Exactly.

She beams. "And for Dada it's me and you and Al?"

You've got it. And for Al, it's me and you and Dad. That's what we have. We have each other.

"And Loki?"

I laugh. *We love Loki, of course. But the most important are the people: me, Dada, you, and Alexander. We're the unit. That's the family. Forever.*

I wasn't raised like this, but I will it to be true about this family, the one Turner and I have made.

"Okay, Mama."

Wow, that was (almost) easy.

Good girl.

We stumble through the next few days, the pamphlet with the photos of kids that look like Alexander still in my bag. I push past it for my wallet and lip balm a dozen times every day.

I go to a nearby naturopath. Or maybe she's a homeopath? My new neighbour recommended her, and I was staring off into space this afternoon for way too long, so I leave Alexander with Turner and go around the corner. I just walk in and she is available, so I get ushered straight into an appointment. I'm in shock, and it must be pretty obvious.

I tell her about Alexander's diagnosis. I hear the words come out of my mouth like they're being broadcast from a speaker attached to my face.

When I finish, she asks, "Do your knees hurt?"

What? My knees have been killing me since we came home from the genetics appointment. It takes me nearly a full minute to climb the stairs in our house. I need to brace my body weight with my arms getting into the car or I yelp. Just the past few days. I hadn't stopped to think about it.

Yes, they do. Why did you ask that?

"In Chinese medicine, knees reflect the state of the kidneys, which are the seat of fear. This diagnosis would be a frightening thing for a mother to hear."

Things spin into focus for a moment. *I'm so afraid. I've been pushing it down, but it's bigger than I can even see. It's blocking out all the light.*

"Okay," she says. "I don't usually do this on a first appointment, but . . ." She goes out of the room and comes back rolling a machine that looks like a radiator. She turns it on and moves a kind of vibrating wand over my legs, rubbing hard into the edges of my kneecaps, the other hand holding the back of my calf, stroking up and down. She is . . . taking care of me. I begin to cry. And just keep on crying as she works. She doesn't look up.

After three minutes, she has me flex my leg, and the pain in that knee is gone.

She does the other knee, and then puts the wand back on the machine. "Come back anytime. I'll do your knees if they're bothering you—no charge. Just come. I'll make a note for reception."

I'm snotting into a tissue, nodding thank you, wondering how much one of these machines are, and it's like she hears me. She pats the box as she rolls it to the wall. "It's a whole process to qualify for one of these—they're really expensive."

Ah, so I won't be getting the home model.

She goes to an unfolding apothecary cupboard and measures some drops into a vial, adds little sugar pills, and shakes the combo up for a minute. "These are for trauma," she says, looking at me as she continues to shake the vial. "Take three at nighttime—each of you, for a week. You, your husband, your daughter."

But my daughter doesn't know. We haven't told her. She's only four.

"She knows. Her body knows. She can feel the trauma on you. You've just moved, and that's a big dislocation. So her senses are heightened." The naturopath nods at the vial she's shaking. "This is a crisis support for you all. These are just sugar pills with tiny amounts of Ayurvedic herbs in a tincture. It can't harm you."

I push to standing and my knees don't hurt at all. I take the vial.

That night I quietly march Turner and Sloane down to the bathroom. We are going beyond the edge of the map now. We have arrived at a place where I dispense placebos to my family. Sloane is in her jammies and doesn't ask any questions about these small new medicines as she stands on the toilet seat, letting them dissolve under her tongue as instructed. Turner and I believe in science. Magic knee pain machines and sugar pills are not usually on the menu. But Turner has been on autopilot for days, speaking only when Sloane needs something or when someone calls on the telephone, and I'm not much different. He doesn't protest. Just steps up and opens his mouth, and I tip the pills in. I take mine too.

Then we stand together in a circle, Turner and I wrapped around and over Sloane. Alexander is asleep down the hall, in the basket in our bedroom. We are all in service to him now.

The sugar pills help, if only as an excuse to commune in the bathroom before bed each night for a week. The pain in my knees doesn't return for a long time. This, too, is something.

It's been seven days since the diagnosis. Turner and I have been travelling around the city together, doing errands, staying in the same room together as much as we can, quiet. Now we're in the parking lot at the Lycée to pick up Sloane, with Alexander in his car seat in the back. We have ten minutes before the bell. I have a sudden moment of bravery. *Okay. Let's look at the pamphlet.*

Turner: "Do you have it?"

Yes. I've been carrying it with me.

We pause. Maybe we shouldn't read the pamphlet.

Turner says, "Should we just get it over with?"

I pull the pamphlet out of my bag and we lean together over the gear shift. We flip it open, scan the pages, reading.

Seizures. Fuck.

"What does that mean? Epilepsy?" Turner defers to me on medical things. I act like I know, and sometimes I do.

"Epilepsy" is a blanket term for "they have seizures," I think. It says seizures cause regression in these kids.

"Regression?"

They lose skills. Look, this kid had nearly two hundred sign language signs and then started having seizures and lost them all. Jesus. Seizures are a horrifying thought, but this bit also delivers good news: that child had learned two hundred signs. That child could communicate—before the seizures.

. . .

"Alexander doesn't have these things: look—" Turner pokes at a paragraph. "He doesn't get fluid in his lungs, does he? When he eats?"

I don't think so. He's not getting enough to chub up, but what he gets isn't going down the wrong tube.

Turner's tone is turning toward hopeful. The pamphlet doesn't ring true for him. "Sleep problems? But Al sleeps great."

Yeah. Maybe the sleep thing develops as they get older. Yes—see? At puberty. Insomnia and . . . oh fuck, catatonia?

"What is that?"

Being catatonic. Not responding. I don't know exactly.

More reading.

Turner sits back, lets go of the pamphlet, gestures for me to hold it. "This doesn't sound like it's going to be Al. He must have a mild form of this syndrome."

Maybe. In Down syndrome there are degrees of severity. The kids in this pamphlet study are having some problems that aren't affecting Alexander. Yet.

Turner takes a big breath and huffs it out. He turns off the car. "Okay. Time to get Sloane." It's less than a minute to the bell now and other parents are emerging from cars around us. I unlock my seat belt and get out, fetch Al from the back, and follow Turner into the Lycée.

We have come away from the pamphlet going in different directions. This is where Turner enters "Well, he's different, but it's not going to be that bad" land. For me, the pamphlet is a list of warnings of what might be. Dire warnings.

I've been trying not to think about the book I finished on the plane home from Europe, *What To Do About Your Brain-Injured Child*, from The Institutes in Philadelphia. Now it jumps into my mind and won't be pushed aside. I don't want to start up that ladder. But when I chance a look around, we're in a walled prison yard with no doors.

That night there's a big dump of snow after dinner and all through bedtime. Once the kids are down and house is quiet, I lie in bed rereading parts of the *What To Do* book. Turner looks over and sees the cover. "Still with that thing? Didn't you read it already?"

Yes. And you have to read it.

Turner looks like a kid who's been given extra chores. "No, Ash, no . . . not right now."

Sorry, but yes. You have to read it. We're going to have to go to this place. You need to know what it is.

I can see by his expression that Turner hopes this is one of my impulsive proclamations: *Let's move to Melbourne! Let's send Sloane to the Punjabi school next year! Let's renovate a sea can into a tiny house!* I want it to be that, too. But it's not.

I try to read for awhile longer, but eventually bounce out of bed and get dressed again. I go downstairs, put on my boots and coat and mitts and hat, and spend ninety minutes outside in the cold, shovelling out strangers' cars and neighbours' walks. Better to be productively exercising than sobbing in the house.

I'm just—mad. Different-mad now. Confused, and wishing I would wake out of this nightmare. *Seizures, for fuck's sake?* This was SO not the life I was going to live.

I see curtains twitch inside some of the darkened houses; it's eleven o'clock and the screech of shovel against sidewalk is loud at this hour. We've lived on this street only ten days—I don't know these neighbours yet.

I cleared your stupid sidewalk and you're welcome, assholes.

I say this to no one. Our new neighbours stay inside their warm houses as I work off my rancour.

I shovel and shovel to the pub at the end of the block and back, both sides of the road. I finally come in, wet and tired, and head for the shower.

When I get back to bed, Turner is asleep. But in the dim light, I see that he has moved The Institutes' book to his bedside table. It has a little bookmark sticking out, a few pages in.

Alexander and I are sitting near the big fish tank in the lobby of the Alberta Children's Hospital. I feel like we are drowning and falling at the same time.

We have been at the hospital for four hours, in the hearing clinic and then Cardiology. At the second appointment we waited in the exam room for two hours and twenty minutes, with the receptionist coming in every quarter hour to tell me it wouldn't be much longer. By the time the cardiologist cheerily bounced into the room I was so livid I could barely speak.

The appointment itself was four minutes of the doctor flipping through Alexander's online patient file, then swivelling on the stool and pronouncing Al's heart murmur a non-issue.

Now we're in the hospital lobby, where I'm gobbling cafeteria sushi to tamp down rage-induced hypoglycemia. I sit here hoping Al will notice the fish, but he hasn't and won't. I'm chewing, zoning out on revenge fantasies for use on obtuse medical specialists.

There is a sudden commotion at the elevators. The whole lobby snaps to attention, focused on parents over there with a stroller who are crackling with chaos. The mom looks like I feel: jacket fallen off one shoulder, hair that should be in a ponytail but is flopping in her eyes as she digs something out of a bag. The father is angrily rubbing a hand over and over his head, throwing defensive "What? WHAT?" glances at the people around him. He goes to stab the up button again as the mom stoops to fiddle with the brake on the stroller, making impatient clicks with her tongue.

An available elevator arrives and we all hear these two parents say, "FINALLY." They roll toward the doors, forcing the people trying to get off the elevator to squeeze out around them. A few lab techs and cleaning people follow them in, but doctors and other parents with children step back to wait for the next one, not wanting to become a target for the couple's free-floating anger.

Alexander and I stay at the fish tank for a long time afterward. These parents are a vision of my potential future: *Get the hell out of my way, I have a fucking kid who needs to be at the hospital twice a week here . . .*

Hoo. Sobering.

I resolve right then not to lose my shit here—ever.

From now on I will be an exemplary representative of my new identity, "the hospital parent." I will dress properly for each visit: clean clothes, earrings, eyeliner. I am here to fight for Alexander, and half the time I'm here I want to destroy furniture, but I need to remember my humanity and manners. We are surrounded by people whose job it is to work with people like us every day. So I will always arrive in plenty of time. I will drive slowly in the parking lot. I will wipe down the bathroom sinks with my paper towel. I will move consciously through this environment.

I may never have wanted to be this, but I am a professional mother now. This will be a workplace for me, too. Over time I will build routines. Eventually, it'll be easy.

(Eventually.)

The fear of what is happening keeps me reading online, and ordering books, and asking for more information. I am going to become the fucking world expert on how to train, cajole, encourage and force a chromosomally gibbled infant toward human functionality. I'm full of pure and manic fury, because it feels like the only way out. But The Fear has also been punching through, into my physical and subconscious worlds. I have a rash under my eyes and a buzzing carpal-tunnel arm at night. I've had vivid visions of Alexander's death in which he somehow perishes through no fault of ours, of SIDS or a tragic accidental head injury. These are hard to pass off as just "worries." But it also feels dangerous to talk about them to the counsellor at the Children's Hospital or any of the doctors we see. I don't want social services ringing our doorbell.

Christmas has been a good distraction, with holiday obligations and days off for tobogganing and doing puzzles. At night I've been working on our application for the five-day intro course and clinic evaluation at the Philadelphia Institutes in April. It's a long application of both fill-in-the-blanks questions and essays. It takes me four evenings of holing up in the master bedroom to get the application done, while Turner and his family—his parents, Margo and JT, and his brother Johnny—revel downstairs.

The in-laws are game to help with new therapies for Alexander, so we've been experimenting with the physical patterning recommended by The Institutes' book. "Patterning" involves Alexander lying face down on a table, with three adults moving his limbs and head in sync, replicating the movements of opposite arms and legs working together. This patterning teaches the brain and muscles the memory of moving in right-left cross-body sync. After just a few sessions at this, we've seen Alexander "swimming" in place on his own a few times, moving his arms and legs while balanced on his belly—a developmental precursor to crawling. This is a big leap in just a few days.

Right now, Alexander is seven and a half months old and still small, so small: 13 pounds, maybe 14? It's easy to carry him upstairs, lift him into the bath, swing him into the car. But someday he's going to be 40 pounds, 80 pounds, 120 pounds. It won't be fun anymore, trying to lug him around. So not-crawling is not an option. In their book The Institutes say that children who can crawl on their tummies can learn to creep on their hands and knees, and that children who creep can learn to walk. It's an incremental matter of increasing their strength and stamina, encouraging them to go a little farther and a little faster each day.

Our first step is getting Alexander to move on his own, which, so far, he is either not interested in doing or not strong enough to do. Today my father-in-law JT and I went to Home Depot for plywood and foam padding to construct an inclined "crawling track" per The Institutes' specifications. The finished product will be a padded ramp, like a short, puffy slide. The idea is to put Alexander on it, face down, and then elevate the top end to a height where, if he moves at all, he will start to slide. A baby has a natural physical reflex to brace against the pull of gravity, so this crawling track will teach him to control his progress (sliding in sputters, because of the incline) by coordinating his arms and legs. So say the Institutes.

As he gets better able to move down the track, we will lower the top end bit by bit, so gravity does less and less of the work and Alexander has to do more to move himself. Eventually, the crawling track will be nearly level with the floor and he will crawl off the end—moving on his own on a flat surface. That's the goal.

We finished construction today, and the track is outside, off-gassing glue and vinyl fumes. As soon as it smells better, we'll start the "inclined floor program."

Today is January 3, our wedding anniversary. Turner and I have left both kids with his family and are out for a date afternoon. We choose the Glenbow Museum downtown, which is hosting an exhibition of Ron Mueck's giant baby sculptures. While we're wandering through, we are joined by a twenty-something young man, who is "different" in some way and walks around and between other groups visiting the exhibit, commenting loudly on obvious things:

"I GUESS IT'S GLASS OR SOME KIND OF PLASTIC FOR THE EYES!" and "THIS IS WHAT THEY MEAN BY SOMEONE HAVING A BIG HEAD!" His mother, an older woman, sometimes gently waves a hand to quiet him down.

I listen to his loud lip smacks and unmodulated voice, and my brain jumps to "Is this what Alexander will be like?"

Bruce said yesterday, "He's cute now." Meaning, Alexander won't always be a baby and he won't always be cute. Someday he may be an awkward young man with a shiny yellow jacket hanging over his shoulder, hulking around a museum, making loud pronouncements in an otherwise quiet exhibition hall.

And then I hear inside my mind, *It could be worse, you know. He might not speak at all. Or he could be incomprehensible.*

To have a messy-haired trailing adult son announcing "THE BACK IS HOLLOW, THAT MUCH I KNOW FOR SURE!" suddenly feels wildly desirable. If it's a choice between that and nothing. The goalposts are moving. I'll take communication over its lack. We all would, as parents, whatever it sounds like, whatever the other people in an exhibition hall think.

Give me a child I can understand. Please.

Our guests have gone home, and this week Sloane is back at school.

Today, after I pick her up, we go to visit her favourite classmates, triplets who live up the hill. The kids are playing in another room and I sit with the boys' mother in the kitchen, drinking coffee and holding Alexander. I confide that we are considering a clinic for Al in Philadelphia. She perks up: "Oh, The Institutes? I used their books with my boys. I have some of their materials downstairs—let me get them." No one before now had heard of The Institutes, so this is a surprise.

She comes up from the basement carrying eleven-by-eleven-inch printed cards with red dots on them that I recognize from that old '80s movie, *Parenthood* (in which a hyper-competitive father played by Rick Moranis used exactly these cards to train his four-year-old on square roots and exponents). She remembers the movie too.

Is that what this is?

"Sort of—but not really. It's about exposure to learning at all levels. My boys were preemies, so they had some delays and I wanted to work on catching them up. I did these cards for a few months when they were really little, and they were really interested. It was surprising. But I don't need them anymore. You should take them." She hands over the stack of number cards, along with another Institutes book, *How To Teach Your Baby Math*, with the same cover design as the introductory one I have at home.

I look at the backs of the cards, which list equations that use the number on the front. I don't understand how they work. *So—they memorize the number of dots on the front? Or they learn to count them up really quickly?*

"I think babies' brains see volume or numeracy differently than adult brains. They can see the difference between the numbers. It works—I just didn't keep going with it. You can teach them all sorts of math with these cards, addition and multiplication, whatever."

Now she's is telling me about her friend who has a child with Prader-Willi syndrome (a complex genetic condition in which a primary symptom is the constant feeling of hunger, which makes them want to eat all the time). She says those parents have been grieving the diagnosis like a death. For three years.

I'm shocked. *Three years?*

She tips her head sympathetically, nods. "It takes a long time. They're really worn out. It kind of never ends."

Oh my god. I've been thinking we would absorb Alexander's diagnosis way faster than in the scale of *years*. Will we be sad and mad and disoriented and upset by this even two years from now? . . . Or always?

January is my first month of not-working, at all, in more than a decade. I never had any intention whatsoever of being a "stay-at-home mom" (despite previously working from home, and already being a mother). When she was a baby, Turner and I had traded Sloane back and forth during the day until she was old enough for daycare, and then we shipped her off, no regrets. This is not an option for Alexander.

Tonight we finally set up my "office" in the basement guest room, creating a small area of order for me to pay the bills and check my email in what is otherwise a still-mostly-unpacked house. Holy, we only moved in here six weeks ago. It feels like a lot longer.

I'm hit with a huge wave of sadness as I unpack my files and equipment. I touch all my camera lenses, re-placing them into their slots in the big storage case. These gorgeous objects and well-used trappings of my career represent so much of who I was in the world not that long ago. I set up the desk, putting pens into a jar and tucking cords down the wall. I'm sad for me tonight, and I know it's fair to be sad. I stare into the black screen of my big editing monitor for a long time.

Then Turner comes down and sees me, and comes around the desk, puts his arm around me and leans his head into my hair. He says, "You can carve out time. Block it into your calendar. Nothing else goes there. You can still do it."

I exhale. There's a lot in that sigh.

I do end up running downstairs a few evenings a month to get some mindless bum-in-chair time organizing my archives of past photo shoots. If Alexander hadn't been diagnosed in December, I would've been leaving for Dubai at the end of this month. I can't think through the loss of this yet, or the long-term impact of Alexander's diagnosis on my career. Obviously it's not good.

But . . . maybe it doesn't all have to be black and white. Maybe I can still do a few projects a year? Once we really know what we're doing and what to expect with Alexander. Maybe then?

I'm spending more and more hours each week at the Children's Hospital, going between ear, nose and throat, audiology, neurology, radiology, and urology appointments. We are establishing baselines for Alexander's hearing and vision and brain development to date. He will also need surgery in the spring to put in ear tubes, and repair his abdominal hernia and a defect they've found in his urethra. The Infant Team "team" involves a bunch of specialists too. The appointments are endless.

And worse, I leave every appointment unsatisfied. I say to everyone, *Please, I need to help him develop. Tell me what to do. I will do it. Tell me who to call, what books to read. I will do whatever you say.* None of these many qualified professionals look me in the face and give me any advice other than "Relax." It drives me bananas. And none of them have heard of The Institutes in Philadelphia.

In the second week of January we're in an Infant Team appointment with an occupational therapist I've never met before, who's about to go on maternity leave. As Alexander lies on the mat, looking at his hands, she pulls out a goals worksheet on health region letterhead.

"So . . . let's do some visioning for Alexander for the coming year. It helps the team here build strategies for him. Does that make sense?"

What have we been doing in here for the last two months?

"Well, I'm not sure. I'm not actually technically on your team, but evaluations are important, getting a baseline on how Alex is doing, seeing how he is developing." She takes a big breath, looks keen.

"So. Goals. What would you like to see him doing a year from now?"

I'd like to see him walking.

This isn't the answer she was expecting. "Okay . . . so . . . this is what you'd like to work toward, so that in *a year*, this is what you'd want him to be able *to do*."

Yes. Walking. This kid can learn to walk. He's already four times faster at going down the crawling track, and we only just started with it a few weeks ago. I want this Infant Team to help us work toward walking.

The OT looks uncomfortable. "So this is . . ."

I play dumb. *Okay, you tell me what goals I should choose.*

"Oh. Ha ha, no, these are *parent*-led goals . . ."

Well, in a year he'll be twenty months old. Most kids walk by twelve months. So absolutely, I'd like to see him walking before he's two.

She looks at me with big bright eyes. "Okay, like, what we're working on here are *realistic* goals—"

I'm not swallowing this today.

Lookit, I am a photographer. I have degrees in Women's Studies and Rural Planning. I'm not trained or qualified in any of this [waving my arm at equipment around the room]. *I'll totally do my part, I'll work with him on whatever this team assigns. But I don't know what's he's supposedly capable of accomplishing by next January. You have years and years of education and experience in child development. So you'll have to tell me. Or maybe the physio or the speech people, who aren't here, can tell me what's possible.*

But, if you are really asking me, as the parent, to set goals, "walking" is what I want to work toward. I want exercises and guidance in *helping him to learn to walk. At home we're doing a learn-to-crawl program for him, and he's doing better every day. I want him to speak, and I want him to read, and I want him to go to school eventually. I'm ambitious for him. That's the point of coming here.*

She backpedals. "I'm not saying at all that he can't learn to walk. It's not my field; I'm fine motor. But today we're looking for realistic—"

You keep saying "realistic." I don't know what's "realistic" for him. So put down "walking," please. I nod at the sheet on her lap, and widen my eyes just as brightly.

Now it's assuage-the-parent time. "Okay, sure, okay, I will put that here—walking. Walking in a year. Okay." Big smile.

I watch her write it on the sheet, and add a bracketed note: (*parent goal*). Ugh. If a higher-up audits this piece of paper and thinks, *Who the hell said this kid could walk in a year?* she's covered Infant Team's ass.

When I leave the appointment, I'm holding yet another pamphlet, a different one about FSCD, which was one of those acronyms the geneticist mentioned last month. It stands for Family Supports for Children with Disabilities, a provincial government program. The occupational therapist tells me to self-refer: "Just call, leave a message. They'll get back to you."

I go home. I call the FSCD number again (I left a message on this line after the genetics appointment last month). The voice mail says to leave *one* message and they'll call within two weeks. I leave a second message. From now on, I call the number every two weeks and leave a message, even though the voice mail greeting keeps emphasizing not to leave multiple messages. I won't hear back for almost three months. Everyone talks about how important "early intervention" is for children like Al, but there's no urgency here whatsoever.

But later that afternoon, I open my email and finally get a rush of elation about Alexander's prospects. Because here it is: our acceptance from The Institutes' registrar.

I jog upstairs to tell Turner and his face says, "Oh, fuck. She actually applied."

I laugh. *We're going in April. We have to actually <u>do</u> something for Al or I'll end up injuring one of those schmucks at the hospital.*

He turns back to the computer. "Okay. I'll look into flights."

—

The acceptance to The Institutes comes with one condition: before we arrive in Philadelphia we need to complete three months of a self-designed program of therapies based on the *What To Do* book. To get us used to working with Al every day before they slap us with a huge "here, do this forever" program. Having a plan and some action is energizing. I'm feeling better about things, less stuck.

But after a few days, I start to worry about something else. We know from talking to Gillian in Toronto that running an Institutes home program for Alexander will require us to have volunteers to help with the patterning. "We had forty-five people on a roster," she says.

Forty-five? Who? Family?

"Family, friends, neighbours, local teenagers, people who heard we needed help and just volunteered, my husband's colleagues, my brother's wife. Tons of people. You'll be amazed at who comes to help."

I'm not so sure. In fact, I'm sure almost nobody will come to help. Even if I ask.

At the hospital appointments, they regularly inquire about our support network. "Any family in town?" they say.

Yes, I always answer. *My brother and father live here. My mother-in-law comes from Nova Scotia every few months to stay with us for a couple of weeks. My cousins visit pretty regularly.*

These statements are true. But in the face of needing forty-five people who can actually support this coming program, I am daunted. It feels like most of the people we could count on for that kind of help live in and around Toronto.

But, but . . . I did grow up here, so I have some childhood connections left; a few of our Ontario university chums have found their way west, and there are family friends who might step up. I could reach out to colleagues and clients from old jobs, maybe? And Turner and I know people in the arts community. Gillian said people come. She said they come if you ask them to. And everyone always says "Don't be afraid to ask for help," right?

I sit with my day planner and bring to mind each of the people for whom I have phone numbers written in the back, running my finger down the list, one by one. This is my actual local network. It's a stretch to consider asking these people—even my brother or my dad—to come to my house on a regular basis and help me with Al's therapies. We were detached from having to truly need people here, by design. We weren't super dug in, on purpose. We travelled a lot.

I really don't want to have to ask the people on this list, or anyone else. I really really *really* don't want to ask. (Would you?)

But . . . I do believe it takes a village to raise a child. And now we all-caps NEED a village.

So I compose an email to our friends and family, with (cringing) lots of Calgary people included, finally announcing Alexander's diagnosis. I explain that we're going to Philadelphia. And I finish off like this:

> Why am I writing this email? Well, we don't want to *not* tell people about Al, and we spent most of December hunkering down and not-telling people, because, "Oh, it's Christmas," and "Oh, it's a bummer," and "Oh, people don't/won't know what to say."
>
> We don't want to make a big deal out of it. We don't want to be those people whose lives caved in and weren't fun anymore (but we might be those people—we're not sure yet), and we don't want to lose any of you because you can't handle our little tragedy . . . which isn't little, and isn't a tragedy, but sometimes feels like an apocalypse and sometimes feels like "well, that's life."
>
> In truth, it's a messy and complicated mental puzzle and I'm really struggling with it. I love our son, he is fantastic—it's me who needs to figure things out. I never thought I'd be raising a child with developmental challenges, particularly such profound ones, hard-wired in his DNA. I worry intensely. There are so, so many questions. You can imagine them. You'd have them yourself.
>
> You may be one of those people who haven't heard much from us in awhile. Before we knew for sure what was going on, the worry around Alexander has been eating at us quietly for many months. It's made it hard to be whole. At times since the diagnosis I've been completely paralyzed

by the cloudy and scary future inside this syndrome's prognosis. Certainly the biggest problem has been over-coming the complications of ego and expectation in adjusting to being the parent of a "disabled" child. The day-to-day reality is completely manageable, but the lurking dread inherent in "this was not the plan" is insidious and destructive and creeps up in quiet moments like a haunting. In retrospect it feels like our lives have been bifurcated, into Before This and Now What.

You were part of our world in the Before This time. Part of why I'm writing is because we're going to need you. Because we love you and we're scared, and because Alexander's coming therapy program will need volunteers to assist with some of the therapies.

If you can, bridge these worlds with us. We really hope that Now What doesn't have to be so different.

11.

The hospital's Infant Team program is billed as a collaborative group of specialists who address the needs of severely delayed young children. Each "team" is comprised of a physiotherapist, an occupational therapist, a speech pathologist, a social worker, a nurse and any other professionals who need to consult. We're all supposed to meet, together (*go team*), at least once a fortnight. But the service is so overbooked and oversubscribed and under-resourced that even with me overruling constant requests from the team to change the schedule, Alexander gets appointments with each specialist only once a month. Since these are the only formal therapies we have access to so far (other than private physio at $125 a session, for which we have to pay out of pocket), of course we go. If we find out in Philadelphia that The Institutes can't provide what we need, the Alberta healthcare system is all we have.

All five of the staff on Alexander's team were at the first meeting, but since then it's been two, with a third sometimes poking her head in on her way to another client. Al's team lead is a physiotherapist named Sheena. Other than her, we don't often see the same people. The staff turnover is relentless, a product of burnout from overwork and shitty management.

At every meeting I ask, *What else should I be doing? Are there other resources I should be tapping? Should I be calling my* MLA? *Someone else? Are there other specialists he should see, anything?* The team members look around at each other. The OTs and speech specialists visibly wring their tied hands. They know about services and programs I don't, and they know phone numbers and supervisors

I could call. But in 2010, the provincial health system is cutting early intervention and disabled children's health budgets, so only those already in-the-know make it onto waitlists. Under threat of termination, these specialists can't tell me what's going on, so they just look around at each other until Sheena finally says, "Infant Team is a good resource for your family at this stage." So little happens in these meetings, I resent having to pay for the hospital parking.

Still, I keep bringing Alexander. And I keep trying to find the secret phrase, the right tone, that will unlock the doors to the actual help these experts could offer. I can tell they don't like my calm delivery of a very long list of researched questions each time, my clear frustration with how few answers they provide. Other parents don't act like this, apparently. Maybe they are able to come in here and chuckle along at the weather banter and leave satisfied with the "He's doing well!" comments. But I can't. I want them to tell me what to actually *do* to help this child. And that makes us all uncomfortable.

The appointments get shorter, and further apart. The team members look Al over each time, but they check their beepers and day planners when they're not speaking directly to me. They give me a new exercise (one, max) at each appointment, but no answers. Yet they always take the time to tell me I need to calm down and take it easy.

Uh, I have a severely disabled kid here. There is no "relax" in this scenario.

But out loud I say, *Ha ha, yes, I do get out of the house every day* (I don't), *I take time for myself* (I don't), *don't worry about me.* Then I bring it back to Alexander: *What else can I do?*

They shift in place and glance at Sheena. I don't really understand what is going on. *Why* would professionals being directly asked what-more-can-be-done not respond? I'd take *any* answers, really. They don't give them, and I take it personally.

Today we're here for a dietician consult. She arrives fifteen minutes later than the usual fifteen minutes we have to wait, clutching pages about Alexander's syndrome that she's printed off the internet (I recognize the website). Alexander remains below the point on the chart where the height and weight percentile rankings starts, so that's why we're here: I need more ideas for how to put some weight on this kid. Only the dietician and a hospital services coordinator that reception rustled up last-minute are in this meeting.

I explain our daily food routine, telling the dietician how we're supplementing Alexander's pablum with olive oil to make it more calorie-dense, that I'm still waking him to nurse at night, that we're feeding him seemingly all the time. And I emphasize that I've been really looking forward to this meeting, because I need more ideas.

She shifts in her chair and says, all vocal fry, "Well? Yeah, this syndrome is just, so *new*? We just don't know much. Does that make sense? So I really don't have anything to suggest. It sounds like you're doing fine."

No, that does not make sense. We are not doing fine. I need help, concrete ideas, a plan.

I don't say any of that. *Maybe I should cut out dairy? Swap out Ensure for his liquids? Feed him nuts? Like, I know you should wait for the year mark for nuts, but they're good for putting weight on adults . . .*

"Oh, no. No—that's not necessary."

I wait. She looks back at me, genial but unmoving.

Oh no. She actually has no suggestions.

But he's underweight. His first pediatrician was super worried about this. I am doing the best I can, and this dietary consult was initiated last week so that you could help me get his intake and weight up.

She says, "Are you familiar with the Canada Food Guide . . . ?"

Oh my god. I mentioned the Canada Food Guide not ten minutes ago while I was explaining what we're feeding Al. Was she . . . not listening?

I look across the table at her, as expectantly blank as I can manage. We stare at each other in the silence. Finally, the services coordinator jumps in, cheerfully summing up, "Well, okay! It sounds like you have some good strategies in place at home, Mum. Canada's Food Guide is a *good* resource for you. . . . So that's great." She tells me to go home and just keep doing such a *great* job.

I have a sudden heady moment of unreality. I have to press my hand into the table to keep myself steady.

The taxpayers of Alberta are paying the salaries of these two people. Taxpayers bought the chairs, the whiteboard on the wall and the toner for the printer that produced those pages about Al's syndrome fifteen minutes ago. Yet again I will end up paying $16 in parking for this meaningless smileyfaced banter. I may have resolved not to lose my temper at the hospital, but I promised nothing about pretending I'm grateful for having my time wasted.

As I get up and start to clasp Al into his car seat, my body language says loud and clear that I'm completely ticked. The dietician turns back from the doorway and says that, actually, she could loan me a tilted foam chair? where Alexander can sit while I feed him his cereal mush? She says it probably won't make much of a difference, but I can borrow the chair . . . if I'm interested?

Yes, I take the stupid chair. Just to make her go get it.

That night I leave the house dressed to walk, and it is bone cold: –25 degrees Celsius. The snow squeaks underfoot, *squit, squit*. I'm out here because I can't be inside that unfamiliar house, this radically changed life, tonight. At the moment we have no living-room floor. You can look from the kitchen into the basement, like a bomb went off. They're putting in the new subfloor tomorrow, but for now it's a perfect metaphor for our lives.

I walk up the block, every house blowing thick steam out the top, furnaces churning in every basement. I turn the corner at the end, walking fast, covering lots of ground, almost floating. Except for the sound of my steps, the neighbourhood is quiet, like it can be only in the last week of January when Canada is in full hunker-down-and-outlast-it mode.

I cross the main road, pass the Safeway parking lot, and go over the transit tracks. Then I'm suddenly running, bolting, just five or six steps, but at a full sprint. *Whoa.* Involuntarily trying to escape, but my body came along? I don't know where I was going just then. Just away, just out.

I stop in the middle of the road. Two streets head in different directions. One leads into a neighbourhood full of little houses and apartments against the hill. I don't know anyone that way. I search my mental map for someone whose house I could aim for. I can picture ringing a doorbell—it's not that late. I see myself crashing into a vestibule, flushed from the cold and laughing, flopping down into a chair for a quick visit. But with . . . who? I could shake off these lead boots in the warm front room of someone familiar-but-apart-from-everything. But there's no one that way, no one in this city to humour me. This city seems to suck the "sure, come over anytime" gene out of anyone who moves here. These nighttime inner-city roads and houses are empty of warmth, there is no available surprised embrace to push away the frostbite and these escape reflexes. The Calgarians I know do not delight in the zane of an unexpected visit.

The other road goes to the river.

My calves are feeling the cold through my jeans: *Move, you need to move. Make a decision, whatever you're going to do.*

I don't even shiver. I'm just turning into a pillar of frozen salt standing here in the half turn near the C-train station. The world I thought I was heading into is still so real-ish, almost right there, but not where I'm going anymore.

Fuck it, nobody's watching, the world is empty—I plant a foot and pivot. *Squit.* On one foot, then the other, pivot, pivot. Me in my twenty-year-old hiking boots, turning circles in Sunnyside, pretending to be point guard with no ball or team. Crouching inside old muscle memory.

Finally I stop, facing the tracks, and move forward at last, reluctantly toward home. Through the silent gate and back over the rails. But wait, the grocery store. Yes. Closing in a few minutes, but open now. I hustle through the doors and walk the aisles, my eyes catching on items I always brush past. I pick up two Hungry Man meatball dinners in tall cans. I stand there looking at them, thinking, *We can trade these for spices or something, after the apocalypse.*

I walk home, dragging the grocery bag, its plastic flapping brittle in the cold wind. I come quietly in our front door, step out of my boots, don't call out my return. Instead, I go straight to the basement and hide the Hungry Men on a shelf behind the Christmas decorations. I know it's not okay to secretly buy food in preparation for the End Times, that this is a sign that Something Is Not Right. But I don't want to answer for these cans and why they appealed to me. I'm stocking up. It makes me feel like I am doing something tangible for our family. *I'll save us.*

From now on, everything I do will be to save us. Even in secret.

I shift the bin of decorations to better hide the bag. It'll be eleven months before this Christmas stuff will get touched again. By

then I'll know what to do with these cans of bright processed food
I've never even tried, or if I'm going crazy. For now, they're there if
I need them.

> It's oh very holy here on the kitchen floor
> Crying drool slipping dripping to the vinyl
> Over this boy born, almost but not normal
> Only barely minutely incomplete
>
> Please and please and I need another word for please
> Help me break me crack me up
> Take the part of me that can't have this
> Fit our jagged unfinished edges flush
>
> His missing piece and mine
> Make us whole.

At the hospital there is a resource counsellor I've been to see a few
times. I unpack some of my frustrations and fears in her office, and
leave always feeling wrung out and hungover. She doesn't give me
anything to do, no homework, no further resources, although I ask
for them, and for a referral to a counsellor who specializes in families
with disabled children—surely that is a thing?

At the third appointment, I realize during the session I've forgotten my wallet at home and can't pay for my parking. I won't be able
to get out of the parking garage. I break down, panicking, and there
is a flurry of activity that ends with a paid ticket being pushed into
my hands by someone from administration. Later as I drive away, I'm
gripped by terror that the counsellor's job is solely to monitor whether
I may become a danger to my child. I stop going to the counsellor. She
wasn't helping me, anyway. I should find an actual therapist.

But what I really need is a doctor.

By the start of February, I clearly have delayed-onset postpartum
depression. Or I'm still processing the shock of Alexander's diagnosis. Something. I need help, but I have no family physician; Alberta is
experiencing an historic shortage. I ask for referrals from everyone I

have access to in the health-care system, from my dad to Al's new pediatrician to the health region psych hotline. They all say there's nothing they can do. The internet has a list of Calgary clinics that may take new patients on walk-in. I call and all but one say they're not even accepting one-off walk-ins at this time.

This last clinic is way over in the city's southwest, at the far end of an under-leased mall. This is one of those February days when summer never existed and it starts to get dark right after lunch. Just walking from the car to the door of the clinic is a guaranteed stumble across a jagged field of scalloped ice.

Everyone in the waiting room is testy and sick, the overwarm air full of farts and coughed-out lung bits. Children in jackets are tugging at their miserable mothers, and people exaggeratedly step over slumped legs on their way to the desk to ask, "Please, be honest—how much longer?" It is one of the places with lots of those ABUSE OF OUR STAFF WILL NOT BE TOLERATED signs pinned around the room, their paper edges rubbed and curling.

There are no jovial Great White North stereotypes on parade here. No one would set a Canadian Tire or beer commercial in a winter walk-in clinic waiting room. (Though someone should. Retail therapy and alcohol are the only escapes at this time of year.)

I am eventually called in to see a Nigerian doctor, who announces at the start that he's only been in Canada for four months. He has a huge noggin and lovely shiny skin, his forehead reflecting individual lights in the ceiling. I tell him what is going on. For real. The son with the chromosomal deletion, the crying on the kitchen floor, the walking into the dark night and buying emergency Hungry Man rations, the home therapy program, the obsessive worries.

I don't want to tell him this stuff. Half my head is pondering the African medical brain drain and the weird broken system Canada uses to pull doctors in from all over the world. There aren't enough residency spots for most to get their full licences, so I've read they sort of languish in a halfway netherworld of medical-ish work. When we were in Toronto, I'd had a lump in my breast and the ultrasound tech was a fifty-year-old man from China. "I'm not allowed to tell you, because here, I'm technician. There, I was radi-ologist, doctor, sixteen years. You don't worry. This is benign lump, no problem." What a waste of their expertise not to arrange to let these people practise.

But here is this calm Nigerian with irises bleeding unevenly into the sclera of his eyes, listening to my stupid sad February face tell my story, his whole experience of Canada so far having been four months of the worst of winter. Seeing patient after patient bumble into this ugly strip-mall clinic, all of us with first world white-people-problems. I hear my own voice going on like a self-indulgent neighbour you can't get off your porch. *Oh, I'm sad, my child has a rare diagnosis I'm afraid of, I can't sleep, I don't know what's going to happen to him, I have a good marriage and lots of friends, and we have a normal older child and a house, but it's not enough, help me, I'm devastated, I'm breaking.*

But he listens to everything I say, then speaks in a rounded staccato. "Well, this is very reasonable. You've had a very hard time. I think you would definitely benefit from a short course of antidepressants. They would help you adjust and get through the shock of the diagnosis." He pronounces it "shok," with a space after the last sound.

"From what you say and what I can see, you're under a lot of strain. You're not coping. You have to take care of your family. You are The Mother, right? You have to take care of your son and get some help. Supports. You don't want to spiral down any further.

"But I can't prescribe antidepressants to you, because I can only see you today. It's a new policy that this clinic can't take patients into follow-up care. You have to find a family doctor who can follow up with you."

I ask how long he expects to stay at the walk-in clinic. Is he going to leave, perhaps start his own family practice? I'd be first in line.

He smiles. "Actually, I have a background in research. This clinic position is just a placeholder, arranged by my employer. I have my work permit in Canada through a partnership with the pharmaceutical company. I'll be leaving here once the paperwork is done. I'll be doing clinical trials. Actually, it pays better too."

He re-ups my thyroid medication, but that's all I get. Almost all the people he sees here need a family doctor, and there's no one to refer me to. I cry most of the way home in the car.

—

So. I have no doctor and no antidepressants, and if I start drinking I won't stop.

A few years ago I did a running clinic with a friend. I have always hated running. If there's no ball to chase, what's the point? But running three times a week, even when it was –25 Celsius, made that winter way more bearable. I prefer dancing, but I'm far too old for the club scene—and I'd never make it to midnight, when the good music starts. Adult dance classes, which I've googled, are criminally expensive. Running is nearly free, and I need the exercise, badly.

So . . . running it is.

One thirty in the morning, random February night.

Turner, rolling over, eyes cracking open, seeing me awake: "Ash? What's going on?"

Me, staring at the ceiling: *Worried about the other women.*

Turner, mostly asleep: "What women? Where?"

The women with special-needs kids who don't have the advantages I have. They are fucked.

Turner: "Oh, no. No, they're sleeping. They're okay right now. You sleep too. Shhhh." He wipes his hand over my face, manually closing my eyes.

But I can't. I'm English-speaking and Canadian-born. My father is a doctor, and I'm a cancer survivor, so I am not intimidated by the health-care system, and have back-door access to things sometimes. (Remember Bruce pulling me out of Emerg when I got bumped?) My marriage is stable, we own a home, and I only have one other child.

The other women with disabled children visit me in the night: *What if you are new to Canada? What if you are ESL, or only speak Urdu or Amharic? What if you have three other children? What if you have no spouse, or your spouse is a dick, or they have to work all the time and are never home? What if you have three jobs? Or what if you just don't know how to function within the health-care system, or don't have the bandwidth to advocate for yourself and your kid?* These faceless other women tap at my chest in the little hours, going, *Hey? Hm?*

Round and round my brain runs on the insomnia hamster wheel. In the morning I call every clinic on the health region website again to see if they're taking patients now. They still aren't. The website lies. I send a complaint into the feedback-button ether.

So I run. Outside, in the cold, with a bunch of strangers who are all much better (more willing) runners. I hate the running. It's terrible, but it helps.

Other things help too. Alexander at nine months old is a snuggly, uncomplaining, lovely soul. He's started gripping onto us when we hold him, bending his body to better balance in our arms. He seems more "in there" to us now.

Sloane can sometimes make him laugh so hard he chokes, but Turner and I only manage to earn nasal coos. Yesterday we saw him roll back to front, without help, for the first time. (By contrast, most babies his age are already crawling.)

Recently I've been getting the distinct impression that the open-mouthed lunges Alexander makes at my face are actually attempts at kisses. And tonight he learned to splash in the bath. Many of the parents of 9q34.3 children report that their kids *love* to play in water (I found the Facebook group for this condition, finally), so I've been encouraging Alexander for a long time to try bashing in the bath. Tonight he figured it out. We spent the next twenty minutes *splash!splash!splashing!* non-stop, and by the end he was even frogging his legs. When Turner came in with a towel for him and saw his moves, he said, "Okay, c'mere, Little Tadpole."

I do a whole bunch of daily therapeutic activities with Alexander now, from flashing a light in his eyes in the dark (triggering his "visual pathway" by getting his pupils to constrict) to vestibular exercises where I swing him around to activate his inner ear and work his balance. When I post a video of this exercise series on YouTube, it gets dozens of comments in different languages from around the world. Most of them say I am damaging my child's brain, and a few call for my arrest. Five people write to ask for more information, to help with their own disabled kids. (I contact these ones directly, then disable comments for the post.)

Al is finally starting to do things like pushing up with his arms when lying on his belly, and he is able to balance at a low table on his knees for about thirty seconds (I place him in this position and help him to hold it), which increases his hip strength and muscle endurance. Maybe he'll start to do these things on his own if I get him to a certain point. I don't know where that point will be, but somewhere. The comprehensive program we'll learn at The Institutes will help him catch up. It has to.

In the last few weeks, Alexander has also finally noticed Loki. I've seen him reach out to stroke-stroke-stroke him in imitation of how I myself gently pet the cat. Most children this age will just bang at an animal. I know I did, and Sloane did too. But Alexander seems to be petting the cat deliberately and gently: plucking softly up his ears, carefully along the tail. There *must* be ways to help him generalize this kind of learning. But . . . I don't know how. Much of each of my days is spent like this, trying to think laterally in a way I've never had to before.

This tactile angle is an obvious route—Alexander's gnostic development seems skewed but keen. He has a severely delayed reaction to cold on his hands, but his feet are properly sensitive. His current favourite thing is a feather cat toy that he pulls between and through his hands, and rubs on his face. So I wrack my brain for more types of activities like pet-the-cat/feel-the-soft-feather-toy that could be good learning tools. It is 2010 and the internet isn't yet full of lists of things for me to try. I read academic studies and bring home books about treating fine motor challenges in Down syndrome (the Down syndrome community is large and well organized in North America, so their accessible research and available treatment materials vastly outstrip those for any other developmental syndrome). But I can't learn fast enough.

Alexander's speech and communication are still nearly non-existent in comparison to neurotypical babies his age. He is *able* to make noise— like, if he's hurt, he'll cry now, and when he's done his nap, he's started to let me know with a calm series of (quiet) yells. But he doesn't try anything more complex.

Unlike our daughter and other "normal" children, who pick things up by observation and inner motivation, Alexander may have to be taught and reminded of each and every skill he develops, step by step by step, as he grows. This is monumental to think about in terms of the long-term reality. I focus on that cliché: I'm trying to take things one day at a time. (And failing.)

—

When I'm not thinking about The Diagnosis and all its implications, we're mostly us—we're good, we're fine. But the quiet just-after-dark time from four thirty until after dinner is very hard. As the sun sets, I become capable of only menial chores like emptying the dishwasher or folding laundry, but mostly I stare off into space. Sloane's really been burning up the TV after school these days.

Turner seems to be doing better than I am, though I suspect much of it's a brave front. There's no time to fall apart amid the mess of our house renovations. But he has also been very wise and quietly kind, including leaving me to sleep on several blurry mornings where it was definitely my turn to take Sloane to school. We're doing our best. There's not a lot of room for anything else.

12.

Remember that email I sent out a few weeks ago? In its wake, many, many people have reached out to tell me I'm brave. I'm finding I can't write those people back.

Because what can I say?

Being told I'm brave feels like these people want to shake off the messiness of our situation. Being told I am "able to handle anything" is like being pushed away. Our people are afraid for us. (I would be, for them.) For our sake, and theirs, people want us to continue to be who we've always been. They hope I'll handle this the way I've handled other things in the past, things they maybe thought were hard and scary but I didn't, like going to live in India or having cancer at eighteen, where I just plowed ahead.

This feels so different. I'm trying to make it into an adventure or something we can conquer, but how it will roll out is beyond a time scale I can grasp. This will probably define everything about our lives from now on, for years and decades to come. I'm still wrestling with how to change (should I change?) the way I think about our lives, how to think about Alexander, what to expect from people, how to ask them to be part of things as we move forward, now. There are still so many questions and unknowns. The only thing that feels honest is to address it all straight on.

Tara Nazerali is a dear old friend from my Ontario life, one of the most competent people in the whole world. I was adopted into her family years ago, and they've been sending specific little pings of support to me by email since Alexander was in the NICU. Tara is the only person I know who really understands about how it's no consolation at all to be considered competent when your life caves in. I've been writing up long, long missives in group messages to Tara, and her brother, my old love Sean, and their mother, Sheila (a doctor), explaining what's happening. In telling them, I'm trying to explain everything to myself. One (or all) of these three will know what to do. They always do. But even they say, *We don't know how to help. How can we help?* They're far away, and my focus is narrowing into a circumference just barely out of my direct reach.

In this life, I'm advocating not just for Alexander but for my marriage, for my daughter, for our family. For me, for my future too. I need help, but I don't even know what to ask for, how to find what I need. I need a community, here, in town, but the one we have is scattered and uninvested. Even farther afield, our people have no experience with a child like Al, with knowing a family like ours. Are we really breaking new ground, suddenly the test case for everyone we know?

By the end of February I haven't yet heard from some key long-time friends and family who received our "announcement" email. Statistically you'd expect a certain percentage of people to be unable to cope with this kind of news. But it's hard to realize that some of these people just don't want to get involved, whatever "getting involved" means to them. That we now have a disabled child and are having a hard time is too much for these friendships to bear.

A crisis does bring your relationships into close focus. Most of the people who didn't respond to our announcement email turned into the ones who walked away from us long term. It started here.

If you are wondering whether that friend of yours who has a disabled child—be the diagnosis autism, ADHD, lissencephaly, cerebral palsy, whatever—has noticed that you have not called? . . . believe me, they have. Others tried to carry on like nothing had happened, but couldn't keep up the pretense and disappeared later. That was worse.

Late February. On Fridays I drag down to the farmers' market for a regular meet-up with some friends who have kids the same age as Alexander. One of them has twin daughters who were diagnosed deaf at the end of January. Today she tells us about her girls' new speech and development aide, funded by FSCD.

Wait, you have an aide already?

"Yes—she started this week."

I have left many messages over the last few months on the FSCD intake line answering machine that specifically tells callers not to leave more than one message.

But the girls were just diagnosed at the end of January, right? And you already got a call back?

"Well, I hope so, it's almost March now! Actually, they called me back right away. We had the intake interview a few weeks ago, and the aide just started on Monday. It took a long time to set up, but she's *great*. Haven't you heard from FSCD yet? Alexander would totally benefit from this program."

I go home and call FSCD again and leave another message: *I've been leaving messages since early December. My friend applied to FSCD in February and she already has a service contract for her daughters. Call me back immediately or I'm calling my MLA.*

On Monday I call FSCD again and their voice mail has been altered to include a renewed promise that callers will be contacted within two weeks. I leave another message, referencing my Friday message, and say I look forward to hearing from them.

Two weeks pass with no callback. I search online for other numbers at the FSCD Calgary offices, and find absolutely none. It's like the entire internet has been scrubbed of data about how to contact this office. So I start calling numbers in sequence from the number of the intake line, and the phones ring and ring. I finally connect to the voice mail of someone in FSCD accounting, and I leave a long message explaining about all my attempts to contact them via the intake line but nobody calling me back, that my friend got her kids evaluated and an aide set up within two weeks . . . I say everything.

After the weekend a caseworker calls me back. Not *my* caseworker, understand. Just *a* caseworker telling me that I've been assigned a caseworker (who is not her) and that "my" caseworker will call me within two weeks.

Name, please?

This caseworker: "My name?"

Sure, but I'm asking what my caseworker's name is.

This caseworker: "I—I don't have it here."

Then how do you know I've been assigned a caseworker?

"You have. She'll call you within two weeks."

So our caseworker is a she?

"Yes."

So what's her name?

". . . I don't know. I don't have it here."

But she'll call me within two weeks.

"Yes."

That won't work for us. It's already been two weeks of waiting times seven. Fourteen weeks since I first started calling. Presumably you're only calling me back now because I managed to leave a voice mail with one of the people in accounting.

"I'm calling you back because you left a message on the intake line."

I nearly guffaw. *Really.*

This caseworker: "Yes."

I don't believe her.

I don't believe you, but fine. What's our caseworker's name? I need to follow up so we don't get lost in the system for months and months again.

"She'll call within two weeks, I promise."

My son needs help now. And I need the name and phone number of our caseworker right now, or I'm getting off this call and contacting my member of the provincial legislature.

This caseworker: "I'll have her call you today."

Big smiles all around. *Oh, that's great! Thank you! I'll wait here by the phone for her call.*

I do dislike being made to get on my broom. But I'm learning.

Our FSCD caseworker calls later that day, and she is pleasant enough, but I have to push hard to make her commit to an intake meeting. She's "really busy." I'm not having it. Four days later, she arrives at the house.

In preparation for this meeting I have read every online document I can find pertaining to FSCD. I have read the provincial legislation governing its programs, front to back, and have written out a list of things to ask for. I have spoken to two women who have FSCD service contracts and visited one at their home while an aide was working with her daughter. I asked Moonira what else I should do. It's been a busy week.

I take all the advice to heart. I haven't brushed my hair yet today, on purpose. I haven't picked up the house, on purpose. When the caseworker arrives, I show her in and we spend an hour on the couch, with me explaining Alexander's diagnosis and emphasizing how *hard* it's been adjusting to the news. I tell her about The Institutes, and all about the therapies we're running at home in preparation for going to Philadelphia. I show her the crawling track and the checklists of exercises on the wall. I explain our frustrations with Infant Team at the hospital, and how difficult it is to get help for Alexander from such an overtaxed system. I even manage to cry. She takes a lot of notes, on what looks like triplicate carbon paper with Alberta government letterhead.

Finally, she says, "Well . . . I think I have everything I need, here. Alexander is really an excellent candidate for the Developmental Aide Program at FSCD. The only thing we need now are evaluations stating that he's severely disabled in two or more areas of his development." She wears very shiny lip gloss. It stays on, even while she's drinking the tea I made.

Genetics already said he's profoundly disabled.

"Oh, that you have a confirmed diagnosis is really helpful, yes. But for our records we need to see that at least two areas of his development have been evaluated as 'severe' delay."

Shitty that there's another hoop to jump through. But we have an Infant Team appointment this week, and I'll just get the evaluation documents from them then.

I'll send them to you by email, okay?

She says she'll approve the developmental aide contract as soon as she has those evaluations in hand.

Fine.

Except, not fine. At Infant Team Sheena explains they haven't done any evaluations on Alexander yet.

I'm floored. *We've been coming here for four months. What have you been doing if you haven't been evaluating him?*

Sheena: "Well, we've been evaluating him informally."

Wait now. *How many of the patients in Infant Team end up in* FSCD *contracts?*

"Probably all of them." She blinks at me. Surely this is an act.

So every client you have here ends up at FSCD, *and when they do, they need evaluations to prove they're worthy of an* FSCD *contract. So you end up doing evaluations on all your clients.*

"Pretty much. Though some parents take their kids to private evaluators."

Why would they pay out of pocket?

"Just to get it done faster."

But evaluations are covered by the health-care system if you do it here at Infant Team, right?

"Yes."

So why are you doing <u>anything at all</u> before you do evaluations on the kids in this clinic? Like, why aren't official evaluations the first thing you do when kids come into Infant Team? To get a baseline on what we're all working on here?

Sheena: "Oh, we're happy to do the evaluations for you . . ."

This isn't what I'm saying and she knows it. *We can't get the* FSCD *aide help until they have evaluations from you. So I need evaluations done on Alexander in all the areas. Immediately.*

"Oh, well," Sheena chuckles. "That'll take a few appointments." She glances at the speech pathologist, who smiles. "It's a pretty involved process to do official evaluations. We have to test him on all kinds of things. Does that make sense?"

Christ on a cracker.

I imagine it can be rather involved, but I really wouldn't know. This isn't my field. But we'll bring him anytime to get the evaluations done, even daily, even for a full day if that's needed, or more than one day. This is a top priority for us. I'm shocked that it wasn't a priority for <u>you</u>. I would love to compare his progress from November to what he's doing now based on formal assessments, does THAT make sense? I'm sure it would be helpful to see how far he's come.

"Oh, probably."

Oh no. I look at my hands in my lap. *So . . . let me just be <u>really clear</u>. You have no official baseline data on Alexander to this point. Please make a note in your file: "Parent is very disappointed that the team has compiled no official data or baselines after four months of*

appointments." The only priority now is official evaluations, what-
ever needs to be done, <u>whatever</u> it is that you need to submit to FSCD,
whatever you do for all the other clients, since "probably everybody"
ends up getting referred. And we need to get these squared away as
fast as possible. We are going to Philadelphia in a month, and I need
to have the FSCD *contract finalized before we go.*

Sheena sits back: Hardball, eh? "We can do most of the evaluations next week. I'm training for the Boston Marathon, so I am more
booked up than usual. But I'll have reception call you."

Absolutely not. I'm not waiting for callbacks anymore, and I tell
her so. I stand motionless, smiling, at reception until all the appointments are finalized.

Lookit me, learning.

13.

That moment in January 2010 when I stood pivoting in the cold, dark streets should have been the lowest point. In the movie version it would be. Then the music would change and slowly rise into an inspirational melody over a montage of slow gains and battling upward, a winter-to-spring blooming. But in truth, that night was just the most cinematic of dozens upon dozens of awful low moments.

At the end of March I sink to the kitchen floor, crying. Can't get up. I am sobbing woolly tears, with a view of the cat dish and the underside of the microwave. This is too hard. I can only see a future where tomorrow will be harder.

My mother, Val, is here on a rare visit, sitting in the chair by the window. She doesn't move. "Now what's happening?" she asks, all sardonic.

I think . . . I think I need to see someone.

She says, "What kind of 'someone'?"

A doctor. I don't have a doctor right now. I'm on waitlists, but . . . I really need to talk to someone about antidepressants. I need something. I can't do this.

Val sits forward and points at me. "Oh? You think you're sad now? You go on antidepressants, you'll gain twenty pounds like [clap] *that*." She sits back. "*Then* you'll be depressed."

I am thirty-seven years old. My mother is over there, looking at me, waiting me out. I feel a familiar, fuzzy shame: I'm "overreacting" again. I am eleven years old and frantically upset, and she's rolling her eyes at me, "Oh yes, here come the waterworks."

I've got too much saliva in my mouth and can't swallow, so I wipe it on my sleeve. I'm running three days a week, as hard as I can, doing hills now. I ask for help from everyone around us and nothing is changing or getting better. The only thing left is drugs. My mom is a psychiatric nurse, a counsellor herself. She would know whether antidepressants would help—wouldn't she?

My legs say I'm fat enough. My belly says I'm curving and bulging and coming up on middle age, so I cannot, should not get bigger. But something else is shaking my shoulders: *Wake up, wake up! You need help, don't let weight shame worm its way into this!*

Two sides pulling, the childhood ignominy versus a life raft.

My mother can be curiosity alight, her intelligence fierce like a flaming sword. But not in this. She has a foot planted hard, resisting being in this with me, insisting *absolutely not, nope.* Once she's set, she won't break character, ever. I don't know why. I resolve, there on the floor, that I will not be like this in my own mothering. Never.

I lean there, blinking back tears, looking at the grimy edge of the floor where it meets the wall. I breathe deep, pull myself together. Sloane will come downstairs soon. She's up in the bathroom, brushing her teeth. It's bedtime for her, my job. I sing to her every night as she snuggles in. It's time to snuggle her in. I have to be the mom.

In the moments before I rise, I reach for my emergency reserves, jars of light, filled years ago, saved to be one-time boosters, and pour them into my engine. No one is coming to save me. I need to take care of myself and these children and my husband. I need a doctor and I need to get us to Philadelphia.

I find a counsellor at last, recommended by Moonira. She's our age. Her office is a renovated house, sweet and stylish. The first thing she says as I start to sit down at the first session is that her rate is $285 an hour.

Suddenly I am crying, and I stand to leave. She is very surprised, as though no one has encountered sticker shock in this office before.

I can't . . . I can't stay. The FSCD funding will only cover $92 an hour for counselling. And the contract isn't signed yet, I'm still waiting on the evaluations from Infant Team, but we will get the contract, my son is qualified . . . I can't stay. I don't have any other money.

She insists I sit back down. She didn't know I was an FSCD client, she says. Yes, she'll take the $92 an hour. She won't charge me her regular rate "for now." She can give me three sessions at the FSCD rate, and then she'll "review" and see if she "needs" to raise it.

I'm not even relieved. I can only think that three sessions won't cover half the mountain of anguish I'm trying to scale. As she begins her script of introduction again, I'm half-gone, recovering, embarrassed for bursting into tears. And distracted. Anyone whose usual rate for services rendered to parents of disabled children is $285 an hour should be considered a war profiteer.

Afterward, I sit crying in the car. I have done a lot of crying in this car.

At the next counselling session, I am calmer. Moonira has assured me that this counsellor is very experienced with the system around disabled children and will help us. That other families love her.

I don't need to love her. If I only have three sessions (two, now), I need strategies for dealing with the crazed fear that's closing my throat. I need a reading list and resources to help me get a handle on this grief and shut that shit down. I need her to identify other services in the system that will help support Alexander, and me, and the family. I have to focus.

As I get settled in the office, she goes to get us tea from the reception area. I look around the room more closely, now that I'm not crying. Her counselling degree is on the wall: Gonzaga University. Sounds made up.

She comes back in. Her hair is long and elaborately highlighted. She has a huge diamond, and the pen she's holding is fancy; its cap makes a hefty clink on the table. . . . This better be good.

Counsellor: "So, last time, we talked a lot about your financial concerns. I haven't heard much about your family yet."

Me: *My family of origin?*

Counsellor: "Yes—so, your father I've heard a bit about. He's here in Calgary, yes?"

[I nod.]

Counsellor: "And your mother?"

[I immediately begin crying.]

[This continues.]

[Five minutes later:]

Me: *My mother . . . is not really in the picture.*

Counsellor: "Can I ask . . . has she passed away?"

Me: [snorting, *hoo-hoo!*] No. She's alive.

Counsellor: [making a note] "Okay . . . let's . . . just . . . leave her just for a second." [She looks up.] "Siblings?"

Yes. A brother and a sister. They're twins.

Counsellor: [giving the *Hmm, interesting* look I've seen thirty thousand times when people hear my siblings are twins. It never gets old to the general public] "Where?"

My sister is in Ottawa. My brother is here.

"So it sounds like you have some support in town. Your brother, your father . . ."

I haven't seen my brother since last year. He used to live three doors down from me, but then he moved to the far south, far suburbia.

"You don't get along?"

We get along great. But his wife didn't want to live so close to his family. My brother travels for work and hasn't been around much since they moved, and he won't let his son come to our house now. The official reason is that our place is "dangerous" because we're renovating. I'm not going to try to explain this like it makes sense or say that I'm okay with it. I am not okay with it, but I can't change it.

"So you haven't seen your brother since last year."

No.

"Not at Christmas?"

No. He called me a few days after Christmas to ask about Alexander's diagnosis, but he and his wife wanted to spend Christmas on their own. I should mention that around Christmas his youngest son was born a bit premature, so my brother was understandably busy. I haven't met that kid yet.

"So that child is . . . about five months old now. You haven't met the new baby?"

No.

"Any plans to?"

I'd love to. But "not yet." And they don't want us to drop by. I have invited my brother to come over on his own, but he's busy with his life and work and the kids, and his wife needs to keep a tight rein on all the plans. I get it. And so he says my house is dangerous—it's a rationalization. I've said this already.

"But is it? Is your house dangerous?"

No, my house is not dangerous. Look, I love my brother, and he is smart and hilarious, and when we're right in front of each other we get along awesome. But he lives far away now, and he doesn't respond to my suggestions that we get together. I have lots of love to give to my brother's children. I'm a fun auntie. I think the baseline situation, where his children were supposed to grow up a few doors down from mine, versus now, where they live twenty-five kilometres away and we never see each other, is bonkers. I will not participate in pretending that that's normal or okay with me.

I've been told most people don't say the things out loud that I say out loud. Fuck it. Life is short.

. . . Goddammit, I got sidetracked with these family questions. The session ends and I didn't have time to ask for resources or referrals. Next time.

The Infant Team assessments are done. After the physio evaluation Sheena hands me the document and asks me to come for our next team appointment—our last before we leave for Philadelphia—on a specific Wednesday. It works with her training schedule, she says. We put it in the family calendar.

The evaluations get to our FSCD caseworker at the beginning of April, and they disappear into the bureaucratic machine. I leave messages every day for a week on her voice mail, asking when the contract will be signed and when we can expect our copy. It's being sent by mail, she says. I check the mailbox every day.

In the meantime, I start the process of finding a child development agency to oversee the FSCD contract, because it's mandatory to have an agency "deliver" and oversee the aide-provided services. Agencies are privately owned companies that employ specialists such as speech pathologists and occupational therapists and developmental aides who work directly with delayed kids. These "service providers" have a minimum nine-month waiting list. Moonira puts me in touch with a friend who owns an agency, and over the phone I explain to the owner about The Institutes program we will run after we get back from Philadelphia. She is nominally on board to support us within the structures of the FSCD contract, and we make an appointment to get together in May, after we return from The Institutes.

I also start the process of hiring the aide to work with Alexander, who will be "overseen" by this agency. This person will be trained and paid directly by us. We will be reimbursed by FSCD for a portion of their wages. I write up an extensive explanation of what we are looking for and post it on Kijiji, nanny and au pair sites, and circulate it in our networks. We get exactly one applicant. Four days before we leave for Philadelphia, I hire her.

At our final Infant Team appointment, Al and I are met by the speech pathologist at reception. These sessions have never started on time, before. She shows us into a room, where it's just her and me and Alexander. After ten minutes of making notes and trying to get Alexander to repeat sounds, she puts her pen down and turns to me, looking suspiciously pleased. She announces that she is leaving the hospital system to start her own practice. She gives me her (new) card. "It'd be covered by private insurance for a few sessions," she says. We do not have private insurance. Her new office is way, way down in the far southeast of the city. Goodbye forever, I guess.

I finally ask, *So . . . where is the physio? Sheena specifically requested we come on this day, at this time.*

The speech pathologist explains that Sheena said we could see her for a few minutes at the pool, if I wanted.

What pool?

Turns out the hospital has a therapeutic pool. It's in the basement. So we go. Lovely pool. Saltwater. Lots of equipment and toys, a long ramp into the water. Things hanging from the ceiling. And nobody in it. But three moms sit in a nearby hot tub with Sheena, chatting and smiling. I make my way across the deck, carrying Alexander.

Sheena looks up, all bright, and says, "Oh, sorry, I double-booked you with this group. Thanks for coming down here." She gets out of the tub and puts a towel around her waist, goes to the locker room to get her notes.

Two of the moms are holding babies a bit older than Alexander. They all look very comfortable. Like they know each other. Like this hot tub session is a regular thing.

I say, *Is this a regular thing?*

One mom: "Yeah, we meet every Wednesday at one. It's been . . . what has it been now?"

Another mom, with no kid: "Two years!"

The first mom: "Yeah, two years, every week. We just chat, it's good. You can bring your kids, or you can come on your own if they're sick. Her daughter's at home today." She points at the other mom, who nods and smiles at me. "You could come next week."

But uh wait wait wait just a second. They've been meeting every Wednesday at the same time for two years? So why did Sheena ask me to come specifically at this time?

Soooo is this, like, a therapy thing with Sheena?

Second mom: "Oh, not really. Things come up sometimes, but mostly we just chat. It's mom time. Social. You have to take care of yourself, too."

Sheena comes back, waving me to a towel she's laid out on the floor beside the hot tub. We sit.

"So, how is Alexander doing?" she says.

He's fine. Are you going to assess him today? I need some suggestions for the next month while we're away.

"If you want me to."

Yes, I want you to. He can't put any weight on his legs, and he can barely hold his head up, for fuck's sake. This is the purview of physiotherapy intervention, if I'm not mistaken. So yes, if it's not too much trouble to exit the hot tub social club for a few minutes before your next marathon training session or lunchtime meeting with HR or therapeutic massage, yes, I want you to fucking assess him. The pool deck is really not my preference, but if it has to be here on the pool deck, with these other mothers watching, fine, yes, absolutely yes, for chrissakes, yes, assess my kid—YES.

Yes, please.

Sheena moves forward and starts looking at Al's flexibility, testing his neck strength, moving him through roll-to-sit motions.

The first mom is watching. She says to me, "Oh, he has vision?"

I glance over at her. *Vision? Yes, he can see.*

"Mine's blind," she says, nodding down at the baby girl she's holding, who lies there with her arms raised and head stretched back. Her eyes are rolled up, flickering. The mom sees me looking.

"She's having a seizure," she explains.

I am speechless. *Uh, a . . . seizure, right now?*

"Yes."

Should you . . . do something for a seizure? Shouldn't you do something for a seizure? I'm a doer and I don't know what to do. We are in a hospital, and surely there are first responders nearby . . .? This seems like an emergency, but the mom is calm. So I just keep kneeling there.

The mom senses my mute question: "Oh, there's nothing we can do. She has them all day."

This baby has seizures all day? And—but—but is there nothing you can do for all-day seizures? That can't be possible. I look at Sheena. She is apparently so focused on moving Al's legs up and down that she can't hear us.

I can usually come up with something, but I gots nothing. I just sit there, crouched over Alexander, as he's moved around by the physio and the baby continues to seize in her mom's arms.

I finally manage, *I'm sorry to hear that.*

Now Sheena looks up. "He's doing well."

I snap back to her and Alexander. *Thanks.*

"He's doing really well."

What more should I be doing for him?

"Just keep doing what you're doing."

I'm running a daily program of stuff sort of cobbled together from a bunch of places, my friend's old occupational therapy work guides, online descriptions of vestibular training, my gut, the things you tell me, and the intro book to The Institutes. Please give us more exercises to do. I'll do them with him.

"I really don't want to overwhelm you or give you homework. It's going well. He's doing well. He's doing good."

Thanks, but—

"He's doing *very well*," Sheena says then, pointedly. She looks hard at me, then flicks her eyes toward the women in the hot tub. None of them are looking in our direction at this moment. Her head does a tiny nod toward them. "You can be grateful he's doing as well as he is."

I . . . am, I say. But, did she really just—what did she just do?

Sheena sits back on her haunches. "Good. You should come to this hot tub group. You can join us next week, or any week, if you like. Except the third week of April, when I'll be away. These mothers have a lot of the same challenges. It's a good group."

The mothers are listening again now. They nod at me. They've been listening to everything, probably. I'm feeling weird and dizzy all of a sudden.

Okay. Well, we're away after this week. Thank you, though. Um.

I find a spot in the change room to get Al into a new diaper before the ride home. The moms come in, hot tub time all done. The one with the seizure kid says, "Sheena told us about how you're doing some stuff with The Institutes in Philadelphia? You're going there?"

Yes, next week. (She told them that?)

"Yeah, I looked into them. It's expensive. And they want your kid to do this huge therapy program that takes all day, even weekends. I have enough trouble running her ketogenic diet—I don't have any more time. I have other kids, plus this." She gestures to her stomach. She's pregnant.

Ketogenic . . . ?

"It's high protein, high fat. It causes ketosis, so the body burns fat instead of sugar. It's getting really popular. But I have to weigh everything she eats, grind it up—she's tube-fed."

Why is she on that?

"It helps with the seizures."

But she was seizing today. *Did she used to have more seizures?*

"Oh yeah. She used to have a hundred a day. Now we're down to about . . . sixty?"

A day.

"Yeah, a day. Every day. It's hard for her to develop, because she's seizing all the time, basically. But the diet helps."

And it takes all day to do that diet?

"It's lots of prep and cooking and weighing and measuring. It's a huge pain in the ass. I'm not sure I can keep going. We've been doing it . . . about six months? I don't know how much longer I have it in me!" She laughs. "I have other kids. I have to focus on them. I have to think of them."

I run away, take the stairs up, with Alexander under my arm like a rugby ball. I am panting. I jog through the hospital lobby, pay the parking fee, run all the way to the car. I strap Al into his car seat, fling myself into the driver's seat, pull the door closed and yell honking, crying rage into the steering wheel. Alexander is unfazed; he sits, twiddling his fingers. I sit there and howl for so long the windows fog up.

When I've finally yelled myself out, I sit there in the ticking silence for another five minutes. Then I turn on the car, roll down the windows, breathe in the late-winter parking garage humidity, turn on the defrost.

I drive home super slowly. I don't turn on the radio. I just pilot the car and listen to the gears and my heartbeat in my ears. When I pull up in front of the house, I put the thing in park, turn the whole machine off, get out and quietly unstrap the kid, and go in. They win. We will never go back to Infant Team.

PART
TWO

To risk all
is the end-all
and the beginning all

BJÖRK, "MOON"

14.

Picture flying to another country to attend a kind of . . . educational clinic you will pay thousands of dollars for. To an institution that has published books about child brain development that are in every public library, but has a laughably terrible website. Picture being told by this place that for the first week you'll attend mandatory lectures from nine in the morning to at least eight at night, and only if you make it through them all will you be allowed to attend a clinic where they'll create a program that will fix your child.

Picture persuading your spouse to do this thing with you. And picture bringing along your neurotypical daughter and, for moral support, your dad, your mother-in-law and your spouse's aunt. You'd need a giant rental car and a borrowed house big enough to hold everyone. Picture knowing that this institution has been helping parents like you since 1955, but no one at the hospital at home has heard of it.

That it was unlikely you'd end up here is an understatement, wouldn't you say?

We fly into Newark with Bruce, where we meet up with Turner's mom, Margo, and his aunt (one of Margo's sisters) Mary Elizabeth. We find the New Jersey Turnpike in the dark.

Inside the vehicle we go over recent family news as we drive past hundreds of warehouses with trucks at their docks, lounging like sows with thirty nipples each. Then Alexander falls asleep, and Sloane falls asleep, and we do miles and miles quietly, looking out at unmistakably American 10,000-lumen billboards advertising hospitals and wrongful injury lawyers.

We take the bridge over the Delaware River into Pennsylvania, and thickets of dark forest start to appear, flanking the highway. We bypass Philadelphia proper, driving overtop and into the north-western suburbs, heading for Chestnut Hill.

The well-kept area near The Institutes for the Achievement of Human Potential is quiet at eleven thirty on a Saturday night. All around us are the original country homes of American railway barons, centuries-old gardens, and trees coming into the fullness of spring. There is a trolley line and big parks with wooden playgrounds, and the nearby high street, Germantown Avenue, is so quaint I can barely stand it.

Before we find our rental house, we drive to The Institutes on Stenton Avenue to check the place out. The grounds have a long, down-lit wall along the road, lined with flapping foreign flags. A large, illuminated sign marks the entrance, and we turn in, driving through the campus in the dark. There are several acres of trees and large buildings from different eras, with walkways in between and formal English landscaping and tall white pines. It looks like a Viceregal Lodge: its main building has wide stone steps leading away on two sides, etched glass windows, curved balustrades and walls covered in ivy.

As we roll past what looks like a Seven Sisters undergrad residence, and then a brutalist theatre, I'm leaning out the open window, breathing in the humidity. There's a growing trill in my chest. The Institutes in real life is grand, and substantial, and somehow familiar.

We are about to learn that this is a universe of its own, a place with definitive answers to difficult questions. The Institutes runs like a field-tested psych evaluation from a time before the internet, when anthropology and biology were similar disciplines. The staff here exist in a bubble in which they've never seen the *Star Wars* movies and gothic script on letterhead still means serious business. There are rules, and there are hierarchies that won't be questioned, and the staff all call you Mrs. Turner even after you tell them you are Bristowe, because they exist in a time when a family only has one surname.

With all this hinted at in the books and on the phone, I *really* hope they're not all-hat-no-horse or—god help us—somehow religious. We really really really won't countenance Jesus freaks, and will most certainly not be signing up with a the-Lord-will-be-our-kid's-saviour cult. Oh fuck no.

After coming all this way, of course I hoped we wouldn't arrive at a conference room in a hotel, but I'm desperate so I would've been okay with an oversized storefront with folding chairs, or a stale hospital boardroom. I didn't dare hope for a leafy stone campus and a circular driveway with pebble gravel, or for flags of the world and magnolias along the pathways, ready to bloom. And never could I have imagined the dark, knowing humour that inspired the erection of a SLOW: CHILDREN sign on one of the trees at the bottom of campus.

But here it all is.

It is now Sunday. We're setting up our Chestnut Hill house for nine days in situ. We get groceries at a typical ridiculous American supermarket that has four kinds of spray cheese and a mystifying product in the deli case called "scrapple."

Me: *Is it scabs and apples?*

Turner: "Let's hope not."

We walk the neighbourhood as a pack, Turner and the kids, his mom and aunt, me and my dad, looking at the houses and gardens and shops and helping Sloane explore the playgrounds. In the evening we all go over to The Institutes for the mandatory check-in.

We are greeted by staff in the doorway of the clinic, who spookily know us on sight. "It's the Turners!" (Later, I will remember that the application form required a large photo of the family.)

We stand in line to speak with Harriet, the registrar, who gives us binders full of information and schedules, and an invoice for the lectures. We stand in a second line to pay the fees. Milling around are families from all over the world: Singapore, Namibia, Poland, India. Their children are in wheelchairs or in arms, or absent.

We check out this space, the clinic where we'll be next week, after the lectures: an unusual space, like a library without books or shelves, with offices along curving hallways and stairs going up and down in three places on each level, all surrounding a large square mat in the lobby that looks like a gymnastics floor. Around the edges of this mat there are benches where parents are perched, speaking to staff members or changing diapers. Overlooking the main room is a huge, thick-brushed ecclesiastical painting of a scene in which sheep and people are being lit by the glory of the sun/god. Um.

On the lower levels, the walls are dotted with awards and framed medals, unreadable certificates in calligraphic hand and faded block-mounted photographs of disabled children grinning with staff that we already recognize from upstairs (though they are younger in these pictures). In the bathroom lobby there is a bust of a man labelled DR. RAYMUNDO VERAS, and nearby, a photo of him laughing his guts out with the founder of The Institutes, Glenn Doman. I lean in to read the inscription. Oh—looks like this jolly Raymundo guy died in 1999. Bummer.

Once all the parents have had a chance to check in and pay the fees and mill around a bit, an invisible timer seems to go off and the staff are suddenly keen to see us out.

"Go home and get ready for tomorrow, everyone," calls Harriet, from the desk. "This week will be demanding and you need to be rested. Please remember that the lecture hall will be at sixteen degrees, which is the optimal temperature for learning. . . . For the Americans here, sixteen Celsius is colder than you think! Please dress accordingly!"

She raises her voice a few decibels. "BE AT LEAST FIFTEEN MINUTES EARLY. YOU WILL NOT BE ADMITTED TO THE LECTURE HALL IF YOU ARRIVE LATE."

Okay, okay, they've only told us four times in the last hour. Gee whiz.

We all file out, families sneaking looks at each other (*What does their kid have, do you think? . . . I hope the Asians have toques and scarves for tomorrow*), find our cars and leave.

Monday morning, our first lecture day at The Institutes. I wake up half an hour earlier than the alarm. It's cloudy, but not dark. I have been running with the Calgary group since February but have never gone out solo. Over the last few months I've progressed from one-and-ones (one minute running followed by one minute walking) to ten-and-ones (ten minutes running followed by one minute walking). This is the best my cardiovascular fitness has been since I've had children.

I still don't love running, but before I can change my mind, I throw myself out of bed and pull on tights and shoes.

Turner: [rolling over] "Wait, where are you going?"

Me: [hauling sports bra on] *I'm going for a run.*

Turner: "Now? Today? What if you get lost?"

I won't get lost—the streets are a grid. I'll be gone twenty minutes.

Turner: "We can't be late."

We won't be.

I stretch in front of the rental house. There is dew on the grass. Philadelphia in April is already fully warm and green and alive. When we left Calgary two days ago the city was still covered in snow. Canada's climate fucking sucks.

I don't have a watch, so I count the sets in my head. I run up our road to the high street, go one block over and run back down, and keep going, up and down. I circle back to the house in time for the end of the third set of ten-and-ones.

My legs are buzzing as I walk in, proud of myself. Turner is there, buttering toast for Sloane. He looks over his shoulder. "Where the fuck've you been?"

I was running! First time all on my own!

Turner is annoyed. "Great, awesome, but you said you'd be gone twenty minutes."

I was! . . . Wait, how long have I been gone?

"Are you kidding? It's been nearly *forty* minutes. You need to get ready *right now*. We have to go."

I've never run for that long, maybe ever. A personal best! I'm certain I only did three sets of ten-and-ones. In the shower I do the math. Oh.

I throw on my clothes and grab our stuff as Margo and Mary Elizabeth talk with Sloane in the kitchen. Turner stands at the open front door, calling last-minute directions to his mother: "She's fine with a granola bar if you go to the park. She doesn't like them, but don't just buy her lunch if she says she's hungry, Mom. She can make do with a bar. You hear that, Sloane?"

Sloane: "Gramma, I want *three* pieces of bacon."

Margo: "Well, darlin', why don't you start with two, and we'll see how much there is when everyone's had some."

Sloane: "I want three, Gramma!"

Turner: "Mom? There's lots of books in her backpack."

Margo: "Okay, Chris."

Mary Elizabeth comes toward us, flapping "get out" with her hands. "We've got it, Chris. We can handle everything here. Don't worry. We'll figure it out. You go, have fun now. We're good." She gestures at Alexander, who is watching bits of reflected sunlight moving across the living-room ceiling.

Margo calls, "You don't want to be late. They said you're not allowed in if you're not on time."

I hear Bruce say, "I'm just waiting on eggs. I can drive you kids over."

No, Dad. We can make it. It's only three blocks. We've got lots of time. It's fine.

As we walk out the door, Sloane calls, "Hey, Mama! Have fun storming the castle!"

We walk over to The Institutes campus and head to the brutalist theatre building. In the lobby there is a huge stained glass window of a youth in mid-stride: the symbol of The Institutes. Rainbows of light filter through it onto the floor. A woman in a green blazer ushers us toward the auditorium doors, past six Institutes staff in a smiling line. "Go inside," she says. "You will find your names at your seats."

We enter a formal mid-twentieth-century lecture hall, with long desks on banks of risers. Big white name tags indicate that Turner and I are together. (Mine does say ASHLEY BRISTOWE.) Below our names, in capitals: CANADA. We look around the room, which is still mostly empty. We sit.

For the next fifteen minutes, pairs of parents come through the double doors and down the stairs, searching for their name tags. The room grows full but stays quiet. There is an air of "first day of school" about everything.

At 8:59 the door opens and Janet Doman, director of The Institutes, enters the room and walks down to the lectern. She wears a lavender skirt suit with lavender pumps and gold bean-shaped earrings, her hair backcombed into an elegant roll. She goes to the lectern and looks out at us for a full minute, waiting for the clock to hit 9:00.

A series of chimes ring through the speakers in the ceiling. The doors at the top of the hall are pulled closed by a staff member, and almost immediately we hear someone tugging on the handles, then knocking. The beige-blazered staffer at the doors opens them a crack, whispers something and then closes them again. Whoever was knocking has not been allowed in.

We all turn back to the woman at the lectern, who raises her hands, raises her voice and begins to speak: "Welcome. Welcome, all you parents. We are so glad to see you here. Today you are taking the first step toward saving your children's lives."

Hmm. Good start.

"You all have something in common, something incredibly important, that brought you into this room. It's the most important thing in your world: your kids.

"Your kids are hurt, and you want to help them. We are going to help you do it. This week we are going to teach you everything you need to know about how to start. Then it will be up to you to go home and *do* something."

She pauses, steps out from behind the lectern and walks to the first row of risers. She rests one hand on the desk and looks around at us.

"It is a frightening thing, for parents, to have a disabled child. I'm very sorry to say that the medical world doesn't have very good answers for you. And worse, the school system doesn't want to teach your child.

"You love your kids like crazy, but I bet you were not prepared for the arrival of a hurt child into your family. Were you?" She looks down the row of parents in the front seats. It's a rhetorical question. Nobody moves.

She continues, "Love is great, but respect is far more powerful. What your kid wants more than anything is your respect. And you're going to give it to them. The medical world doesn't respect your children. The school system doesn't respect your children. But we do. We are going to show you how to help your children be extraordinary."

Janet Doman is now in charge of this room, no question.

"Your learning curve with your kids has been steep. A lot of parents go to all kinds of hospitals and clinics before they finally arrive at The Institutes. We hear about the Mayo Clinic and Johns

Hopkins and special places in Europe and Japan. All kinds of places. But eventually the hardest-working parents find their way here. Because there is no magic pill. You can't pay to make the problem go away. If there were something you could buy for your kids to fix them, we would all be doing something different today. But that's not what's happening. We know you love your children, and you are here because you need to do something about them. And we are going to show you exactly how."

Okay. This place is definitely different.

"My father opened The Institutes in 1955. Over the years we have worked with tens of thousands of families. Our kids recover. They become well. And they excel.

"We listen to you—keenly. We know you ask yourselves: 'When will it be normal? Will things be normal again?'" She pauses.

"Normal like before? Oh: never. It'll never be normal like before."

She pokes her index finger up the air. "But it *will* be wonderful."

She turns and heads to the lectern. Oh, I love Janet Doman already.

15.

Over that first day's lectures we are introduced to the various institutes—physical, physiological, intellectual—for which the staff wear corresponding blazers in black, green or beige. So this finally explains why the name of the place is plural. The speakers talk to us about the history and epistemology of The Institutes' work, the brain and the body's neurological systems, why the regular and historical medical models of brain injury treatments don't work.

The chimes sound every so often and we are released for a ten-minute break. The women run to the bathroom, and the men move on a table laden with coffee and apples. We are reminded at each interval that we will not be admitted to the lecture hall after the end-of-break chime rings. They are training us with blatant cues and consequences.

For the first few days someone is left outside after every break. On day two it is me. Another mom, too. We are led, like misbehaving children, to soundproofed booths overlooking the auditorium where simultaneous translators are turning the lectures into Spanish, Russian and Chinese for parents listening on headphones below. We are guided to chairs in the dark and watch the lecture from above. We parents come to call this "the penalty box."

During the longer dinner and lunch breaks the staff open the bookstore across from the lecture hall, which stocks Institutes publications, "intelligence" materials like flash cards and posters, and nutritional supplements (available by "prescription" from the clinic and stored behind the counter). There are CD-ROM teaching units about the Romans, reptiles, astronomy and the American Revolution, flip decks of types of trees and butterflies, math textbooks. We learn in the lectures that we'll need this kind of stuff once we get home and start running our therapy program. Since anything we don't source here will have to be handmade by us or purchased online, everyone is browsing and buying.

But the bookshop is lacking in Institutes-specific souvenirs. After dozens of hours of lectures the materialist in me wants branded mugs and T-shirts. I want one for Sloane with something like MY LITTLE BROTHER WENT TO THE INSTITUTES AND ALL WE GOT WAS A HUGE HOME-SCHOOLING PROGRAM AND NOW I CAN'T HAVE ICE CREAM written on the front. Only . . . snappier. I might get something made back in Calgary.

Our fellow parents here become familiar, like classmates. We see their kids, who have a vast range of neurological and physiological problems and chromosomal irregularities, only at mealtimes. Many of the kids have types of cerebral palsy, a brain injury condition caused by oxygen deprivation at birth. One child from Ukraine fell through the ice at a pond near her home. She was dead for twenty minutes while CPR was performed, and when she was finally revived, she had catastrophic brain damage. This girl is eight, no larger than she was at four, and curls in a jagged ball on the floor, jaw misaligned. One woman's daughter was normal until eighteen, but one morning she had a seizure and ended up in a coma. Now she can't speak or move one side of her body. Two women have infants with Down syndrome, floppy, cross-eyed girls, one of whom has a feeding tube set into her stomach wall. Alexander is the first 9q34.3 telomeric deletion syndrome child to come to The Institutes.

The days of lectures do contain bits of whimsy, parcelled out over long, long hours of stories and slides and notes and demonstrations, and much repetition to drill in the lessons. Our adult lives at home are full of our choices, our priorities. Not here. You cannot leave the auditorium during lectures, you cannot bring drinks into the theatre space. No phones are allowed on campus. While no questions are allowed during the lectures, staff from each of the institutes line up near the coffee tables and along the hallways when the chimes ring. We are reminded each time that the staff are available to us during the breaks and encouraged to ask them anything.

These people occupy a hyper-specific and secure world. Their approach to disabled children is completely—utterly—different from what's happening outside The Institutes' gates. They are so at odds with the common wisdom and yet *so* sure of what they know. It is singular. It is humbling.

Because it becomes abundantly clear that they are certain. They *believe*. They know they're taking us somewhere we can't picture before we arrive. They're very kind about it, really. But doctrinaire. Single-minded in a way I've never experienced with any institution.

And really, they must know that most of the questions we parents have are some version of, *But how do we actually do all of these things with our kid, at home? How do we fit it all in? It seems like a lot, it seems crazy, it seems like way too much . . . doesn't it?*

Glenn Doman himself gives the intelligence lecture on day three. He enters the auditorium after the chimes ring and we are already in our seats. We parents are well-trained now, all attentive and compliant. No one has to go to the penalty box anymore.

Doman is ninety-two years old. He proceeds slowly down the side stairs, assisted by a black-blazered woman whose name, we will come to know, is Rosalind. She helps him into a chair and puts cue cards into his hands. "Thank you," he says, and nods once. She retreats to a chair at the side of the room.

This is the founder of The Institutes, a Second World War veteran and physiotherapist by training. Doman looks up at the room. All eyes are on him.

He has thick white hair, parted on the side and yellowing at the tips. He has giant jug-handle ears like my grandfather Alec, a man who also liked teaching things, who was also patient and matter-of-fact. He knew about automobiles and chores. Glenn Doman's world is handicapped kids.

"The world doesn't understand children," Glenn Doman begins. "And, even more so, it doesn't understand disabled children. To the world, your hurt children are not human. They're thought to be irrevocably broken. Around the world, disabled kids are utterly ignored. For millennia children like yours have been left to rot in the corner, because the world doesn't understand them and doesn't even try.

"We are introducing you to your child's brain, and the miracles that it can perform. No matter how hurt, your child's brain is capable of growth. It is capable of repair and change. Brain development can be deliberately sped up. We know this is true because we have fifty years of experience with the results. [Though the idea of brain plasticity is widely accepted now, it was still very new to mainstream medicine in 2010. Most medical practitioners still believed that the deficits caused by brain damage at any age were permanent.] Out there, the medical world is still saying, 'We really don't know much about how the brain works.' . . . I say: 'Speak for yourself. We do.'

He takes a beat, and lets that sink in with us.

Then he says, "When I was in school, I played football. I wasn't very good. I was one of those guys who stands there and gets hit so that the quarterback has a few more seconds to throw the ball. But I grew up understanding the idea of being on a team. And I was considered an athlete. The world understands a hurt athlete. They don't do him any favours, but they understand him. If an athlete goes to war and comes back with one leg, or gets in a car wreck and breaks a cervical vertebra, there's plenty of pity and money to help someone who *used* to walk."

He peers at us. "Your children don't want any pity. They want your respect, your companionship and your love. Your kids are ferociously intelligent inside, and they desperately want to learn. And you are their only chance. Hurt kids have physiological barriers to their growth and learning, so with your kids we have to *over*do our efforts, we have to do more than what the world provides to regular kids. If you're a swim champion, you didn't just learn to swim. You swam and swam and swam and swam and swam and swam. You are an *over*-swimmer.

"When it comes to intelligence, the world will do in anyone they think isn't intelligent. The world thinks your kids are stupid. *They couldn't be more wrong*. Every child is a genius. Your children are geniuses. . . . Believe that. Your hurt kids are intelligent beyond what you can possibly imagine."

Before this lecture I had never heard any man, let alone a very old man, talk about children like a crusader. I never anticipated hearing anyone say that the strength and grace and stamina of special-needs children have humbled them in their life's work. But Glenn Doman does this.

"Believe it, because it's true," he says.

"As they grow and have to live in this world, your hurt kids will be subject to prejudice and ignorance from every quarter. Your kids' only safety is being *above* average in intelligence." He says the next part slowly: "They have to be over-knowers. Over-learners. And we're going to show you how to make that happen."

The day after Sloane was born, a staccato beat for her arrived unbidden in my head. This is how it goes:

When I mentioned this beat to people, nobody could grasp wtf I was trying to explain.

Them: "A rhythm? That represents the kid?"

No. Like . . . it's Sloane's. It's hers.

"So it's the vibration that Sloane gives off?"

No. It's kind of a drum line. As her mother, I bestow it on her. But it was given to me, for her.

This sounds a bit woo-woo, even to me and especially to them. "Ummm, given from who?"

. . . The universe?

Everyone, deadpan: "Um, my children do not have 'rhythms' from 'the universe.'"

I stopped talking about it.

While I was pregnant with Alexander, I wondered if this baby would have its own rhythm, or whether perhaps the first rhythm I'd heard wasn't just for Sloane but actually for "motherhood."

When Al was born, it was clear that the rhythm I already had was Sloane's alone. And I didn't receive a different rhythm for Alexander. As his first year went on, when I listened for it, trying to tune my inner ear to bring it in, there was an absence. Like birds flown away.

I wondered whether it was because he was a boy. Then I wondered whether it was because he was disabled. That maybe he wasn't "enough" of a being to need one.

I also worried that not receiving a rhythm for Alexander meant I hadn't, on some astral plane or something, asked for it for him. That my disappointment and self-pity was interfering in his rhythmic birthright as a child of mine.

But one day at The Institutes, I am walking across campus to lunch and thinking about Alexander watching sunlight shards reflecting around the rental house living room. In time with my steps, and in that image, this arrives:

I walk up the damp slab stairs toward the dining hall, clicking through this rhythm with my tongue and breath. It is already familiar.

Now I am grinning. I realize I'd been doing it for Alexander last night in the bath. I'd jiggled him back and forth to this beat for this morning's vestibular work. I'd been saying *Tiggy-tiggy tig-tig tig-tig tig* while tickling him at dinner on Sunday.

My son's song. It arrived here, in Philadelphia.

16.

On day four, after a break, a boy's parents carry him into the auditorium and down the left-side stairs, *step step down, step step down,* to the floor. The child twists in his father's arms, his hands curled up hard near his face like a praying mantis. The eyes roll in his head, his mouth hangs open. A bag of bones and sound, his moans fill the space. When people see this kind of child in public, everyone pointedly ignores the fact of them, carrying on, pretending nothing is wrong. But so much is not okay. Smiles get stuck, pauses lengthen, and everyone's ears are on the door, hoping it will open and take this body away.

But the people with this body are smiling, calm, proud, carrying their boy to the front of the room. Fifty pairs of parental eyes, our eyes, are watching.

I think, *What is this? Oh god, what is this? Is this where they show us the tricks they've taught a super disabled kid? Oh no.*

Susan Aisen, the director of The Institute for the Achievement of Intellectual Excellence (beige jacket), says, "Now we have a very special guest, twelve-year-old Javier, and his parents. This family is from Mexico City. Javier has been on the program for five years. They're here for a programming visit and have generously volunteered to be part of this next session. Javier is going to show us the facilitated communication program we just explained to you. We have a translator because Javier and his parents speak Spanish."

Through the translator, Javier's mother says they raised their son with no therapy supports for years. A brain injury during birth had left Javier "spastic" and non-verbal, so they cared for him and tried to find ways to enrich his life, but the only health care he received within the Mexican system came when the parents would take him to hospital for chest infections or fevers.

The mother says, "We were encouraged to leave Javier's illnesses untreated, with the intention that he might pass away from 'natural' causes. For the first seven years of his life, we kept on like that, keeping him safe and trying to reach him ourselves, but getting more desperate and hopeless. We really felt there must be something we could do to teach him to communicate, but we didn't know what. And then we found The Institutes. We took the What To Do About Your Brain-Injured Child course, just as you are doing right now. We were you, in those seats, learning the same things." As the translator says this part in English, Javier's parents nod up at all of us in the auditorium.

Javier's mother continues:

But then we went home to Mexico and started the program. Even right away I experienced a crisis. What was I doing? Was I pretending this child could talk? Javier can't feed himself, he can't control his bowels, he can't always even look in the direction he wants to. He seemed unreachable. I talked to our advocate. He just said, "Keep going. Keep going. Javier will show you the way." And soon, Javier started answering my questions. I spent a week thinking, *I'm answering these questions myself. I want my child to talk to me so much that I'm moving his hand, even though I don't think I am. I'm going crazy. I'm using my child as a puppet!*

So I called The Institutes again. "He's speaking to me now, but I don't think it's him. I think I'm having a conversation with myself."

Our advocate said, "Is there anyone else there?"

I said, "No. Just me."

"And Javier."

"And Javier, yes."

The advocate said, "So you're asking questions, and you think you're answering the questions yourself because it's facilitated communication."

"Yes. I think I want him to speak so much that I am creating these answers!"

He said, "Let me ask you, in these conversations, has Javier told you anything you couldn't know?"

I said, "Well, yes. For example, I asked him what he did with his grandparents when I was out, and he told me."

"Did you ask your parents what they did with Javier while you were out?"

"No."

"So, how would you know?"

"Well, I'm inventing what they did."

Our advocate said, "You could check this, though, right? You could ask your parents what they did with Javier while you were out. Right?"

I hung up on our advocate right then! No goodbye, I just hung up and rang my mother. I said, "Mama, two days ago when you were here with Javier, what did you do? Did you see grosbeaks at the feeder and a zanate chased them away? And did you go and fill the feeder again?"

She said, "Yes, love—how did you know?"

I hung up on my mother! I called our advocate back— "Javier told me the truth! He was right!"

And our advocate said, "So who is answering the questions?"

I finally believed. I ran to Javier and apologized to him! I gathered him up and said, "I'm sorry, I'm sorry," over and over. "Oh my god, my child, I didn't know." I cried and cried, and he cried too. I said, "I didn't know that you were speaking to me. I'm so sorry I didn't believe it. I love you, forgive me! Forgive me!"

It is a great story. I am happy for this mother. The story pulls at me. I want to believe it.

I glance around at the other parents, from England and Cleveland and Russia. They look like how I feel: *Well, that was very inspiring, thank you. Very good, really excellent. . . . Unfortunately, this won't work with my kid.*

But now the translator and the parents set up on the floor on a mat, with Javier lying slumped half sideways on his mother's lap. The mother pulls out a laminated alphabet-number card, and Javier's left hand swings up, penduluming in the air above it. Javier's mum catches his hand lightly by the wrist and guides it down, toward but not touching the card.

Susan Aisen crouches down across from them and looks up at us. "Usually when we do these demonstrations, it's hard for new parents like you to believe what you're seeing. We have a lot of empathy for that. But we've also been doing this for a lot of years, so it's basic stuff here.

"Don't worry about the how and the why of what we're showing you right now. We're going to have a conversation with Javier using the facilitated communication method."

She turns to the mom: "Ready?"

The mom nods.

"Ready, Javier?"

Javier's finger pokes the *Sí* box on the card. He isn't even really looking down at it.

I reach over and put my hand on Turner's leg under the desk, clutching the fabric of his jeans. *Oh god.*

Susan Aisen: "Javier, do you have anything to add to what your mother just said about the facilitated communication?"

Javier's finger staccatos across the board, poking out the words letter by letter.

Javier, in Spanish, through his mother and the translator: "First I will say hello to the parents here."

Susan: "Okay, go ahead."

Javier: "Hello, parents."

Susan turns to us, expectant. There is a scattering of hellos from the room, including mine. I'm a joiner.

Then poke, poke, Javier's finger picks away at the card. As the words are completed, the mother says them aloud, and at the end of each sentence the translator repeats them in English into the microphone. It takes a long time for the message to come through.

Here's what Javier tells us: "The facilitated communication program brought me to life. Before, I was in darkness. My parents did not know me. We were together every day, but I was like an animal. I could tell them nothing. I was angry. I could only watch. I had pain and could not explain. I had no words for the world. The program let me speak through the letter board."

The poking-out-words stops. The mother stops, the interpreter stops.

Susan crouches, casually waiting, like this is all really normal. That it's normal for the bouncing wrist of a writhing child to spell out the words that are making these sentences. We parents in the riser seats are all frozen, barely breathing.

Susan, speaking to Javier's mother: "Is this true? What do you think?"

Javier's mother: "*Absolutamente.*" No translation necessary.

Javier begins to poke again. "I want to tell the parents here something."

Susan: "Sure."

Javier shifts and moans. His mother repositions him so he is facing out to the audience. The poking begins again, loud now. We can hear Javier's fingernail hitting the laminated cardstock, *pek-pek-pek*, as he spells out the words.

Through the interpreter: "You have come from far away because you can't talk to your children. You don't know how to help them, but you want to help them. Your children are like me. Your children want to talk to you. Every day I thank God for my mother, who did not give up. She taught me how to speak to her through this card and there was an explosion. I had words for the world. I swam into light after years of darkness. My mother discovered that I was inside this body, that I am me.

"Do not give up. Your children are waiting for you."

The whole world shatters.

Oh my god, there is a child trapped in that body.

Oh my god, disabled children are prisoners of bodies and brains that won't obey them.

Oh my god. We are failing them all.

17.

On day five, we parents spend all morning reviewing how to perform The Institutes' therapy program at home. Everything is based on the philosophy of high frequency, high intensity, and short duration of each therapy, and stopping before your child wants to stop. We are wrung out after the week of lecture days and the session with Javier, which really brought home the reasons why we're going to take on the wall of work looming ahead.

I look around the auditorium. Damn. We look beaten down. I sit up straighter. *C'mon. We can do this. Let's do this.*

Glenn Doman is already seated at the front of the lecture hall when we start to trickle back in after the lunch break. "I know the staff have spent the morning consolidating the program for you," he says. "You may be feeling overwhelmed. You're about to leave here and go home to a life that is very different from anything you've seen before. You didn't picture this world before you arrived. There will be days when continuing the program seems impossible. We know this because parents call and *tell us* that this program is impossible. They tell us that it's too much to complete in a day, that they can't get everything done.

"But I promise you . . ." Glenn Doman peers around at us, taking his time. "The staff here at The Institutes stay up late at night trying to think up *more* things to add to your kids' program. To make it harder." He chuckles. ". . . More *effective*. That's our promise to you."

He points at us. "Every day that your children aren't learning and growing is a day that they are falling further behind their peers. You must put away all your regrets and heartache now. You don't need them.

"We give you hours and hours of work to do each day, every day of the week. Parents tell us that it's unreasonable. But I'll tell you what." His *wh*'s are soft off the top, like Foghorn Leghorn's. "We're asking *you* to be unreasonable.

"There are lots of reasonable programs out there. They'll take your money and give you reasonable goals, reasonable tasks."

He straightens the cards in his hands. Then stops, and looks up at us. "The problem is, the reasonable programs don't work."

Turner and I drag our asses home at the end of this final day of lectures, utterly spent. Our brains are fried and our hearts are full. We have this weekend to rest up before the clinic appointments for Alexander start on Monday.

It's eleven o'clock and we're sitting with Margo and Aunt Mary Elizabeth, who are keeping us company while we stuff down some leftover perogies. Sloane and Alexander and Bruce are in bed. This rented house is made of old wood covered in new paint, and the narrow floorboards creak quietly under our chairs as we shift our bums around.

I feel like I should be standing to eat. I don't think I've sat so much for so long in my entire life.

Turner: "Me too, but I'm too tired to stand."

Margo says, "They're on to something, these Institutes. They've got you right where they want you. You've got nothing left but their way after wringing you out all week."

She's right.

I have no idea how we're going to do it when we get home, but it actually feels like everything is going to be okay.

Turner: "Well, Ash, everyone kept telling you to lower your expectations and stop being unreasonable. But here they're saying, 'Yes! Be unreasonable!'"

It's true. I don't even care if they're brainwashing us. They're the only people who believe.

On Saturday morning I feed Alexander early-early and then put him back in the crib and go for a run. Going out on my own has become way easier, even after only a few days. When I'm done, I creep back to bed. Turner and I try to sleep in as long as we can, but stupid birds are chirping their guts out right at the window. We lie there aching as the house awakens around us. It feels like we've been put through a punching machine all week.

At midday, Mary Elizabeth flies home to New Hampshire and Bruce to Calgary. In the afternoon, our friend Carla comes in from New York City to spend the night. We lived with Carla in India, and studied Hindi together, up in the hills at Mussoorie. She's a religion prof in New York now, and returns to a shrine site in the northwest of India every year for her field research. She knows from intense experiences. We spend Saturday night out at a restaurant in Chestnut Hill, repeating our stories from the week for Carla, doing the voices of the lecturers, playing out our incredulity at everything we've just been through. She's a great audience.

And in the telling it's clear how preposterous and funny this whole situation is. We've not only drunk the Kool-Aid, we're about to run a Kool-Aid stand at our house for the foreseeable future. We laugh until we can barely breathe. (Turner and I may be somewhat delirious.)

The next day, I open Facebook for the first time in a week and the 9q34.3 parent group has news. Alexander's syndrome has been renamed after one of the Dutch researchers who identified it. Alexander's alphanumeric diagnosis is now called Kleefstra syndrome.

Monday morning. Sloane is exploring more of Philadelphia with Margo—the aquarium today, I think. We're back at The Institutes, in the clinic building with the gymnastics floor and the huge wall painting, and Alexander is with us.

Over the next two days The Institutes' staff will design a customized therapy program for our boy, and teach us how to track and report on his progress. We could have gone home and figured out a therapy routine for ourselves after last week's lectures. It costs more for this clinic visit, but I know I need the accountability and support of being officially "inside." I need The Institutes' full, ongoing involvement. I need the cult. So here we are.

I see a few families who attended last week's lectures dribbling into the room, but most of the families are new to us. We all find places around the floor and, as instructed, place our bags and jackets

inside the bench seats to keep the room clear for the kids with mobility issues.

Our assigned "advocate" is Rosalind Klein Doman, the director
of the physical institute (black jacket), who will oversee Alexander's
file and take a specific interest in his progress. She speaks with a
Bronx drawl and has a large, beautiful birthmark on her upper lip
that I watch as she talks. She goes through Alexander's entire history
with us, following the account I wrote in December for our application. She asks for more details about my pregnancy, has extra questions about the birth, and wants updates on all of Al's medical
appointments right to our departure for Philadelphia a week ago. We
talk for more than an hour while she takes notes. Rosalind often
addresses her questions and comments directly to Alexander. He sits
quietly propped in Turner's lap, looking at his hands (or the ceiling).
We answer for him.

All day Turner and Alexander and I move back and forth between
various large treatment offices and the main gymnastics floor. There
are long, long intervals in the main hall between appointments, with
Turner and me trading off the baby. There is no posted or discernible
schedule, although the clinic director, Emma, seems to be managing
things according to an internal order or system not shared with us
parents. Clinic staff regularly remind us that appointments take as
long as they need to take for each family, and that other parents and
children are receiving the staff's full attention behind the closed
doors. So we wait.

The staff in our appointments really do not rush. They speak
slowly and clearly. In each session we are handed colour-coded worksheets on which to write down the programs Alexander is assigned,
and we copy verbatim what the staff tell us to write. We have to read
back what we've written. They make us demonstrate that we understand what they've explained. They are very definitely in charge, and
we do what they tell us to.

When we're finally released for lunch, we sit with a boy and his
family from Singapore. Two years ago he was hit by a car. He lost most
of his speech and fine motor control, and hasn't grown since the accident. He takes a shine to Alexander and wants to hold him. The parents are surprised we let their uncoordinated son cuddle our baby; he

strikes most people back home as frightening. I think for a moment. I can imagine what these parents have been through, losing their "normal" child, who has been replaced with this jerky, slurring kid. Actually, I can't imagine it. All the parents gathered in this leafy corner of Philadelphia are living through particular private tragedies. But after the lectures last week, and after Javier, this small Singaporean boy isn't intimidating at all. The frightened contempt I can now admit I've carried all my life for disabled people has been completely burned away.

In the afternoon The Institutes' medical director (black jacket) takes a full baseline of Alexander's physical measurements, using caliper tools that before today I've seen only in old anthropological photographs. The doctor and his assistant record Alexander's weight and height, the circumference of his head and chest. They test his reflexes, measure the flexibility of his joints and the depth of his breathing; they look at his fingernails and the width of his heels. We leave with instructions to get hair sampling done for the whole family (to test for heavy metals in our home environment), and a long list of different kinds of bloodwork to request from Alexander's doctors at home.

At the nutritional consult we are greeted by Charlotte of the physiological institute (green jacket). The shelves in her narrow office are lined with nutrition texts and worn recipe collections from around the world, books on macrobiotics, traditional Japanese cooking, a few Moosewoods, *Eating Right for Your Blood Type*, nursing textbooks, a whole Ayurveda section and a copy of *Gray's Anatomy*. We sit across the desk from Charlotte as she methodically works through all the nutritional history I provided in our December application, reading parts of it back to us.

Everything stops when she sees that we had been feeding Alexander ricotta cheese.

"Now, in the elimination diet, he will have no dairy at all," Charlotte says.

Yes. No problem.

"It's very important that you stop feeding him ricotta, and remove all dairy from his diet."

Oh, we will. We have. We did the lectures last week. We really understand. No dairy.

"Are you still interested in giving him ricotta?"

No—no.

She waits. So I explain, *I had just sort of discovered it back in December as a kind of supplement to Alexander's diet, to help him gain weight. His first doctor at home was really worried about his weight. So I was feeding him anything he'd eat, and cheese is fatty, so . . .*

She straightens and sits back. "But that's not going to be an issue now. We're not concerned about his weight. He'll gain weight on the nutritional program we've assigned. You will be writing down everything that he eats every day on the charts—" She sits forward again and flips to a pile of green spreadsheets on her desk. "We'll get to the charts in a second. But if you feed him dairy, it should be reflected here." She points at the page. We saw slides of these food-tracking sheets last week in the nutrition lectures. We know we'll be recording the descriptions and weights of everything that goes into Alexander's mouth.

Yes, we've totally got it. Don't worry. There won't be any dairy on his charts.

Her eyes widen. She wants to be sure I'm not trying for some wiggle room. "But, wait now—you can't give him dairy and not write it down."

Oh jeez. No, no—*we won't give him* any dairy, so that's why there won't be any dairy to write down. Really.

"Because at the mid-term report, if we see any dairy in his diet sheets, we'll ask you to take it out. That includes *all* dairy."

One hundred percent. We agree.

Turner reaches over and takes my hand, but he doesn't have to worry. I'm 100 percent on board. I'll just keep talking until we get past this. I'm looking Charlotte in the eyes, reassuring her. *We've got it. No cheese. No milk, no ice cream, nothing with dairy in the ingredients, no yogurt. We won't give him any dairy.*

"And no ricotta."

Yep. No ricotta. Promise.

". . . Okay." She gathers herself.

Now she asks us to take verbatim notes about the prescribed protein-carbohydrate-fat balances for each of Alexander's three daily meals and two snacks. There are sections in the green pages on ingredient substitution and rotation, parts about constipation, reflux, the necessity of refrigerating oils other than olive and coconut, and far more—much of which we covered last week in the nutrition lectures, but which is repeated here in different form, alongside diagrams and places where we fill in Alexander's assigned foods in grams and milli- litres and calories per meal per day. This personalized eating program has been designed based on Al's history and the recommendations of the medical director.

Alexander is also prescribed a list of supplements—vitamin B com- plex, Kyo-Dophilus (a probiotic), chlorella (a protein supplement made from green algae) and others, with different supplements for an "anti- stress" protocol we will use when he is sick (even just with the sniffles). And we have to buy a kitchen scale that can measure down to hun- dredths of a gram. (I have no idea where we will source a scale like this. Eventual answer: bong shop, duh.) This appointment makes it clear we are going home with a nutritional program of even more substitutions, restrictions and complexity than we'd anticipated from the lectures.

We have been told over and over: "If you do *nothing* else, run the nutritional program." But as we walk out of Charlotte's office, I wonder if we will ever manage the whole thing, let alone the rest of the therapies. (We will. And for years and years—right to the present day.)

Finally, the clinic manager releases us for the night. We stagger home, carrying Alexander, and find the house empty, Sloane and Margo still out at a nearby park. We put Alexander to bed in a back bedroom and fall zombified onto the couches, eating the spaghetti Margo left out for us. As the light starts to fade outside, Sloane comes bursting through the door, flops over the back of the couch, throws her face right into mine and, in a funny low voice, growls, "Hooyyy Mawwww-mawww."

Hi, my lovey love.

Life keeps going.

Day two at the clinic is longer, and lunch break is later. Today's appointments build on the ones from yesterday. The inspiration of last week's lectures and the weekend's rest is wearing away in the face of the work piling up ahead of us. But the staff are of one voice: *Leap and the path will appear.* So I am leaping—and will haul Turner and Alexander and Sloane along with me.

Today we are given customized programs for Alexander in reading (numbers of sets of words and phrases to show him) and math (using the dot card system). Another appointment takes us through the intellectual development program (encyclopedic information presented on any topic, eventually focusing on areas that Alexander shows specific interest in, a philosophy known as "Follow the Child"). Al is assigned a physical program (crawling with distance goals and hanging from his hands to build up his shoulder strength) and a neurological program that includes hot and cold compresses to stimulate the nerve endings in his hands and ears. We are also retaught the cross-patterning protocol we learned in the lectures, and are assigned six to eight patterns a day to do at home, for which we will need adult volunteers (Sloane, at five years old, is not yet strong or tall enough to be a patterner for her brother).

Each appointment gives us more and more to think about. At lunch we hear parents at every table talking about how we all wish there was a dorm here where we could live, a working program clinic we could all attend each day with our kids. None of us want to go home to our old lives and try to upend them with all this therapy. But it's clearly the only way forward.

In the late afternoon we are finally taught the masking protocol. This is the backbone of The Institutes' brain oxygenation program. We know from the books and the lectures that masking helps prevent seizures, builds diaphragm strength, increases breathing depth and helps disabled kids be more alert in general. The Institutes' custom-made plastic masks fit over the child's nose and mouth, with a thin elastic strap that secures the mask behind the head. The child wears the mask for up to one minute at a time, breathing largely their own exhaled air, though the mask has a small tube at the bottom through which new air can enter. As each family learns the masking protocol for their child, we begin to see them masking on the gym floor as we wait for our own session. We try not to stare as the plastic fogs up with the kids' breath. It looks exactly like something you're not at all supposed to do with a child. But none of the kids seem to mind. It just looks scary to us parents.

When it's our turn, Dr. Ernesto, the director of the physiological institute (green jacket), has Turner and me try the masking ourselves first, to show us what it feels like. I wear the mask for over two minutes, and although the air inside starts to feel warmer and my breathing speeds up, it doesn't resemble holding your breath underwater, where you run out of oxygen and have to rush to the surface. Rather, new air comes into the mask through the tube, and some in around the face—the mask is not designed to have a perfect seal. So breathing inside the mask is like breathing into a paper bag, as you are told to do when hyperventilating.

Exhaled air contains about 5 percent carbon dioxide. While you keep rebreathing the air in the mask, it becomes increasingly rich in carbon dioxide, causing hypercapnia—the term for the body's response to increased carbon dioxide. Hypercapnia triggers vasodilation (the expansion of the body's blood vessels) and an increase in heart rate, breathing rate and breath volume. Translation: you begin to breathe more quickly and more deeply, which over time strengthens the diaphragm and builds lung capacity; it's akin but not identical to the process of adapting to higher altitudes. In the presence of increased carbon dioxide, blood hemoglobin increases its relative uptake of oxygen, becoming more efficient, relatively speaking.

Masking periods are short and done at intervals between which the child breathes regular air, so the body isn't overwhelmed. When the mask comes off, the brain gets a relatively large "hit" of oxygen from the room air, which verbal Institutes kids describe as delivering a kind of "kick," like the caffeine from your first cup of coffee of the day.

Alexander's prescribed masking periods are only thirty seconds for now, with at least four minutes between each masking. Eventually we will increase the masking duration to forty-five seconds, and then sixty. At home we will use a timer with an alarm to let us know when each mask is done, and when the interval between each masking is up. The Institutes' staff stress the need to set such alarms, since we will be running many simultaneous therapies at home and will need auditory reminders. Alexander's assigned program will see us work our way up to forty masks a day. *No sweat*, I think.

As evening comes on, families start to emerge from their final appointments. They shake hands and hug staff in doorways. Everyone looks relieved, ready to get the hell out of here, get dinner, head to the airport. Parents gather their things from the benches and make for the door, giving quiet thumbs-ups as they pass families still waiting. "See you at the revisit," they call. We are all scheduled to return to the Intensive Treatment clinic in six months.

Finally, it's our turn for the closing appointment. It's with Susan Aisen, the senior director who did many of the lectures last week, including the one where we met Javier. Susan does a complete overview of the program they've built for Alexander over the last two days, literally reading over everything with us, page by page. She does not rush. I feed Alexander under my shirt and Turner takes notes in our program binder. We've both been wondering if there's some kind of book or article that can come out of all this. ("One Family's Radical Approach to Special Needs" by Chris Turner will be the June 2015 cover story of *Reader's Digest*.)

When she's reviewed the entire plan, Susan opens a folder that's been sitting on her desk since we came in and presents us with the Intensive Treatment Program contract, made out in our names. It states that one parent will take on the full-time role of therapist; that no one other than Turner or me will run the program with Alexander; that we will not send Alexander to school; and that we will get our local pediatrician's written permission for every part of the program, including the masking.

Susan sits back and holds out her hands, palms up. She has narrow, silvery fingernails, unpolished. She says, "Take your time. This is a momentous decision. We're here to help you, but it's up to *you* to save your child. If you can't sign the contract, your family will not be in the Intensive Treatment Program. You're welcome to do portions of the program on your own at home, of course, with the skills and knowledge you've gained from the books and lectures and the clinic this week. You can return for the following sets of lectures. You're not 'out.'

"But in the everyday work, you'll be on your own. Being in the Intensive Treatment Program means you are accountable for tracking his progress daily and sending in the mid-term and final reports. It means you can call us at any time for support and we are always available to you. It means you understand your responsibilities and you know that we will fulfill ours.

"So, do you have any questions? Please, ask every question you have now, before you sign." She waits.

Turner and I look at each other. Any questions we have are moot, because they are about things we know aren't allowed. Can we send him to a special-needs day camp when he's old enough to attend? How about a day off the nutritional program so he can have turkey stuffing on Christmas? No and no. What if we hire someone to help us with this? How about if Gramma or someone who really under-stands, who we teach and mentor, helps us with the program, or even just masking? We know these are absolute no-gos.

All of us parents are wondering how to actually do this program day after day after day when we get home. If we find and arrange people to run the program with us or for us (instead of us), we'll have to navigate that prohibited space by ourselves. If we tell The Institutes we're not doing it on our own, we'll be booted from the program.

So we cross our fingers and sign the contract.

That night, Alexander is sitting on Turner's lap in front of the com-puter while Turner scrolls Twitter, strung out after our final day at The Institutes. Al turns to face him and says, "Hi, Dad."

Turner comes pounding out of the bedroom, carrying Alexander and crowing. We all say, "Hi, Al! Hi, Al!" at him the rest of the eve-ning, but he just smiles at us.

The next day we are leaving for the airport. There's luggage everywhere. Margo is cleaning out the fridge.

Sloane and I are throwing on jackets and putting on shoes. Turner goes to pick up Alexander and says, "Hey, buddy. Ready to head to the airport?"

Alexander says it again: "Hi, Dad."

We all hear it.

We all cheer.

Oh my god, it's happening.

18.

The southern Alberta weather is turning. A few May chinooks have thrown the city into dampness, and spring is coming in earnest now—our first in this house. I'm paying attention to rhythms and symbols, trying to wring inspiration from what's in front of us. I needed someone to tell me what to do for this kid, and The Institutes sent us away with a binder full of what to do. I will do it. So let's do this.

But before we even start, The Institutes have been very clear: we must spend a full four weeks detoxifying our house, gathering up recruits to volunteer with the coming therapies and, most importantly, establishing the complete nutritional program.

Neither Turner nor I are neat freaks. Our environments tend toward entropy with clean spots, but given what we're about to embark on, I needed to make certain someone is (at least) doing the laundry. So with the government money Al now qualifies for, I hired Kelsey, who starts a week after we return home.

She's young and beautiful, with long, fancy fingernails that I think are fake. (I'm a bit afraid of the fingernails, actually.) Before this gig she was a waitress at a boozy restaurant around the corner, but got sick of it. After some soul-searching she decided she wanted to work with children, and saw our job posting the same day.

Kelsey takes Alexander in the mornings while I clean the house, per Institutes protocols. She keeps the dishes washed and the laundry folded. I don't know any other twenty-somethings, and I'm sure we're the only Gen-Xers in her world. We are working in parallel, in tandem sometimes, getting used to each other. At her age I was in my last year of university, just home from the Philippines, about to go to grad school. Kelsey went to high school in rural Alberta, where on weekends the teachers got drunk with the students. Her grandfather is my dad's age, and one day she says she'd arrived home the night before to find sixty dead ducks in the backyard, the bounty of his day's hunting. I don't understand her world, and I don't know why she would want to work with us, but I'm grateful she's here.

We've been in this house five months. I push the boxes I don't know what to do with into corners and cover them with throws. I wish that we'd chucked out three-quarters of our belongings when we moved and just restarted with an empty house. But I carry things down to the basement to think about "later," so I can carve out an unobstructed area in the living room. This is where we will start unfolding the therapy miracle next month.

Each weekday Kelsey arrives at eight thirty and we walk through the house, opening the doors and windows to air the place out. A few days in, she pulls all our bedding off the beds and out of boxes and drawers and carries it down to the laundry room in unwieldy arm-loads. Everything goes through the wash twice on the sanitize cycle. The Institutes want us to replace any pillow over a year old, which would result in us having zero pillows and a minimum $400 pillow bill. I only get rid of the two oldest, pancake-flat ones and resolve to buy new pillows "soon." Those we keep follow the bedding into the sanitize cycle, and then all the towels go through. We only have an apartment-sized washer and dryer, so it takes days and days to get everything washed twice and dried and folded and put back away while keeping up with the regular laundry.

The house is chaos, but I scour every corner I can reach, wipe down every windowsill, clean the toaster innards, free the plants of dangling dead leaves and wipe out the kitchen drawers per Institutes' orders. We did most of this when we moved in, but there's been con-struction and Christmas and the whole winter since then. We wash the walls and the stairs, wipe down the furniture, clean the oven. Kelsey and I vacuum the entire basement ceiling one afternoon while Alexander is sleeping.

This century home has mice, so we stuff the cupboard cracks with steel wool and I go to Canadian Tire and buy plugger-inner things that emit a pitched-beyond-human-hearing whine meant to make mice vacate the premises. The previous people also had a rabbit, which they swore was an outdoor-only pet, but we are still finding little rabbit poops under the fridge and between the cracks of loose fireplace bricks. We borrow a steam cleaner and boil every floor surface, including the basement concrete. If we hadn't ripped out the carpet before we moved in we'd be ripping it out now—because of the rabbit, and because The Institutes bans having carpet in the home.

Once the house is sanitized—and by the way, we're supposed to do this again in six months, floors to ceilings, and all the corners—we can start the nutritional program.

Food is a hard one. People got emotional during that lecture in Philadelphia, shaking their heads and complaining out on the terrace during the break. Parents said things like, "You can't tell me the kids can't have a Dairy Queen after soccer on Saturdays!" But Turner and I just shrugged. We'll do what they tell us to do.

Humans think we can outsmart our own unconscious selves. But we can't. You say you eat healthy, right? So how come you've got that jar of jelly beans on the low shelf beside your desk? Do you sneak off to have a chocolate milk every afternoon in the cafeteria? Or grab a samosa on the way home to take the edge off? Yes—because the food and the treats are there, because it's easy, because it's tradition, or because it reminds you of your mom, or of camping trips when you were a kid, or because you're being "polite," or because your blood sugar was tanking and there was no time to find something healthy. Or just because it tastes good. All of these. The Institutes knows we will all go home and be faced not just with our lifetime of eating memories and habits, but also our existing stores of food.

I am facing mine. Kelsey is outside with Alexander and I'm standing in my kitchen, looking at two full pantries and the open refrigerator. I'm scanning boxes of crackers, cans of New England clam chowder, ramen noodles, sauces sent to us in care packages from Margo. There are cheeses, salad dressings, miso and yogurt in the fridge, and bagels and bags of perogies in the freezer.

Before he went to Chicago for research this week, Turner said, "It'd be a waste to throw it away. We'll just make sure we don't give any of it to Alexander. We can just slowly eat it down."

I know that won't work. I know it all has to go. If it's in the house, we won't learn how to make food that sticks to The Institutes' rules. I'm an uninspired cook at the best of times. I don't want to learn how to eat on this new program. But I know it will be better for us all if I do. If we all do.

I pull everything out of the cupboards and fridge. Muffin mixes and cereal. Canned baked beans. Hot chocolate mix and Ovaltine. A new box of cream cheese we hadn't even cracked before Philly. Nearly two pounds of butter. And boxes and boxes and boxes of pasta—every kind—cute alphabet ones, spaghetti and spaghettini and fettuccini, fancy multicoloured spirals from the Italian store by the airport.

Everything we can't have anymore goes onto the counter or the floor. I stand above it, staring down and around at the piles. Holy god, this is a lot of food.

I parcel the mass out into five big grocery bags, distributing the expensive unopened condiments among them, putting pasta and cans at the bottom of each bag. I try to make each one feel like it's a present.

Then I walk through the neighbourhood, carrying Alexander in his sling. I hook one bag on our friend Jenny's doorknob, give another to a neighbour out hoeing her garden. I give one bag to Kelsey to take home, and drive the last two to friends in other parts of the city. I pick up Sloane from school and we all come home to an empty kitchen.

It's only now that I realize I can't make dinner. I stir up pablum with cooked carrots for Alexander, and Sloane and I get Vietnamese from around the corner. Mid-bite I suddenly realize the pho and salad rolls will be okay for Al once he's on full solids. Oh, thank god. One comfort food stays on our list.

I devote part of every day this month to finding recipes and thinking up meal ideas. I write lists and notes of ideas that will eventually float, untried, into stacks of mail and down into the space between the fridge and the wall. I'm not good at this.

Twitter: @Hilksom, June 3, 2010
Anyone know anyone who has done The Institutes program? Needing recipes, meal plans, YYC/AB families to swap with, anything.

My tweet gets no replies. I post the same thing on Facebook. Nothing.

The Institutes were very specific about us needing to include vegetables in breakfast. As a first try we use zucchini and cucumbers. Then I drive to Community Natural Foods. The store smells like organic bulk foods and natural cleaning products. I start walking the aisles, looking. I find rice pasta and a kind of spelt bread, which we can eat. Damn, these are expensive.

Chill, it's fine, just start. Start as you mean to go on, Ashley. Open mind, open heart (and open wallet).

I push a mostly-empty cart, pacing through the whole store, stopping to examine all kinds of products I've never peered at closely. After twenty minutes of wandering I have the pasta, the bread, a head of lettuce and a jar of organic mayonnaise in the cart. When a second staff person asks me if I need any help, I say yes.

"What are you looking for?"

My son has been assigned a nutritional program that's very restrictive. He has to have leafy greens plus two other vegetables at every meal. Organic produce and local and freshly made everything. He can have meat and eggs, but there's a lot of stuff we can't give him. Our whole family has to go on the program. I'm at the very beginning of figuring it out. I came here to look for gluten-free stuff to avoid the wheat, but it's more complex than that.

I show her the paper where I've written a quick list of what we're eliminating:

- wheat
- soy
- dairy
- corn
- bananas
- tomatoes
- citrus
- sugar (other than natural fructose in fruit)
- added salt

Bless her, she's unfazed. She asks about allergies, and fermentation. Then she remembers the store has a printout of gluten-free products they can hand out. She finds two copies and we work our way through the store together. We look at every . . . single . . . package and box and bottle, trying to find items Alexander can eat. (Most natural grocers now make gluten-free products obvious on the shelf price listing, but this wasn't commonplace yet.)

Before today I had no idea that sausages have flour in them. I didn't know bacon has added sugar. I didn't know tomato soup contains cornstarch. After two hours at the store I walk out carrying a few small bags of groceries that came to $85. I was in there hoping for some packaged-food eating shortcuts. There aren't many we can afford.

A few days later I explore the regular grocery store. Local fruit is out of season for a big stretch of the year in Canada, obviously. Nearly everything we used to eat as a family seems to have wheat in it. At this stage I have never heard of kombucha, or amaranth, or ajvar, I have never cooked with coconut oil, and I have never kept nuts in the house except at Christmastime, let alone stored them in the refrigerator. I grew up being told too much about calories and being made to wait, hypoglycemic and shaky, for dinner to go on the table. I worked hard to create an adulthood at peace with the idea of food as fuel. Sometimes I eat cheesies because I love them, but mostly I don't, and if dinner happens at 5:30 p.m., I can live a normal life.

Now I'm taking a master class in the art of the elimination diet. And as I learn, I still need to feed my kids three meals a day. Help.

I email Claire, a former journalist we know through Calgary circles. I'd heard from someone that she's into alternative foods, foraging, substitutions for the usual ingredients. We really don't know each other, but I ask if she'll come to the house. Maybe she can boss us around a bit.

Claire arrives bearing agave syrup and millet, and shows us how to steam kale and chard because they're bitter when eaten raw. She explains how to make nut milk, but it sounds complicated, so I begin buying it at the nearby hippie grocery. She tells us about kefir, and sauerkraut, smilingly reassuring us there's a whole world inside this new diet. She's seems delighted by the challenge of our weird restrictions. It's a relief to find someone here in Calgary who gets it.

Following The Institutes' instructions, I source a massive, two-tiered, eight-step water filter, the purchase of which becomes a gift from my in-laws. It has a ceramic strainer and a charcoal tower and rocks at the bottom that alkalize everything. We are to use this water for all cooking and drinking. I marker Al's name onto a glass bottle and make a line at 750 millilitres, his assigned daily liquid intake, part of the anti-seizure protocols we follow because Kleefstra syndrome kids are at risk of "silent" seizures when they're young.

From the very back of one of the kitchen cupboards I pull out a small food processor my mother gave us years ago in a box full of kitchen hand-me-downs. We've never used this thing before, but its engine becomes a familiar sound, ten times a day grinding up flaxseeds and radishes and walnuts and plums. (This little food chopper will finally die in a quick snort of electrical fire after two years of constant use, RIP.)

Though I'm a competent enough cook under duress, I've never been naturally curious about cooking. So I'm having trouble learning what I need for this new program quickly or laterally. The food prep is an extraordinary effort for me; I'm having to train my brain to care. We cannot afford Vietnamese takeout more than once a month, and the new groceries are dear, so I'm doggedly careful with using them all up. Safeway deli chickens are a boon, and we lean on them hard, being mindful to avoid looking at the ingredient list in case this is another no-go food. I could really use a personal shopper, not to mention a personal chef. Or a customized cafeteria—honestly, that'd be ideal. A modern-day lunch counter that cooked to our specifications? Perfect. But no, the cook is supposed to be me, and the cafeteria our kitchen.

Two weeks into the complete overhaul of our eating, I finally serve our first program-perfect breakfast: green eggs (containing minced spinach and broccoli) and ham, with two hazelnuts on each plate, a small pile of brown rice, a cauliflower floret and rooibos tea. This and subsequent meals look strange on the plate, and we aren't used to eating these combinations at all. Though there's a reasonable amount of food for each of us, Sloane and I are always unsatisfied when we're finished eating.

Hereafter, every meal is to the letter of The Institutes' program. Turner likes cooking and is starting to come on board. By the end of the second month we've got some things figured out. Turner has started making a verde to keep in the fridge, a green chopped-herb-and-oil mash we use as a condiment. It helps make the unfamiliar tastes more appetizing.

They warned us in Philadelphia that it would be tempting to make "regular" food for siblings when they demand it, but that this is a slippery slope into the parent becoming a short-order cook three times a day. A fellow Institutes parent, five years further along than we are, concurs: "My daughter refused to eat on The Institutes' diet. I was really afraid she would grow up resenting our son, so I just broke down and made two sets of meals for years and years. It was SO much work. *Don't do that.* If you can, have everyone eating the same thing. That's my big advice."

I am good at taking good advice. But Sloane is not a fool. At five years old she obviously knows what ice cream and buttered popcorn taste like. She does not want to have cauliflower or gai lan for breakfast. We are having to be relentlessly upbeat and dishonestly one-note about this new eating program to keep her onside. *Yes, it'll be so good for all of us! The Institutes say we can put some of the things back into our diet in a year or two! The time'll probably go really fast . . .*

We present it as The Way We Live Now, no other options. I make a big deal of taking photos of the meals as I put them on the table, encouraging her to make goofy "Okay, Mama, but whaaaat?" faces for the camera. Turner and I are careful never to complain about the food except in whispers, behind closed doors, after she is asleep. We know her buy-in alone will save us thousands of hours and acres of heartache. So we're constantly sneaking glances at her and each other: "Is she buying this?" (Thank christ, she is.)

But at the end of the first full week on the nutritional program, Sloane comes into the kitchen at bedtime and asks for a Popsicle, even though she knows there's none in the house. Then she asks for hot chocolate, although it is warm outside, basically summer. Now she's fretting, eyes darting around. She starts to drag the stepstool over to look in the cupboard above the stove. She says, "I want . . . I want . . . honey!"

Honey surprises me. The ferocious delight of sugar and its hold on our biology: wow. Her brain is working hard tonight, finding sweet options that have never before been "treats." But there's no honey in the house anymore. And before she asks, we tell her there's no maple syrup, no juice, no mints or gum. *There's no sugar here at all now, love.*

Suddenly she begins to cry, and it's the most plaintive sound. Any five-year-old's sugar detox is hard, but I didn't expect this. We scoop her up, Turner and I hugging her together, rocking. Food is love. Our girl, who never finishes her Halloween treats and always shares goodies, who has never begged for candy at the grocery store—even for her, this is an anguish.

Looking at me inside our hug, Turner lifts an eyebrow: ("Maybe . . . ?") Me, stern-faced: (*NO.*) We cannot crack. We're at the very beginning; there are years of this to come. We have to hold the line.

I say into Sloane's hair, *We're doing this together. We're in it together. We love you, and love you, and love you, love. Come, get a drink of soda water and then head upstairs. I'll make you a tray of cut-up apple and tea and rice crackers. It'll be a really awesome tray. And I'll give you a nice scratch before bed.*

She breathes in big, breathes out big. A pause. Turner and I hold our breath.

Then: "Okay, Mama."

Fewf.

Her parents' first real yearning is for tomatoes. It's inconvenient to remove wheat and corn, and there is something so sad about getting rid of dairy. But what we come to miss most is that tang of acidity from tomato sauce, salsa, dollops of sriracha. We begin a weekly taco night with rice tortillas, and after a few rounds of tweaking and with Turner's verde, it's almost tasty.

There are also failures. For awhile we have avocado on kamut toast every morning, fooling ourselves that this is getting our "greens" for breakfast. But then we ask The Institutes, and damn, avocados are considered a fat, even if they're green. Back to chopping cabbage and carrots into eggs.

In August, Turner and I manage a date night. We go to the pub and have pints of beer with nachos. Wheat, dairy, corn and tomatoes all at once, for the first time in three months.

The next morning our room is wreathed in a low-hanging fug. I open the balcony door. Turner turns over, pulls the pillow over his head, flaps a hand out at me: "Nooooo . . . cold!"

Me: *Smells all like bumholes and beer in here.*

From under the pillow, Turner: "It was worth it."

19.

Alexander is sick and moody today, teething. Tomorrow he heads into surgery to correct his epigastric hernia. He gets two days of being carried around, being babied. And then, in the second week of June, we start the customized Institutes therapy program, a huge list of things we do with him over the course of each and every day.

It's taking an unexpectedly large amount of brain power to move into this new rhythm, despite our resolve, my many lists, and The Institutes' lectures. I have no mental muscle memory for trying to make a baby do things-he-can't-yet this much, day in and day out. I don't know how I'm going to find the people to help keep us going, enough people to build a real village so we don't drown.

But I'm keeping at it, starting new therapies and ramping them up each day, trying new recipes, calling new volunteers. I should be exhausted by bedtime and I am, but I find myself lying there blinking at the ceiling most nights. I'm wrestling with how to roll out and, daily, complete the full program, raise our other child, stay married. The hurt kid is The Institutes' only priority, and everything else comes second, full stop. I get it, but hate that there's so much to maintaining the equilibrium of everyday life that there's no room left for "now." When I try to mentally step back and look at where we are and how things are going, some urgent and un-put-off-able thing comes chasing through the room or my mind, and my musings have to be shelved. I envy the Indian parents their joint family households, their staff. . . . Should we be looking at moving back to India? There's no time to give this enough thought to weigh whether it's escapist whimsy or an actual option.

Turner's office is in the third bedroom upstairs, the room with the most light, with a sliding deck door and a huge balcony. While I'm downstairs doing chores with Kelsey he's at the desk up there, working on the first draft of a book that will come out in 2011* and magazine work he's pitching here and there. We're trying to leave him alone as much as we can, because we need every dime Turner can drum up. But I have to call for him to come pattern with us way too often, distracting him and reducing his hours.

I, too, could be working. A few times a week, I turn down offers, hand gigs on to other photographers, recommend other researchers. I bang out the *rats-I'm-booked* messages and send them off before the what-ifs can swim in. Every one stings, every one diminishes my chances of being able to return to my career, to get back at it again, eventually.

But I have to focus on what's in front of my face: this kid, these tasks, turning myself into an unpaid therapist for my own son. This kid's worst-case scenarios are just too awful to spend time taking photos for faraway clients. Alexander is everything right now, and so much work, and the worries about the future never let up. The Institutes program is our beacon, our unreligious star in the east, and I'm marching us ever toward their promised land. And so far we are doing . . . okay. Other than the insomnia and the worry. There are some giddy points every day, at least. And we stave off the periodic evening lapses into despair with beer and dance parties in the living room.

When they hear about Alexander's syndrome, his prognosis, the therapy program, many people say, "Okay, but just make sure you keep living your regular life. Fit this in on top." They don't want to hear that our old life plus-one-disabled-baby is not what's going to happen. The more we do now, the more he'll be able to do later. I hope.

I'm terrified of allowing my faith in The Institutes to falter or wane. I have to insist we're on the right path even if the people around us don't understand. Because I'd get plenty of support for parking

---

* *The Leap: How to Survive and Thrive in the Sustainable Economy,* by Chris Turner, published by Random House Canada; finalist for the 2012 National Business Book Award and longlisted for the BC National Award for Canadian Nonfiction

Alexander at a daycare and finding a job downtown. Or hiring a nanny and going back to work, returning those calls and getting back on the freelance horse. God, I want to go back to work. And I really, really want the reassurance that my family would pile on—oh, absolutely, get someone else to watch him. He can go on around the block with the helper, you just change his diaper at night, just put him in the "special" class, where they spend twelve years teaching him how to button his shirt and then he "graduates" from high school.

That's the kind of "help" that's waiting for us, that well-meaning societal bigotry.

It's a terrible danger to Alexander, to us. The world considers it the default thing to park your disabled kid inside dismally low expectations. If I side with my child and try to build a world in which he can live and prosper, I'm very clearly on my own.

Not even my parents are going to participate in the ground game of this world-building for their grandson. They've both all-but-yelled, "I'M TOO BUSY, THAT SOUNDS WEIRD, DON'T ASK ME TO DO THAT." But I'm a never-learner. I want them to swoop in—to not just care, but to show it by doing things I've never seen them do, like the dishes in my sink and reading The Institutes' books.

One hard night before we went to Philadelphia, my mom was visiting. I was cleaning the kitchen and Val was sitting in a chair by the window, and she asked me how I was doing in her "Tell me what's really going on—really" voice. I always fall for that voice.

So even though the previous month she'd told me not to go on antidepressants, I try again.

I say, *Actually . . . it's like being bashed against rocks. I'm a little boat in a cove of cliffs. I can't leave and I can't see the end. I'm only deliberately putting a smile on my face. This has already been the hardest thing ever.*

My mom sits back and says, all droll, "That's parenthood, kid. We've all been there."

I think she thinks she's being funny.

But I am walking past her and up the stairs, unbuttoning my clothes. I step straight into the shower. The water comes on, freezing, but it's the only half-escape I have, this liquid wall to put between me and that throwaway quip. I stand there and let the water blast in my face as the temperature rises. I scrub all the walls, clean the tub, and rearrange the shampoos and razors and soap, shoving them into place: *Stay*. Where's a waterproof StairMaster when you need one? *What-the-fucking-fuck-fuck-fuck*, right left right left.

I'm working out the logistics of shower aerobics (a harness hooked into the ceiling so you can't slip?) when someone flushes the basement toilet. Everything goes white-hot and I can hear a woman screaming. (*Oh hi. It me*). I end up out folded over the sink, sobbing, a washcloth stuffed into my mouth to muffle the noise of my howls, for a long time. No one comes.

Finally I get dressed, careful of the pink stripe all down my side from that blast of hot. I fetch Alexander out of the kids' room, where he's been napping. Tomorrow there will be a huge purple bruise on my leg where I rebounded off the wall corner escaping the shower.

My parents raised me, of course. They put me through university and call on my birthday and feed me when I'm at their houses. But when I literally ask for help, from favours to *hey, gimme a hand with th*is, both my parents' default answer is no (unless it's something to do with my physical health). I have never understood why. It's like they think I'm out to trick them or something, corner and trap them. But sometimes they smile upon me without warning. One winter Val handed me her old sealskin boots, expensive and beautiful things: "Just take them. They're warm. You'll love them." But, years later, she wouldn't let me have a blue plastic nail brush. We'd just spent three weeks touring my mom and stepdad, Michael, around India, where Turner and I were living. As she was packing, I saw the nail brush on the bed among her toiletries and picked it up. *Hey, can I have this?*

Val snatched it out of my hands. "No."

Sometimes it's about money with her. *I, like, just paid $75 for your departure taxes.* (She'd run out of cash and hadn't wanted to exchange more traveller's cheques.)

She snapped, "You cannot have it. It's mine."

I will happily give you the dollar it would take to replace that thing when you get home.

She stuffed the nail brush deep into her bag. "No. You're not getting my good things!"

I started to laugh. *Jesus christ, Mom. That's a cheap drugstore nail brush. You've probably used it every day while you were here, right? I should have brought one with me from Canada. I haven't seen one for sale here anywhere. I've looked.*

"No."

My smile was gone, now. *I'm actually serious. It would really help us keep our hands properly clean. It's another four months before I come home. Please give it to me.*

"Get your own!"

I turned and appealed to Michael: *We can't get them here.*

He shrugged. "It's hers."

Oh my god.

I had to pay for their taxi to the airport too.

After we came back to Canada, Val gave me nail brushes for the next two Christmases and birthdays.

But that was ten years ago, and this, now—this is life-and-death, isn't it? Surely, she can see that I need my mother. That my children need their grandmother. That I've been handed a potentially very bleak future from which we're trying to save ourselves. I've spelled out for her that this storm seems to be swallowing me. Surely she isn't saying, "Oh sorry, I'm busy with my own stuff just now." But that's what's happening. I . . . think that's what's happening?

Since Al's arrival, when my mother visits, she has about an hour of incredible, golden, wondrous energy. She pours this late afternoon light into Alexander and he comes deliciously, incredibly alive, in her thrall. That magic gift lasts for days after she departs. It's one of the only reasons we keep inviting her back.

Last time my mom was here, we were in the kitchen in the magic hour and she was petting Al's head. She said, "You know, I'm good for him. It would be very helpful for him if I lived here. I'd come over all the time." Alexander was waving his arms, trying to get closer to her.

I replied, *YES, YES, PLEASE, MOVE BACK HERE IMMEDIATELY.*

"Oh, ha ha, no, I have my house, I can't leave all that."

Come more often. Please, come pour your light into this boy. We're doing everything we can, and it's not enough.

As Val headed outside, I looked to my stepdad. *Please, tell her I need her.*

"I'm always happy to come visit," he said, rubbing the dog's head. (They bring their dogs. Also excellent.)

You can come on your own if she won't come. Please, come more.

"Aw, naw. Val won't want to stay home alone."

I put up my hands: *Fine, good, come together, bring all the dogs, stay as long as you want! You're all welcome. How can we make it easier for you? We can make it work.*

"It's not up to me," he said, shrugging.

It prickled, but it's impossible to be angry at Mike, or resent his unquestioning loyalty to our mother. He has a truly beatific smile, a beam.

As I watched them drive away at the end of this visit, I looked down at Alexander, who could benefit so much from my mother's steady presence in his life, but won't. Val will do only what she wants to do. We went back into the house.

That night I found a little note taped to my computer monitor: *The world breaks everyone and afterward you are stronger in the broken places.* Just that line, in my mother's handwriting. She's saying that what's happening in my life isn't uncommon or terrible (though it's definitely uncommon and feels terrible), and in the end I'll be better and bigger (which may be true, though I can't see an end to this, yet). By inference, the quote and her leaving-it-behind-to-be-found-and-considered-later makes the point that "someday" I'll be better able to appreciate things I cannot possibly understand now, and anyway, I should just get over my self-pity.

I want my mother to stroke my hair and hold my hand and walk through this fire with me. I want her to be something she cannot be. Which is here for me.

After the note, I stop inviting them to visit. She never asks to come again.

For his part, Bruce has already tried to sabotage the nutritional program. He says, "You don't have to do this *every* day!" as he folds ice cream into Al's mouth.

I come running over. *Dad! Don't DOOOOOOO that!*

"Ashley, it doesn't matter. Kids like ice cream. Relax."

I take Alexander out of his arms, wipe out the boy's mouth with a paper towel. *Dad, we're doing a whole thing here. Can you please be on board?*

He rolls his eyes. "You know what I think of all this."

My doctor father has never suffered "alternative" anything gladly—massage, chiropractors, self-help courses, even podiatrists— let alone the truly out-there stuff. The only reason he is not openly antagonistic to The Institutes is because he can see the hope and new energy the program has given Turner and me.

My father's support, when he gives it, is big ticket—help with buying our house, for instance—or big gesture, and he prefers sur- prises to things we've said we need. Like, he arranged for a friend in the electronics business to break into our house while we were in Philadelphia to mount a huge flat-screen TV on the wall.

But . . . where did it come from? I said, staring at this massive thing after we walked in the door from the airport, not grasping the obvious.

Sloane fiddled with the clicker, trying to turn it on. "Musta been Grampa."

The TV came to life and the picture was so high-resolution it nearly hurt my eyes. *But we didn't need a new TV . . .* I turned around and there was a clear spot on the credenza where our old TV used to sit.

At that moment Bruce called from the speakerphone in his car, sounding delighted. "Hey, you're welcome! That's a very good TV!"

But now we're into this therapy program, and he comes over a few times a week (he does come, and I'm grateful) but just looks around for a few minutes and then leaves. I hate watching myself chase after him: *Stay. Please stay. Just hang out for a while.*

He puts on his sunglasses. "I can't, I'm going to be late! Sees-yuh!"

Late for what? On this occasion, it's a Sunday.

He gives me a look: "Ashley. Stop it."

To me it feels connected to Alexander. To the fact that this little boy is too much, too less-than.

These moments strike a dark, low note in me, a warning that Alexander and this program will become an insurmountable obstacle for my family. That their historic reluctance to join my team and schemes will create an undeniable "us" and "them." If it comes to Alexander's needs versus their wants, I'll have to push them away. I know they won't be part of this, but I can't stop wanting them to be. It's achy crazymakey.

Finally, Bruno asks the big, simple question out loud for me. An older friend, fifteen years ahead of us on this mortal coil, Bruno is having a slow week at work, so he's over helping me strip the dated vinyl kitchen wallpaper. Alexander is with us, sitting in a bouncy chair, looking at his hands. Bruno pauses in his scraping, looks at Al and then just says, "Ash, where's your family? Why am I the one doing this? Why aren't they here?"

I . . . uh, they are . . . my dad is. He came to Philadelphia.

"But, Ashley—" He gestures around at the walls, at himself. "Why is it *me* doing this? Like, I love you guys, but what the fuck? Your brother's here in town, right?"

I . . . uh . . . um, he has a new baby.

"And your mom?"

She visits, she . . . comes with her husband sometimes.

Bruno drops his scraper and, as he bends to retrieve it, his voice squeezes higher. "But are they *helping*?" When he straightens up and sees the look on my face, he moves on. "Your stepmom, your parents' friends—where are they?"

My . . . my parents don't really have close friends in Calgary.

My mother lived in Calgary for sixteen years, was a nursing prof at the college and a fitness instructor all over the city. She is the kind of person to whom people suddenly bare their souls in elevators or in line at the grocery store. A low-key but unwieldable magic runs in our maternal line; sometimes Val knows things she can't possibly. When I was a teen, there was no fooling her. She is clever and funny and assured and irreverent, she was the "cool mom" who would offer my friends cigarettes and give invaluable, bald advice when people asked for it. Everyone she ever met still asks about her. But Val will tell you Calgary is ungracious, and that she made not one friend here, other than my stepdad, Michael. Now they live in the Kootenays.

My father has work colleagues, golf partners, political compatriots who think the world of him. He coached kids in hockey and soccer, knows every one of their parents, and has famously trained (and terrified) generations of young doctors on rotation throughout the city. He's done provincial negotiations and medical advocacy for decades, is admired and valued, and is a good sport. But he doesn't really socialize. We threw a huge surprise party for him when he turned sixty, stuffed with people from his life in Calgary, and he was shy and embarrassed the whole night. I know those people who clapped him on the shoulder and grinned at him—folks from our old suburb and the golf club, long-time partnership chums and their wives, friends from the trenches of provincial medical politics—would help us, would spread the word, would contribute to our future fundraisers or volunteer to help with the program, and would know others who would help us too. My dad won't ask them. Absolutely not.

And my dad's wife, Peggy, grew up here, was a teacher for decades, and knows everyone on earth in this city. Her son, my stepbrother Jeff, was my sister's friend in high school and is quadriplegic, from a rugby accident when he was nineteen. Peggy has two other kids, too, and little grandchildren Alexander's age. Peggy and I got along fairly well until some point after Alexander was born. Maybe seeing the bottom drop out of our lives is a horrifying threat to her at some fundamental, involuntary level. I'm sorry Peggy can't be part of what we're doing, because she's organized and connected, and has expert-level experience in epistemology and dealing with children and disability and "the system." Maybe our enormous ongoing crisis reminds her too much of what happened to Jeff, the years of chaos his accident brought into her world. Whatever the reason, she can't abide being in proximity to us anymore, and eventually I and my children will be pointedly unwelcome at my dad's house. But that's still ahead.

I say none of this, about my mom and dad and Peggy, to Bruno.

He sighs again. "And your sister is in Ottawa, right? What's her deal?"

She is . . . she . . . I think she's visiting next month. Ainsley is definitely visiting next month. With her kids. I already know she's not going to like what she sees here, but I don't say that. I protect these people, but I can't explain them.

. . . Because, maybe it's something about *you*, Ashley, hmmm? *You* aren't someone people want to help, because *you* expect too much, hmmm? My family says that right to my face: "You ask too much of people, Ashley." I've never understood what they mean.

There are people in my life I would never say no to, even when they ask way too much, and my family members are among them.

I live for demonstrations of loyalty. If you need me, sure, I'll plan the day-after-your-wedding brunch for forty people that you said you didn't want but have now changed your mind about, right there at the wedding. Absolutely, I will spend four days of my five-day holiday helping dig up the hillside to find the possible slow leak in your water line. I will bring food when I come and make all the meals and trim the blackberries and chop wood and stack it nicely. Yes, you can crash on my couch, here's a key to my door, eat anything in the fridge and drink the booze. Use our parking pass, have my Aeroplan miles, I'll get up early to drive you, I'll miss my own graduation to attend yours. I will help you move and introduce you to my friends and host Sunday dinner and drag you along while you build a life, and later I will abide by the new rules when suddenly nobody can drop by without three days' notice. I will answer the phone late at night when I have a sleeping baby if you call. I will spend hours and hours and hours listening to your problems and drama, and, in good faith, offer advice when asked because I know you are calling for help.

My family likely have reciprocal-type lists in their heads of the things they've done for me. (I definitely got wayyy too drunk that one time at family friends' in the Laurentians.) But what I hear is only: "Ashley, you always ask tooooo much of people." I have no idea what they're talking about.

And yet, every few days, a new person emerges to volunteer—a friend of a neighbour, new moms in our circle who are at home with wee babies, a friend's mother, a woman from a workshop Turner did last year. I don't know why they volunteer. It might be a religious thing for some of them. But I don't want to know. For any of them. I'm terrified to ask. It would be weird in the extreme, right? A question that leads to other questions.

Why are you volunteering to help with this?

Uh, you said you needed volunteers.

We do.

So why are you asking why I'm offering to help?

Because, um, my family told me I shouldn't ask people for help.

That's . . . really weird.

Maybe. It makes me feel like probably I don't deserve the help . . . You know?

How are you going to do all these therapies that need other people to help, if you don't ask for help?

Well, obviously we have to ask for help. The Institutes recommend you ask everyone and be persistent, and then people come together around the program and sign up. A lot of families talked about having a volunteer who coordinates the other volunteers. I feel like that's not possible in Calgary or Canada or something, but god— wouldn't it be amazing?

Okay, but wait, your family think you shouldn't ask for help? Like, your parents say that? They're not part of this at all?

No, no, my dad is here, he helped us pay for Philadelphia. And he brings over wine sometimes, and takes us for dinner. And he gave us that huge new ridiculous TV . . .

Well—Ashley, okay! I thought you were saying your family wasn't involved at all.

It's . . . but that's not the help I want.

Oh my god, don't be such an asshole—your dad is helping.

My mother says I should be grateful when people help me in the ways they can, on their own terms, and not ask for things that they can't do.

How do you know what people can't do unless you ask?

Right? You can't know. But my family say asking people to get involved in this is not fair.

Fair?

Because people will feel obligated, and then they'll feel bad when they don't help. Because people are busy and you need to let people do their own thing and not ask them to get involved with your life. But, like, so, you volunteered to help . . . How come?

Because you said you needed help, . . . but now I'm wondering whether your family has just gotten worn out by decades of unceasing and extreme demands that I don't know about or haven't encountered before now . . . ?

—*Maybe they're right, but I would never ask for something I wasn't willing to do for other people. Do I maybe have no insight into how I function in the world? Do I wear people out and they have to push me away because I'll suck them dry? My family are maybe giving it to me straight because they love me? . . . But then I think, that's not how it is with Turner, with our friends . . . that's just the role I've been assigned in my family. The role of "pain in the ass," and—*

So, um, listen, sorry to interrupt—but next week, I have this other thing I have to do. I can't come, but I'll email you.

I . . . ah. Yeah, that's okay. I get it. Thanks for coming today.

Oh, of course! You're welcome. And Alexander's doing really, really just *so* well, you know? This whole program is going to be really awesome for him. You're really brave. I'd help, but I'm just really, *really* busy.

I get it.

[Gathering up keys and bag, heading for the door.] But I'll see you in October, right? At the big Halloween party at Jenny's, right?

For sure.

So I don't want to know why they're volunteering. There's no reason good enough, no explanation clear enough, to erase the fear. What spurs them to walk through the door is none of my business. A fragile magic is moving them that is unknowable and, I'm certain, temporary. If I question it, the soap bubble will pop.

20.

Our first day of starting the full program of patterning and masking and physical therapies alongside the nutritional program is in mid-June. The volunteer patterners are scheduled for next week, friends and neighbours and friends-of-friends. But this first week we will do it all with Sara.

Sara is engaged to my friend John Johnston, and came into our lives just before I got pregnant with Alexander. She is empathetic and insightful, has thousands of stories and a million practical skills, and pays attention to everything. Even before Philadelphia, she noticed and asked about my discomfort at the prospect of needing volunteers. Her fiancé is my close friend of decades, so she's been privy to more of the raw grief of the last year than most people we know.

Remember in the last chapter where I was moaning about having no help? That's happening at the same time as this: Sara comes every day for three weeks as we start to roll out The Institutes' therapies. She cancelled everything she had on the go and committed to being at our house every day, all day, so we can get our bearings and learn how to do everything with a "safe" helper. So we don't have to learn how to do the program ourselves at the same time as managing new volunteers. She's here to help *me*.

Sara shows up in the morning, every morning (and on the weekends she brings her two kids, Laura, six, and Emerson, four), and she stays for at least six hours. She does patterns with me and Kelsey, and watches as I make lists and chop ingredients and clean. She listens to the babble of my unspooling worries and paranoia and responds with intelligent (even related) facts and anecdotes. She says

"Yes, and" to everything. Sara is doing something women have done for millennia: making the drudgery of "housework" feel normal. She's keeping me company as I struggle with how to make this new thing all go. She's saying, by being here, "This sucks, but it can be a world. And you're not alone."

She is also asking questions, learning the more detailed what-and-why of all this, and she often says "Oh! That's so interesting!" (And she seems to mean it.) By the time other volunteers begin coming to help, Sara knows the workings of the program nearly as well as Turner and I do. And better, she is fully separate from the bottomless need I'm sure I ooze. She can call our volunteers to the table without fear, the firm and polite instructor.

She lets me pretend to be preoccupied with Al's shirt collar or the hem of his leggings while she explains to newbies why we're doing what we're doing with Alexander. As we push and pull his limbs, she corrects volunteers' form and explains that they need to keep each stroke smooth, to cross Al's midline with his hand at the top and bottom—acting the taskmaster, so I can smile and quietly say, "Hm, yeah, that's it," encouraging them, pretending I wasn't watching closely, furtively, myself. From behind my hair I watch Sara explain how the masking benefits Alexander, all the science The Institutes explained to us (and that I, last week, explained to her). How she moves her hands, when she pauses, where she puts the emphasis: I'm recording it all in my mind, for later. Because I know if I was doing the instructing now, amid these myriad and ferocious new responsibilities, I'd scare everyone away. Together, we pretend she's just taking initiative as a close friend, helping share the burden of explaining things over and over. But we both know that Sara is showing me how she manages these people, how she corrects them and redirects them, so I can model myself on her.

After three weeks, Sara hands the director's role off to me. I don't want her to go, but (of course) she has a life beyond this house. And it's time for me to be fully in charge. Sara continues to come four days of every week for the rest of the summer, to keep me company, helping and listening and asking questions, letting me talk through what I'm thinking and planning and trying to do.

We could not have, I could not have, established The Institutes' program at home without her. Though Sara doesn't really show up in the book after this, she's part of the story from now on. As you continue to read, even the parts where I'm wailing about being o-solo-mio, remember that Sara and Turner and others are invisibly walking alongside me, and things couldn't've kept on without them.

I should tell you about the masking, which we start once the patterning has been going for a week. Al wears the mask for thirty seconds at first, and then the timer goes and we take it off. On the first day we do five masks. The next day is six masks. Then seven. The Institutes are geniuses of adult education, honestly. They prescribe this incremental adoption so you can build it into your day. Gradually we work up to forty masks a day, sixty seconds each.

The masking freaks a lot of our friends out. Tara Nazerali is a child protection lawyer, and reacts by email with total alarm: "The 'masking' thing terrifies me. If I were not your friend, but someone in a professional relationship with you, I would be obligated to report you to child services. Although I trust you absolutely and completely, and know you are doing it with the best of intentions, the potential for something to go terribly wrong is huge. What if Sloane wants to 'help' and masks her brother when you are off going pee? What if Sloane thinks 'if this is good for Alexander, maybe I should try it?' What if a government worker becomes involved who thinks the only way to respond is to remove your children (and yes, they would likely take BOTH)? Or what if, and this is probably the worst of the horrible possibilities above, what if the masking causes Alexander to stop breathing and he can't be revived?"

Her brother Sean, who lives in Mozambique, is also deeply concerned, but after I explain it more fully to Tara and Sean and their mom, Sheila (in an email that includes photos and a printed study from The Institutes), he quickly writes back, sending hugs and this: "I didn't think it was quite the baby-in-a-Ziploc thing."

I can withstand and address these worries because the masking makes such a huge impact on Alexander. A week after we begin, when he's not even at twenty masks a day, Al's vocalizations are discernibly louder. After two weeks we hear him sneeze for the first time. After four weeks he is grunting while pooping his diaper. He has begun to aurally inhabit this world. His diaphragm is getting stronger. His colour is better. "He's so much . . . brighter, just after a few weeks!" people say. It's evident to everyone why the masking, which looks ridiculous at best and irresponsible at worst, is actually very good for him.

For the first many days, managing the masking is no problem. But I'm not a natural when it comes to scheduling, and in the midst of the increasing masking we're continuing with the patterning (with volunteers coming in shifts, twice a day) and (per The Institutes' schedule) introducing reading, math, gnostic sensation, visual stimulation, auditory pathway creation and distance crawling sessions. We are using the microwave timer for some therapy intervals, and eyeballing the kitchen clock for others. Kelsey and I have stopwatches on the counter, and make notes in a little book, but we are failing to make this into a routine.

By the time we get to forty daily masks, our therapy day feels like a relentless, frantic sprint. My brain is pulled in eight different directions all the time. We are still—still—unpacking boxes around the house. Thank christ for Kelsey, who keeps our clothes clean and the dishes washed, and answers the doorbell. I'm running around doing these things too, and making more word cards, planning the next intelligence flash card sets, changing diapers and answering the phone. Many days we only make it to thirty masks. When I riffle through the pages of our therapy books from this period, the program records show us falling short again and again.

"It's okay, Ash," says Turner every evening as I fret. "We're doing everything we can. We'll get there."

But I can't relax into it. Will not. Won't.

At the core of me I don't want to do this program, live this life, fix this slow-motion emergency. I don't want to do it so much that if I let my foot off the gas for one moment I know I will slide and years will go by . . . and oh well.

So I am, by force, walking up a scree mountain with sliding-downward steps and the ascent is interminable and I strain every single second, but I am making myself be in it and become OF it.

Because no one else will push even half as hard as I will, not even Turner, who has to work, who has to pay the bills, and is ultimately not built to apply brute force to a problem. I can. I don't want to do this alone, and I can't do this alone, but I will if I have to.

I will.

(I do.)

One morning I leave Kelsey to run the program and walk through the neighbourhood, looking through local shops and at café menus for prepared foods that might work on Al's diet. In a high-end kitchen store around the corner I find a three-item countertop timer. I snatch it up and nearly run to the counter so I can own it faster.

In this first year of the therapy program, I will touch this timer more than anything I've ever owned. When it dies after ten months of every-day, constant-constant use, we keep it in the kitchen as a revered retired friend. We go back to using the microwave timer and the stopwatches on our phones for a week before it finally dawns on us one day that there might be an app for all this. And of course there is. Within five minutes we all have the perfect timer, down-loaded free from iTunes, on our phones. I move the old three-way kitchen timer to my bedside table, where I touch it before bed each night, like a talisman.

The weather is so beautiful that we can finally spend the day outside. But there are poplars all around this house, and we're beset by those assholish sticky things that fall when the leaves emerge. Alexander's knees and socks are stained brown-yellow, a mehndi mess of poplar sap. Turner tracked a bunch up the back stairs and I stare at the stains, thinking, *Lord have mercy.*

School is out for Sloane. When Sara is here with her children, the kids sort of entertain each other. But some weeks Laura and Emerson are at their dad's, and we can only afford one week of day camp for Sloane, and not until August. So she's underfoot. Many days she is wringing-her-little-hands lonely in this new neighbourhood. "Aren't there any kids here?" On our block the only kids are babies and early teens. Nobody her age.

One day Kelsey can't make it to work. Turner's first chapters of the new book are due in a week, and he's locked in his office fourteen hours a day. I'm at the end of my rope trying to run Al's program on my own. But Sloane's face, all little-kid sorrow and bereftness, aw. I have to do something about this.

I grab the kids and a pen and a stack of sticky notes. We walk up and down the street that backs onto our alley, ringing doorbells. I leave handwritten notes at every door where it looks like the house has children: *Hi! We just moved onto 10A. Our daughter Sloane is 5 and looking for friends. Do you have kids? Want to have a playdate? We have a trampoline! Call or email Ashley.*

Sloane is reluctant to approach these strangers' houses, pulls against my grip on her wrist. This girl just didn't inherit some crucial sliver of my extroversion genes. You have to ring doorbells sometimes, kiddo.

Nobody's home at any of the houses, so we don't talk to anyone in person. Gradually Sloane cheers up as it seems like we won't have to ask anyone to be friends face to face.

We leave behind at least ten stickies, and she even skips on the way home. Later that evening, we kind of wait by the phone. *Someone will call, love. Remember the place with the bikes? There's kids there, for sure!*

But nobody calls. Days pass. Nobody emails.

The weekend goes by. Out our back window, we see kids running between the houses on that street across the alley. I'm pissed at their do-nothing Calgary parents. But I put on a fun voice and say to Sloane, *Oh hey, look! Those kids, let's just go meet them! We can cut through the yards.*

Sloane: "No. They got the notes. They won't want to be friends."

I know that expression of hers. If I drag her over there, it'll be a fight, she'll sulk. I consider going by myself, talking to the kids, telling them about Sloane, finding their mothers, suggesting the kids invite her over. But I've tried this before in Calgary. It never works. In fact, it's considered weird, almost impolite. I grew up here but I don't understand this city.

Over the coming years I will meet some of those one-street-over neighbours-with-children at community events or parties, and can't resist mentioning the notes we left.

Them: "Oh, right! I remember that! We got that note, yes!"

Me: *And?*

"Well, we . . . we just didn't . . . I mean, Jack/Jill was at camp/had a nanny . . . and in the evenings we're just, like, so busy, you know? There's lots of kids on the block, and ours've already sort of got their friends and routines . . . We knew she'd find some other kids to play with." Not-it.

Right.

21.

Our society functions with an obdurate certainty that people should carry full responsibility for their health. Antibiotics and antidepressants and step counters and birth control and keto apps are within our grasp. The pandemic has since moderated this view, but many of us, with our squirt bottles of hand sanitizer, our masks and social distancing, still seem to believe that only the uncareful or the unfortunate get sick, and that the wary and worthy will be spared. This extends to everything.

So many of us live far from our people and the places where we grew up. Every government comes into office wanting to "find efficiencies" in already underfunded social services. We are living a collective delusion that success and peace are within reach, inside a decluttering spree or a white noise machine, in more privacy and less obligation. We feel justified sneering at kids who toddle noisily past our brunch tables because their mother was taking off her jacket and lost track of them for a second. Few of us simply see the situation for what it is—normal, understandable—and get involved (talk to the child, put out a hand to block their path) just enough for the mom to get her bearings. We seem to expect people to be capable of carrying on no matter the breakdowns in family support, no matter their mental health or marginalization. Absorb the shock, the loss, the inconvenience, the delay—and be bigger, better, and capable anyway.

My sister Ainsley has brought her sons from Ottawa for a week's visit in Calgary. She has known since Christmastime about Alexander's diagnosis and The Institutes. She followed the photos and reflections

I posted from Philadelphia on Facebook and Twitter. On the phone before she came, I explained what it would look like when she is here. It was crystal clear that the daily schedule involves volunteers, and that the volunteers come every day.

Every day, I told her, we do patterning and masking. We run a visual and audio stimulation protocol with Alexander six times daily. He has distance goals to achieve, so we coax him to crawl across the floor every second he isn't being shown flash cards or eating or sleeping. Every hallway and room in our house has been measured and marked with tape so we can detail his distances accurately in the program notebook. I spend hours preparing Alexander's food. At night we make educational materials.

"You can take *one* day off," she says. "Can't we have one day together? Without all . . . *this* . . . going on? Ash, it's not a big deal to take one day off."

The Institutes warned us that people would say exactly this—that it's not a big deal to take a day off. They drilled into us that we must put the child first. Especially for the first two years of the program. That our child's life is at stake. That this kid's brain will never be easier to retrain than it is *right now*, today.

I see it from my sister's perspective, though. If I were visiting, I would think, *What's one day?* You think a one-day break doesn't matter when it's not your force of will keeping the train in motion. At this point I am terrified that if we stop for even a few daytime hours the accumulated exhaustion will swoop in and I won't be able to start it all up again.

We're doing this huge thing, Ains. It's so critical we don't let up. We have momentum.

"Ash, you're *always* doing some huge thing."

Ainsley, this is obviously different.

"Is it, though?"

She can't possibly mean that.

We are in the kitchen and I start chopping chard for Alexander's lunch. Then I weigh flaked bits of cooked chicken, down to the gram, making note of the quantity. I have Alexander in the Bumbo on the counter so I can show him a set of reading cards. Every day, and especially today, with Ainsley here, I'm trying to make it look like I'm taking this program in stride. That it's intense but normal, complex but possible. I am faking it until we make it.

Summer is coming in the side window, crabapple branches bobbing against the glass. A delicious breeze is rolling through the house, carrying the smell of water from the hose on the trampoline. Our kids are screeching outside, laughing. I want to be out there with them. I want to go double-bounce my nephews and have a tickle fight with the pile of kids on the grass. I pull the ice pack out of the freezer and push it onto each of Al's palms for thirty seconds to stimulate his cold reflex. I put the chard and chicken and some baby carrots in the little food processor and grind them up into a paste, adding pumpkin seed oil and gluten-free baby food mix at the end, stirring it in.

As I spatula Al's lunch into a baby bowl and start feeding him, Ainsley is leaning on the counter, trying to find another topic. "So it must be really hard to find recipes for all this stuff," she says. She picks up the baby food box. "Do you really need to cut out wheat? It's apparently very trendy to be gluten-intolerant right now, but actually most people really aren't."

Ainsley is ferocious-funny, wicked-smart. I have nearly laughed myself dead at her zingers, her hilarious cackle at her own jokes. She is determined and disciplined and athletic. She is organized and plans her time and knows exactly what's in her fridge, down to the number of slices of deli meat. She is blond and green-eyed and svelte. We don't even look like neighbours, let alone sisters. Though we're both goofy, no-bullshit moms, and have the same voice on the telephone, everything else about us is utterly opposite, too.

When we were little I was pinchy, punchy, mean. I'd leave her out of games because she was younger and shy and held on to the kite for too long even though I yelled NOW! She and our brother are twins, and they left me out, and I didn't fit anyway, jealous of their shared glow and secret language. I've spent decades trying to make it up to her. We're in our thirties now. We both want to just get on with being adults together.

But we can't. She tries with me, and I try with her. Her world is too orderly, ironically enough, given what I'm dealing with now. I'm messy. There's always laundry in the basket. My stories make her shudder, my instincts make her anxious, and my extroversion is a burden. To her, my everyday life is like a bag of superbounce balls that's been dropped just as a steeplechase detours through our dining room. And she loves me in spite of the stress I invariably cause her. But it's hard on Ainsley, having a sister like me. *I'm always doing some huge thing.*

The countertop timer is still counting down the intervals between kitchen therapies. I carry on, pouring water through the filter and wiping the counters and measuring out millet to put on to boil. Ainsley is now standing at the back window, looking down at the kids in the yard. She has already refused to pattern Alexander with us. If she's going to be no help in here, I want her to go out there, hang out with Sloane. In the midst of this circus, my girl could really use an auntie. But I think it's taking everything Ainsley has just to be here at my house, amidst all these moving parts.

I glance over at Alexander and he's staring at his hands, as usual. With the diagnosis, he'd fallen plink-plunk into a new category. Defective, full stop. Not just for my family. I felt it too. I fight that vicious ableism every day. The voice of the world is telling my sister that none of this is her responsibility.

And it's probably too terrifying. Alexander makes the randomness of the universe real, peels back the facade that something like this could never happen to people who have their lives "together." We all live inside the fantasy that our choices make our destiny. If we don't like our destinies, we should have made better/different choices. But the black balloon can land in your yard no matter what you do, who you are, how you plan, or what you want.

Today I'm the older one and I'm the fatter one, the poor chooser and the faulty planner, the moral failure in size twelve pants. I know I have to be the one to understand Ainsley, and everyone else who can't join in with our new reality. I want my sister to grab me and hug me hard and say in my ear, "This is a fucking mountain you are trying to climb. Most people wouldn't try. I know this is the worst goddamn thing, and I know you don't want it, and that you are doing it anyway. I'm far away, but don't doubt for one second that I'm cheering for you." She can't right now.

I know Ainsley tries harder with me than with anyone else in her life. But I piss her the hell off. And now I've been silent for too long,

unable to respond to her comment about gluten. I can tell she's thinking about packing up her kids, taking them to the zoo or just heading
back to our dad's. Then we hear Turner coming down the stairs. He
walks into the kitchen. "Everything all right?"

   . . . *Yeah. Everything's fine.*

Ainsley turns away, doesn't say anything. She wants to get out of
here. I want her to stay and help. I want things that can't happen. So
my sister will have to be mad. I can't try to take care of that anymore.
I was never good at taking care of that anyway.

Turner gives me a look that asks, "Everything really okay?" I shrug
and nod. He puts both palms up and lifts his chin, signalling to me:
"What more can you do?" Then he trots out to say hi to Sara in the
yard. When he comes back through the kitchen and heads upstairs to
work, Ainsley sighs.

There's a hole in the bucket, dear Liza.

22.

I go and get all my glorious hair cut off. Since the genetics appointment I've been asking for shorter and shorter hair, and the hairdresser always talks me into less-short than I want. Not this time.

Cut it off or I will walk out of here and never come back.

She cuts it very, very short. I am delighted.

I arrive home looking like Sheila E. minus the shoulder pads. In one double take, Turner is every man whose wife just made an extreme move at the hairdresser. I cackle. *I'll do this for awhile, and then in a few months maybe add those fabric dreadlocks we saw in Copenhagen. Bright blue!*

Turner says, "*No.*"

(I still might.)

Every part of our household has now been adapted and altered per The Institutes' orders. For instance, there's a ball thing we soak in the bath to dechlorinate the water. At one time, not very long ago (a period that could be measured in weeks), I would have needed more science to rationalize floating a sack-full-of-I-dunno (feels like rocks?) in the bathwater for ten minutes before my son goes in it. I listened to The Institutes' lecture, I did . . . but is chlorine really so bad? We put it in swimming pools, don't we? It's in our drinking water, I think (though the complex water filter in the kitchen now takes it out). . . . But I can't invest the time right now to do the research and decide for myself.

The Institutes said to do it. I will do it.

The shower water pours through a new filter (fitted yesterday), but when I reach up to wash my hair—*squip*—I've taken too much shampoo for what little hair I have left. I'm in the shower with Alexander, who is sitting unsteadily on the floor of the tub, so I use the excess on him: *Scrub scrub scrub! Clean-clean-clean with the extra shampoo, clean-clean!* It's still a lot of soap, and in all the bubbles, he slips down the tub, onto his back. I lift him to rinse him off; he has soap on his face, bubbles at the edge of his mouth. He blinks at the little flecks of water and residue getting in his eyes, but he's not complaining. *Aw, my boy.*

Our daily shower is a great place to help him learn to "anticipate." I always say, *Are you ready for the dip-dip?*

Alexander's eyes start to go wide, processing, processing.

One . . . two . . . three . . . dip-dip! and I move him into the spray, letting it fall on his face for a moment. Then I pull him back out. His tongue emerges for one lick. He's considering, absorbing what just happened . . .

Okay. Ready for the dip-dip again?

This time Al realizes what's going to happen half a tick before the water hits his face. It gets him full in the open mouth. I pull him back out.

Oh, that was a good one! Wow!

I wipe his eyes, then lick his nose. *You had water on your nose! There are drips coming off you! That was a lot of water!*

He hums a giggle: "Hnnnnnn!"

Okay, we're going to do another one! Here comes the dip-dip! One . . . two . . . three . . . Alexander's eyes go wide.

The duvets have been outside in the sun today, along with the mattresses. The house is smelling good. I take Alexander into the rocking chair to sing to him before bedtime. There are new pillows on his bed, a new mattress cover underneath the sheets. Our old air purifier has a new HEPA filter, the machine *vrrrrrrr*ing away under the window.

Every night I sing the same songs: "Black Boys on Mopeds" and "Three Babies" by Sinead O'Connor, and "No Need to Argue" by the Cranberries. Then I put him on his stomach, kiss his head, say good night, turn off the light and leave.

Al falls asleep nearly right away, and he sleeps solidly through the night. He never calls out. He never has nightmares, or, none that we hear about or notice. It is the miracle of this child, the only actual miracle in play, here. Any parental sleep deprivation is our own fault for staying up too late. These unbroken nights are a gigantic gift. Without them I don't know where we'd be.

I go to our room and stand in front of the mirror, pulling my short hair into ridiculous shapes. I can be new inside this haircut. If you only loved me for my hair, you can't love me now. This haircut suits the Ashley doing an intensive therapy program for her kid every day of the week. This haircut suits a woman who's stuffed her hesitation and fear way, way down, underneath the cleaning regimen and the therapy routines and the singsong monologues into her son's mostly-blank face. I am paying the toll to cross the bridge and save my boy: here's my hair, my friendships, my career. Here, take it all.

Turner comes stumbling out of Sloane's room, having put her to bed. He looks at me blankly.

What? I say.

"*Diary of a Wombat* is a very satisfying book title," he says. "And I learned something. I was under the impression that a wombat was somehow bat-like."

Oh my god, you're delirious.

"Yeah, maybe."

Let's go to bed.

"Nah, gotta close up the house downstairs . . ."

C'mon, let's go to bed. Like adults who want to stay married.

Double take. "Oh. Right. Yeah, let's do that."

23.

I continue to struggle with how most people don't say anything when confronted with our new reality. New friends, old friends, cousins, health-care workers, Facebook friends. Most people say nothing because they don't know what to say. Maybe they assume we heard them think, *Oh jeez*. Maybe they didn't want to be a burden, so they stayed away, carefully not acknowledging the huge monster eating our souls.

I'm learning that unhappy times like these are characterized by silence. "I didn't know what to say"? Fuck you. Say something. Anything.

It's midsummer and Alexander is crawling his distance program out front. I mask him and chalk the names of things like "oak" and "gate" on the sidewalk as we go along. Part of the everyday all-day literacy exposure.

Without warning, a neighbour I've barely met comes across the road. She says, "Hey, I wanted to tell you, about your daughter—you're not ruining her life. She's going to be fine."

What?

She says again, not bravely, not hesitantly, not cluelessly: "Your daughter. She's going to be good. It will be okay for her."

I look at her. Dianne? Dee? Something like that. I knows she runs the bed and breakfast. We've never spoken, really. Hello on Halloween—that was it.

Oh, I say.

"My parents went through this. My younger brother is disabled. He's about eight years old? In his mind? About that. He's an adult now, but he's only about eight in what he can do. How he can reason. I have him over sometimes, he shovels the walk for me. He lives in a group home. But I wanted to tell you, growing up was okay for me. My parents worried a lot. They worried about him, they worried about me, they worried that they weren't doing enough for me because everything had to be for him and they were so scared and there was so much to do.

"So I wanted to tell you. Your daughter. She's going to be okay. You're not ruining her childhood with all this." She gestured at the mask and Alexander crawling ahead on the sidewalk.

I say (and *wow* do I mean it), *Thank you.*

"Okay! I'm around all the time, pop in anytime. Bye, Alex!"

Al doesn't turn, engrossed in a leaf stem on the sidewalk, rubbing it in his fingers.

Dee—yes, it's Dee—goes back across the street to her yard, picks up the garden claw she'd been using and gets back to digging.

That's real-life bravery, right there. *That's* saying something.

24.

It has been raining for two days.

The phone rings. Unknown caller.

Hello?

A voice responds. "Hi. So . . . what is this?"

Zero introduction is weird, but it's clearly not a telemarketer. I can hear papers being shuffled in the background.

Sorry?

The voice: "I'm looking here and I don't know what you mean."

I think about hanging up, but this is possibly Alexander-related.

The voice, already annoyed: "Are you there?"

Alexander starts to cry in his Bumbo. I say, *Who's calling, please?*

Voice: "I'm with accounting. What do you mean, here?" Presumably she's stabbing with a finger at some line item in front of her.

I suddenly clue in. *Are you calling about my reimbursement paperwork? Are you with Family Supports for Children with Disabilities?* The countertop timer goes off to signal the next reading set, and Kelsey grabs the flash cards and steps in front of Alexander to show him the words.

FSCD woman: "Yes. So what do you mean here under 'respite'? We don't fund this rate!"

I don't quite know what she's talking about. *I can't see what you're looking at.*

Sloane arrives with questions. In an aside to her, I say, *Just a sec, I'm on the phone, just go ask Dada—wait, ask Kelsey. . . . NO! Just . . . Justwaidaminnut!*

Back to the phone: *Which . . . which month are you talking about?*

FSCD woman: "All of them. We don't fund this rate."

Okay . . . I need you to back up. What paperwork are you look-ing at? (There are three different types of government reimbursement paperwork that replicate each other but have different final destinations within the bureaucracy.)

Her: "Right here. You're asking for $16 per hour. We don't fund this rate. But wait . . . Okay . . ." More paper sounds, a loud exhale. "I'm confused. Just a second, are you . . . ?"

I bite the insides of my lips, hard, to keep from yelling that she should call back when she knows what the fuck she's talking about.

Her: "Okay. I *think* you need to resubmit this form."

Alexander's mask timer goes off.

Sloane, just ASK DADA! Kelsey, can you get Alexander's next mask going?

To the FSCD woman: *Please, can you just pay out the portion that's covered and ignore what we've said on whichever form it is? The contract says we get reimbursed $11 per hour, but we actually pay our aide more. The forms ask "What do you pay?" so I put in what we do actually pay. Please reimburse us for whatever our con-tract allows. Redoing the sheet is super time-consuming.* (They have to be handwritten. Blue or black pen. In triplicate. If you make a mistake, you have to start over with a new form. Sometimes you run out of forms and have to request more and then wait for them to come in the mail.)

Her: "Your form—"

Sloane is now yelling "Daaaadaaaa!" in the living room, Alexander is crying as Kelsey tries to fit the mask over his head, and I hear Turner's feet pounding down the stairs.

Lookit, I have to go. Please pay out what you can. Ask our case-worker about whatever is still confusing you.

Sloane runs back through the kitchen and bumps hard into Kelsey, who's holding Alexander.

Sloane! No! Into the phone: *PLEASE. I have to go.* I want to bash the phone handset into pieces against the kitchen counter. God, that'd be satisfying.

Her: "Uh . . ."

I hang up. Turner arrives in the kitchen. "Ash. What. The Fuck."

Kelsey disappears into the living room with Alexander. She slaloms this house's moods like a champ.

I'm sorry. Paperwork call from the government people. She didn't understand what I'd entered, even though it's the thing they ask for—

The masking timer goes off. *Kelsey! End of mask! Distance now!* Kelsey calls back, "K!" *And they don't—*

Sloane slams into Turner's leg. "DADAAAAAA."

Turner: "Sloane. SLOANE! You need to stay downstairs. Ask Mama if you need something. I am *working*. You come upstairs to the bathroom or your bedroom, that's it. Don't knock on my door in the daytime."

Sloane: "Mama said to ask you."

It's true. I did. He whirls back to me.

She wouldn't shut up, and I was on the phone with FSCD, and the timers were going—

Turner: "Ash, I am barely starting a thing before I get interrupted. I can help with the patterning if I have to, but I can't get enough work hours into the day. I should book a time to leave the house to work. Or I'll have to stay up at night, and you don't want that."

Okay. Yes. You should probably work out of the house.

"A few days a week, at least."

Yes.

"I'll look at my schedule and I'll start—maybe next Tuesday." (Turner will say he needs a regular day working away from the house for the next several years. He will actually manage it three times.)

The phone rings again. Call display shows that it's the FSCD woman calling back. Why didn't call display tell me it was the FSCD the first time?

Turner says, "I'm going back to work," and leaves the kitchen. I let the phone ring, start tidying the counter. Sloane says, "When's dinner?"

The timer goes for the next mask. Kelsey carries Alexander back into the kitchen and puts him in the Bumbo. "I have to go," she says. "I'm going grocery shopping with my grandpa today."

I look at the clock. It's after four. Already?

Yes, yes, of course, sorry to keep you. Today was bonkers.

She laughs. "Yeah, it was! When Turner came down, I was like, whew, almost time to go home!"

I'm jealous that she gets to leave. And she's pooped—this is a job, for her. I look at the program book on the counter. Still at least a third of the program to do before Al's bedtime. Kelsey's already in the front hall.

"Byyyyyeee, Kellllseyyyy," Sloane calls, leaning out the kitchen doorway.

I hear the front door open. Kelsey shouts, "See you on Monday!"

Oh fuck, is it Friday? No no no. Two days of weekend program-without-help. I call, *Have a great weekend! Thanks for everything!*

"I will!" The door slams.

Sloane asks, "What's for dinner?"

When does school start back again? I glance at the calendar. Not for a few weeks. I might kill her before then.

The phone starts ringing again. It's Bruce: "Hey! You kids want to do early dinner at La Viena? I can meet you there in a half hour."

(Yes, thank you, christ)—yes!

"Okay! On my way!"

25.

I can't tell you everything. I'm already saying too much. But the following week, Kelsey comes into the kitchen and says, "Um, water is still dripping on the electrical panel."

What?! "STILL?" *What do you mean?* Pretty sure my voice rises to full screech.

I run down the basement stairs, Kelsey following. "I told Turner about it a few days ago," she says. "I noticed when you were out with Al at that physio appointment."

We get to the breaker box. Water is dripping from a pipe in the ceiling onto the silver rectangle that houses all the electrical circuits. I cover my hand with my sleeve (protecting myself?) and pop it open, carefully. Everything inside looks wet, but the lights are still on around us. I am not an electrician, but it seems a genuine miracle we haven't shorted out the whole neighbourhood.

Jesus fucking christ.

I look closer. The drywall behind the panel is soaked and bulging unevenly. A puddle spills from below the box into the corner.

Quietly: *Kelsey, please bring three black garbage bags and the duct tape.*

She goes upstairs and I go over to the laundry for towels and rags. I bring the thick extra bathmat, too. *Whaaaaaat the actual hell.*

I bunch a towel in my hand and mash at the panel to soak up the drips across its face and breakers. God help me, I am going to get fucking electrocuted. When Kelsey returns, we locate a slow leak on the pipe above and duct-tape it closed. Then we cover it with a garbage bag and tape that in place, then tape a towel around the bag, and another garbage bag around that. Then a huge seal of duct tape. This will surely buy us a day, at least.

We sop up the floor, using every towel in the laundry, and all the rags. I drag over a standing fan and point it at the drywall, and together Kelsey and I secure a garbage bag over the electrical panel in case the leak finds a way around the temporary plug above.

Once the situation is absolutely under short-term control, I turn and say, *Okay. Tell me again. When, exactly, did you tell Turner about this?*

"Um, Tuesday?"

It is now Thursday.

"Yeah . . ." Kelsey looks sad.

It would be better to go deadlift the car or chop down about ten trees. But from the basement I pound up the two flights of stairs to Turner's office and straight-arm the door. *THERE WAS WATER DRIPPING ON THE ELECTRICAL PANEL AND KELSEY TOLD YOU TWO DAYS AGO.*

He is already deflating as he turns to me. "Oh, I . . . forgot." He starts to get up.

Where the hell are you going? As IF we didn't just deal with it! It's fucking done!

He sits. He looks at me.

You forgot? You forgot water? Dripping? On the electrical panel?! OUR HOUSE COULD HAVE BURNED THE FUCK DOWN!

What a good wife am I.

WATER DRIPPING ONTO THE ELECTRICAL PANEL IS A FUCKING EMERGENCY, TURNER.

Wife of the year.

"I know. I forgot."

Now he glances at his computer, already looking like he's wondering how long I'll be mad for. (He never gets enough time to work + "Ashley is always angry about something these days . . .")

Oho? Yeah, guess what? YOU call Brad.

"But . . . you said you fixed it." Turner hates the telephone.

Now comes the terrible moment where I wish our wiring had fried entirely and the house had burned down to punish my husband's detached cluelessness. I speak slowly: *Yeeeessss, we duct-taped the pipe that was dripping. But me and Kelsey MacGyvering some towels and tape onto the basement ceiling pipes is not the adult-land end of this story. You do not leave your basement ceiling like that.*

I tilt my head for this next part: *But oh, are you going to fix the leaky plumbing?* (Rhetorical. He will not and cannot.) *Kelsey told you about it on Tuesday, so, like, did you have it pencilled in for the weekend?*

By the way, there are ten thousand other moments when he's a goddamn saint.

Do you even get that everything could have shorted out? We could have had to replace every wire in every wall. This is not necessarily true. I don't really know anything about electricity. Maybe it would have flipped all the breakers in the box and that's all. But I am feeling apocalyptic, so he gets to hear all about it.

It is INCREDIBLE that the house is still standing.

Now he's waiting for me to finish.

We need to call Brad, because a qualified plumber has to come fix the leaking pipe. And you, my friend, are the one making that fucking phone call.

He'll do it.

Make sure you tell him you knew water was dripping onto the panel two days ago, but that you couldn't get around to dealing with it.

Okay, I'm done.

Gimme a kiss.

Still, and so you really know: I am thankful for Turner. His cluelessness aside, I love his arms, the line of his shoulders inside his shirt, his mind. His love, just clean and there, unwavering. His soul, the blue flame of his being. The understanding and cover he provides for my feminist rage in this world. His values, his focus, his squinty choking chortle when something's *really* funny.

I am thankful for Sloane's words, so articulate, all kid-truth and real wisdom. She is witnessing too much angst and anarchy here, and we can't prevent it. She is part of us, she is immersed in it, being baptized by this firefight. My girl. I want to shield her from all this, and I can't.

I am also humbled by Bruce continuing to come through the door. I know he doesn't want to. I'm grateful for his extra thinking, for the worry, for the groceries. For showing up and showing up. We four are stumbling forward together, imperfectly.

All for this little boy who has become the fulcrum of our lives. I am thankful for the brief glow of Alexander's gaze when I catch it, his smile when I earn it, the lessons he is bringing into this house.

I am thankful for the tall trees out the windows, the high ceilings, the wood door frames. I would have flung myself into traffic long ago if we were trapped in the suburbs.

26.

Sep 2 (2010)
Hi,
I noticed a small thing in the video you sent that I wanted
to mention. When Alexander was securely planted at the
couch he reached forward and attempted to "type" on the
computer keyboard (lots of finger action). . . . He's watching and is doing what is modelled by those around him. I'm
just saying . . .
Love Mum

Sep 18
Dear Ashley,
I viewed the recent blog post. Alexander's "signing" is most
impressive and he seemed so attentive. . . . You must be so
very proud of his progress. The work that you are accomplishing with him is remarkable. Being able to see what is
happening is gratifying to me. . . . Thank you for putting
the time and effort into sharing the progress you're seeing.
Love Mum

Sep 21
Dear Ashley,
Your most recent post about Alexander's program was
incredible. Your family's incorporation of principles behind
the program, that understanding, and the routine involved
in performing with him each and every aspect of its

prescription (and the documentation) has been daunting
indeed.
Love Mum

Sep 25
Dear Ashley,
Maintain patience and persistence with Alexander's program. When he walks—as he absolutely will no matter
what the supposed predictions—it will be truly a gift to
you, Turner, Sloane and most importantly for himself. So
very well done; I am proud of all of you.
Love Mum

Sep 30
Dear Ashley,
When are you to return to the USA with Alexander? We
can accommodate Sloane during your next visit, if that is a
concern. We could arrange to meet her at the airplane in
Castlegar and return her to Calgary by plane. Please let us
know.
Love Mum

My mother did try to stay in touch. But I didn't respond. I couldn't.
I had to push her away.

27.

Alexander is a wonderful baby, this is truth. But he is nearly seventeen months old; his peers are no longer infants. They're walking and talking. Sloane at this age was yammering in full sentences, driving us crazy with cogent arguments. Turner and I would look at each other proudly: *Ah, our maddening, delightfully articulate child.* Alexander just exhales a sharp "ah" sometimes when it seems like he wants to say "yes." It's hard to feel wild parental pride about deliberate breathing.

My worry that he'll never be a normal child is bottomless and exhausting. The genetics test proved he's not a normal child. I have no language, no vague mental stencil even, to draw an outline of future-him to fill in. I cannot picture what he *will* be, I only have words for what I don't want. A "retarded" child and everything that means crowds the frame. This has fuelled me since the start. I'm sorry that I am not braver, but this cowardice has made me strong.

Tonight Sloane and I go out to fetch housewarming mums for John Johnston. It's mommy-daughter time. We buy the flowers at Co-op, drop them on the porch at JJ's new rental nearby and then go for a drive.

Sloane gives a big contented sigh as we roll slowly along McHugh Bluff, looking at the downtown towers. "Can we get milkshakes, Mama?"

Sure, love. You want a hamburger, too? Such a treat in our reconfigured universe.

I take her to the drive-in on 16th Avenue and then head slowly home. In front of our house Sloane climbs over the centre console, holding her too-big burger and too-thick shake like prizes. She wants to stay out here to eat, to stretch the time alone together. I tell her about my brother and sister, who at five years old, cut two peepholes in the side of a box. They put it out in the middle of our street and sat underneath, watching the cars drive around them.

Sloane is shocked, laughing, "Oh, Mama! That's so DANGEROUS! Where were you?"

Dunno, camp or something. I heard about it afterward.

She has her legs over my lap in the dark, we are warm in our shared glow, her eyes are shining. My darling girl.

She says, "I don't think it's usually regular that moms laugh with their kids."

No no! I did! My mom was hilarious. SO funny.

"Oh, I didn't know. That's good you had a mom like that. That's how you know how to laugh with me."

I don't think she connects stories of my mother with her fading memories of Granny Val, anymore. I have stopped trying to mash these disparate characters together.

We sit in the car, goofing around, until nine thirty, way past Sloane's bedtime. Eventually Turner comes to stand in the doorway, turns the porch light on and off to get our attention, and does "Come into the house, get in here, you assholes" plane-directing arm waves. Sloane and I finally tumble through the front door, laughing. Turner sees the milkshake cups. "So you went to Peter's. But you've been gone for hours. Where were you even going, originally?"

To get mums for John's porch. Planters.

"Flowers."

Yes.

"For outside."

Yes. He wasn't home. We dropped them off.

"Snow is forecast Thursday. You bought plants that will just die on the porch in two days?"

HA! Yes. (Not necessarily. John can bring them inside, if he remembers to.)

Turner rolls his eyes.

Sloane: "Dada! It was for a good cause!"

Turner points at us. "You two. Get upstairs. Brush teeth, Sloane." To me: "Tomorrow morning's going to suck."

I'll get up with her.

"Oh, you betcha you will. I'm not getting her up tomorrow. This is *your* doing."

Sloane flings her coat on the floor and flaps her elbows, waggling her bum at me: the piggyback bird. I carry her upstairs to the bathroom and plonk her on the toilet lid.

She sucks on her milkshake straw, leaning over to watch herself in the mirror, holding my neck to steady her lean. I say to her reflection, *You are my favourite girl, love.*

Sloane grabs my cheeks and mashes me against the milkshake and her face: "Oh, I *knowwwww*. And you are my favourite MAMAHHHH!"

We hear Turner's feet on the stairs, calling as he comes, "You jokers stoppit! Get your teeth brushed! Go to bed!"

Sloane and I start snort-snickering, quick-ripping off our clothes. When Turner arrives in the doorway, we are naked and clinging to each other, pretending wide-eyed surprise.

He's unfazed. To Sloane: "Jammies, darlin'. *It's time*. No books tonight."

Sloane rolls her eyes at him, huge. "Okay, Dada, we geeeeeeeetttt it." She jumps down and runs to the bedroom, with Turner calling after her, "Keep it quiet! Your brother's asleep!" She yells back, "YES, DADA," as the door to their room bonks loudly off the inside wall.

He exhales and turns to point at me. "This is your side of the family. My people don't go in for this nonsense. . . . Gimme that." I hand him Sloane's abandoned milkshake, still three-quarters full. He takes a sip. "They do good shakes."

Tonight was so good with her.

"I know. I'm glad."

I love her.

"I do too. But she needs to get to sleep earlier."

Sometimes it's worth it to just drive around and talk. This was not what I thought her life would be, y'know? She was going to grow up going to India and knowing our Ontario people, and— My mouth waters, tears rise. *We're so tamped down, here, now. Staple-gunned to this place. You know?*

Turner steps forward, pulls me in by the back of my head, his hand on my hair. "It's okay. She's doing good. She's okay. We're okay."

Into the shoulder of his sweater, I say, *I think we need a weekly thing. I need to see her more, so I can just be me with her. Wednesdays I could take her swimming in the afternoon. She needs to know how to swim, Turner. She's not safe by herself in the water yet. She needs to know how to swim! She's five!*

Turner pets my hair. "She doesn't have school on Wednesday afternoons anyway. It would work."

I sob, once. I want good things for my girl. I want to give them to her.

"Something just for you two," he says. "Yes. It's a good idea."

28.

Alexander happened inside my body. I made him in me, of us. Physically, literally. Turner came, I came, it was over, we lay there listening to each other breathe for a minute, and then we fell asleep. And sometime in the following minutes or hours our gametes met and combined, tra-la-la, and the cells started to divide.

By the time I was in Victoria two weeks later, for the memorial service for my paternal grandmother, our future Alexander was well on his way, growing, growing.

I peed on a stick when Sloane and I returned from the funeral, and two lines showed.

The radiologist said, "I'm really not sure why you're here. It's so small we can only see the implantation site. We can't tell you anything at this point—"

Me: *How many?* As the older sister of twins, I didn't want that for Sloane.

Him: "Well, honestly, it's so early we can barely tell you anything except that you're pregn—"

ARE THERE MORE THAN ONE, OR IS IT JUST ONE?

"Yes, it's only one—"

K, fine, I'm good.

But by then, Something Had Happened, but not a something anyone could see on an ultrasound. That one bottom gene gone, a genetic gecko tail that can't grow back, and the baby's cells dividing and replicating that omission, on and on, and even now, right to this day.

—

When they told us the diagnosis, they made sure we understood that no one was to blame. But when you have a special-needs kid, you wonder (ten trillion times), How did this happen? (Howdidthishappenhowdidthishappenhowdidthishappenhow?)

What's to blame?

Who's to blame?

Are *you* to blame?

Actually, maybe it was me. (Probably me.)

The Possible Reasons Why
My Baby Is Missing a Gene

Pollution at the Lakehead. Born in Thunder Bay, I spent my first four years in the fallout shadow of the Fort William pulp mill. Mercury and other effluent puffed into the sky, making the southern clouds, I thought, of my early memories. An eye-watering sniff of pulp processing on the air makes me feel just-hatched young. I read in *National Geographic* years ago that scientists can match isotope signatures in your adult teeth to the distinct geographical water sources you drank from in infancy. My adult mouth would tell of toddler teeth absorbing strontium from rain falling into Loch Lomond on Mount McKay, way on the other side of the mill, then pumped into the city's drinking supply. If my teeth are so marked by long-half-life pulp-mill pollution, why not my ovaries?

Vast Quantities of Diet Dr Pepper. When I was ten, we moved house and my parents bought a new fridge. It arrived filled with various types of Dr Pepper, a thank-you gift from the appliance dealer. The kitchen pantry shelves bowed under the weight of so many cans. We kids were certainly, without-a-doubt, absolutely *not* allowed to drink it . . . but there was so very very much. Pop is crack for children, and our parents didn't maintain a careful inventory. If we were smart (take from the back, arrange the six packs at the front so nothing looks disturbed), they didn't notice the stores depleting. My brother and sister and I guzzled our way through hundreds of Dr Peppers in the following weeks, stuffing the empties way deep into the trash (no recycling in those days). All summer we suppressed strings of tin-flavoured burps as we jumped on the trampoline and played BurgerTime in the back room. A lifetime glutton, I probably consumed more of that pop than my siblings combined. Here in the twenty-first century, science is still studying the suspected genotoxicity of aspartame.

Bug Spray on Lake Louise Way. There were swarms of wasps at our next house. In the Calgary of 1989 you could get a licence from the City for super-strength insecticide. Our controlled substance came with a long straw on the end of the nozzle, and spewed a stream of liquid death. When Val used it on the wasp nests, everything in them died within minutes. We had a few blessed wasp-free weeks, and the death can got put in the garage. We kids eventually located it, and I recall us screwing around on our parents' bedroom balcony, spraying it at individual wasps alighting on the nearby elm branches. Later we began to notice dead-everything on the patio and dining table below—where we ate on warm nights. Before dinner we'd just swipe the dead bugs off before setting the table. Our family were not disciplined before-dinner hand washers. Num num.

I Was Asking for It. In 1990 I went to France on a high-school summer language program. For our final project my friends and I presented a scene from the movie *Dirty Rotten Scoundrels*, which had been shot in nearby Villefranche. I'd suggested this hilarious scene because I had it memorized in English, so we'd only have to translate what was a sure winner. In it I played Ruprecht the "monkey boy," the repugnant and imbecilic character Steve Martin's playboy uses to drive away the women who want to marry Michael Caine's suave larcenist.

Amy: *"Pourquoi a-t-il un liège sur la fourche?"*
Jenn: *"Pour ne l'empêcher pas de se faire mal."*
Ashley: [stabs self in eye with cork-covered fork]
. . . And so on. We got a 95%.

The Toxic Stress of Math. In the 1990s, and even now, you had to pass high-school math to apply to university, and I am no good at math. Every day I woke up with math lurking at my shoulder like a pulled-back fist. I had math class every weekday, attended in-school tutoring twice a week, and went to a private tutor on Tuesday and Thursday evenings. Because I forgot the principles almost immediately after "getting" them, my homework took hours and hours and agonizing hours, and even so, often I didn't finish. Every non-school moment not spent sleeping, eating, or playing soccer involved math revisions, worksheets and "extra help." It was deeply, vastly, black-hole-no-escape stressful, no way to live.

Though it was obvious to high-school-me that mathematics explains and makes possible things the world needs explained and done, it was equally clear to me that I would not be the one wielding any of the crucial math for society. But grade twelve math was a poisonous wall I had to scale in order to escape to a faraway university. Math gave me insomnia, made my stomach hurt every day, and impacted all my relationships. When I earned 52% on the standardized province-wide final exam, I was *so* proud of myself. I would not be surprised if those years of unnecessary and extreme math stress epigenetically damaged my eggs.

A Family Predisposition to Hashimoto's Disease. . . . Which leads to hypothyroidism and a host of other problems, including a proven link to Hodgkin's lymphoma, a type of lymph cancer I developed at age eighteen (not getting into it here; whole other book), which led to my treatment with:

Radiation. You'd think this would be the obvious answer to what happened to Al, but I'm not so sure. Still, it makes the list, because, well, *radiation.* A mini Chernobyl, all for me, at the outset of adulthood, yayyyyy. The doctors in Kingston, where I was attending university, warned of post-radiative leukemia and other cancers that could occur in my forties. But the Calgary doctors said their radiotherapy was so focused that it wouldn't affect my ovaries, and I was going to be fine. (These are the guys who also said they'd protected my lungs and heart, but they fried them, and my thyroid, and the tops of my kidneys, and half my salivary glands. So a few stray beams across the ovaries isn't beyond the realm of possibility.) . . . Maybe I shouldn't have had children? Too risky? Was Sloane a lucky neurotypical anomaly?

Baby Powder All up in My Business. When you're a curvy lady working in Asia, someone eventually suggests baby powder as a solution to some of the heat-related thigh-rub challenges you face. In recent years, studies have shown that talcum is bad-bad-very-bad for our lady parts. After years of underwear stuffed with baby powder, perhaps my fallopian tubes let a few grains slip through, and they messed with the egg that became Alexander? . . . Hard to say.

The Hand of God. The least/most satisfying of explanations is a giant Monty Python finger reaching down to flick off the tail end of that one allele in Alexander's DNA. "You think you've got things under control? Think life's pretty good and you get to make the choices? Don't believe in Me? Ho ho! How about *this*?" Many amazing and unexplainable things have happened in my life. But this was the first time it felt like I was dealt a hand *because* I thought I could avoid it. I could not avoid it.

But there's another thing, though. It's big.

Before Alexander, I thought I wouldn't love a boy child.

I thought I couldn't. I thought I would need to abandon any infant boy of mine on a mountainside to be picked at by birds. I thought I would end up emasculating any male child I had, involuntarily making him sorry and smaller by being his mother. Deep inside, I felt I could not collude in raising a male child just to have him snatched away by the world and turned into a blithe and chuckling monster by the patriarchy, etcetera. (Recall my Women's Studies degree.)

Growing up, I couldn't picture having a husband or even a baby of any kind. Then I met Turner and things shifted. I saw a glimmer through the trees: *Hmm. Maybe.*

If you're wired to want children, and it turns out I eventually was, by and by you get reckless or you make a decision: (*Okay, I will push down my fear and go for it*).

I sure didn't want a disabled child, because I had shit to do (!) and most certainly did not have it in me to raise and support a subnormal dumdum. But in my guts, deeper down, I didn't want a boy. I picture the conception, the winning sperm being a Y, and my frightened soul going, *No no no no*—interfering, wrestling with it—*no no no, we can't do this, no no NO!*

But the spark of life is muscular, involuntary, bigger than my wants. That Y chromosome shoved its way to the front. I couldn't handle a boy who would become a man, so I got a storybook boy, a child who will never grow up.

Alexander will never be a boyfriend or a husband or a father. My son will never mansplain. He will never announce at dinner that it's obvious professional women don't prioritize their careers like men do. He will never offer to have friends smell his fingers as proof of recent sexploits. He will never loom over a seated woman and warn, "Don't you DARE." He will never ask his girlfriend to pretend that a classmate didn't attack her in a sudden rage at a party, out of embarrassment that she "probably made him do it." He will never sneer that some women are unfuckable because they're fat. He will never be thrown out of a bar for harassing an ex-girlfriend and have his teeth smashed in during an unrelated fight outside, and then show up at the woman's house the next day to demand she pay for the dental repair because if he hadn't been thrown out of the bar he wouldn't have picked that fight with a stranger. He will never slip and call the female employees "sweetheart" and then lay them off because they remind him of his daughter. He will never yell, "You're the kind of woman that makes men beat their wives."

I got a boy stripped of the repugnant male potentialities I have seen in this world.

I didn't think I could love a boy, so I was given a boy I could love.

29.

I can't believe it, but I'm still running. By myself, and often, and I finally love it. I run in the evenings, all summer, all over the neighbourhood. I jog through parks I've never seen and down alleys with old rusted house numbers screwed onto tree trunks. I flush pheasant and giant jackrabbits, get bugs in my mouth, cut up my legs on sharp hill grasses.

I've registered for a 5K in September to have something to work toward. I chose an event in Canmore because triathlete types would overtake us on after-dinner walks there with my Aunt Jackie and my cousins when we visited them. The event update emails feature photos of grinning joggers with Ha Ling Peak in the background. They'll pin a number to the front of my shirt. I will cross an actual finish line at the end.

I never thought I'd run for running's sake. But at this moment of my life, running hard up hills far from the house and then coming back home feels like controlled flight, and eases the clutch of fear in my chest. I'm often visited on these runs by a vision of myself as a pilgrim on my way to . . . somewhere. Each time out I resolve anew to bring my full energy to the program and our family life. When it's time to go for the evening run, I feel a quickening. On my rest days I miss it.

Then Turner gets a Toronto speaking gig for the day of the Canmore race. We need the money. He'll be gone that whole weekend.

I check the event website, and there will be no child care. My aunt has moved to the West Coast, and my Canmore cousins are long gone. I call around and search the internet and there are no just-book-it babysitting services in Canmore or even Banff. At least, not that I can find.

I call my dad: I'll go straight to the Canmore event and directly back to pick them up, okay? Bruce sighs. That is too long to leave them, he says. "You can't ask Peggy to do that."

Can't ask Peggy to do what? Watch you watch the kids watch two movies?

"*Don't,* Ashley. It's not realistic for me to take the kids. This isn't the only race. They happen every weekend."

True, but . . . *Dad, please. I've been training for it, really. It's my first-ever one. I'm registered. I paid. I want to do it.*

"No! Pick another one! In town! When Turner is here so the kids can stay with him!"

I try the being-his-daughter angle. *Dad, come to Canmore with us. You could come cheer me on.*

"I don't want to!"

I'll do the race and you just take the kids to lunch. I won't be running for long. You don't even have to watch me run.

"Ashley! I'm not going to Canmore!"

I close my eyes. The Man U crowd is ululating on the TV. He just wants to be left alone to watch soccer.

I break my own heart. I can't speak again without risking tears. After thirty seconds of sitting quiet on the line, I hang up.

I email the race organizers, hoping they'll at least refund my money. Nope. If I cancel, I lose the race fee. $85 feels like a lot to lose.

So one by one, I call everyone we know in town to ask if they'll come to Canmore with us. I know what the answer will be before I even start. Everyone has their own children and activities, work obligations, weekend plans. Of course they do, of course. Understandably.

Alrighty. I'll take the kids to Canmore with me and duct-tape Sloane's wrist to Al's bouncy chair. It'll be fine. I'll prop up a sign for passersby: *Their mother is running the 5K. They're dressed for the weather and completely okay. Pretend it's the '70s. I'll be back in twenty minutes.*

. . . But, fuck it. In the grand scheme, me wanting to run this one race is inconsequential. I should find another event, sign up for something in town.

*Whatever, the running is about taking care of me, anyway. I don't
need to run an official race. I'll just keep going out, running in the
evenings. It's good for me. I will.*

I do.

Then, a month later, on the Canmore race day, Bruce shows up
spur of the moment with my brother's older boy to take me and the
kids out for lunch. I get the fennel and arugula antipasto. It's delicious.
Alexander pulls at salad greens I've placed at the far end of his high-
chair tray and pushes them slowly into his mouth for consideration.
Sloane and my nephew Liam jump around the booth, all hepped up on
San Pellegrinos.

Dad and I talk about his upcoming travel plans. He and Peggy are
doing a canal cruise in Panama next month, and then on to Palm Springs
in November. They've decided on Costa Rica in February this year, with
my sister. —*Wait, what?* February is when *we* go to Costa Rica. Or did.

He says, "You could go down before Christmas. It's nice then.
The air is fresh."

*Dad. We're going to Philadelphia for our Institutes revisit in
December.* He knows this. He's helping us pay The Institutes' fees.
Then we're going straight to Nova Scotia for Christmas.

"Well! You're getting around, kid! Must be nice!"

*It's not a holiday when we're in Philly, Dad. We're at The
Institutes, like, twelve hours a day.*

"I don't know, flying around to the States and the Maritimes
sounds pritty-good to me!"

I drop it. I shoulda gotten a glass of Pinot with lunch. Two.

Our waiter brings the bill and the machine. As he pays (Bruce
always pays), my dad says, "So you're on your own with the kids.
What's the plan for today?"

Look at my father's face: such lovely lines around his eyes, those
green-brown irises. His nose is an older, male version of mine, unre-
markable except our uneven nostrils. His upper lip has a faint scar from
a brother skating over his face when they were kids. I love this face.
I want it to say, "Actually, sorry. I *do* remember there was that race
you wanted to run today, and I wish I had it in me to help like that. But
I'm not taking the kids on my own, and I can't ask Peggy to help with
them. I won't cause that kind of trouble for myself. I'm sorry."

But that's pure fantasy. He has no idea that today's the race, because I never told him the date. It is a crisp September Saturday, and the sun is shining. He's just bought us an expensive meal. There is no subtext or admission in his question about our plans for the day.

I start to pull Alexander out of the high chair. *Oh . . . just Alexander's program. That starts back up as soon we get home. No days off.*

He rolls his eyes. "Dear, you have to take a break from all that busywork. Some of those exercises are fine, but I don't see it changing anything for him. You need to get out of the house more. You should take the kids to the zoo today."

I took them just before school started. And Al's really not at the stage where he likes that kind of stuff yet. (I'd take them again, but the zoo is expensive: $50 for a few hours of wandering around the gardens, and Sloane just wanted to go to the playground, anyway. There are free playgrounds.)

"Okay, I hear you, the zoo's been done—check. Find something else."

Um. *Dad . . . in reality, every activity-type-thing is expensive. And the kids are too different in age to, like, go to the wave pool with just me, alone. I need another adult with me to manage both kids.*

He's not coming with us to the wave pool or anywhere else.

"Okay, do your thing. I will just [motions zipping his mouth closed]." Then he shakes his head, play-sadly, "Ashley, I gotta gooooo, I gotta get this kid back to his parents."

Liam and Sloane are giggling under the table, test-bonking their heads against the tabletop to jiggle the glasses above. Cousins.

We walk back to the house. Bruce straps Liam into the car seat and turns, puts $40 into my hand and drops himself behind the wheel. Not looking at me: "Take the kids out and do something. And call your mother. She wants to hear from you."

I shift Alexander to the other hip. *Does she?*

He glances up. "Don't start, Ashley."

I can say anything, even the truth, in the last moments of a visit—that's the unspoken rule. *She doesn't call me, Dad. I do a full-time therapy program for my disabled baby and she complains to Ainsley that I don't support her enough. I'm fucking busy. Val can call me.*

"Okay, whatever. You don't look that busy." Pulls the door closed.

The window comes down as the car starts to roll. "We loves-you. Bye, Sloane!"

Then to me, "You're not too busy to call your mother."

That day, the running balloon develops a slow leak. What's the point of running, again? *Because I feel better, it helps me cope.* That thought isn't enough to get me out the door much anymore. I'm down to three days a week, then two. *Does it even help? It's not helping enough.* Come October I'm sleeping less, drinking more with dinner. And afterward.

I start to go out tipsy, mashing on my shoes and already heading out the door when Turner realizes I'm leaving. "You going out?"

I'm often wearing jeans or a not-good-enough bra when the impulse hits, but the point is to go. If I can get out the door, I can keep going.

I trot over to a nearby elementary school to run the outside metal stairs, probably the original fire escapes. Now it's nine o'clock and I'm drunk-running in the twilight, going *dong-dong-dong* up the stairs, *fuh-fuh-fuh* down. The stairs are dusty. It's just my footprints on these treads, put down over the last weeks. I deliberately run different trajectories on different days to make more prints.

Stars are appearing in the deepening blue above when a creeping fear billows into my gut: *I'm an adult on school grounds after hours. Would me running these stairs be questioned, by . . . someone?*

I'm alone so much of the time now, my grip on what's okay in the real world is slipping.

This is a public building, isn't it? Surely I can run on unused stairs at a public school after hours?

The bannisters are narrow and cold under my hands. I hold them anyway. *Careful on the way down. Focus on the feet.* Fuh-fuh-fuh. *Don't want to trip and go flying.* ("Oh my god, how did you break your TEETH, Ashley?")

Beyond the playground I can see silhouettes of women, moving with purpose along the sidewalk. Yoga ladies carrying yoga mats in special yoga mat bags, striding into the evening class at Bodhi Tree. It's lovely in there, that yoga studio. There are nebulizers in the change rooms that spritz essential oils into the air. I went three times for $18 on an all-you-can-yoga special back in the spring. I would definitely go to yoga instead of running, but for returning students it's $22 a class. . . . Like, as if.

Stop it, stop it. I jog over to the stairs on the east side of the school so I don't have to see those serene assholes converging on the studio.

I begin to climb, muttering *Running is free free free, running is free* in time with my steps. Up up up, down down down, all these footprints, all of them just me, out here by myself. *God, I'm lonely.*

Such melodrama. *Shut up, Ashley. Suck it up.*

In the shower later, I find myself cupping my boobs like I'm protecting baby chicks. This road is getting harder.

I order a book online called *Spiritual Tasks of the Homemaker*. It's about building holy satisfaction into the routine of daily chores and responsibilities. I keep it in the kitchen, read random parts between Al's flash card sets. I need to accept these doldrums, embrace them. I tell the counsellor (I'm still seeing her, she's still just charging the FSCD rate), *I'm struggling against everything. I'm not settling into this. It's going the opposite way. I'm falling out of myself. Most of the time I'm actively "acting." I'm playing like I'm calm. Inside I am not calm.*

She says that I'm building the habit of being calm. That I'm teaching myself the pattern, and it will get easier. By my birthday in early November, I've stopped running the school stairs.

Now I just stay home in the evening when I'm drinking, which I'm doing more. Fuck it, amirite? I call my cousins and clean the kitchen while we joke and chat. I tickle Sloane toward the bathroom to brush her hair and teeth and fart around before bedtime, hold my breath when I hug her. I give Alexander his nightly full-body rub and fall into the rhythm of the strokes and the song, pushing at the tendons in his legs, getting him all soupy with endorphins. I read in bed with the lights down dim until Turner falls asleep. Then I get back up and wander around the house, doing random chores. I am always tired and never sleepy.

I lose track of where my running shoes are. There's a hole in the right toe, anyway. *I put a lot of miles on those old shoes. Maybe when we have some money, I'll order new ones, start in again.*

But we don't. I don't. I won't. That light has guttered out. Then winter sets in.

PART

THREE

Do I wear you out?
You must wonder why I'm relentless and all
    strung out
I'm consumed by the chill of solitary

ALANIS MORISSETTE,
"ALL I REALLY WANT"

30.

It's bitter-cold and I am standing outside the Braeside mall, under a knife-edged chinook cloudbank, holding a cheque for $24,000. Calgary parking lots are full of gravel, even this early in the season, little rocks crunching underfoot during thaws. I am here to deposit this money onto our line of credit at the bank branch here. The cheque will erase part of our debt, make it disappear, and is a gift from my father before he decamped to Palm Springs.

I am staring at this cheque, made out to me. Here are thousands and thousands of dollars. I don't know how we arrived at this number; there's double this on our line of credit, and more on the credit cards. This must be the maximum that my dad thought our debt could possibly be. (It isn't.)

I keep looking at the number. Wasn't there a game show pyramid of this amount? With $24,000 I could start a new life. It's not enough to leave easily, but it is enough to leave.

Sloane is at gymnastics class at the nearby leisure centre. I have enough time to deposit the cheque and turn it into a prepaid credit card, oh, plenty of time for that before the class is over. I could pick up Sloane afterward and later, while Turner is making dinner, grab my passport from the wooden cigar box behind his desk. I could put some underwear and my thyroid medication and my 24-carat gold wedding bangles in a bag and hide it in the basement, then wake up early in the morning. I'd tell Turner I was going for a run, a long one. *Please take Sloane to school and bring Al with you.* Kiss him as he rolls over, look in on the kids. I could take the train downtown and then get a cab to the airport. Hurry through security with my carry-on and the money.

I could disappear into the world. Goodbye.

I suspect I could live without my children, and they could live without me. Alexander is a tiny child who doesn't make eye contact. And Sloane is what, five and a half? She might not remember me, after awhile. (False, of course. I'm rationalizing.)

But Turner—I would miss him forever.

This is where duty saves me, and saves our family from me. Duty is something I didn't understand, before. You hear about it in the context of military service. Or civic action. I'd thought duty was a feeling in your gut, like conscience . . . I need to help that woman whose coat is caught in the escalator mechanism, or, it's my obligation to cheer loudly at Take Back the Night to set an example as a feminist. You do what you are supposed to do because your gut tells you to do it and you just *know* you should.

But duty is different, actually. Duty is the last stand of what must be done before all is lost. It's not something you necessarily feel. In fact, I know from experience now that duty can drive the bus when you feel nothing at all. When everything's gone numb and surreal, duty can push you from the outside, somehow. You can allow duty to drag you forward when you don't have anything else left.

The list of really excellent reasons why I should walk into the credit union and put the cheque toward our debt are right here in front of me. But they don't push me forward, those responsibilities. Nor does my integrity, whatever that means now. Nor does the image of Sloane, twenty years in the future, sitting in a therapist's office, explaining her abandonment issues. These things do not factor in to how this day ends.

The real reason I crunch across the gravel and pull open the wood-handled mall doors, walk the shiny '70s mall-floor brick, find the bank and stand in line (lick a finger and wipe under my eyes to clear any smeary bits of eyeliner, check my purse for ID); the thing that pushes me into a chair to explain my business, what makes me sign over that cheque and put the money into our line of credit and take my receipt and walk back across the gravel in the slushy parking lot to my car, and get in and sit with my chin on the wheel, staring into the sun, burning my corneas until the sun's centre goes blue and begins to dance . . . Only duty made that happen.

—

Today I get downstairs after Turner has taken Sloane to school (with Al along for the ride). There's clearly been some spreading of condiments in the kitchen. Four knives splayed across the counter, smeared with almond butter, peanut butter, jam, butter. *Why you gotta use so many knives, Turner?*

There are toast crumbs everywhere, eggshells on the counter, the fridge door is ajar, the dishwasher full of clean dishes, the water filter empty. It takes me nearly twenty minutes to undo the mess of the morning routine, put the vocab cards back in order and the paper clips on the word sets, wash the frying pan properly, unpack and pack the dishwasher.

At night I've been looking on the internet at school buses that people have renovated into rolling live-in campers. If we lived in a school bus, we'd only have room for one kind of nut butter. We could drive out to Newfoundland, and in the mornings I'd look out the window and through the fog there'd be houses painted fun colours and my soul would be glad. I make a note: *Renovate school bus— driving-around life.* I put the sticky note on the fridge, then in my pocket, then go upstairs and stash it in my bedside drawer, under my journal. On the fridge Turner would see it and think I'm going crazy. (I am, but have to hide it as best I can.)

I spend most of my waking hours in this kitchen. There isn't much of a view from the window. Believe me, I've looked. I have put in lifetimes gazing at the three houses over there, such boring colours: pus yellow, dirty white, brown. When we first moved here, I introduced myself to those people, invited them over, shared our trampoline with their children. Now if I banged on their door to borrow a cup of sugar or even warn them of a coming tornado, they'd likely ask who I was. I was raised in the wrong city, the wrong century. Something.

I glance at the clock: 9:05 a.m. Turner and Alexander will be back soon. I check the program notebook: Turner only did two masks on Al this morning. Four kinds of toast but only two masks. *Jesus fuck.*

I think about going to the basement to touch my photo equipment for a few moments, to think with it in my hands. It's been a long time. Halfway down the stairs I hear the front door open, so I stop in the laundry room and flip the clothes to the dryer and head back up.

Turner has taken Alexander upstairs to see if I'm still in bed. These are the last fleeting moments I have to myself before I start training my doll-boy again. I listen to Turner walking around up there, gathering the overnight water glasses. One minute left before I'm on.

Standing there, hand on counter, I feel like an empty cup with dirty rings inside. I read in a feng shui book that you should clean your kitchen sink twice a day, morning and night, to make your whole world clear. I turn and wash the sink. There's a discernable pleasure in this kind of work that has an immediate result: the metal shines, there is coffee residue on the paper towel I use to wipe out the drain. I can see the impact of my effort immediately. These tasks mean nothing in the long run, but they are all I have now. I was never going to be a housewife. And now I am a housewife.

Turner walks past me and out the back door, saying "Hi" as he goes. Garbage day, I guess. Then Alexander pulls himself into the kitchen, sliding along on his leg warmers. Those little toes. He doesn't look up. He's heading for the metal bowl on the floor at my feet. He pulls it over and spins it deftly. The metallic putter of that bowl is the primary audible thing Alexander makes happen. I wait for it to clatter to a stop and then I pick up my boy. *Hello, little Al, little Al!*

He looks down and away. Tongue going in and out.

I say, *Hello, my boy!* and throw him lightly up in the air, his warm armpits landing in my hands. He comes to attention, looks right at me, gurgle-hums a bit. That's better.

This weekend I am making flash cards for Alexander's intelligence program:
      Inuit women's art
      Bones of the body
      Breeds of cows
      Trees of North America
      World leaders in history

I bubble with flash card categories for adults without disabled kids too:
      Indicators of dangerous isolation
      Mental-health impacts of chaotic environments

Average in-office appointment wait times, by medical discipline
Interpersonal NIMBYism

Nobody wants these flash cards.

Taking care of a baby, any baby, is mostly boring for their first three
months. Then they sort of wake up, come alive, and you're on the
go forevermore. But even now, a year and a half into his life,
Alexander's constant quiet is a sinkhole. He won't look at anything
farther away than the end of his arm. His hands move, to rub and
explore each other, but often he just sits there, hunched to one side
in the Bumbo, blinking slowly at nothing at all. The signs of in-
there-ness are unpredictable.

I am bothered and frightened that he still won't point. He can't
say "Mama." He doesn't really seem to recognize people other than
the ones living in this house. The doctor says the hypotonia affects
everything, including his face. So the eyebrow twitches and small
mouth movements that elicit great joy and flurries of photos with
most babies have always been absent in this boy. He moves and
gestures, but not enough. Not enough that we are predictably able
to say, *THERE. See right there? That was a reaction to what we
said. Yes!*

Turner and I are showing signs of wear and tear. Last week he
went to pick up Vietnamese takeout around the corner and was gone
an hour. I was sure he was sitting in the restaurant, having a couple
of beers before coming home, but he said he wasn't. We are keeping-
going but not coping. There isn't infinite space into which trying-to-
save-Alexander can expand. There are limits. We are reaching them.

I've been having suck-me-hollow dreams about Sloane dying.
Turner dying. Bruce dying. I am walking a dusty suburb, looking for
Alexander. He is somewhere here, spinning a bowl under a roof
overhang, out of the wind, not hearing my calls. I find him around
a corner, dirt caked into the folds behind his knees, and around his
knuckles.

Dregs of this dreamscape follow me into the waking world.
I throw away some batteries, picturing dump scavengers of the future
finding them and rejoicing at the tiny bits of energy left inside them.

Turner keeps a bowl of dead batteries in his office "to go to recycling eventually," another errand that will never be done. He fishes mine out of the garbage and adds them to the bowl. He doesn't know that when I sneak them into the trash I'm sending resources to myself in that dystopian nighttime world.

31.

I'm at a sushi restaurant well after lunchtime. Nobody knows I'm here—by "nobody" I mean Turner and Kelsey. I told them I was going for a walk, but I came straight here. I should be home, doing Alexander's program, but I'm pushing raw fish into my mouth instead. Gulping down little cups of green tea, asking for a teapot refill.

Sounds: trembly guitar track, the clack of hard plastic cutlery. Around the pillar from where I sit, one man is bluntly coaching another on how to negotiate the sale of his oilsands services company. The older guy is laying it all out for the younger man: the human resources systems on-boarding he needs, pricing the company at $260 million on the TSX, arranging the Christmas family employee party at the Calgary Soccer Centre. "That's how you go. Then it's easy." Never in my life has anyone given me advice in that tone. I need advice in that tone. I have never needed cheerleading so badly. I order more salmon nigiri.

When I get home, Kelsey is gone for the day. Turner has already picked up Sloane from school. I enter the house softly and hear noise in the kitchen, Sloane's little-kid falsetto, Turner's lower tones. I'm full of sushi rolls and self-pity. I go quickly quietly up the stairs and put on my wedding bangles. I squeeze them slowly over my knuckles, let them *ting-ting* onto my wrist, then pull my sleeve down to keep them quiet. I grab my thyroid meds and put them and my wallet into a purse I never use. But I need to hold the passport. I need to hold it.

I go back downstairs and am breathing hard as I put on my warmer coat.

Turner comes to the kitchen doorway. He sees the passport in my hand. He approaches and says, quietly so Sloane won't hear us, "You're going out?"

Yes.

His eyes are soft. "Do you know when you'll be back?"

I just shake my head, sorry.

Pause. "Will you be back today?"

I don't know.

He takes a big breath. "Okay. Let us know where you are. When you can."

I picture a giant airport board with all the places I could go. Calgary doesn't have one of those, but I picture it anyway. Vanuatu and Buenos Aires and Edmonton and Cairo. But heading for the airport is too much. A big show, a big mess, smashing sideways out a high-rise office window, holding a pickle jar full of coins. Not a path to peace.

So instead I am standing near the Safeway in the slush. At home I'd stupidly changed from boots to shoes, bad footwear for fleeing. My feet are already getting wet. I am turning in circles. I do have to go somewhere. My brain is twirling. *Where? Where that's not here?*

I see a bus coming. Turns out I'm just steps from the stop. I don't know where it goes, but I get on.

I choose a seat at the window, looking out at the oncoming traffic. Poplars and flat, melty lawns and dirty cars flow past. Somewhere beyond the hospital, the humidity and soft vinyl seat lull me down. I lean on the foggy window as we roll past the big mall and out to a cul-de-sac that overlooks the river valley. The bus idles here for fifteen minutes. Then we lurch along the reverse route, slosh of turning wheels, hum of engine, slowly back to the Safeway. I'm the only one on board, but I ring the bell to request my stop. I stand up, leave quietly. I pause on the sidewalk for a full minute, assessing. I feel not better, but not the same. At least no longer desperate. I walk home. I have only been gone an hour.

When I come through the door, Turner is visibly surprised. Sloane yells, "MAMA!" She's been told I would be gone awhile.

The house pulls me in. I take off my shoes and jacket, and the forward inertia captures me. *Hello, hello, here I am, I'm fine, it's okay.* I go to the kitchen, running my hand down Turner's arm as I pass him. I start packing the dishwasher, take over masking Alexander, feed the cat, boil the kettle, make tea.

Turner is watching me. He's not scared, but he's not relieved, either. He can't ask, "How close were you to actually leaving?" You can't say that in front of the children. (And bedtime is hours away, but we won't talk about it then, either.)

It has to not matter that I left. There's too much that needs keeping going. The timers keep beeping, the toast pops up, you put butter on it, you cut it in half, and you push it across the counter. Next.

32.

At the end of November, my mother sends an email offering to pay for bookshelves for the kids' room. She also mentions she'll get a few weeks off at Christmas, which will be a nice break for her, that she's looking forward to having time at home, alone.

Again I don't respond. I don't want her to pay for bookshelves. I don't give a shit about her solitary holiday time. I want her to be here, to be part of this, to grab my wrist and say, "You can do this, kid. You can. I'm right here with you." Ainsley says I can't expect our mother to be involved. But I miss her. Involuntarily, desperately. And full of rage.

So many people have told us they've said to others, "If there's anyone who can handle this, it's Ash and Turner." But they can't possibly know my mother could be but isn't standing with us in the middle of this hurricane. That key Toronto friends have vanished, including people who said we were family, people we stood by when it really mattered (for them). What does it say about me that I do not inspire hard-times loyalty, or that I somehow chase it away—*shoo, go*—even as I crouch inside this catastrophe, keening, calling for help?

In the midst of me "handling" this (the giant forever-ness of it), I am failing that hazy old-Ashley identity I built in other people's minds. Not just the people still in our lives, but "them": the people I knew in high school, at university, at jobs, soccer, friends of people I dated, old bosses and colleagues, Rotarians who saw me speak. I'm the sort of person people remember.

Apparently most people feel something of a fraud. I never did before, but was I always actually a fraud anyway? Was I such a self-duping charlatan in all those charmed years before Alexander that I was blind to my own fantasy? Everyone wants to seem strong, singular—was I just singularly successful at conjuring an illusion, telling myself a story of who I was, and believing it?

The sameness of my days now makes everything blur forward and backward in time. I know what I did yesterday, and the day before, and that I will be doing the same thing today, and tomorrow, and the next day and the next day. Every day I think of the things I have lost, lists of them swim to mind. There is such ugly, ugly self-pity in all this. Things and people and opportunities occur to me when I am sitting on the toilet, as I am heading up the stairs to read Sloane bedtime stories, when the phone rings and I know it is not for me anymore anymore anymore. . . . *Danger, Ashley, danger*.

I'm re-prickling at the thousand times I missed various chances, different opportunities, before Alexander. All the ridiculous things I did because I "had" to, or thought I should, all the wasted time on people who didn't matter, who didn't last, who got from me time and shine they'd never reciprocate. Years of energy and love invested in those people, years. I poured so much of my young concrete into leaky frames, and now I have nowhere to stand.

It's been nearly a year since the diagnosis. Today is a deafeningly cold late November day, with the sun pouring yellow through the house. Turner and Sloane are skiing, taking a daddy-daughter break away. *Go, do it, please,* I said to Turner. Take Sloane to the mountains, she'll remember even though she's little still. It'll be a goodness anchor in her memories, riding the chairlift with her dad, looking down at the lodgepole pine-tops. I helped them pack last night. Got them out the door early so they could get the first chair at Louise. *Have fun, have fun, it's a clear day by the forecast. Take lots of pictures!*

So I am at home alone today with the boy. It must be a weekend, because even Kelsey isn't here. I do Alexander's program, as ever, masking and log-rolling him on the living-room carpet, and most of the day passes, the stretches and the feeding and the crawling-down-the-track, around and around. We work through the program and I joke into the quiet, talking to him as "we" putter through the house, me carrying him and him being carried. I note his progress in the book. It is everything and nothing, this kind of being, an everyday day, the same as dozens of weeks' worth of days this year.

But this day is different somehow. By midafternoon the house is dazzling inside, a golden-floodlit trap, a honey-beam purgatory. We can't go outside because it's winter at every door. We don't have a solid snowsuit for the boy, just a bullshit hooded thing with feet that looks the part but is only good enough to get him to and from the car. We haven't bought him something better because have you seen what kids' snowsuits cost? And how much do we really take him out, with this home therapy program going all the time? (Not much.) And—where would we go? What swimming pool? What playroom? What groups of other-mothers-with-kids? I don't know who would want us, who would gather us in. And there're the entry fees. The juice boxes he can't have, the cute baby containers of Cheerios he can't eat. I'm not doing that to myself, pushing us into that toddler world he can't inhabit. I'm supposed to be home, anyway. Do the program *at home*, they said. Save this child *at home*, they said. I told them to tell me what to do, and they did.

But today it is hard, hard again like it's always hard, yes, but today somehow even more harderer. This world contains only the hum of the refrigerator and the invisible vibration of the nerves buzzing down my left arm. Our breath. The shuffle of my feet on the floor. Alexander is in the sling on my front, and I come to a stop in front of my reflection in the mirror. Who is that woman? Consider these jowls, emerging. I am becoming only the lumbering ox who pulls the carriage for this child. I go to the kettle and pour hot water into a mug, chug it down to clean myself out.

On the second cup, I can't swallow, and have to turn and spit into the sink.

Turner will come home later and find me locked in a loop, trying to drink water and having to spit it out, like a crone fountain.

What a boring horror movie.

I try to fill my lungs, but my windpipe is all narrowed. By nothing. By everything. I look at Alexander. When I was his age, my mom was teaching me:

- to make cookies (*Never touch the mixer when it's moving, you can lick the beaters when it's stopped*)
- to balance on the ride-along bicycle seat (*Don't lean!*)
- how to call my grandparents (*344-1643*)

I remember the smell of rain in the drains near our Thunder Bay house. Pussy willows in a jar on the back of the toilet and being careful as I petted their tiny tails. My grandfather Alec taking me to watch the grain elevator burning at the docks, the fire higher and higher, orange and huge in the night sky.

I pet the baby, stroke-stroke, through the sling, thinking of the pussy willows. Folded into me like this, this boy's body is again an extension of my stomach. *You are mine* [pet] *you are mine* [pet], *let us live* [pet], *please, I need a way through and out.* The only way out is through.

I step into the living room and the therapy program notebook is there, open to today's page. The rest of Alexander's distance work isn't going to get done, not with me in this strange, wigged-out frame of mind, now. There are toys and clothes on the floor, the disaster of our objects and belongings, boxes and piles everywhere. . . . Christ, how do I have two irons? There's a shelf full of feminist textbooks, a painting of Turner's great-grandparents' farm in New Brunswick, a formal salwar kameez I'll never wear again, an incomplete alphabet of fridge magnets. *Why did I keep these glued-together Ukrainian dancer figurines?* It all looks like kindling.

Alright, alright. I carry Alexander up the fifteen stupid stairs, counting out loud as I mount them, as they creak underfoot. Fuck these stairs, this house, this world, the golden light. Go into the bathroom, slowly. Press my palm to the old wood, push the door closed, turn on the fan. Then undo the sling, undress the baby and put him, uncomplaining, down on the floor to wait. The *zzzzth* of the zipper on my threadbare jeans, *foosh* of knit past my ears. Focus on the small things, make everything a meditation, be present to the immediate all around me, the movement of my limbs. I step to the tub, turn on the water, wait for it to go warm. Then we go in, Alexander in my arms.

The bathroom is a refuge with a lock on the door even though no one is home. Hot and hotter, the shower tamps things down, a bit, for awhile.

I wash the baby's front, his shoulders, his feet. I sit down and wash between all my toes and say to him, *See? Mine are same-same but bigger.* I take his finger and put it on my toes, one by one. *Mine are really big, and yours are really small.* He stuffs his other fist into his mouth, looks away. He's getting hungry.

I stand and shut off the shower. Pull us both out and onto the mat, dry the baby's face and his neck and arms and bum crack, all his folds and flat parts and the thatch of hair on his head. The room is warm and humid and smells good. I rub a hole in the mirror steam and pluck my eyebrows as he lies on the floor. Still daytime out the cracked skylight—still, still daytime. Time has no meaning anymore, in this cold, except dayness and literal darkness.

I sing to the baby in the reflection: *Oranges and lemons, say the bells of Saint Clement's . . . You owe me five farthings, say the bells of St. Martin's.* Does it matter to him? Is it going in?

When will you pay me, say the bells of Old Bailey. When I grow rich, say the bells of Shoreditch. My voice is thin and hitches. *When will that be.* When will this kid look at me? *Say the bells of Stepney. I'm sure I don't know . . .* My voice trails off, and I hear it trail off, and I think, *My voice is trailing off. Because I'm singing to myself.*

Swallow. My mom got this record from the library for me so many times. I'm singing my childhood into this boy, even if he doesn't seem to hear. Somewhere in him, he hears it. He must.

Here comes a candle to light you to bed. Here comes a chopper to chop off your head! I bend and chop-chop at Al's tummy, then tiggy-tiggy at his neck, his armpits. His mouth is open, tongue stuck out, and he breathes a bit different. It's just enough.

I carry Al to my bedroom to get dressed. Everything in the drawer is scratchy and ugly. I wish I still had soft socks. They wore out. I stand there, staring at the drawer.

Fuck it, no socks then.

People have been going on recently about Cormac McCarthy's *The Road*, about how it's the final word on the brutality of becoming parents, what we are capable of, how far we will go. One friend said,

"Good god, no woman should read this book, no mother. It's terrifying, it breaks everything. Don't." A sudden self-destructive glee strikes me. *Oh.*

Woe is me today, is it? Do you hear that feathered air under Kali's sword, the electric crackle? I'll make it worse—try and stop me. With new energy I stomp into Turner's office and pull *The Road* off the shelf.

I spend the rest of the afternoon walking through the house with Alexander in the sling, reading the book. Into the light, into the shade, letting my hips sway. I put my feet here, here, here. I walk with that man and boy, I am walking that road. Oh, I understand this book.

I read it all the way through in six hours. Turner and Sloane come home while I'm stalking around the house, and I hand Turner the baby and just walk away, reading. I get into pyjamas and start walking the house again, reading to the sound of Turner putting Sloane to bed upstairs, the dishwasher running after Turner has loaded it with my day's dishes.

When I finish the book, I throw it across the dining room. *Fuck all y'all men who said this book was too hard. You are such soft meat.* There isn't anything I wouldn't give my children, this child. What wouldn't I give my own blood? I'd give him everything. I *am* giving him everything.

The Road has given me strength. I bare my teeth at my reflection in the dining-room window. *Fuck you. Try me.*

. . . Well, I'll try her again tomorrow.

I can't breathe all the way in.

Turner: "What's going on?"

Can't breathe.

Turner: "Hmm."

He's heard it lots. The head and shoulder rubs he gives help shut me up. They're not a cure, just a sort-of-helping thing. They distract me, help me doze.

I tell my father, Dr. Bristowe: *I feel like I can't breathe all the way in.*

"That's the way it goes sometimes, kiddo," he says.

But . . . I don't think it's normal to not be able to breathe, sometimes?

"Suck it up, kid. Life in the fast lane."

I tell my son's pediatrician, the Indian South African who calls me "Mum": *I have trouble with my breathing. I don't black out, but I can't get a full lungful of air.*

"You maybe need to take it easy, Mum. You think? You are a hard worker. Relax."

I'm not doing well. I can't get my thoughts straight.

"You should not worry so much. Alex is doing great. Get some time for yourself."

No one mentions the word "anxiety." I don't know what anxiety is. I can't name what it would be in myself. An old housemate used to say she got nervous sometimes. I never understood why she'd be nervous about renting a car at the airport or not having dinner reservations. I thought "nervous" meant you didn't like being on stage giving a speech. Or that you'd worry about probably running into your ex if you went to that party.

But now I think she meant anxiety. That paralysis of thought and crowding-out of real self from the head by the clanging mental and physical noise. I should've been listening better.

For me, apparently nothing's wrong, or everything that's wrong is obvious and none of it should make me unable to get enough air. If I feel like I can't breathe for months at a time and it never comes to anything, doesn't that just mean it's nothing? Hypochondria? But . . . it's like something heavy is parked on me. A big square combination safe or an anvil, fallen out an apartment window. I'm pinned to the sidewalk of my life: Okay, breathe. That's it. Keep going. This is just your life now, kiddo. Accept it. Life in the fast lane.

People tell me I need to exercise more. I do need to exercise more. I go out for walks, I jump on the trampoline with Sloane. But I would like to dance, it would make me feel much better, but I can't go out to the bar: I'd never make it to midnight, when the good music starts. Where are the mid-afternoon raves for aging Gen-Xers with kids?

I take to drinking more. Always loved to drink. Now I am

drinking often. In order to sleep. To smile. To be distracted and get on with all-the-everything. To feel something other than the ratchet strap around my chest. I wake up with a headache every day. Then I discover you can buy over-the-counter codeine at the pharmacy. They take your name and write it on a list, I guess so you don't go home and chop it up and snort it or whatever people do. I don't care what other people use it for. I like that it punches my headache down.

Stay down, says the codeine to the headache. *Shut. Up.*

I hold onto Turner's hand in the doorway as he's trying to leave.

Don't go.

I hate to share him with the political people and environmental groups who want him, with the writer bois and journalists, with anyone here in Calgary. Fuck this place, they don't deserve him.

He lifts my hand with both of his, looks me in the eyes: "I love you. I'm done my book, free of it for awhile." Yesterday Turner submitted the manuscript for *The Leap*. "I have a thing this morning where I am the expert and they want me and they're paying me. I said I would go. So I'm going, and I love you, and goodbye."

We need money more than anything right now. I unhand him.

Turner has been the most bulletproof endlessly forgiving gentle unfazed kind and strong man through all this. And I'm being no kind of wife to him right now. Or maybe I'm a new kind of wife, one off the edge of the map of the things I was going to be when he signed up for this marriage. This is why wedding vows are so vague but all-encompassing. Shit happens. Cancer. Fires. We'd been together twelve years before Alexander arrived. We thought we'd run the gamut of big stuff to encounter before old age set in. Now we're like people changing a tire at the side of a highway during a blizzard, shouting directions to each other over the wind and traffic. No mitts and the flares are wet.

I am leaning on him, leaning, leaning, just ridiculous some days, the angle clownish. I'm worried he'll crack under this weight—that the day-after-day-after-weeks-after-months of my leaning will wear him out. But Turner is holding us. He's planted, he's braced. I can lean. For now.

So I shut the door and face the house, yet again. I'm not much of a calendar watcher, but tomorrow is the one-year anniversary to the day of Alexander's diagnosis. We've been at this therapy program for six months. Forever already and years to go. I'm so impatient. I want Al to "catch up" to his peers. I chew the inside of my cheek. In the kitchen, Kelsey is masking Alexander and clearing up the breakfast dishes. When I think on it, we *are* slowly seeing a little boy emerge among us, a no-longer-infant who sort-of participates. He is trying. At the therapies he is obviously trying.

Even as I despair that nothing is happening, that this is all just busywork, I admit he's obviously coming along. Just not quickly.

In ten days we head back to Philadelphia on our first return visit to The Institutes. I have to have all of Alexander's paperwork in order, all the diet sheets filled out, all the program documentation, all the revisit forms filled in before we leave. I have been working on the report for eight days, and I'm only nine pages in, with many more to go. It all has to be handwritten. I haven't seen this much of my own handwriting in years.

Many hours and days later, I am done the report. I am cross-eyed and I went through two pens and my hand might be broken, but we can leave for the airport tomorrow morning. Now to panic about packing. And also, yes, to panic that Kelsey is leaving us to go back to school, as she should. When we get back from Philadelphia with a new-and-improved (tweaked and expanded) program, and from Christmas in Nova Scotia, and from a work trip to Cuba that Turner and I are doing on our own while his family takes care of our kids, we'll need to hire someone new here to help with Alexander.

For now, though, Onward.

(That's Calgary's official slogan.)

33.

Philadelphia in December, 2010. I am sitting in the kitchen of another rental house, feeding Alexander, Sloane smooshed in beside me. The floor is old, thin hardwood, crinkly under decades of orange Varathane. The dishwasher is running, warm against my back.

This Philly row house is straight out of *The Sixth Sense*: "I'll show you where my dad keeps his gun, c'mon." I tamp down a snicker. God, I am happy here. We went for groceries first thing, gawked again at the scrapple, then took the kids to the park while Margo organized dinner. I love that she joined us again for moral support and comfort, along with our friend Mark, who came in from New York. Margo made crab cakes and found dessert across the street, in a little house that holds a tinier restaurant selling takeout jam tarts. Now we are up late from jet lag, settled in and giddy, anticipating returning to The Institutes for lectures tomorrow.

Here, I am able to love my boy on his own terms. For so long I could only see what was wrong. All the things he wasn't. The possible and predicted complications, all the ways our lives would be different and worse than they could have been. Being in Philadelphia again is such a shot in the arm. Here, I can see Alexander inside the diagnosis. I so clearly behold my boy coming forth, a different frame making his colours pop. As I do the extra dishes, Alexander is at my feet in a mask, petting the seam of my jeans, Sloane is reading with Gramma on the couch, Mark and Turner are bantering at the table. This is life. It is not parenthood or domesticity that is breaking me, back at home. It's the isolation and aridity. Everyone says you need routine. But predictability is great unless more of the same is nowhere near enough.

I have been alone in our Calgary house for nearly seven months, limited to Kelsey and the patterners and my dad for news from the outside world. Philadelphia is an escape, it is learning, it is community. It is another place, The World. It is big whiffs of humid wind in my nose as I throw balls with Sloane in the park behind the rental house. I am elated the whole time, my wild grin undeniable in the photographs.

For this round of lectures, the parents include Indian couples who wear full hats-scarves-coats and mitts in the chilly auditorium. There are other Canadians, from Montreal, and Ukrainians, Belarusians, Bermudans, Chinese. Americans from the southwest and California, tanned and fit.

A Mexican-American couple from Cleveland look familiar— I realize they were in our original cohort here, last April. The woman runs up to me at the first break and grabs my hands. "I would not have made it without you!" she says.

I recall that her baby has Down syndrome, but I don't remember her name. It is Angela.

"I've thought about you every day! You said, 'Tell me what to do, I will do it.' Every day I did the program with your voice in my head. This program is impossible—I would have stopped. But you kept me going. Thank you!"

Me? Holy shit.

Janet Doman stands at the front of the lecture hall to deliver the anti-seizure lecture. I picture her closet: rows of lavender blazers, beige turtlenecks, black pumps after Labour Day, camel pumps for summer. Miles of them all, curving dimly into the distance.

Janet presses us to have our water tested when we return home. To remove any carpet left in the house, to throw out pillows we haven't replaced this year. Did we switch out all our household cleaners as we were told to? Have we had our insulation tested for asbestos?

And if we haven't, what are we waiting for?

Money, half the room silently shouts.

Janet says, "Are you waiting for the money?" She looks around the hall slowly. She takes her time. "There's a lot of concern about money. Let me assure you, we hear you. You've paid to come from around the world to sit in this lecture hall. We know you're devoted to your hurt child. We know you'd do anything for them." She looks out at us. We believe that she knows.

"We also know that when you go home it's different from being here, on campus. Here at The Institutes, everyone understands what is best for your child. The staff are of one mind: the directors, the advocates, the people who schedule the appointments, the folks who work the AV equipment and everyone who makes the meals and cleans the dishes in the cafeteria. We all work only toward the goal of saving your children. And you do, too.

"But we know that out there in the world, people will tell you water purifiers and natural cleaners are ridiculous, unnecessary. We understand that you may wonder if the financial outlay is worth it. Do these things really make a difference? . . . Don't wonder. You've spent your valuable money to come here to learn what's best for your children. The staff here at The Institutes know these things aren't frivolous or even optional. Read your binder notes when you go home. Trust that a detoxified environment is *essential* for your child, like food and a roof.

"Many of you have moved house to be closer to medical treatments your children need. So don't let the detergent you use be the thing that's aggravating your child's breathing challenges. Maybe you don't want to have the conversation with your neighbours about using fertilizer on the shared lawn. Your neighbour isn't going to pay for your child's hospitalization for gastrointestinal or lung complications. You are working so hard on behalf of your kid's neurological system, and neurotoxic chemicals are undoing your hard work. Your child is already behind. They deserve every single advantage you can give them. Don't let your reticence stop you. You can't be shy. You're saving your child's life. We're giving you permission to be ferociously on your child's side, always."

She turns and walks back to the lectern, then turns and points at all of us. "Get your water tested. Get your pipes replaced if you need to. Filter the air in your child's bedroom. All the instructions are in your course binders. *Do it.*"

Boom. Unequivocal.

Janet opens her binder to the next section, and the slide changes on the wall screen. "Okay. Let's talk about nutritional supports for your child . . ."

But the chime sounds in the ceiling. We are released for lunch.

That night, we walk back to the rented house, blurry-brained after another eleven hours of paying attention. We're over-hungry and wrung out. The slate sidewalk slabs are damp underfoot, high pine branches gleam in the streetlights. It smells like a chilled garden out here. Turner and I walk up Stenton Avenue and cross into the three-hundred-year-old neighbourhood of sleeping oaks and stone walls. I'm glad to have this time to move after all that sitting.

To the beat of our steps, I hear these three things in my head:

1. They're telling the truth.
2. They believe in Alexander (more than I do).
3. They're helping us.

That's it. That's enough.

We arrive home to find Sloane asleep and Margo dozing on the couch, holding Alexander, damp cloth alongside. He'd spent the whole day barfing his guts out.

The next morning Sloane says solemnly, "Gramma is a hero."

Glenn Doman intones, "The brain-injured child's greatest enemy is time. Every day your kids aren't better, they're worse. Because all the other kids are better and yours is being left behind."

He slips the front cue card to the back, but doesn't look down at the next one. "So to combat this, we've created a twenty-four-hour-a-day program for your kids. And by the way, we have no guilt about filling your days with work that will save your children."

He looks up and around the lecture hall at us parents. "This program gobbles up the lives of the families that take it on. Right?" He nods along with us. "It certainly does. Because there's a whole world of things to understand, so much to learn how to do, and then hours and hours of each day to do the program and prepare your materials."

New card. He still doesn't look. He knows this lecture cold. "*You* have to fight for your child's place in this world. Families have to be the fences and defences that keep the hurt child safe. The outside world is ignorant about injured children. The world thinks they are animals that should be kept in cages, away from the 'normal' people, who are all running around doing 'very important things' and can't be disturbed or inconvenienced. We know that is wrong ethically— but that it is also, absolutely, untrue."

At the mid-morning break, Turner and I are standing at the coffee-and-apples station chatting with the parents from Bangalore. And I am hit with an unrelated-to-our-conversation epiphany. I realize that I believe in The Institutes like I've never believed in anything. They offer salvation in exchange for obedience. The program is way too much, and I can't do it by myself, sure. But I can sign on with absolute faith to their mission that we embrace, without proof or societal support, our children's hidden potential, and relentlessly pursue unlocking that potential. They command an assiduous commitment to excellence and (essentially) ascetic discipline.

I can do this. I can keep doing this.

Six weeks ago we sent Al's hair samples for chemical analysis. Kelsey and I had to shave him completely bald to get enough hair for the sample. Now the clinic director brings us the results: Alexander's levels for antimony, cadmium, gadolinium, tin and uranium have all come back above the normal range.

What *is* gadolinium, even? Three years of staring at the periodic table in high-school chemistry and I have no memory of that element. Must be one of the stragglers in the bottom rows. I google it after the appointment, sitting in the large waiting hall of the clinic build-ing. . . . Radioactive. Used in MRIS. Okay, that makes sense, given how many tests Al has had.

Turner leans over. "The gadolinium? Yeah, I googled that too."

The rest of them, though. Tin—seriously? And cadmium? I overheard another parent saying that cheap Chinese porcelain is often contaminated with weird metals, and that they had to replace their mugs and plates. I think of our kitchen dishes at home, col-lected from various Asian groceries over the years. Hehhhhh. One more thing.

—

At the clinic visit, we are assigned respiratory patterning for the next phase of Alexander's home program. The therapy will involve Alexander lying prone on a table, inside a sort of jacket with lengths of fabric that attach to dowels. Two adults sitting opposite each other will "pattern" Al's breathing by pulling on the dowels in time to a set metronome speed—it almost looks like the adults are rowing—so that the jacket gently squeezes his chest. Alexander is meant to fall asleep during the twice-daily forty-minute sessions. Once he is fully used to it and we have at least a full month of every-single-day manual patterning in the can, we can switch him to a mechanical respiratory patterning jacket that hooks up to an air pump. This machine will pattern him while he sleeps. We already own it, this machine, sent to us by another Institutes family. It's sitting in the basement, awaiting deployment.

On Wednesday afternoon we wander down Philadelphia's German-town Avenue in a jailbreak daze. We're all done at The Institutes for now. We leave tomorrow for Christmas in Nova Scotia.

Sloane and Gramma are up ahead, Margo pushing Alexander in the stroller. Turner says, distantly, "There were a lot of possible outcomes from the year since Al's diagnosis. Looking back, a year out, from that day? This is the best possible one. This is on you. You made this happen."

I did. *But it's complicated. I feel guilty about it.*

"Don't. Who cares what people think? If they think this is a holiday or it doesn't help Al, fuck 'em."

No, no, of course. But I'm not working, we are taking on a lot of debt. Al's progressing, but is this going to <u>fix</u> him? How long is this going to take? Are we still going to be coming here in ten years? I don't think I have that in me. There are frilly still-green bushes with red berries around us. Yews, I think? This world doesn't freeze solid and die down to the bare earth in winter.

Turner shakes his head. "We don't need to have answers to those questions yet. I'm still getting work. The Vietnamese dinner fundraiser worked. Your dad is helping. My mom will come to Calgary whenever we need her. Don't focus on things we can't know yet. We just need to keep going."

Kelsey did a lot of it, but now she's gone. But even when she was there, I was the only one doing it every day. . . . Like, if I don't push the boulder up the hill every day, it doesn't get pushed. It's on me to keep it going. You do it, but you don't really do it, you know?

"Nobody's going to do it the way you do it. But you also push yourself too hard. I think there's a way to have more balance."

We have to do the whole thing or I can't do any of it. It's crazy-making, but it's very all or nothing. The Institutes' staff say it themselves.

"But Ash, *they* don't have to do it with Al day-in and day-out like we do. They're just telling us what to do. . . . They're *right*, but they're also insane."

. . . I think they're the only sane people in the world, on this stuff. I stop, put my hands out like I'm presenting myself: *And I'm sane here. I know what we're doing and that it's right and that it's the only important thing. But at home, I'm a basketcase.*

"You're not, really. It just feels like that. The kids are happy. We are okay."

Margo is way ahead, now bumping the stroller over the sash of what I'm sure is the toy store.

I'm worried about when we leave here, Turner. Like, worried. The program feels so doable when we're here. Maybe we should move here.

This idea has clearly never crossed Turner's mind. "Ash, we can't move to Philadelphia. We aren't American."

But you can get that whatever-whatever-extraordinary-artist visa. You qualify.

"We don't know anyone here!"

We do! And I feel like I'm talking to intelligent adults here. The Institutes is something I understand. Maybe we could run their communications—the website is a shambles. And there's a cafeteria full of Al-friendly food. Remember the sign? "There are patterners all around you." There're other people in the same boat, other families coming. We'd make friends. I'm full of hope here, Turner.

"Ash, how am I going to get actual work here? I've been trying to place articles in New York magazines for ten years. And what, we'd sell our house and buy something . . . around here? Put Sloane in that shitty public school down the block? The property manager guy said this neighbourhood school is rated one of the lowest in the city. And forget French, if she's here."

We start walking again.

. . . That palace near the ravine has ten bedrooms and is only $750,000.

"No. What? How do you even know?"

I was looking online at house prices.

"Ashley. Stoppit. Don't do that. And $750K in American dollars—that's a million Canadian. No."

I'm kind of chasing along beside him now, ridiculous. *I know, of course. How would we even heat a ten-bedroom stone mansion? But it's a recession here. Even a railroad baron estate on two acres is a relative bargain. So we could get a four-bedroom row house in Chestnut Hill that would be bigger than our Calgary house—for the same price.* (Philadelphia is Zone 7a. Loquat, magnolias, sugar maple . . . Makes me want to weep.)

"This is not happening, Ash."

I'm in the house all day, Turner. Just the chaos of it all, all day, being in the kitchen, doing the program all day, the data sheets all day. Being alone. The patterners come, but it's not like an actual social life. I'm burdening them. I'm always afraid they'll stop coming. I have to take care of them, feed them, chat, catch them up. And now, after this clinic visit, the program is even bigger. I'm glad it's different and more, but I'm terrified. I need to know what to <u>do</u>.

"What do you mean? You know what to do."

I need a bulletproof schedule that includes, like, everything. A comprehensive guide to what I need to do, all day, so I don't have to think about it each day and each time something comes up or interrupts. All the details of what needs to be done, all the what-ifs, in one place. All the permutations and combinations.

Turner flaps his hand at my head. "But you know that! It's in there. You don't need that written down."

Being in a different place doesn't change how Turner thinks. But I shift depending on the container, like water. I need to make him understand the schedule thing, *here*. When we get back to Calgary, I won't be able to explain it.

I need a colour-coded visual. I need to look at something that's taped to the fridge. So I can know when it's okay to stop and make materials, or meals, and when I have to be doing something specific on the program.

He's not getting it. "But you *do* know what to do. We've been at it for months. You can do the program without specifically writing it down—"

Holy fuck, why are you fighting me? You asked what I need. It's not just the program. There's too much in each day. I never get everything done. I can't keep everything straight—what I've done, what's to be done, what I missed and needs to be made up for, what I need to prepare ahead for the next day, what needs to be set in motion now so that it's ready next week. All that stuff.

But really, it's the day-to-day. I feel like I'm losing my mind at home. I get all whirly and can't concentrate. I never get all the reporting and paperwork done, it's always just sitting there, half-finished.

"I can start picking up Sloane every day. I can take that off your plate."

No! Fuck no, that's the only thing that gets me out of the house. The Institutes would want me to stay home and not drive her, but I need to get out of the house once a day!

"Okay. Okay."

I really need an actual written schedule that I can look at twenty times every day that tells me what to do. I can keep going if I know when I can stop. I know it seems like I should be able to handle making those decisions on the fly, but it's just too much. In Calgary I can't keep my thoughts straight. There's no more room in my brain.

Turner starts to say that he is also constantly interrupted, and I wave him off. *I KNOW. But you have an office with a DOOR. You don't shut it, but you could.*

We have arrived at the toy store. We stand outside to keep talking.

In The Institutes' data sheets there are whole therapy days missing because of some fucking two-hour morning meeting with a government person while I'm bouncing Al and keeping him moving and then his nap started and I got going tidying our room and then I deflated because it was raining and in the end nothing got done that day. *The Institutes expect me to answer for all the days not accounted for in the data sheets. It's distance Alexander "lost" because we didn't do it with him.*

Turner leans on a decommissioned parking meter. "They have to be all doctrinaire about it so that we actually do it. But Glenn Doman himself said it was too much to get it all done. There's always more."

I GET IT. But I'm the taskmaster. On days that I can't get out of bed, the program barely runs. And if I don't try to do it all, it won't happen, and I'll drift back into work.

"Oh, not after all this time. You're not going to just stop. You just need to ease off a little. We need to decide where to draw the line so there's more time for you—"

A streetcar rumbles past. The din lets me yell without seeming totally deranged. *Turner! Every day I don't want to do the program! I just make myself! But I can't keep the house and the volunteers and the data sheets and the laundry and the driving and the meals straight! I need a SCHEDULE!* The streetcar is past, and I pause.

Turner says, "I make most of the meals."

I look at him hard, head cocked. Yes, he makes most of the dinners. But the breakfasts and the lunches and the two snacks and all the associated chopping and prep is me. I let it go.

It's not just the program. It's the still-moving-in and the renovations and my dad coming over, saying, "You know, you kids should . . ." And I have no friends.

Turner: "What! You have *tons* of friends!"

The program is working, but I'm really trapped, inside it, at home. I need to actually be doing it or ignoring it to do other stuff— not FORGETTING it or getting distracted or sad or pulled into a phone call with the aide coordinator and then feeling like a shitty failure. Fitting everything in as it comes at me is not working. There's enough work and logistics for five people, and now it's only me. I get time "off" when I break down completely and can't face leaving the bedroom. It's not sustainable.

Turner says, "I know. It's just, I've been desperately trying to carve out some time when I know I won't be interrupted. If I know I can count on the time to be left alone, then we can schedule in the time for me to come trade off with you."

Holy fuck, dude. This is my whole point.

Inside the store Sloane is jumping up and down at the till, and Gramma has her wallet out, talking to the clerk, paying for something. Al looks asleep in his stroller.

"Ash, we can make the overall schedule anytime. Don't worry. It won't take long."

I'm always in it. It's all a mess in my head. We need to do it together.

"Okay. We will. We'll do it."

Got him. *When? When will you focus and do it with me? When, exactly?*

"In Nova Scotia. There'll be lots of time at Christmas. We'll do it in Antigonish."

Aaaaaahhh! Turner!

"Fine, Ash, we'll do it on the plane! We'll start it on the plane and finish it at my parents' house. We have two weeks there, we'll get it done."

I pout on purpose to make things a bit lighter. He thinks it's easy. I hate that it's not. Two years ago I could have done this by myself. Now my brain is like an overfull blender without the lid. Here in Philly it's on low, slopping a bit over the edges, but mostly contained. In Calgary I'm on pulverize every day, splattering everywhere. I need something to tether me to reality. *C'mon, schedule.*

Sloane is coming toward the glass door, now, a big sucker in her cheek, looking very pleased. My mouth waters just thinking about the sugar. Gramma is managing a huge bag hooked onto the back of the stroller. Early Christmas gifts. A grandparent's prerogative.

I sigh big. Turner reaches to squeeze my neck, massaging me as we wait for them outside. "Shut up, shut up, it's fine. Don't worry. We'll do it."

(We won't.)

My Nova Scotian in-laws roll out a cozy, boozy Christmas carpet. Their Antigonish house is filled with heirlooms and tiles from around the world. There are tin boxes full of chocolate peanut butter balls and other Christmas cookies lining the kitchen island. The fridge is stuffed so full it's Tetris to get anything in or out. Another full-sized fridge in the basement clinkitty-sings when you pull it open, the shelves and door packed tight with eight kinds of beer. The largesse is way overboard. It's a calming balm.

We drive to chop down the Christmas tree on Crown land, a spot under the power lines where they'll be shorn in a few years anyway. Sloane gets to wield the big axe, every nearly-six-year-old's dream. Alexander has a proper snowsuit now, thanks to Gramma, so we bundle him along on all the errands and adventures. One afternoon we make snowfolk on the back forty and spend an hour tobogganing down the little hill there. Alexander goes, "Uh! Uh! Uh!" panicking against the feeling of free fall. But The Institutes say to keep him physically stimulated, so we shrug it off and send him down again.

Turner's brother, Johnny, and his son arrive on Christmas Eve, stepping out of their rental car wild-haired and triumphant after a harrowing, stormy drive from the airport. Everyone piles into the house, the fire literally crackling and the Barra MacNeils on the stereo, stomp stomp in the narrow hallway and it's all coat hangers and pulling suitcases across the living room. Now the Turners are all together for the holidays and loving it, within the hour peering long-armed at wine labels, arguing, considering croque monsieurs for tomorrow's lunch.

On Christmas Day there are a truly preposterous number of presents under the tree. Uncle Ron lives up the hill at the original family house, and comes down with another of Margo's siblings, Aunt Andre (in from Halifax), for dinners. Predictable and decades-long political debates get fired back up. I retreat downstairs to our room with the kids at eight thirty each night while the rest of them stay up, sharing out Armagnac and Calvados, shouting each other down over family memories and points of order about their old military postings in Germany and Canada's North, and hand-washing the last of the wooden cooking spoons.

"Why does Dada's family yell so much?" Sloane asks over toothbrushing.

They're happy to be all together. (And drunk.)

"Is it okay?"

Of course, love! We get all loud at dinner parties at home, right? This is a big, long dinner party, all Christmas.

"We don't have dinner parties at home."

I think about this for a sec. Huh.

. . . *We used to. We will again.*

"Will it have to be loud?"

I laugh hard. I've been drinking since five o'clock myself. *Yes!*

These in-laws, most familiar of strangers, are carrying me. They're probably liking me less by the day, but when they welcomed me into the family years ago, they meant it. I'm "theirs," part of their sphere, non-negotiable. They are proving to be an imperfect but solid scaffolding in this time of great strain. They love Alexander to absolute bits. He's one of their own, full stop. And they show it in all sorts of ways.

Earlier today we picked up Al's respiratory patterning jacket, which looks like a sleeveless straitjacket. A tailor—the woman who sewed Margo's wedding dress forty-one years ago—handmade it according to the blurry mimeographed instructions The Institutes provided.

At the door the tailor said, "Oh, Margo called ahead. It's been paid for. Here you go." She handed us a brown paper package, tied up with string.

34.

Finally I have a panic attack. My first.

We're in Cuba, on a working vacation after Christmas, just Turner and me. A travel magazine editor friend had heard about Alexander and pitched us an assignment. "Hey, maybe you need to do a piece for us this winter, okay?" It's a gift.

The kids are far away, with Turner's parents back in Antigonish. But I still can't breathe, even as I'm setting exposures to capture the gloaming light against the cathedral from this balcony, even as I charm the people with my shitty Spanish and big gestures, chumming up to the man grooming his fighting cock, the restaurateur with a Santeria shrine behind his house, children on the primary-painted swings. It's always there, the clutch around my throat like a slipknot necklace, pulling.

In the bathroom of our inn in Santiago de Cuba there are five bullet holes in the ceiling, smoky around their sharp edges. Someone had a temper tantrum in here. Water has condensed around the ceiling holes over and over, making loopy orange rings. The bathroom walls were recently painted purple, but the ceiling is old beige plaster, flaking. I am like this ceiling, those bullet holes, I think. Obvious, ignored.

A despair has begun to visit me during the night, especially if I've been drinking. Deep wells of disembodied detachment, spiralling loss. Last night I woke to a new kind of pounding headache and The Fear. I took some ibuprofen and lay there waiting for the pills to pull away the pain, drain its bad magic. These long night hours bring deep dread, existential consideration of my own demise, that my death must someday come, that it will be upon me eventually, and perhaps soon, and what will become of Alexander and Sloane thereafter? Everyone says things will be "okay," but things may *not* be okay. This spiral may be a death spin, not temporary, not a phase. This journey could be too long, and final.

For the last days of the trip we head to a resort that caters to Quebecois tourists. Ostensibly we're reviewing the place. There's a beach and a pool and scuba diving and vacation sex and buffet meals. The people we meet here come every winter, know the resort staff, treat the place like a tropical cottage.

An older anglophone couple from Montreal are here with their disabled adult son. Their young man wears headphones and shuffles around in huge unlaced running shoes. This family is apart from the rest of the Quebeckers, unilingual, shut out of the *bahnnnnn-oui* poolside chatter. I notice them, of course I do. The parents look old and worn, but the father is on one of our afternoon reef dives. He's a good sport.

One night the resort schedule includes a small piano concert. In Cuba the all-inclusives employ the most incredible musicians the country produces; it's the best gig for a musician, money-wise, no matter what their instrument. These virtuosos play white-people-chucking-down-piña-coladas music, honking out "Sugar Pie, Honey Bunch" on the saxophone and trilling Bob Marley's catalogue on eight-string classical guitars.

Tonight's concert is in the lobby, and the pianist is working through a bunch of standards and Disney songs. All afternoon I've been reaching up to pull at my throat: the choking is getting worse. I need to go to the doctor (find a doctor—I'm still looking) once we're home. We pause while passing the concert, on our way to sit at a rooftop patio to talk. The anglophone couple are there in the back of the crowd with their son, and he is rocking back and forth, and singing along.

The piano guy begins playing "Memories" from *Cats*. I'm muttering at Turner, *What a waste of these musicians. Why not actual Cuban music?* Then I notice the Quebec tourists are turning around, glancing and then staring, and now glaring at the disabled son. His parents are sipping their drinks, listening to the piano, maybe inured to such attention after all these years. Their son does not notice the glares and continues to hum, open-mouthed and off-tune. Some of the people nearer to the young man begin to say little *shhh*s. My heart skips badly. When he doesn't stop, the eye rolls begin, one person to another across the small crowd, and especially from one obvious woman in her early sixties in the centre of the chairs and couches. Standing where we are at the edge of the crowd, we have a clear view of the whole thing unfolding. I am becoming breathless, horrified.

The woman now sits exaggeratedly forward, frowning in concentration, leaning her head to one side to playact trying to hear the music. Her posture shouts, "I'm trying to *enjoy this*, but there is a *disturbance.*" A huge hatred in me snarls awake.

I want to march over and slap her. *You are perched on a fuchsia ottoman on which ten thousand other bums have perched, listening to Andrew Lloyd Webber standards bonged out by this piano master. That disabled young man and his parents are also paying guests. They too took a long flight and a three-hour bus ride down that potholed highway to be here. Is this guy's genuine enjoyment of the music bothering you? Because you do seem <u>very</u> bothered.*

I am nearly frothing. How can I intervene? Stand over her, block her view of the piano and just stare, judging her openly? Then, one by one, find the eyes of everyone who shushed that young man? Point at the boy's rocking and singing and be like, *This? You're being a shithead about <u>this</u>?*

No. But least—at least I should go to the boy's parents and stand with them. Near them. Show solidarity, somehow.

And I can't. If that glaring woman is a longtime guest, if she comes every year, I would put the staff in a terrible position if she complains that I embarrassed her. I whirl away instead, and Turner follows. As I stomp past the bar, waiters see the flaming anger in my face and glance away. This force of rage is frightening.

The shushers don't know, that woman doesn't know she's being horrible. I realize this. In their minds, the irritated tourists are well within their rights to be put out. People with special needs, with cognitive disabilities in particular, are not entitled to live out loud in our mainstream world.

That woman thinks she's right. She thinks her body language is speaking for the rest of the crowd. It probably is. It's not my role to kick over a table of rum and Cokes and shout in the face of a fellow Canadian being a bigot in a foreign country.

. . . Or is it? I think it maybe is.

I don't know. Alexander is so young. He isn't here. I will stand up for him when he's older, when he's bigger and less cute, when exactly this sort of thing happens to him and us. But by then will I be exhausted? Like these anglophone parents getting on with their lives as best they can, their radical act simply being bringing their son along on vacation?

Maybe I have to act now, while I'm still young-ish and strong-ish, before time wears me down and the fight goes out of me.

Turner and I walk out to the pool deck and then head up to the quiet rooftop patio. We'd come down early, before dinner, to finally do the big schedule I've been asking for. This is my last chance to lock it down, before we're back home and I'm back in the legtrap again.

I am carrying a pen and a notebook. Turner says it'll be easy, don't worry. He's been saying this for two weeks. But we leave Cuba in two days, and when we get back to Canada it's immediately kids and packing and returning to Calgary, and then on Monday (four days away) the volunteers will flood back in and Turner will need to disappear upstairs to his work. And I will still be there, the sad ringleader in my mashed top hat, holding the whip, with everything waiting on me to announce what's next.

We lie back in the deck chairs and look up at the stars, but my leg is bouncing. It is warm and windy, the nighttime hug of humidity holding me in my clothes. This has always been my favourite weather. Turner says, "Let's just enjoy this for a minute as we finish our drinks." The thin waxing moon is lying on its side, but my blood is pounding in my ears, the volume rising.

Suddenly I can't breathe at all and I start to cough. Turner is saying, "Ash? Ash?" and puts a hand on my arm. I slap him off— *No! No! Don't touch!* I roll out of the chair and then flail back into it, rubbing my hands down my legs, hearing myself panting as I can't get air. I can't even make a schedule by myself and my son is disabled forever and I can't breathe. I can't hear and I can't focus my eyes. I close them and rub hard. All at once I realize, *Oh, actually, I am dying. I am dying right now, for real.* This is what dying feels like.

I'm alone, utterly, in this death. Turner is there beside me, saying my name, worried, but I can't take care of him, I can't take care of my own kids, it doesn't stop and goes on and on and I can't live inside this and it must end. This utterly new experience is unbearable. Literally I am unable to bear it, and yet it continues.

All at once, an egress that's never been there pops out of the solid wall of my life, somehow already ajar, eerily beckoning: *Through here.*

Oh, I see. I realize I may have to *make* it end.

On this rooftop in Cuba, as I'm choking on the nothing that's crushing me, it's then a far-too-small stumble to: *And I'll have to take them with me. They'd be a burden to the "them" that would have to help, the people who would have to bear the responsibility and appointments and lifetime of work after I'm gone. The kids are my responsibility.* Val had once yelled that at me, made sure I knew.

They are my blood and they come with me. I don't want them to be afraid, don't want a mess. Kinder to use the river in the middle of the night. Cold and fast.

Juuuuuust gunna stop for a second here.

No one can say they haven't pictured their own death. As a teen, I detachedly imagined riding my bike out into traffic, the resulting mess and noise, and most particularly the horror of the driver who would involuntarily hit me. We all picture these scenarios, and indeed are presented with them by parents and teachers and television to convince us to take care of ourselves, lest we die. German children's literature and books like Edward Gorey's *The Gashlycrumb Tinies* are full of vivid reminders of our frailties as a species and the bringing-about of one's own death via poor morals or bad luck. But these are essentially brain exercises, common to all religions and cultures. What happened on that rooftop was not this kind of thing at all. It was not melodrama, and it was not self-pity turned up to eleven. It was involuntary. And inside it, there was a kind of peace.

At this point in our story I am in my late thirties. I had of course heard of suicide, and I'd even known suicidal people. When I was a kid, my mother, a psychiatric nurse, would come home with stories of chasing down patients who'd escaped the ward. (The St. Boniface

Hospital mental ward of the late 1970s obviously needed better exit protocols.) In one case she'd spectacularly tackled a man who'd nearly made it to the bridge over the nearby Red River. I'd grown up equating suicidal thinking with severe mental illness. But when it happened to me, it was a simple realization. It wasn't about wanting to die. What I was experiencing (my first-ever panic attack) was horrifyingly scary and could not continue. My brain pulled the "we cannot endure this" rip cord and gave me a new option. Suicide isn't about desiring death. It's about requiring release.

When this panic attack subsided, I was clear-headed in a way I hadn't been in months, even clearer and better than in Philadelphia. In the days that followed, I thought, Oh wow, I'm out the other side! Things will be completely fine now—sure, a freak-out was probably inevitable, but yay, now I'm all sane and fixed.

Here we go into the future. Hurray!

Apparently it doesn't quite work like that.

The panic attack buys me about a month of clear thinking and stability. Back in Calgary, we make the new schedule, including the new program goals and extra therapies. I rehire for the programme aide position, we start the respiratory patterning with new volunteers, I return to running the therapy program, and everything is rolling along. Huzzah, as they say.

Then I start to wobble.

There's no reason why things cave in again, nor why they're worse this time, though not having a family escape to Costa Rica this year didn't help. In February I begin to cry, and I cry through many days of darkness, and then I'm fine. Back to feeling rational. Then I go numb and silent for a whole weekend, standing and rocking back and forth in the late afternoon with Alexander in a sling, staring at the street outside. I can't pinpoint what's wrong, because nothing is really "wrong," these days. Our lives have settled down enormously, and the new Institutes programming is being phased in step by step without too many glitches, and Alexander is vocalizing probably five times better than he was last year—making new sounds, more sounds, more "talking" overall and at new times of day, at new volume.

My brain has perhaps decided it's safe to unpack all the extra-special Crazy and Fear I've stuffed down since Al was born. One day I will feel balanced and completely myself, but the following afternoon I'll be sobbing into a dishtowel, ostensibly missing my grandparents or worried sick about needing new attic insulation. The counsellor says that it's grief and post-traumatic stress, all finally catching up with me. She has advised me to breathe. I'm doing my best.

And the therapy program continues every day. Though Alexander is a pretty genial kid and we do the respiratory patterning with him on a soft folded blanket, who wants to fall asleep face down on a table in the middle of the day? There are still no curtains on the dining-room windows. And it's long, repetitive, quiet work for the adults doing it; relentless, daily, and easily blown off. *Oh, he's over-tired because he was late to bed last night and I just want him to have a good nap—let's forget about the midday pattern today.* And *Oh, Sloane has gymnastics and we'll get back pretty late; let's not do him before bed tonight.* Forty minutes twice a day sounds like not much when we're earning our way to a machine that will do this work thereafter and forevermore, right? But we're failing at it.

Bruce comes over and finds me counting loonies and toonies out of a leather piggy bank. "What's all this?"

We were supposed to get HEPA *filters for the house after Philly. We had one for his room, but it conked out months ago. Now I almost have enough for a replacement unit. They want a filter run-ning in Alexander's room while he sleeps, and others in the rooms where he does his program.*

"No, Ashley. You already have a filter on your furnace. Everyone does."

I look at him. *Dad, no. Maybe you do, at your fancy house. But our furnace certainly does not have a* HEPA *filter.*

"Come with me."

I follow him to the basement. We stand looking at the shitty old furnace in my shitty old basement. He points at the filter hole: it is empty. "I stand corrected! You do not have any filter on your furnace whatsoever! Let's go to Home Depot!"

Another program day upturned. But, how can I say no?

At the store Bruce fills the cart with light bulbs and packages of paper towels and batteries and furnace filters. He's stocking us up. He grabs my neck, squeezes. "You're not talking! This is not happiness!"

I can't. I am tearing up, suddenly snotty. He stops, changes tone. "Dear, what do you need? Your dad is here. Let's get what you need. Don't cry. Everything is completely okay."

He leads us to the appliance aisle and puts two freestanding HEPA air filters in the cart and gets packages of replacement filters. I'm ashamed.

He grabs me around the shoulders, squeezes hard in time with his words: "Ashley. Stop it. This is your dad. I'm here to help you." He shoves me away genially. "Buck up! What do I say? *Just win.* We're in this together."

He pushes the cart, gestures around. "Do you need anything else?"

Of course we do. We need everything. I shake my head.

"Then let's get out of here."

All month this month, we only leave the house to drive Sloane to school and to take out the garbage. No snow falls. The world is frozen solid, every day –20 Celsius. The nights are very clear, the moon bright.

I'm in a standoff with our new house helper and aide, a musician with beautiful eyes and a beautiful voice who won't do the dishes (it's prominently in the job description, taped to the fridge). I remind her to please pack the dishwasher each day, and each day she does not.

The house is becoming dirty. I can't keep up with the cleaning she's supposed to be doing. A rind of grime coats the kitchen vinyl. One black circle of mung below the stove has been there for months. I finally swipe at it with a wet paper towel between masks. *Made a clean spot. Fuck.*

By late February it's breaking-hard to do anything that isn't ingrained daily habit. I brush my teeth because I brush my teeth. I brush the kids' teeth because I brush the kids' teeth. I say hi to the neighbours because I say hi to the neighbours. I drive safely because I drive safely. Anything that already "is" seems okay, continuing on autopilot. Anything that needs more from me is like lifting a refrigerator with burned hands.

I periodically feel weird pricks of loss, but not how you'd think. Sometimes I'm throwing something away, something small, like a wad of chewed gum. Past tense useful, present tense worthless. Not Important. I fling it over the bridge railing. As it leaves my hand, past the point of no return (even if I regret the harmless and only technical littering, which I do, deeply), I have a sudden stab of fear. I jerk forward, thinking I'm throwing something away I shouldn't (not just littering-shouldn't but *shouldn't*-shouldn't). I get this crazy crackle of terror; for a half second my body reacts as for a devastating error, an alarm-jolt in my chest.

This fear-stab comes when I'm throwing away compost, a broken dish. It's never Alexander—I'm never throwing him carelessly out the car window, or into the recycling bin. But some part of my gut has become a suspicious watcher of all the things that pass through my hands. It's just been loose hair from my brush and vegetable ends, so far.

So far.

But my shattered reality might hide what is real until after I chuck it. There's a misfiring guilt trip message in it: *You don't know what you have, what you are holding. It is infinite and everything, and you might throw away. You did this, are doing this, to yourself.*

. . . I don't tell Turner about any of this. How do you explain crazy?

Alexander is coming up on two years old. At this age Sloane was speaking in full sentences, had favourite songs she'd request in the car, was doing sleepovers at Grampa's house. Alexander cannot walk, will not feed himself, and can only say "uh" for yes. He does not nod or shake his head, will not look at us when we call his name and may only ever wobbly-stand-while-holding-furniture. That we will some-day move on from manual respiratory patterning to the overnight machine is a vague concept at best; I cannot hold on to the connec-tion between this work and his future, even a potential month away.

Who cares if he breathes in a pattern? Did the rate at which I breathed when I was sleeping as a child help me learn to read and walk? Is this patterning the best use of eighty minutes of my day, and his day, every day? Are the patterners leaving determined not to come back? Do they see this whole thing as Sisyphean? Do I?

(I do.)

But we keep on with the respiratory patterning, because they told me to do it. It spirals scribble-scrabbly across the calendar. I ask new people to come, and they come, and these are the times Alexander screams and cries; these are the times Sloane totally loses her shit, yelling from the stairs and I have to keep calling across the house, *Sorry, love, I can't . . . Sorry, love, no . . . Sorry, love, it's another fifteen minutes until the end of the pattern*, while the metronome clickity-clicks and our neighbours and friends sit across from me, pulling on the in-click and releasing on the out-click, helping but horrified, and only coming once each.

We subject so many people to this intimate view of our lives. Deep in my soul I know it's actually healthy to experience this crazy reality together. But most folks don't want to see your soft pink underbelly. It's scary or embarrassing to them. We avoid bearing witness to the full spectrum of each others' domestic lives, nowadays. This sort of shit wouldn't have fazed my grandparents. They were all, "This is what we were told to do. It's understandable that kids will cry and act up, but we committed to this, so let's get on with it."

I know the respiratory patterning gives some of the volunteers their last-ever other-family glimpse of domestic complexity before they pull the veil of self-reliance tighter over their own heads. Do they go away vowing to themselves and each other: "Let us never require help to moil for gold"?

The roster of patterners thins. I shouldn't have needed other people so much. At Moonira's son's birthday party months and months later, I am still carrying around a paper calendar, cornering our friends and their friends. When I ask them to help, to volunteer to pattern, people say no. Even people who said, last year, that they'd be happy to help and have not yet helped. Now they "level" with me, saying they can't, they just don't have any time. Then they put their hand on my arm and ask me how I'm *really* doing, their faces all concern. They've already forgotten that a few seconds ago they crushed me cold. They even suggest we hang out for drinks sometime.

It takes everything in me to just smile and say *Maybe*. On the inside I am all, *I will not be meeting you for drinks, I just told you I am fucking patterning my disabled son at my house every fucking night. I can serve booze if that will get you over to help.*

I cry in the bathroom, then wash my face and go back out. I still need to fill the volunteer calendar. After an hour and a half of cake and awkward conversations, I have asked everyone at the party other than Moonira's parents, who live in BC. I have three new patterners for the schedule.

What kind of person am I, that these social workers and science geeks and environmental activists look into my face and say, "Actually, no." People don't tell me outright that they think our efforts are futile, but they won't waste their time, working with this little boy. Turner has never been able to ask people for help. He says he can't. He says it's too hard, that it's too uncomfortable. It's been excruciating for me, too. I should have taken a lesson from my husband.

We leave the party into a windy, spinning-leaves day and drive straight home. After this, I stop asking people to come. I stop asking everyone. It takes a village to raise a child, but apparently that's just regular kids. Disabled kids don't get a village unless you pay for it.

People who are getting $18 and $35 and $78.50 an hour will show up, but not even they will arrive on time. We are deeeeep into the line of credit now, hemorrhaging money into . . . just everyday life. Gas for the car and Sloane's school trip fees and cat food and the hydro bills—and people to come to the house to help us. Costs for Turner's speaking gigs out of town (flights, hotels, car rentals) go on the line of credit for weeks and often months, the interest piling up as we wait for reimbursement cheques to arrive, no recourse. We just have to keep bleeding.

I'm lying awake, again, it's nighttime, again, and darkness rules the land. Turner is snoring and I'm inspecting the scalloped ceiling above the bed. I always said I have amazing friends, but many of the ones right here are obviously assholes. My faraway beloveds don't say no, but perhaps because they don't have to. If they were closer, maybe this whole gong show would have shoved them away, too.

Breathe . . .

Another hour of exhaling the heartbreak in the small hours of another night. Heart bits dribbling into another gravelly roadside ditch.

So be it, so be it.

We will do it ourselves.

The Institutes' regulation brachiation ladder arrives on the week-end, made for us using the instructions from Philadelphia. Alexander will learn to walk underneath it by holding up his own weight using the rungs above him.

We can manage these sorts of outlier activities. We can remove all the furniture and install a giant wooden therapy frame that takes up the whole living room. We can have the neighbourhood kids in to cheer Alexander on his maiden runs across the ladder, and serve everyone lemonade and sandwiches afterward. But the everyday activities of normal life are non-existent chez nous.

Can I keep my legs shaved? Nope, I can't.

Can I get Sloane to school on time even two days this week? No, evidently not.

Many incredible things go on here every day, every week. A lot of work for tiny victories. I can't celebrate them, can't feel proud of this shitshow. This morning I'm frustrated with Alexander for not using the choice boards. It's been months trying to get him to use them, to point at what he wants. I tell him, out loud: *This is ridiculous. You can use this thing to communicate with us.* I poke the laminated board like Javier did, *pek-pek.*

The Institutes say you have to use this board.

He wants some of my cereal and reaches, but I pull my bowl away.

No, I'm not sharing with you. You have to use the board.

He cries. But today I've got it in me to push.

Are you hungry? I hold out the choice board with a red YES and NO printed on it. He refuses to touch it.

I take his hand for the hundredth, five hundredth time, hold his wrist lightly. I say, *Are you hungry?* (He is obviously hungry.)

Yes? I touch his hand to YES. *Or no?* I touch his hand to NO.

He looks at me, yells, "Aaaaah!!" Mad.

Tough shit, kid.

I ask again, calm, pointed: *Are you hungry?* Janet Doman is standing at my shoulder: "That's it. Wait him out. He's testing you. You're the boss. Be the boss."

Again: *Are you hungry?* . . . I wait.

Finally, Alexander gently reaches out and touches his out-stretched fingers to the card: YES.

You want cereal?

Alexander's fingers go again to YES. Still gently, lightly. He's acquiescing: "Fine, I'll use the stupid board."

I push one step further. *Cereal?* (I show him the ASL sign for "cereal," a pointing-curling-pointing finger, travelling in front of the chin.)

Alexander brightens and moves his hand to his face, and curls and straightens all his fingers under his chin: "Cereal."

You beautiful little turd.

The next day he refuses the choice board.

35.

March. Hard days. Feeling hateful. My mind has been replaying the scene from *Igby Goes Down* where Jeff Goldblum calmly beats Kieran Culkin in the stairwell. Over and over. I say to Turner, *I probably shouldn't be around the kids by myself with that scene on repeat in my head.*

When I hit "tilt" and need to walk away, Turner does step in. After this exchange I am hiding upstairs and he is running the program in the kitchen. I can hear the timers going off. I think I scare Turner these days, but he still holds me close.

Tonight I buy Alexander $30 shoes. I wanted to buy him boots. Boots for a kid who can't walk (except while holding an overhead ladder, indoors), but that's what I wanted. I figured they'd support his ankles better as he learns his walking program.

There are two kinds of tiny-kids' boots at the store, the $70 ones and the $85 ones. Even if I buy the $70 boots there will be no money for groceries at the end of the week. . . . Can I get to the kids' second-hand store? It's far, and even their consignment kids' boots are expensive. I check my watch.

. . . Fuck it, he can't walk yet, anyway. I'm just carrying him to and from the car, to and from the stroller. It's not like he's walking on the snow. I could be layering his feet in four pairs of socks and put a shopping bag and elastic band overtop, really.

Stupid expensive kids' boots. I buy the shoes.

Turner goes to Montreal for a conference and meetings. With him away, things are getting weird at home. I feel like I'm living a really boring shroom trip. I have only a thin grasp of what day it is. I check the calendar over and over. I remind myself of a hyena I saw as a child, pacing its cage. A zoo employee told our class, "They call that 'the dance of death.' When an animal starts pacing like that, it's very bad news."

This morning I get Sloane a third of the way to school and realize I've left a pancake cooking on the stove. First hit of adrenaline in months. I U-turn and floor it home, and run into the house to find the kitchen filling with smoke and the cat yowling. I've ruined that pan. When I go back to the car and open the driver's door, Alexander is crying. Sloane yells, "What happened? Mama? . . . Mama, why aren't you talking? . . . Am I going to school? I'm going to be late. I'm not supposed to be late any more days this month, Mama."

I know, kid. I know.

The Lycée requires tardy students to be accompanied into the school by a parent. This walk of shame is familiar to us. You present yourself at a little window that looks into the office. The woman there says, "Pourquoi l'étudiante est-elle en retard?" You tell her and then write the reason into a special late-student book and initial it. Then you stand there as the woman explains (again) that it's very important not to be late again. Jamais. You're released from the interaction at her "tss" and a flick of her chin: the child can go inside.

It's a performance. They are very French about it.

The first of many times Sloane was late I apologize in French and stumble along trying to explain the actual reason we were late. I eventually shorten it to *Je m'excuse* and continue in English, seeking absolution.

When I complain at home about this rigamarole, Turner just says, "Haaaaaad to put her in the French school, eh? A regular bilingual program wouldn't doooo, had to be the French-from-France place."

Shut up, Turner.

Today there is a father ahead of us, dropping off his son. I happen to know this guy is an orthopedic surgeon, but he has to grovel at the window like the rest of us schmucks. His reason involves a project that requires a muffin tin. His boy is standing with one hand on the door, muffin tin under his arm, awaiting the chin flick. He gets it. The father turns, chastened. None of us like this dance. One day I saw a mom slam the minivan trunk door on her daughter's head in her rush to get the kids inside.

As he passes me, I say quietly, *First time?* The dad replies, low, "Usually my wife drops him." He pushes out the doors, into the winter wind.

Our turn. The lady's seen me so many times I don't even get the full grilling anymore. "Raison?"

I decide to tell her. *We were actually on time this morning, but I realized I'd left a pancake on the stove and had to drive back home. I caught it just in time.*

She ne cares pas. "And what shall we put in the book?" Blinks at me, blank. The French really do disdain best.

House fire.

I push Sloane toward the doors. *Go in.*

I turn and leave.

We need a fucking break. I'm going crackers. I pull Sloane out of school the next day and take the kids to Banff. People do that, right? Go out of town to clear their heads?

So we go. And the world-famous Banff scenery is shrouded in ice fog. We have rented a "suite" up on Tunnel Mountain, which consists of a tiny kitchenette in a freezing living room, and a roasty-boiling bedroom. The thermostat is broken, and snow is collecting inside the poorly fitted glass slider. The raw wood–panelled walls shed splinters into my sweater. This room was the best internet deal we could find. Quelle shithole.

I miss my aunt Jacqueline and her warm house in nearby Canmore. I want her to be loving up Sloane with tea and banana bread, using her baby voice on Alexander. I can't blame her for leaving. Way better winters out on the West Coast, and her brother, my uncle Alan, is descending into dementia. She is out there to support my cousin Samantha, now, helping her take care of Alan in Victoria. When I was seven, Jackie visited us and brought me the *Evita* soundtrack, making me promise to learn the words to "Don't Cry for Me, Argentina." Much later, when I was grown up and heartbroken, she cast me in a local play she was directing. We got six weeks of rehearsals and sleepovers, learning each other as adults. She understood loss and how to be stoic and gentle inside it. I can't even miss her properly, I need so much these days. The water from her kitchen tap tasted amazing. I'm sitting on this grimy Tunnel Mountain loveseat really really wishing I could be at Jackie's house instead. One more thing I can't do anymore.

Keep going anyway, I guess. I am doing Alexander's program here in the hotel room. I'm only half-hitting our therapy target numbers, masking and hand stimulations and intelligence flash cards, going through the motions in the dim bedroom. An hour in, I wheedle Sloane into doing math dot cards with her brother so I can use the toilet by myself. *That'd be fun, right? Showing him the cards?* She does two sets and bails, complaining loudly outside the bathroom door. She wants me to read to her. The kid is six and refuses to learn. I suspect she's already literate and just a big faker. (I'm right.)

After an hour of books we're feeling the cabin fever, but Sloane gives an emphatic "No" to a car ride up the parkway. Can I justify the cost of taking the kids to the hot springs? I guess I can't. Instead, to kill some hours we go to the tiny motel pool, housed in a separate building off the lobby, with no change rooms. We cross the icy parking lot in towels and boots.

What am I doing? We will be wet on the way back.

And we are, but Sloane and I scramble to the room at a run, Alexander bouncing in my arms under a damp towel. When we burst through the door, our hair is crispy and we are breathless and laughing. I get a big, deep lungful of air in. *Ahh.*

Sloane flings off her wet towel. "I'm hungry. Can we watch TV?"

Heh. Of course, there is no television. Sloane refuses the granola bars from home. She wants to go to a restaurant, and so do I, but I open the soup I packed and heat it up on the kitchenette stove. I serve it to her, she doesn't like it, won't eat it, and I get cranky.

Just eat the fucking soup, Sloane. We are not going to a restaurant.

Alexander begins twirling his hair into knots, his avoidance stim.

Looking around, I spot the fireplace. That'll be a nice distraction, a fire. I open the flue, but the chimney is somehow clogged. The fire smokes so much we have to keep the sliding door open for the next hour. I run over to the motel office, but the staff are all goggle-tanned stoner Australians who don't care and won't help. This day is cursed.

The sun we can't see falls behind the mountains at five o'clock. At six I shut the curtains and turn off the lights, announcing bedtime for everyone. There is zero fun left in me, I am all done. I lie awake alongside a flipping and jerking Alexander (seizures in his sleep? I can't deal with this right now), with Sloane on the pullout couch in the other room. I write a despairing email to Turner and resolve to buck the fuck up tomorrow.

The next day we have a long morning shower all together and spend a few hours running Al's program: I sit Sloane on my lap and she shows Alexander the reading cards while I whisper the answers in her ear. Then I take us to the Whyte Museum. I'm starved for culture, and at least the kids get in for free. I walk slowly through, studying each painting carefully, even stubbornly, reading the labels to Sloane as she talks overtop my art-voice drone, yanking on my jacket, begging to go to our sushi place for lunch. I don't want the canned Italian wedding soup waiting back at our room, either.

After a half hour of this I'm ready to belt her across the exhibition hall.

"Sushi, Mama, please. We'll get the mugs without handles!"

Hehhhhhhhhhh okay. Fuck it.

It'll have to go on the credit card. Like everything else.

Pulling open the door to this familiar room on Caribou Street gives me a rush of pleasure. The warm umami air rolls over us as I usher the kids to a spot on the far side, pull off their mitts and jackets. We snarf down stacks of edamame and sushi from the coloured plates touring the small restaurant by train. Sloane and I are on stools and Alexander sits in a high chair, transfixed by the ceiling fan as I pile rice and bits of fish into his mouth. New snow is flying sideways past the windows, but I'm grounded here. This is the Banff I know. Yes.

Later, after changing Alexander in the bathroom, I push through the hanging curtain and get a momentary outsider's snapshot of Sloane perched on her chair. Unselfconscious, perusing the sushi rolling by, dipping a finger in her soy sauce and licking it off, drinking up the last of her mug of green tea. My glorious girl is six years old, the picture of childhood contentment, deft with her chopsticks.

Maybe my grief isn't ruining her. Maybe I tell her enough of the truth and balance enough of the impatience that I'm not handing her a well of resentment to work through in her thirties. Maybe the wave pool on Wednesdays, the bedtime trays, the tickle fights and car songs are shoring up her edges enough. . . . *Please, let it be enough.*

Though this mini break seemed a waste of money while we were gone, on the drive home it's clear that being out of town has helped us all. The urban landscape looks slightly new as we crest the last hill before the city limit. I can keep going. Until Turner gets back, at least. The forecast says there's a chinook on the weekend.

But the dishes are not done when we return.

This afternoon the aide is off. I turn from the sink to find Alexander staring intently at the tip of his finger, which he's brought up way too close to his eye.

What the fuck fresh hell is this. His fingertip is less than a centimetre from his sclera.

I push his hand away twice and he just brings it back up to his eye. I step away, then back another step, then sink onto the pantry stepstool and just watch him. Alexander is slowly barely moving his fingertip around, his eye following. Why?

I just can't even with this new thing. He's safe in the Bumbo on the counter, can't get himself out of it, doesn't even try anymore. I lie down on the floor. Loki walks between my head and the microwave, pausing to sniff at my hairline. I grab the cat and pull him onto my chest, and he fights to get away. *Just sit with me here, Loki. Please.* I'm petting him and he's letting me, but as soon as I'm not restraining him he'll run. *Be my friend. Stay.* When I let go, he jumps away.

Up on the counter, Alexander's still looking at his finger. Having never done this before today, he'll do it forevermore if I just leave him to it. I'm the only thing that can get between him and finger-staring, and I know it. At one point last year Al was hitting himself in the head. We stopped that by hugely ramping up the reading program, on orders from Rosalind (Al's advocate at The Institutes). Now what—more reading? More math? I don't think I can do "more" anything.

For another few minutes I stay where I am, looking at the popcorn-spackle ceiling, the broken track lighting. We painted this ceiling when we moved in, so that stain up there is ours. How the fuck do you get a stain like that on a nine-foot-high ceiling?

I stand up and the blood rushes out of my head. I lean on the counter alongside Alexander until my eyes come back into focus. Then I reach and push Alexander's hand away from his face. I say, hard: *Don't do that.*

His hand starts to come up again. I push it down onto the Bumbo's edge and hold it there. *No.*

I let go and the hand begins to rise. I grab it and I put my face right in his face.

NO. DON'T.

He is looking down, off to the side.

Don't you look at your finger, Alexander. That's not good for you. It's too close.

He blinks. He heard me.

Let's do some math. His eyes widen the barest bit.

Fuck, this kid—he's in there. I tuck him under my arm and walk over to where the math dot sets are lying in a pile. We sit down. We do the dot sets.

We do more math this week, and I double the amount of log rolling each day. Plus I stuff in more reading than before. At Moonira's suggestion, I make him do "targets," where I move my index finger up and down and around, and he has to reach up and poke my fingertip. (I give a big party-time *WHOO HOO!* every time he touches my finger with his.) He loves it. We do it ten times a day.

He stops looking at his finger.

Sometimes I wonder what Alexander dreams. It seems easier to ponder this than to wonder what he thinks about when he's awake. And easier than "How does he see the world?" Or "How is he different from me, from us, from 'the rest of us'?"

Dreaming, his feet move: he's running. One night in the dark, Turner was checking on the kids and heard Al say "Go! Go!" in his sleep. This kid who can't walk on his own and never speaks words aloud is speeding along in his nighttime world, free from the forced march of daytime therapy in this house. I hope he's dreaming about his own future.

Maybe he dreams about masking, about patterning, too. He often signs "more" when the mask timer goes off. One time I asked him, *Do you like doing the masking?* and he looked right at me.

"Ah," he replied—his "yes."

As little as he is (not even two years old yet), he knows it is good for him.

Bruce asks me, "Do you resent him?"

We are at Earl's, having an early dinner. Turner is at home, catching up on work, and Sloane is at gymnastics.

I look over at Al. *No. I don't resent him. I get caught up sometimes in "why" and "why us." But I don't blame him.*

In my place, my dad says, he'd resent the child, the cascade of consequences. He tells me I am a good mother.

I am, but I haven't earned this compliment just by answering honestly.

I don't know why I don't resent Alexander. The fact of him, his obvious blamelessness, is perhaps reason enough. But it's not that. I just don't.

36.

Sloane's birthday falls in the middle of the March. Her peers have parties with science performers or live-musician singalongs, or they're circus-themed at the trampoline park. Sloane brings home loot bags containing movie tickets and passes to Heritage Park. We can't do any of that.

We invite everyone to meet at Eau Claire Market, which has a (free) indoor playground. Sloane had wanted to take everyone to the wave pool. Not a chance. We manage a few games and provide a cake, but we forget to bring candles. At the end, the kids get brown lunch bags (crayon-drawing decorated—we're not monsters) that each contain a balloon and some flower seeds, things we scrounged from the backs of drawers and basement boxes. We prefer to be frugal, but these stingy loot bags make us wince.

Anyway, fun party otherwise.

The rest of the time, every day, all we do is the therapy program. I show the boy words and phrases on the white board. Alexander does walking lengths under the brachiation ladder, supporting his weight by holding the rungs above, back and forth and back. Day after day I plow hours into food preparation, masking, greeting patterners, calculating distance. There are no weekends, no Mondays, no TGIFs, no statutory holidays.

By this point in the story (probably earlier), you are perhaps thinking, *Um, what on earth takes so much time?* And, *Surely this is just "life" by this point, Ashley?* Perhaps also, *Accept your lot already*, hmmm?

I should just fit in the therapies and get some laundry done (and wash that kitchen floor from the last chapter, for crying out loud) and shut up about it, right?

I get it. I do. But.

These are our therapy days:

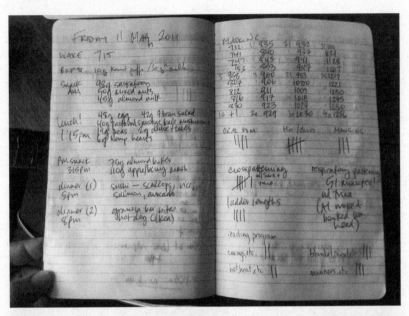

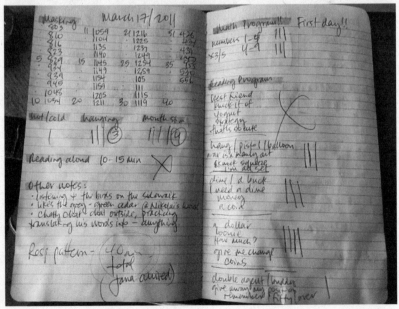

It doesn't matter if you understand what you're looking at here. Just know that each highlighted thing is a type of therapy, each line represents a unit of x or y done to Alexander per Institutes specifications, each time noted represents a sixty-second mask, and so on. It's a lot of stuff.

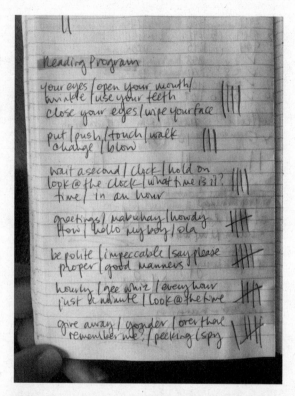

In that last photo, notice that we started the masking at 8 a.m. and didn't manage to complete the assigned forty masks by 8:24 p.m. There's a big break from after lunch until evening, and it's not unusual to have an interruption like this.

And I'm trying to get us into another government program for special-needs children, called Specialized Services, that will help pay for the extra therapy Alexander obviously needs (specifically for speech, occupational and behaviour therapists). If we qualify, this program will pay for more aide hours to help deliver the therapies (and, I hope, some of the daily Institutes work), and for parking at the hospital and driving mileage and more counselling funding for our family. But the application process is deliberately complicated and drawn out, meant to discourage and overwhelm inexperienced parents. Exponentially more children qualify for this provincial program than are approved to receive its funding, so crowbarring its door open involves phone calls and emails and paper letters, messages left on MLA office answering machines, two in-person pre-full-evaluation interviews and a file, compiled by me, of allllllll the assessments and the history of Alexander's situation to date. I have to arrange letters of reference from Moonira and another specialist "familiar" with our family situation, and the second specialist requires a steep fee for her letter. I am told again and again (by our FSCD worker and her manager) that Alexander "doesn't really qualify" for Specialized Services, so I download and read the Alberta government's policy for the program, and then the full provincial legislation—dozens of pages of legalese. From these it's obvious that Alexander is an excellent candidate for this funding.

I address my emails to increasingly senior people, making our case to be admitted to the program over and over. I quote specific sentences in the legislation, I cc the Minister for Children and Families, I attach photographs of Alexander walking under his brachiation ladder. This funding, some aspects of which currently come from our empty pockets and off the line of credit, would make a humongous difference to our family. It's important. We need it.

Because (big breath) the financial stress is no joke. It's constant. Yes, my dad put a big cheque toward our debt, and he took me to Home Depot and even to Costco several times. Bruce is covering most

of the repairs going on around the house and Sloane's tuition at the
Lycée this year. Without him, we'd likely be living without hot water,
because the tank conked out a second time and then died completely.
If he was a different kind of dad, or didn't have the means to help, we'd
have to sell the house, the car, probably move to Nova Scotia. We've
had two fundraisers, set-menu Vietnamese "dinner parties" at local
restaurants who have hosted for us, and we've created a board of directors for a non-profit society that I hope will help us raise money to
cover Alexander's therapy costs, materials, and the trips to Philadelphia.
We're making our mortgage payments so far, and we can pay for most
of our groceries. But nearly everything else goes on credit, though we
don't tell anyone how close to the bone we are living.

Because . . . how can we? If I were working, I'd be earning.
Between Turner's and my income, we'd be fine. Like before. But
we've chosen to throw everything we have, including our credit
rating, at saving Al (and us, from him). Everyone tells me not to sacrifice my career for this boy, but it's already gone, and the money I
used to earn is gone with it. When Gramma Margo's huge birthday
care package for Sloane included two tubes of the natural toothpaste
we use, they arrived in the nick of time.

The spectre of our always-empty bank account invades my ability to make strategic decisions and rational choices about all kinds of
things. I am unaccustomed to this level of brain scramble. Bruce asks
me (rhetorically?) why can't I just put one foot in front of the other
and get organized. In 2013 there will be a study out of Harvard on
how the cognitive load of poverty interferes with executive functioning[*] and I will feel it, hard. This study will help me retroactively
organize lots of vague thinkitty-thinks I've had about the finite nature
of mental bandwidth.

Relatively speaking, we aren't even poor. We have equity in our
house, we have a working vehicle, we have universal health care. I've
lived overseas, and I've known some truly destitute people here in
Canada. I do have some perspective. But there is far, far too much going

---

[*] "Poverty Impedes Cognitive Function," by Anandi Mani, Sendhil
Mullainathan, Eldar Shafir and Jiaying Zhao, in the August 2013 issue
of *Science*

on in our house, too many competing responsibilities, too many expectations, too much internal judgment, too much external advice and
nowhere near enough rah-rah support and money not to be worrying
about all of it every single minute. I'll understand later, or will try to.
For now, I just can't keep a thought in my head, and I don't know why.

There is no allotted time in the program to manage emergencies
like the basement flooding after spring rains. While I'm sopping up
the floor with towels and moving books and boxes to higher shelves,
Alexander is losing out on program time. I spend most of each day
resenting the impossibility of keeping going like this. "My best" can
be superhuman some days, but against the bottomless fear about
what will become of Alexander, the never-ending Institutes program
targets, and the bald lack of actual money to throw at real problems
that crop up, I am failing in all directions. All my pants have holes in
the inner thighs where they've rubbed through, and there's no money
for new pants. But it's not like I go anywhere other than the hospital,
so when I do, I wear tights underneath and a long cardigan and keep
my legs together when I sit down, and that's just how it is. I'm now
a person whose pants have holes.

Years later, I will reflect that instead of hiring someone to help with
the household chores and the therapies, I should have been paying a
roster of people to just come be my friend. Like roadies, kind of. To
stand there and bear witness and lend a hand, laugh with me, think
with me and problem-solve with me, like Sara did in the beginning.
(Sara still comes, but far less often, because she has two children, university courses, and a job . . . and a life!) I need stimulation and cama-
raderie, not employee issues and scheduling headaches. In these years
I often wish there was somewhere I could go where parents with disabled children could meet up and do our therapy programs together,
help each other, keep that motivating spark alive in all of us.

Oh, hey, that's a great idea! You should do that, Ashley! That'd
be a great business!

Suuuuuure. Do you have any idea what rents are like in Calgary?
You'd have to charge an entry or membership fee to make it viable.
And how would families with disabled kids pay for that? It'd be a
barrier to the people who need help and community the most. And
many disabled children have feeding tubes, oxygen, wheelchairs,

medication—how would a business get insurance to cover accidents or complications? It'd be too complex. That's why you've never seen this, even though we all need it.

But you know who could and should provide this kind of space? The fucking hospital! They've got meeting rooms and a gym and tons of equipment, before you even start talking about staff. The clinic rooms are huge. Five full families could hang out in each of them, easy. The Children's Hospital basement pool never even gets used! Remember?

Hey, you know where else we could host this kind of thing? . . . Schools! Most disabled children end up being homeschooled or kettled into "special" programs. Instead, we parents could take our kids to regular school buildings and use the resources and the spaces that already exist thanks to taxpayer dollars. Though real integration is apparently impossible (different book, even a Ph.D. thesis), everyone knows those school buildings are empty most nights and every weekend, just sitting there. Opportunity knocks!

Parents with disabled children need friends. Colleagues. A community. A baseline income to help us make ends meet. But the government would rather pay *other* people to take care of our children than make it possible for us to survive while taking care of them *ourselves*. Our society does not make that kind of community life possible. Shame on all of us.

Anyway . . . where was I going with this?

. . . Oh right. I'm lonely. And the isolation is eating me alive. And I can't dress myself like an adult anymore. And there's no end in sight.

In April Alexander has a brain MRI under a general anesthetic. When the results come back, they show that his white matter appears normal, and he has normal myelination (the "circuitry" of the brain). His pituitary gland is somewhat flattened. And his olfactory bulb is absent. (In 2019, the pituitary abnormality and absence of olfactory neural structures will contribute to ten-year-old Alexander receiving a secondary diagnosis of Kallmann syndrome, which will probably delay the onset of puberty and impact his bone density in adulthood, though no one mentions any of this after the MRI.) Overall his brain looks normal. Many Kleefstra kids have serious cerebrum abnormalities, and he has dodged this fate. Our main takeaway is joy.

Though, obviously, our boy cannot smell. Of the five senses, I guess smell is the one you'd choose to lose if you had to make a choice. I love the depth and ferocity of my olfactory memories: rain on the road, musty basements, Shalimar perfume. Alexander will never experience these kinds of nostalgic triggers. But he won't miss having a sense of smell. We'll make sure there are always lots of smoke detectors wherever he lives.

But it's no wonder he'll eat anything.

37.

Sheila Nazerali and her sister, Cherry, have arranged a bucket-list train journey across Canada, with the implicit intention of coming to visit us and stay on to help with Alexander's program. We are standing on the porch, eagerly awaiting them, when they pull up. When these two dear friends arrive, everything feels surreal. Is this happening?

Sheila sweeps out of the car and calls, "Hello, my dear! How *lovely* to see you. Is this your house? Isn't it *wonderful*. I love the colours and the second floor. Isn't *that* something to have a balcony off the front! *Wow*."

We all come down to the sidewalk to greet them. "And this is Alexander." Sheila leans down, right in his face. He is looking away. "Hello, love. *Finally*."

Cherry comes over to me and grabs my arms: "Hi! Hi!"

She pulls me up the walk, and up the steps. She's all joy at being on my porch. "You wouldn't *believe* how glad we are to be here! Sheila— okay, now wait a minnut." She steps back, puts up her gloved hands: *Get this*.

"We were coming into the city, right? By car. That's our car there." She points at the car we saw them step out of, seconds earlier. "It's a rental. We drove from Banff, right? So . . ." She tips her head, smiles big at me. "So we did what you saaaaaaid, we did the TransCanada into the city. And then we turned after the college! But we ended up in the parking lot anyway! In the college! We got terribly lost. This was just the last fifteen minutes. We would have been here earlier. We knew we were close, but we'd followed the directions!"

I breathe in to say *10th Street, I said you had to come down 10th*, but I don't get it out.

Sheila, coming up the steps: "Let's go in, darling. But I need to say, the signs on the outside of the city are *all wrong*." She stops, renders a big billboard with her hands. "At that Olympic hill there is a sign: TOURIST INFORMATION. And an arrow. So we followed the sign! We thought we'd get some ideas about what's around. We've never been here, you see. So we parked the car and went to the desk, and the girl there had *no* idea what we were talking about! No information about Calgary, no pamphlets, nothing anywhere around." Sheila tips her head forward, looking over her glasses, hair falling from where it's usually tucked behind her ear. "I made a bit of a scene, I'm afraid. I marched out of there."

Cherry, jolly: "Sheila got quite cross. That whole place is very disorganized." Cherry is the younger sister, and relishes Sheila's temper.

Sheila gestures at the door: "Okay, darling, can we go in? It's a bit chilly out here and we've had a long drive. Will Turner be able to bring in our bags? They're just there." She waves back at the popped trunk of the car.

These two are here for a week.

Grandmothers and aesthetes and classic autodidacts who love me, who've known me since I was a teenager, sisters Sheila Nazerali and Cherry Robinson live north of Toronto. Sheila's children, Tara and Sean, are my beloved friends from university. Sheila and Cherry were raised in England, so when you read what they say, imagine the accent. Before Alexander arrived, we visited their Ontario cottage every summer, and during the years I lived out east, I did Thanksgivings and long weekends in Barrie with them. They adopted me into the extended family long ago, and Sheila calls herself my "Ontario mum."

The next morning I arrive downstairs to find them in the dining room, testing each other on the math dots.

Hello . . .

Cherry, holding up a card: "We're doing the dots!"

Sheila, focused, looking right at the card but speaking over at me: "We've been doing them for about fifteen minutes. I've gotten two right."

Out of how many?

Cherry, delighted: "Dozens! She's no good at it at all!"

Sheila: "I'm not. Cherry got *five*. It just looks like a mess of red blaaaaah to me." Focusing on the card: "I think this is maybe about . . . sixty."

Cherry: "No. It's forty-four."

Apparently we can't comprehend the quantity because we're already adults. There was an exercise at The Institutes where we were given a random card, and they got us to try to count the dots. Of all the parents I was the only one who got mine correct.

Sheila: "Oh! Can you see the number, darling?"

God, no! My card was eighty-two! There were so many dots and I lost track when I tried to count them and I just guessed. I was just accidentally right. Some people think the kids are counting up the dots really fast. But there's no actual way to count them, even if you're deliberately trying, with plenty of time. That's what they were proving to the parents in that lecture.

Cherry jumps in her chair: "Oh! I mustn't forget to *tell* you: I've remembered that back when I was teaching in Jamaica I *heard* about this program! One of our teacher friends from America had a student who had done the program. And later I heard about it again, on the television—maybe. At that time it was called the Doman-Delacato 'technique.'"

Wow! Really! So you remember hearing about this in—the eighties? Seventies?

Cherry: "Yes, the seventies. So of course this morning we *had* to try the dots."

Well, yes—

Sheila is a doctor. "I can't say I understand why babies would be able to grasp the numbers beyond about thirty or thirty-five. But their brains are developing *so* fast, and when we're young there's *so* much capacity that later we just lose because it's not needed. Those connections die off if you don't use them, and the parts that are important and used regularly grow. The brain is *remarkable*. Remarkable!"

Yes, they say—

Sheila: "Shall we get breakfast started, darling?"

—

By day three they've read all The Institutes' books. By day four, they've read all the books I've bought by mothers of disabled children. They're the other two patterners for all the patterns. They make all the meals. The scrambled egg I'm handed for lunch on day five is, I think, the most delicious egg I've ever eaten.

What did you do?

"Nothing!" Sheila says. "I scrambled it in oil because you said you can't have butter. There's a bit of salt in it. I whisked it before I put it in the pan, but I don't think it makes any difference."

I look at the plate, embarrassed by my reaction. Am I so starved for care that a scrambled egg tastes momentous? God, I am losing it.

Cherry starts in her chair. "Oh! Listen! We *have* to tell you!"

Sheila, knowing immediately: "Oh, yes, this is soooo funny—"

Cherry: "Sloane was having her breakfast, and we were chatting and everything was just—whatever. Just the routine, chatting away. . . . Right." She waves her hand at me. "You were already gone out to the appointment with Alexander. It was just us, with her."

Sheila is beaming.

Cherry: "And we could see Sloane was sort of sitting there, turning something over in her head. And then she said, 'So, are you two married, or . . .?' And it took us a minute to understand what her question was."

Sheila: "She thought we were lesbians!"

Cherry: "We said, 'We're sisters!' and she seemed sort of disappointed."

Sheila: "Well, you can see why she would have thought it! We're sleeping in the same bed."

Cherry: "And we have different last names."

She's been told a bunch of times that you're sisters. I'm amazed she didn't remember.

Cherry: "It's actually a very rational conclusion. We showed up together, we obviously know each other very well. She said you have other friends who are same-sex couples who are married."

Yes.

Sheila: "Well. It's obvious she's comfortable with the idea, darling. Well done you, as a parent. Though, really—society is finally coming around, isn't it. There have been homosexual people forever, of course. Women living as spinsters together when they're lovers, actually. That's just what we're doing, two widows and grandmothers living together, but sisters in this case."

Cherry: "I wonder who else thinks we're lesbians? Maybe everybody who doesn't know us! When they just see us in the grocery, or at Timmy's, or wherever."

Sheila: "Isn't that wonderful! Life is such an adventure, darling. You never know what people think of you when you're just going along, living your life. I don't think you have any sense at all what an inspiration you are to the people around you, for instance."

Wait, what? *Me?*

Cherry says, "Yes, you!" at the same time as Sheila says, "Of course, treasure."

I laugh. *I feel very small and alone, actually,* trying for a stoic tone to make it okay.

Sheila, soberly: "Yes, I know you do. This is a *very* tough time right now, obviously. But you are doing *brilliantly.* And it's *not* going to last forever. You are going to come out the other side, and what's there, we don't know yet. There are terrible times in life when you have no idea what's next. When Amir died, there were six months when I was just *lost,* and just when I thought I was okay, it would be hard again. Of course I had family, and my friends, and work, and still lots to do. It's a very different thing you're doing with Alexander, of course, but we *do* understand." Cherry is nodding. Her husband died young, too.

"With this child, you said no, you wouldn't just leave him—and now we're here and we see what you're doing and it's *obvious* what a success it is. The doctors who see Alexander must be recommending this program to all their patients with delays!"

They're really not. The pediatrician is the only one who tells other patients about it. He reminds me of Amir, actually. He calls me "Mum." But I think he's sort of humouring me because he can see that I'm going to do it anyway.

Cherry: "You're doing something no one's ever done before with this Kleefstra syndrome. Nobody's ever done this with a Kleefstra child, have they? Right. You're the first. I wish I'd known more about this program when I was still teaching. This program you're doing depends on the parents, and the community you've gathered. You didn't have any background on any of this at all, before, but you can run it."

But honestly, I don't want to do it.

Sheila: "No, darling, of course you don't, but you're *doing it*. Anyone *could* do this program, but they can't, you see. They don't have it in them."

Cherry: "This wasn't the plan. *This was not the plan.* It's very limiting for everyday life. But you're saving his life! And you're saving *your* life, and you're saving Sloane and Turner."

Sheila: "It's remarkable what you've done, darling one."

These sisters remember the best of me, a version of Ashley I can't recall anymore. They are so proud of me, so relentlessly certain that I will survive and thrive. They respect science, and education, and routine, and everything they've read about The Institutes' program from the books and testimonies is so clear to them: this is good for Alexander. *He* will survive and thrive.

But the shambles of my scattered inner world is invisible to them. I'm hiding inside the shell of who they remember me to be. I say, *I'm having trouble*, and they say, "Yes, that's natural, you'll be fine, you're doing fine—better than fine, you're doing extraordinarily." It feels good to hear.

But I'm not saying, *Actually, I'm broken, I am not thinking clearly, but there's no emergency anymore other than that I'm broken, and it doesn't seem to matter because obviously you can be broken broken losing time blackouts broken and keep doing this work for the child, and the emergency the emergency is in my head now.* I'm not saying, *Literally, I'm drowning.*

Because how can you say that? I don't know how to say that. Because what if in this battle *I* am the collateral damage, what if I am the acceptable loss? The magic eight ball says, SIGNS POINT TO YES.

While they are here, I slide inside their delight and ferocious curiosity and admiration. It is such an unburdening to be surrounded by Cherry and Sheila each day. In their company I don't have to be the driving force. We share a work ethic and it's easy, interesting, to spend all the day's hours in their company, prodding

Alexander, cheering him along, pulling out the best of him. I don't want them to go.

Though of course I have to let them leave. They have onward train tickets. They tell me they're counting on me. Their obvious pride in what I've done so far with Alexander shuts me up.

Before they leave, Sheila takes me aside. "I'll come back whenever you need me. You just call. Or if you want, if you need a break, come to us in Ontario for a week or two. I'll pay your flights."

She peers at me. "You'll let me know, right? Promise?" I promise.

(I will never take her up on these offers. I can't let myself believe they are real.)

After they depart, I can't speak for the rest of the day. I just move around the house, working. As the rest of the week unfolds, I can't even feel grateful they came. I'm just empty and wretched, wishing it all off me, wishing it all wasn't, grieving the girl they knew, the woman I used to be.

38.

May 11. It is Alexander's second birthday. Turner's out of town, a symposium in Vancouver this time. I'm on my own again.

I had to get rid of the aide last week. I can't pay someone who resents being here. I resent this place enough for everyone.

First thing this morning my brother, John, posts to Facebook: *Happy birthday, Alexander!* He must have a reminder set. We haven't seen him in over a year.

My mother sends a one-sentence email recommending I read a book by a Spanish writer, no mention of Alexander.

I spend the first half of the day cleaning and masking and doing reading work with Al, and then we meet Margaret, Alexander's godmother, for lunch. It blooms into a lovely warm spring day, with puffy clouds travelling across the sky.

This is a distance program marathon day and Al and I are trying to beat his previous record of 270 metres. We spend the afternoon outside, chatting with neighbours as the boy crawls up and down the sidewalk, making a gorgeous mess of his pants. Alexander's crawling is finally fast and clean, perfect form, cross pattern, left-right-left-right.

Mid-afternoon I get an email from my sister, Ainsley, forwarding a heated rant she sent to our brother about him moving to Australia. There is no mention of Alexander.

John is moving to Australia?

I can't think about that right now.

Alexander still likes to chase his metal bowl that we set to spinning in the distance. He sprint-crawls for it and then spins it himself, still the most dextrous thing he does. Doing bowl-motivated crawling on the sidewalk is always a loud undertaking.

When we head inside for a water break and diaper change, it's not two minutes before the doorbell rings. Our neighbour Lina is standing there, bearing the largest metal bowl you've ever seen, fricken beaming. "Italians use lots of big bowls," she says. "I think I inherited five aunties' worth of these things. But this is the biggest." She heard the distance program this afternoon and went digging around in some old basement boxes. "Happy birthday, Al!"

Then she pivots and yells, "See ya!" and heads back home.

When we pick up Sloane after school, she leaps into the car with a card she made for Alexander, yelling, "HAPPY BIRTHDAY, LIDDLE BROTHER!" She grabs his head, yanks it back and forth in a hug: "Mm! Mm! Mm!"

Alexander grips the card and begins to crumple it in his hands: the old paper trick.

"No, Al! No! That's for you!"

Alexander stops. "Ah," he says. He puts the card up to his face, seems to kiss it. Did he just kiss it? I can't see properly in the rear-view mirror.

Sloane, did he kiss the card?

Sloane is having trouble putting on her seat belt.

It's okay, love, just go slow with it. But look at him—did Al kiss the card?

She looks. "No—hey, Al, no! Mama! He's eating it! NO, AL!" She snatches the card away and hands it up to the front seat. "Keep this, Mama. Let's put it on the fridge so he can see it when he's older."

Once we're home, Bruce doesn't come over, doesn't call, doesn't answer the phone when we try to let him know we're leaving for dinner, where to meet us. We go out for sushi, Sloane's suggestion. Back home, we have cupcakes ready from the local place so Alexander can giggle and fail to blow out the candles. That's what big sisters are for.

Before bath time we open Margo's gigantic birthday box and it's full of presents for all of us: candy, clothes, diapers, organic bum cream, fancy hair elastics for Sloane and a huge card (FOR A SPECIAL BOY WHO IS TWO!), along with a cheque for Alexander's RDSP (the registered disability savings plan, a new federal program for special-needs people where the government matches the first $500 contributed each year at a ratio of three to one).

Later, the kids are in bed and I am standing in the bathroom, brushing my teeth. Brushing, slower and slower, and then I just stop. The house is quiet. I look at myself in the mirror. Alexander's birthday is essentially the anniversary of the end of my life as I knew it.

O woe. I spit into the sink.

Yet this day is a total nothing to my family. They all call on Sloane's birthday, even send gifts or cards, but Alexander doesn't seem to register with them as a real grandchild or nephew. He's a lesser being, his disability a liability. He doesn't warrant their emotional investment.

I want something that is not even on their radar. I want them to care about him. I want them to care about what having a disabled child has done to me. I want them to *want* to know him, or at least to try, to understand that I need some petting and attention around this and that Alexander needs extra thought and love. On this day of all days, please. At least my brother (who is apparently moving to Australia?) put a fucking alert in his calendar. But the rest of them don't and they won't and they have their own busy lives. Very busy. My siblings' own children are their first concern, of course. My mother's and father's and brother's and sister's work lives continue, of course. That I want them to remember Al's birthday is part of the "too much" I ask of people. Caring for and about him is my problem. The Institutes' program is an "Oh right, right-right, that *thing* they do with him . . ."

Tomorrow Bruce will come over, and he'll wave his hand, half-embarrassed when I call him out, and he'll say, "He doesn't even know when it's his birthday. Get real. This is your issue, Ashley."

And he's wrong, but he's right. It's my issue.

I've been keeping a blog of Alexander's progress, and my angst and worries, since just after the diagnosis. I write that it bothers me when people don't see my son as a real person. My sister reads the blog and she calls. About it, but also about our mother.

"I have to walk on eggshells around you in case I say the wrong thing, because you might stop talking to me," she says. "I mean, I get it, there is a lot going on for you. But I don't know what you think people should be doing for you. Mom is getting older and she's gone through a lot this year, she has to adjust to these new contracts she's doing, and Michael has migraines, they have to go to Vernon for tests, they put a new roof on the house, and she had to put one of their dogs down a few months ago. You weren't part of any of that. You haven't been calling her at all. She *needs your support*."

I have mostly stopped answering the phone when my sister calls. I don't want to hear about what a shitty person I am for not being a more attentive daughter. I don't want to update Ainsley about Alexander's program, or explain how hard it is dealing with the government, or talk about the ups and downs of our everyday survival. It always ends up with my behaviour, my methods, my judgment being questioned. Today I answer the phone, though, and find myself talking about firing the aide.

If she wasn't actually drinking on the job, she had alcohol on her breath when she arrived some mornings, and many days she was obviously hungover.

"And why did you hire this person?"

She was very qualified. Overqualified, really. I thought it would be good for Al. I was looking for a therapy aide and a new house helper, but she was out of work and wanted both jobs. She stopped washing dishes after the first week, and it was a challenge about the housework from then on.

"So did you talk to her about this?"

I did, but it was always awkward. She wouldn't do the kitchen work, and she had already been in the house long enough to know that we really needed someone to do it. She was the only solid candidate, Ains. I interviewed twelve people.

"Um, so maybe you should have kept looking?"

We'd already gone a month without someone, and I can't properly do Al's program without help. Hiring takes at least a week, often longer. And she'd brought all this equipment to our house, like a light box that would blink in interesting designs when Al was doing the ladder work, and she was an incredible singer. She did parts of the job really well.

"But she didn't show up? Did you have a clear schedule?"

Yes, but there are changes sometimes—Al has appointments or whatever.

"Well, if you don't have a clear schedule, communication is going to break down."

Ains. She knew we always worked on Tuesdays because that's the morning Turner tries to go to the library. The day before we had a friend over to pattern and she thought my friend's daughter had taken her phone and was angry about that. She found it later though, down near the laundry where she'd left it. And then she just didn't show up on the Tuesday morning. I called her and she didn't answer, and then emailed her and asked if she was coming in, and she emailed back that she assumed she wasn't working that day. Then she sent another email right away saying she'd be taking the next day off too. So suddenly I have no aide for two days. On Thursday there was this weird moment when I called out to ask if she was doing okay and she sing-songed back, "Oh, it's fine, I'm doing my job. It's what you asked me to do, Ashley!"

"Uh-oh."

It was chilling. Right then I knew I probably had to let her go. But I was trapped. I needed to get her to sign all the paperwork so that we'd be reimbursed for her hours. I needed her to come in on Friday so I could get the paperwork done.

"So, like, it doesn't occur to you to stay on top of the paperwork in case something like this happens?"

Ainsley. Of course it "occurs" to me. But do you know how many fucking things are going on at any given time, here? The paperwork is not at the top of the priority list.

"Ash, you have to do it right away. You have to do it, what— every month, you file?"

Yes, in theory. It's very time-consuming. You have to fill out these triplicate carbon forms in pen, and if you make a mistake, you have to redo everything. You have to put Alexander's name, address, etcetera, etcetera, tons of information, at the top of every form. We're backlogged sometimes.

"I'm sure the government has those forms online somewhere. There's no way the only option is a carbon form."

Ainsley, I'm telling you, the only option is a carbon form.

"I don't believe that."

I didn't either and we have been asking for two years for a digital form and there isn't one.

Silence.

Finally: "Okay, Ash, so you fired her."

Well, sort of. I asked her what she wanted from the job. She said she needed to focus on her music and I couldn't expect her to put that aside. I was like, Um I'm just trying to run a therapy program for my kid, and if working here is not working for you, we can adjust the schedule? I suggested she take her stuff home for the weekend and let me know if she wanted to continue working with us. "That way, you'll have all your stuff if you decide no, so you won't have to come back." I was trying to give her the opportunity to have a think on it. But she started stomping around and huffing and going back and forth out to her car. She had a lot of stuff at our house.

"Why? What did she have at your house?"

Therapy materials, musical instruments, all kinds of stuff. She'd been working with us for a few months.

"Still, did she need all that stuff?"

We used it, Ains. It was generous of her to have brought it all over. We appreciated it.

"That's kind of weird. Like, can't you get your own stuff for Alexander?"

Therapists have all kinds of shit for every age level of therapy they do. They have closets and shelves full of stuff, offices full. Anyway, she slammed the door on her way out, and I never heard back from her, so that was the end.

"So . . . I wonder why you end up in these situations, Ash. Like, why do you always seem to end up in these confrontations with people?"

What are you talking about? This is the second aide we've ever had, ever.

"You said the first one was flaky too."

No, I said she was young and had never worked as an aide before. But she worked well with Alexander and worked her ass off for us for most of last year. We love Kelsey. She's graduating from her upgrading program this weekend and we're going to the grad.

"She's upgrading from what? High school?"

Yes. Sara and I helped her get into this accelerated science-credit high-school upgrading program. She's going to graduate with a ninety-one average!

"Ashley, I don't know *how* you get yourself involved with all these crazy people. Like, she was twenty-one when you hired her and she hadn't finished high school? Why did you even hire her?"

She'd finished high school—she needed to upgrade to get into college. And we pay more than we are reimbursed by the FSCD *so we can get better candidates. We can't afford to, but we do it.*

"And this is who you get! I don't believe there aren't some dependable, normal people who want a job there. This seems like an okay job for a student or something, like babysitting but with a purpose. You need to get on a job board and post it more widely or something."

. . . Okay, Ains.

"'Okay, Ains' what? Sorry, but I'm trying to help you, Ash. What is with that tone?"

We are trying. I'm trying to tell her and she's trying to tell me. But we can't hear each other.

39.

Yesterday we went before the multidisciplinary panel to argue Alexander's case for Specialized Services. This funding is for children who have been formally assessed as "severe" in at least two developmental categories. Alexander is severely delayed in all areas, and has been for at least a year. But it's the unwritten rule that children don't enter the Specialized Services category until after they're two years old. Why? I don't know.

Why?

I don't know.

Why?

Why why why would you wait until they're two years old to provide severely delayed children with targeted supports in the various developmental categories?

Because of known (and pointedly ignored) structural inadequacies, is why.

So I am the squeaky wheel. I loathe having to be the squeaky wheel. But Al gets the grease. All my push-push-pushing finally earned us a multidisciplinary panel to review our request for Specialized Services.

I have been completely stressed out about this panel, spent a few hours crying about it last night. After all this effort, they can still say no, and for no reason, leaving us with nearly no recourse. I think I sounded like a mostly-sane human as I described to the four panel specialists what we have been doing for Alexander and why we need this higher level of support. Our FSCD worker told the panel that we are the most dedicated and hard-working family in her caseload. The panel were smiley and seemed impressed, but Moonira says these panel gigs are well-paid and sought-after. So, who knows.

We'll hear sometime next month whether Alexander will receive a Specialized Services contract and what it will entail—what kinds of specialists, number of hours, aide funding, etcetera. Fingers crossed.

40.

There's a pulse in my feet when I stand on them. From getting older and heavier and slumping, longing for my long-agos, when I could walk far. Turn circles with the full moon in my face. Floating, sparkling, effervescent.

Now, even if I could dash and deke and run until my legs fall off, they'd drag me back legless: "Oops, ha ha, whoopsie—there y'go. Back at 'er, eh?"

So, what's my prize? What do I get for keeping on? Ooh, a plastic sheriff's badge, yes. Congratulations, I'm in charge, he's only mine and no one else's. "Take care of your own children!" my mother had once screamed. There's no one else to do it.

Last night I blacked out. I fell through a grey cowl and couldn't think of Turner's name, ended up on the floor with my hand jammed against the bathroom vinyl. Then, finally, a breath, my consciousness flooded back in, and I shuddered and started to sweat, called for help but no one heard. Got up gagging and fled to bed, turning sleepless in the sheets. What has happened to me?

My neurons are all fried? Or I have a broken heart that shouldn't be broken? I'm not allowed to let this child die. But he is allowed to kill me. I'm not allowed to let him drown or drop him down the stairs. Be grateful you even have children, right?

I am a bowl into which much-too-hot has been put. My middle boiled up and away, only ropy melty bits dripping, now. My ragged edges have a secret centre, nougat going necrotic. But I'm spinning these dishes, smiling for the photos. For Sloane, for Turner, for strangers in the produce section, pretending at my life.

But oh-for-sure I'm dead in here. Burned out and away, gone sideways dreaming through the grey cowl. Ha ha, tho. Don't tell anyone.

Turner is in Germany for two weeks at an all-expenses-paid climate thinkers' summit, and afterward has some extra days back in Berlin. He was reluctant to go. I talked him into it, pushed him to stay longer so he could reconnect with some of his book contacts and keep those relationships alive. Dude travels so much that he's sick of it. I have to bite my fists to stop from yelling out my jealousy.

I'm clinging to John Johnston and Sara's wedding in England in August. We are going. Or at least, Sloane and I are going. I am a groomswoman, and Sloane is a flower girl. As we research the flights and logistics, England is even more crazy-expensive than we remember.

By June, our money is so tight we are pushing bills from one line of credit to another. People are delaying paying Turner for articles—usual, predictable, inexcusable—but the timing couldn't be worse. He is getting jumpy and unsure about how we'll get through to the fall, and soon we realize only I can go to the wedding.

Then, a few days before he leaves for Europe, for the conference and Berlin, Turner comes out of his office and breaks it to me: I can't go to John and Sara's wedding, either. He knows how much I want to go, but we just don't have the money.

Then he leaves for Germany.

But . . . But wait . . . Wait . . .

On Canada Day Bruce comes over to tell us about the ancestry research he's been doing online. Boomers love this stuff, it's like the meaning of the internet. Dad is telling me and Sloane about Ireland, where our people lived before they went to Scotland for a few generations and then emigrated to Canada. He is animated, excited to share all this new information. We should go to Ireland, he says. It would be a fun trip together.

Sounds amazing, yeah, I say. I know we are not going to Ireland.

Now he says we should totally go this summer. In August. He means it.

I say, *That would be wonderful. And we could time it to attend the wedding.*

Bruce has known John for years, and he too is invited to the wedding. But Dad says, "I'm not interested in going to England. I've been there."

Um, I say, *but surely . . . if we're all the way over there, we really should go? The wedding is going to be absolutely a ball, and Sara's kids will be part of it of course — Sloane would be in the wedding if she's there, and I'm obviously in the wedding. We could rent a car and take the ferry over, even go to a Manchester game afterward.*

Bruce hardens. "I don't want to run around England on your schedule, Ashley . . . Get your computer. Let's book Ireland for August, so it's not cold. I don't want to be cold, so it has to be August."

I bring my computer and Bruce punches dates and numbers into Expedia.

I'm looking over his shoulder. *So Dad, those dates . . . that's right on top of John and Sara's wedding. We could easily take a few days out, to go to Oxford?*

Bruce takes off his glasses and turns to look at me, hard. "Where are you going to get the money to go to England, Ashley? I'm not paying for that." He gestures at the computer screen. "It is only Ireland I'm offering here." The glasses go back on.

He looks back at the computer. "Let's book it now." He clicks through to the final payment screen and pulls out his Visa.

Wait . . . wait . . . *I need to talk to Turner about it, Dad. Let me clear this with Turner before we say yes.* Bruce gives me the "Gimme a fuckin' break, Ashley" look.

It's very generous and it will be amazing and thank you, but, Dad, I can't commit to a trans-Atlantic trip before even mentioning it to Turner!

"Fine. Call him."

He's on the plane. He'll be home in a few hours.

Bruce flicks his hand at me. "You are *such* a procrastinator, Ashley!" He picks up his hat and sunglasses, stands up to go. "Call me. Let me know and we'll book it. Call me when he gets home."

I offer him our *Father Ted* DVDs to take home as inspiration for Ireland, but he leaves them on the windowsill.

Turner walks through the door ninety minutes later.

A trip for everyone in August? Of course, he says, that would be amazing. Not like everyone going to the wedding, but still . . . Actually, *fuck* yes.

I am on tiptoe now, dancing. *If Bruce gets us to Ireland, maybe Sloane and I . . .*

Turner shakes his head. "We really, really don't have the money, Ash."

Okay. Yeah, okay. . . . I know.

"But . . . if he gets you to Ireland, we'll get *you* to the wedding. Call your dad, let him know it's a yes."

I kind of squeal in glee. *Really? . . . Okay? It can work!?*

Turner: "We'll figure it out. Somehow."

Holy shit!

I call Bruce. When he answers I say, *Dad, I talked to Turner, and we say yes to Ireland. <u>Thank you so much</u>, this is going to be amazing!*

There's a pause on the line. "Ashley, you know how much a trip like that would cost? Get serious. There is no trip to Ireland. I'm not made of money. Get real."

I am speechless. Two hours ago he'd been putting his credit card number into the internet.

"I'll be over tomorrow to see the kids. I gotta go."

I'm actually trembling when I push the button to hang up.

Turner: "What happened?"

I don't know.

I can't breathe. The banshees are screeching. I stare at the ceiling all night. I am definitely going crazy for real now.

When Bruce arrives the next day, the kids are out with Turner somewhere and he doesn't want to stay. I walk him back out to his car, following, traipsing, needing to ask. How did I misunderstand him on this Ireland thing? The edges of everything are shimmering. The world has a tilted feel from my lack of sleep.

I have to ask. I am frightened, of my own mind. I have to push the words out, force myself to say them.

. . . Dad, I don't understand what happened yesterday. Were you here yesterday? Are <u>you</u> going to Ireland in August? You were suggesting we would all go together . . . weren't you? You had five

tickets punched into Expedia, didn't you? You were just about to pay for it.

He gets in his car, leaves the door open, looks at me. "Ashley, you need to get serious. You can't be running off, travelling anymore." He points at the house. "*This* is your life. You need to buckle down and focus on your family. You have responsibilities."

"No, I am not going to Ireland." He reaches for the car door. *Slam.* The window is open. "In August I am going to Sandpoint."

He turns on the car, waves. "Be good!" He drives away.

I stand there in the middle of the empty street. The leaves overhead are going *fffffff* in the breeze. I'm inside a tiny sealed flask, using up the last bits of oxygen.

I look up at those big branches above and think, *In ten years all these old poplars will be gone, this overstory will be gone, the beauty of that elevated world will be gone. If this were a movie, I would be the confused, unbelieving, devastated character standing in the middle of the road, looking up at the trees as the camera pulls out and away.*

Nobody wants to see a movie about a fat old crazy-lonely-broken middle-aged lady in worn-out pants. I turn and go back into the house.

I mask Alexander in the kitchen. Then I take him out back and bounce him on the trampoline. The sun is hot on my arms, but the wind is up and I get a chill. Al doesn't want to be out there either, so I take him inside, but after ten minutes we're back out again. I can't take it in the house. I'm gradually collapsing inside like a dead star, and the walls and cabinets are leaning in around me.

Al is fussy and I hate everything, just everything. So I set him down on the grass and go inside and uncork a bottle of Rioja. I pour the wine into a handleless mug that was a wedding gift, a beautiful blond thing shipped from Scotland that makes me smile. Last year Aaron, the one who gave us the mug, got married himself (in Toronto) and I couldn't go (no money) so I contributed a pittance to his honeymoon in India (*We have forsaken a registry in favour of having friends contribute to our trip of a lifetime*). The online form asked us to recommend what they should see on the Subcontinent and I spent most of an afternoon ignoring Alexander's program to write out a curated list of awesome places with accompanying email contacts on the ground and anecdotes from our time over there. Another program day lost, but it felt important at the time.

The wine slops over the edge of the mug as I gulp. This program day is lost too.

Fuck. It.

Refill. I go back outside and force myself to talk to Alexander between glugs from the mug as he examines the texture of the deck with his fingers and messes with the stacks of intelligence cards I brought out with me. After a few minutes of the wine, the sky lifts and I can breathe a bit, and I hear a happy voice coming out of my face, jollying up my boy. *Therrrrrre we go.* I cannot be even a passably good sober mother today, but I can be a good buzzed mom. The afternoon of wine becomes a dinner with wine and laughing at the table and everyone helping clean up the kitchen. We have an early, long shower all together, upstairs. We do the songs and books and kisses and snuggles and put the kids to bed.

As soon as their door shuts, a thick dome falls around me and closes out the world. Turner knows what happened and that I am scared for my sanity. He knows I don't want to talk about it. He knows I put everything I had left into keeping it okay for the kids today, making it good, being Extra-Fun Mama. Now I am super dooper done.

I put in my earplugs and start to clean, peering at the hoo-rah's nest of every room, slowly gathering pens into drawers and walking dishes back to the sink. Still drinking, just moving, putting on a load of laundry, wiping the windowsills and skirting boards with baby wipes. I go upstairs and change into my nightgown and brush my teeth for a long time, floss twice and use a washcloth to wipe all my teeth hard: I fakey-grin to admire the result. Haven't been to a dentist since well before Alexander was born. Gotta take care of these chompers.

In the mirror I look like I've aged a decade in a day. I used to have great hair, a lovely long neck. I can discern (or am imagining?) a weird pulse in the lights above the bathroom sink. I reach up and unscrew one of the globe bulbs. Dimmer now. Better on my eyes. I picture throwing the light bulb into the bathtub, revelling in the sound of shattering glass. But it'd be so much hassle to clean up, would require a broom and vacuum and the wiping of all the room edges to make sure I get all the shards. And it'd wake the kids. Not worth it.

I read emails in the dining room until long after Turner goes upstairs to bed. Eventually I begin wandering room to room through the dark house, touching the tops of shelves and furniture, a spectre in a nightdress. I go and stand outside on the upstairs balcony, pushing at the rotting railing with my thumbs. A good shove would take down this rail. But two storeys would only be broken legs, maybe a rib. Not enough.

I tip my head all the way back and blare my face at the sky. A bright half moon blinks through the big poplar next door. Some stars are out. I can never find Aries unless I get all my bearings and tip over sideways and I don't have that in me tonight and who cares anyway. So I just stare up and up. It's cold out here, but I don't feel cold.

Turner comes to the slider behind me, bed-headed and confused. He woke and couldn't find me in the house. "What are you doing? You okay?"

I turn and look at him.

Turner: "You. Come to bed. Come in. Get some sleep. Come to bed."

I turn back to the night. He stands for a minute more, then goes back to our room.

The next day I wake with the alarm but I can't get up. I have lead breasts and my hair is made of lead and I get up only to pee, dragging down the hallway like a wood planer. I'm wrung all the way out, shredded. Turner leaves me be. He gets Sloane to school, settles Alexander with the new aide and comes back in the mid-morning to look at me blinking on the pillow: "You okay?"

I look back at him for a long time and then small-shake my head once: *No.* He gets it. Or he thinks I am hungover, which I am not.

Turner brings little meals and tea and club soda upstairs to me on the tray. He is taking care of me. Later on, Bruce drops by and, when I don't come downstairs, he calls up at me, "Ash-LEY?" I hear Turner telling him I'm not feeling well, that I'm napping, so he leaves. I stare at the ceiling stucco. Its swoops were done poorly, long ago. Must've been the guy's first day.

Turner comes to rub my head and doesn't make me talk and basically I lie there silent, then cry until I stop, and then lie silent until I start again. Sloane gets home from school and I don't even get out of bed. When she pokes her head into the bedroom, I pretend I am asleep. Turner feeds Sloane and Al in front of the TV. After the kids are finally in bed, I go downstairs by myself and drink two and a half bottles of malbec sitting in the dining room, looking out at the dark night and at my reflection in the glass. Before bed I throw it all up in the shower. I doze without really sleeping, and spend most of the night looking at the sky out the window, ashamed of everything.

The next day I can't get out of bed again. When I wake up, I'm looking out eye holes from way, way inside my body. I can't speak, and my face is numb.

. . . So this is a nervous breakdown. Huh. I poke my cheeks every couple of hours to test the sensation there. I never thought I'd really go crazy. I worried about it, I got upset and depressed and anxious, but I never thought I'd imagine things that didn't happen. I feel encased inside my skin layer like a pupating, jellyish mass. Maybe this is metamorphosis. I don't think there'll be a butterfly on the other side, though.

I don't read, I don't check email, I don't look at Twitter. I breathe and stare and cry. Turner eventually comes up to open the bedroom balcony door and the curtains, to let in light and air. The warming wind tucks into the room in little gusts. Turner rubs my head some more as I weep and don't talk. He brings Al to look in at me from his arms, around the doorway: *Oho.* Loki is tucked under my armpit every minute. I'm too hot but I can't move.

That evening the house is full of golden late-spring light. I can hear Sloane screeching with neighbour kids through the hallway window. Turner comes up to the bedroom to see if I can join them outside.

I stare at him. I haven't spoken in two days. It's warm and he's right and I should go, because that's best for the kids and probably for me. He looks back at me for awhile—a long while, really. He doesn't want to leave me here; it's not okay, this sudden silence and utter retreat. But he's not the type to wheedle, and he doesn't want to just stand there, so he begins tidying the clothes flung over the cedar chest.

Suddenly I open my mouth and, though I haven't planned any of this, out it all comes:

I've known John Johnston for twenty years and I was always going to go to his wedding in England and if this life means that I can't go to the wedding of one of my most important friends, then I don't know what the fuck this life is for.

If stopping working and doing Alexander's program and being in this house all the fucking time isn't focusing on my family and I should be "getting real," I have obviously lost my grip on what the fuck is real.

What part of giving up every fucking part of my life that was gratifying and made me happy is not "buckling down"? I would way way way rather NOT be doing any of this shit! So what the fuck part of this is me not buckling down?

I see basically no one, I earn zero money, my bras are fraying and my underwear has holes and there's no money for new underwear. I manage the aides and I fill out fucking triplicate carbon-form paperwork and I fight with the government for Al and I make word cards and I spend every day scared and ruminating about the future and I can't breathe half the time. I feel guilty that I'm not doing enough and I never finish his program for the day and it never goes away.

Then my dad says, "Let's go to Ireland," but wait, actually no, we are apparently not going to Ireland and we were never going to Ireland? I'm hallucinating escape fantasies now!

And by the way, I don't know if Alexander actually reads or is learning the math or if it's all a fucking gigantic waste of time and I'm the idiot who couldn't just park him at a special-needs daycare and get on with my career and our lives. Nothing is getting better, nothing is getting easier, and now I don't even know what is real. I am evidently inside some useless self-imposed incarceration bell jar in this fucking house, advocating for this fucking kid, and it clearly doesn't mean anything.

There is no fucking future except fucking years of this same shit, same fucking thing seven days a week, and now I have lost my grip on what is actually real as the moments pass. Am I even in this bed? Everyone says, "Oh, ask for help, you have to ask for help," and Val says, "You have to accept help from people in the way they want to help, not the way you want help." But WHAT THE FUCK—THAT

IS NOT HELP, that's wishing for a letter and getting a mailbox full of flyers. It's just garbage!

Is my life just work I don't want to do and gratification deferred forever? OH, but keep going and somehow pay the bills and don't look desperate and don't lose your temper on the pediatrician's receptionist or the physio asshole or you'll get booted out of the clinic, even though they're phoning it in, even though they can be late or rude or smell like forty cigarettes; their way and their pay is <u>by far</u> more important than the entire-rest-of-our-lives-with-this-kid?

I don't even know: <u>Could</u> Bruce dangle a trip like that and then snatch it away? Did that even happen? What does my father see when he comes over here? Am I sitting around, eating fucking bonbons? Everywhere I found joy has been vacuumed up <u>and</u> I'm not doing enough, even though I can't possibly do any more, and I am doing everything badly and I can't be proud of myself for anything, not even one thing, anymore.

I point at Turner, frozen in place, over by the closet.

What do <u>you</u> even see in all this shit, Turner? Are you just humouring me because this therapy program is the only thing I am allowing to happen? Do you believe in any of it, when it comes right down to it? You're taking care of me right now because I'm silent and devastated, but is this you making sure <u>I</u> can pull it together enough to get back down there and keep going with Al's program? Do you take care of me so you can go back to work in your office with the books and the desk and the door? Because your kid's mother is the child care here and if Ashley goes down, we all go down?

Hey, look—thank you for the rubs and the trays, obviously, and frankly you are a fucking saint and hero, because you know I wouldn't put up with even a fraction of this kind of bullshit moody craziness if it was you doing it.

But really—really: what. the fuck. is any of this?

If this life supposedly needs to get realer than what we've been doing for the last two years and this fucking life doesn't include going to John Johnston's wedding in Oxford after us being friends for twenty fucking years, I DO NOT KNOW WHAT THIS LIFE IS FOR.

Yelling all of this, I am still lying down, in the same position as when I started. Only my mouth is moving. It must be horrifying.

What am I worth? What is what I've lost worth? How much does MY grief weigh?

Then I say it: *I have nothing to look forward to.*

I sit up.

I scream, full force: *I HAVE NOTHING TO LOOK FORWARD TO!*

It rings through the room, rattling the bones of the house. An alarm, truth.

That's what this is all about.

This is bottom.

I lie back again and glare at the ceiling, glowing angry. I'm dangerous, and Turner knows it. He goes to be with the kids.

That night, after Turner puts the children to bed, I get up and drink another two bottles of wine and cry in the dining room while scrolling through Twitter, then throw up again in the shower and fall asleep on the couch, wrapped in towels. I straggle upstairs as Turner is coming down with the kids in the morning, passing them without saying hello. I have another shower and throw up again, just bubbly yellow bile and stringy maroon dregs swimming to the drain. I take a bunch of ibuprofen and codeine and drink a giant glass of club soda and shut the blinds and go to bed wet. Fuck everything.

That day, while I am sleeping, Turner buys me a ticket to England on our line of credit.

41.

I prepare and plan and pack, but cannot believe that I get to leave. The flight stops in Edmonton before flying direct over to Gatwick. As they close the doors at the Edmonton airport in preparation for departure, I involuntarily yelp with glee: *AAA!* I startle my seatmates. I run to the bathroom as the plane is taxiing and whisper-scream into my cupped hands: *Eeeeeee!*

At home I don't want to live, but if the isolation can end, I don't exactly want to die. If I can go somewhere, sometimes, and be part of things and talk to people, sometimes, and if I can be delighted, if I can learn, if I can push myself physically, if I can look up at the stars at night and know I am seeing something other people are also gazing up at, then I can keep going.

Fifteen years ago I visited John Johnston when he still lived in England, and he introduced me to the Ridgeway, an ancient road that stretches from Wiltshire to East Anglia. I was enthralled by the thought of millions (billions?) of footfalls over thousands of years on this ancient road. Turner booked a trip that allows me four days to walk the Ridgeway, starting at Wendover, going inn to inn (my bag being moved each day by a service, surprisingly economical), and ending in Wantage, where the wedding will be.

When I step out on the first day, I have breakfast in my tummy and water in my bottle and a walking pole in each hand. I feel like such a pretender. I've been standing in my kitchen for over a year. I'm not in good shape. What will the other walkers be wearing? Does this outfit look ridiculous? I want to take a selfie with the first Ridgeway sign, but I'm so close to town, I'm self-conscious.

There are little signs featuring the Ridgeway's yellow acorn symbol affixed at intervals along the route so you can see the next acorn ahead whenever the path turns. Within a few minutes I encounter my first stile. Over the next few days I come across all sorts of ingenious ways of making a fence passable by people but not farm animals. Aw, humans are clever. This pleases me very much.

As the path turns upward to Coombe Hill, a thrum is starting in my chest. There are cows grazing around me. From this vantage point above the Thames Valley, I'm looking out at the homes of more people than live in all of Alberta. No wonder the cell reception is so good. I send a video saying hi to the kids, showing them the cows and the view. I play it back for myself. I look goddamn happy.

Then down down down the hill and through rambly woods, past huge beeches with roots that snake around the trunks, and boughs stretching long over the footpath. Old pollarded trunks with fat necks, nests of branches springing up above. Ivy and ferns below. I'm walking through scenes out of *The Princess Bride*, Robin Hood movies, *Game of Thrones*.

By hour three I am for sure the best-suited-to-long-distance-walking walker ever to walk. I will definitely do at least one long walk every month once I'm back in Canada. I resolve to do an annual week-long overseas pilgrimage after I turn forty—surely this utter pennilessness can't go on. (I won't—it will.)

Now I'm in Princes Risborough for the night. At dinner, my waiter has shattered front teeth that look like they've been broken for a long time. He asks me about my accent, and I explain about the Ridgeway. He says he competed nationally at the 400-metre distance back in Slovenia. "You only breathe twice in a race. Once before you start, and one breath in the middle. That's it."

This seems preposterous. I ran the 400-metre a few times in high school and all I did was try to breathe. It's a terrible race, I tell him.

"I loved it," he says. "I could fly." He left home, though, to wait tables in this little Buckinghamshire town, working slowly up from washing dishes. "British people don't like foreigners, but they don't want to wash the dishes more."

He is charming and I am charmed. At the end of a boozy meal he
brings me a triangular glass of some kind of yellow dessert liqueur on
the house. As I step outside, the glow melts away and I walk home
worrying how my Slovenian sprinter could possibly bite into an apple
or a carrot, or even toast. Any Canadian with teeth like that would
consider it an emergency. The restaurant obviously doesn't have a
dental plan. Does he not make enough as a waiter to take the matter
in hand? These teeth haunt me.

I head down the block and go into a pub across the road from my
B & B. A last pint before bed. But the television is showing riots in
London. I go over to the bar and ask the line of men what is happening. They turn, glare, then shift away and ignore me, looking back at
the TV, hands curled around glasses. I tend to enjoy the English, but
in groups they can be such dicks.

I take my pint to a table across the room, near another TV. People
in the footage are shoving each other, breaking windows, running.
There are fires in the streets. Surreal.

My buzzing brain takes a turn. What if this is the beginning of
The End? What if society collapses and there are no more flights and
I can't get home?

I know only two people in Britain who would take me in. I text
Graham in Scotland. It's a bit rainy and windy for year-round living,
but surely he'd tolerate me crash-landing in on him if it's a true disaster.

ME: Uh, London is burning down? Suddenly?

GRAHAM: Apparently so. Fuckwits in charge egging them on,
too

ME: Soooooooooooo if things spiral and I can't get back to
Canada, can you come fetch me?

GRAHAM: Like, pick you up at the train station?

ME: I'm having visions of Partition trains rolling into Amritsar
full of bloody bodies

GRAHAM: Shall we hope it doesn't come to that? The English
are more about sneering and subjugation than chopping people to
bits

ME: You have a car, right?

GRAHAM: Sold last fall, alas

ME: Rats. Borrow car, come fetch Ashley?
GRAHAM: How about I send the helicopter?
ME: Ah perfect.

The banter with Graham lowers the volume on my paranoia. I glug down the last of the pint and walk out, tramp up the tree-lined lane, manoeuvre the B & B's fiddly front door lock.

Upon turning on my room light, I realize I need a shower before sleep. Oh dear. I hope the owner won't yell at me for hogging the bathroom at eleven at night. Afterward I drink three big glasses of water and finally slump into bed. Surely the UK won't collapse overnight. Maybe I have skills that can earn me passage on a boat back to North America. If the flights are down, if the airports are closed, I mean. Surely every seagoing vessel needs an academic feminist aboard.

The next morning, I am unhungover, blessed be. The gods of long-distance tramping are shining on me. Another ridiculously huge breakfast, not served until nine o'clock. The best walking is to be had between six and eight in the morning, in my opinion. This British eating schedule isn't working for me. And honestly, who wants fried mushrooms for breakfast? I eat them anyway. I have twenty kilometres ahead; I need all the calories on my plate.

The other guests at the table are British, and they are ignoring me. They must be in the suites flanking the shower, and have decided to be annoyed that I was up late clonking around in there. I perk up when I overhear that they're going to Roald Dahl's house today.

Wow! How far away is it? In town?

They literally don't answer. I look around the table. The host comes in from the kitchen and says, "Two towns over. It's a museum. Most people who stay here take it in." She turns and leaves. The other guests are unchastened and continue to chat, ignoring me.

Woman, to male companion: "Pass the toast."

Me: *I LOVE TOAST TOO CAN YOU HEAR ME DO I EXIST?*

I don't say that. Instead, I leave.

Off down the Ridgeway again. Within a kilometre of setting out, I encounter a bent old man, feeding birds by hand from a small box.

The robins are making a racket and flitting out from the hedge that borders the path, taking little bits from his grasp.

He looks up at me as I ask cautiously, *What are you feeding them?*

You have to be careful with folks around here, they seem touchy.

But he's noted my accent, and his head comes up. Looks me over, taking in my purple cap, my walking poles. Holds up the box briefly: "Beetle larvae."

Do you collect them to feed the birds?

"Oh, no. Order them. I get two boxes a week by post. These fellows expect to be fed regular."

I chance it: *Can I see?*

"Alright." His hands are reddened, all dry patches, his sleeve ends are frayed. With a big curled finger, he slowly opens one of the lid flaps. The box is full of milky-coloured worms with black innards showing through their skin. He picks one up in his fingers and gestures with it at the hedge as it twists in his grasp. "They wait for me to come—that one waiting now is cheeky."

I look into the hedge, spy a twitching little bird.

"He'll come. He's greedy."

The *Erithacus rubecula*, so much smaller than a North American robin, bounces to the edge of the bush, then flutters over to his hand, quick. The bird cocks its head, grabs the grub from the man's fingers and flits back to the hedge. Other birds are swooping past, and one lands on the man's other arm. What a glorious hobby.

Now he asks, "Are you Australian?"

Canadian.

"What are you doing in England?"

I'm walking the Ridgeway. I hold up my walking poles, gesture up the path. *To Wantage.*

"By yourself?"

Yes, of course.

"You're not afraid?"

Of what, bears?

This wins an open smile. He has a surprising pink tongue. It juts out for a moment as he stands up straighter.

"You're not afraid of anything."

Today I'm not.

"I've never been to Wantage."

It's only just over there. I gesture at the valley. *Did you grow up here?*

"Yes."

Born here in Princes Risborough?

"I was born in Sing-a-pore."

Singapore!

"Father was an officer with a field division. We were out a few years, but they wanted me to go to proper school. Came home by boat. Don't remember."

Have you been back to Singapore as an adult?

"Oh, NO. Too far. Who knows what happens over there, now."

Singapore is fantastic! It's a beautiful city. You totally should go. Such good food, there are these hawker markets, street markets. And lovely plane trees, planted all along the roads.

"Oh, no. Those countries, I can't have any food like that."

You should go. Really.

I'd like to say that he said, "I can't, who would feed the birds?" But he didn't.

I glance at my phone, the time. Lots of miles to cover between here and Watlington, my stop tonight. *Well, I've so enjoyed meeting you, and thanks for showing me the birds. Should keep on, though.*

"Lovely, lovely to meet you. Thank you for stopping." He pauses, then asks, "Can I have a kiss?"

Ummm . . . It's usually my policy not to do this. I check my gut. His world seems very small. I can do this one.

I step forward, turn my head. His hand goes up to my shoulder and he brings his lips to my cheek, kisses me and breathes in, thankful. He steps away with a little hum. His eyes are shining. He is thinking of someone else, another time. I step back.

He says, "Will you be back through?" He is thinking of another kiss now.

No. I'm just going in the one direction. There's a wedding in Wantage I'm heading for.

"Yours?"

No. I hold up my hand, show my ring. *Already married.*

"Oh, well. Come see me when you are here again."

What's your name?

"Gordon."

Gordon from Singapore. Thank you.

"Safe travels." He turns back to the birds.

I walk into Chinnor for a late lunch, and land at a community kitchen. A disabled teenage girl is washing baking pans in the kitchen and later comes wandering through the dining hall. She has an unusual white streak—poliosis—through the lashes of one eye and the eyebrow above, beautiful. As I'm finishing my meal, a man invites her to sit and play hangman. On my way back from the toilet, I glance at their paper, left behind on the table, and see that she solved the word: *cake*. The man is calling goodbye to the woman in the kitchen, putting on his sweater. The girl is stacking trays on the far side of the room.

I am seized by curiosity. Does she work here every day? Does her mom work here? Is she supervised by, like, a program or something? Does the whole community know her? Is Chinnor a specific place with a funded hub, or a . . . local system? to integrate disabled people? into daily life? The girl notices me looking at her and walks away, through the door into the back. I'm the only one left out here, lunchtime long past. It would be awkward to try to find someone to talk to me about who the girl is, how she came to work here. Disrespectful, maybe. I leave.

On my way back to the Ridgeway I pass a tree full of doves.

It's a long, golden-lit walk to Watlington. With about three kilometres to go, my legs begin shaking. Okay, this is new. I slow down . . . and my body takes over, going slower and slower, and I finally half fall into a sit. *Um, okay . . .* I'm giggling at what I probably look like, sitting here in the middle of the path, and then my body involuntarily lies me down, no time even to take off my backpack. My corporeal being is on strike. My body just decided, *NOPE.*

This is an interesting development. I lie there, calm, for ten minutes, on my side, looking at a gravel pit through the trees. Of course, there is no cell signal here. No one comes past. At probably ninety minutes to sunset, I think, *I guess I can sleep here safely enough, but it'll suck if it rains.*

Eventually I am able to sit up, and I drink the rest of the water I have with me, and eat a protein bar. After another fifteen minutes I can stand.

I wobble into town after dusk. If I go to my room I'll be down for the night and won't get dinner, so I bring my backpack to the hotel restaurant and prop it against the table. After the meal I can barely push myself up the stairs to my bed.

In the morning I wake up dizzy and dehydrated. I am clearly not going anywhere. I spend the next six hours gulping down litres of tap water and eating energy bars from my luggage, going between the bed and a hot bath. In the early afternoon the man from the luggage-moving service taps at the door with the inn owner. I forgot entirely about checkout. When I open the door, they say they've been listening through it, worried that I had died.

Died? I start to laugh.

They nod, very serious.

C'mon, I wasn't that quiet, was I?

"The waiter from last night said you looked terrible at dinner and didn't talk at all," says the woman who owns the place.

Oh, I've actually given them a terrible scare. *God, I'm so sorry.*

I pack up as fast as I can and ask the luggage guy, who doesn't seem to know whether he's relieved or angry, for a ride to my halfway point. This is not in the job description, but ten miles is not very far by car. He lets me out and roars away, headed to drop my bags at the next inn.

Here the Ridgeway runs along the Thames, and I walk along the river, thinking about yesterday's slow collapse. I'd pushed way beyond my limit, without knowing. I walk and walk, the river on my left, and eventually come upon a huge field of poppies, like the one where Dorothy falls asleep in *The Wizard of Oz*.

I can't keep going and going at home without a break. It's breaking me for real. There's no fairy godmother to save me.

There are willows growing all along the riverbank here, their long branches draping down to the water between lily pads, minnows poking circles into the surface. The Institutes say to do the program every day, but I can't.

And not "I can't." Rather, I really *can't*.

I did the program to the letter of The Institutes' law for fifteen months. I had to do it exactly as they said. And I did it until I couldn't do it anymore.

When I get back, we need to shift the program to run only five days a week.

I'm the only one who's been feeling like a failure. I'm not failing Alexander. He's thriving by any measure of what he could have become.

We need the weekends. To be a family together. To rest, to break the pattern, to recharge, to have space to breathe.

This decision feels born of deep walking wisdom.

What a simple act it is, to walk from one place to another. We create all these complexities within our lives when actually all we need to do is move and know that the world is under our feet, holding us up.

Final walking day. I arranged a packed lunch last night and this morning set out early for Wantage. Way down a farming road, I'm checking my map and suddenly realize I don't want to do the day's route. I want to see the Uffington monument, an ancient drawing in the earth, five miles beyond Wantage. I backtrack to the main road and catch a ride to the White Horse. This is where John Johnston brought me all those years ago, where I first stood on the Ridgeway. The ground is chalky and grey underfoot.

I spend the rest of the day walking in to Wantage from the White Horse. Sara and John arrive tomorrow from Canada, and their wedding is on Sunday.

42.

That night, in the hotel, I wash my socks in the bathtub and then lie on the bed, scrolling Facebook. There's a Kleefstra syndrome UK family meet-up in Coventry this weekend, but I hadn't planned to attend. I don't have a great grasp of English geography, but Coventry can't possibly be close. I check, just in case.

Google says it's a straight shot up the M40, an hour and fifteen minutes, door to door.

Oh damn. New plan.

Okay, rent a car. Okay, fine.

I drive around the car park to test my wrong-side-of-the-road driving ability, shifting gears with my left hand. Okay, check.

I roll out into the Wantage square, literally saying aloud: *Keep to the left, keep to the left.* Do not crash this rental, Ashley.

It's Saturday morning, and off down the highway I go, whispering, *Keep to the left, keep to the left.* Two blinks later the Coventry ring road appears—*keep to the left*—and there's the hotel: *exit to the left, keep to the left.*

I park in front of a low-slung motor inn and sit in the car. In the days before I departed Calgary, this trip to the England wedding felt like a many-months-in-the-making full-tilt mental-health tantrum where I got my way in the end. It's become about a lot more.

A family pulls up alongside me and parks. And in the back seat is a child who looks like Alexander. I have never before seen another Kleefstra syndrome child in the flesh. She is younger than Al, but has his wide eyes, his flared nose. She is sucking a binky. The parents leave her in the car and go into the hotel.

I'm sure this is . . . fine? The weather is coolish, the passenger window fully open. I get out and stand at her window, looking down at this familiar-stranger-baby. She doesn't look up, doesn't notice me there, just a few feet away. She is so much like mine, they could be related. They are, somehow. I swallow against tears.

Then I remember I am an adult woman standing alone in a hotel parking lot, crying, looking at a child in an unlocked car. *Time to move.*

I literally run to the hotel, breaking stride just over the threshold, and then quickwalk through the lobby. The Kleefstra conference room is marked with a sign, just past the check-in desk. I reroute to the bathroom and mash myself into a stall.

I am shaking a little, but just a little.

Is our future in that room? . . . Is our future not in that room?

Do I even want to know what's in that room?

There are seven or eight families gathered here, littler kids on the floor, playing with sensory toys, bigger ones and siblings walking around the edges. One of the Kleefstra kids, six years old, maybe seven, sneaks up alongside while I am talking to her mum, the organizer. The girl pinches the underside of my arm—that fleshy thin skin near my armpit. I leap up and in reflex nearly strike her. *Holy fuck, that hurt.*

Her mum shakes her head, saying, "Yeah, sorry, that's her trick. She gets me a few times a day with that."

Me: *Ha ha?* I move away.

Note to self: *Alexander will never-ever-ever-ever pinch ANYONE, so-fucking-help-me-god.*

I go stand near a ten-year-old Kleefstra boy holding a simple electronic game, smiling, pitching his head over sideways. He looks up and says something to me, and then again.

I lean in. *What? Sorry, love? What did you say?*

He takes my hand, flops it up and down, and looks right at me, says this nasal singsong thing again. He's smart in there, in his eyes, like an elephant. You can see it plainly.

His father comes over. Northern accent. "He's saying '*Toy Story.*' It's his favourite movie."

I look at the kid again. Ummm, no. He may be saying the words "Toy Story," but this child is 100 percent not simply trying to tell me, "Toy Story."

The dad: "It's all he ever says. It's his favourite. He tells everyone."

None of the other children can speak. Some shriek, but the only one who can talk is this boy, whose entire vocabulary consists of a movie title.

Note to self: *No more pictographs, no computer communication apps, no modified communication. Alexander needs hard-core speech therapy. Right. goddamn. now.*

One of the moms with an older Kleefstra daughter leans over to a new mum with a three-month-old Kleefstra baby. She coos, "How's it going? You doing well?"

The new mom has a fresh manicure, with a small crystal set into her pointer nail, and dyed hair, a run in her leggings.

"Yea, she's a good gell. Qwy-yut. Slepps through the night, nevva bothas us."

Her child is spatchcocked in the pram, eyes at half-mast. I know that look. *How old is she?*

"Ah, she's . . . furteen weeks? Yeah. Tomorro, furteen."

Sleeping all the way through? My son did that. I woke him to feed in the night because he couldn't rouse himself.

"Aw, we just leave ah, gives us a break."

Time to go.

I'm heading for the door when a man arrives at my elbow. "But wait, there's cake!"

Oh, ah, thanks, I can't, I have to get back to Oxford for a wedding.

I have to run away *now*. I have an hour to think about this in the car, and then it all gets locked up and locked down. Tomorrow's the big day for John and Sara, and I have a speech and responsibilities. Everything I've seen here has to be put away until the airplane home, oh-ho-ho, for sure.

So!

THANK YOU, *thank you very, very much.*

Enjoy the cake and I hope I never see any of you again, or I hope you all have a come-to-Jesus moment with your kids, I hope you find a way to make their lives extraordinary. I can't care about you enough to become real friends or get involved, because I live far away and have a shit-ton to do with my kid so he doesn't end up like yours.

I'm so grateful you had me here, thank you for welcoming me.

You taught me more in two hours than I'd ever've figured out on my own. I'm going home to change everything, and you're the ones to thank. It's not your fault your kids have been left behind. No one is telling you your kids can learn. I didn't know, really, until the Institutes told me.

Goodbye!

You British families who graciously welcomed me that day, I'm sorry you're in the book like this. Don't hate me, but it's okay if you do. Because the one time, a year later, when Alexander pinched me? I bawled in his face so ferocious he'll never do it again.

And I returned to Canada rock-solid-certain he needed to learn to speak, so we changed everything to make that happen. By 2012 he could mimic sounds. By 2013 he had phrases, and by 2015 he had scripted sentences. In 2017 he recited "In Flanders Fields" for his class at school. And this morning, Turner asked him, "What will happen next?" and Al answered, "I don't know, Dada—I guess you'll have to wait and find out!"

That he speaks at all now is completely thanks to you. I wish I could return the favour.

I floor it back to Oxford (*keep to the left*) and change into my garden party clothes in the car, parked near John's aunt's house. As I trot into the yard, barely late, Sara spots me and comes straight over. "How'd it go? Was it . . .?" She knows this was big, and unplanned, and . . . big. She looks me up and down. "How *are* you?"

I grab her hand. *It was huge. I'll tell you in Calgary. It's wedding gear now.*

She turns immediately. ". . . Alrighty!"

Sara leads me to the table, full of relatives. "Let me introduce you to cousin Cathy—"

—

When I return from England, Bruce has planned a sudden trip to Hawaii for us all, to visit cousin Jenna, who lives on the Big Island.

It is an unexpected holiday. The old house we rent near Hilo looks east across the water: an unobstructed view of the ocean from on high. There are bedrooms for everyone, with the owner's books and stuffed animals on the creaking, damp shelves. We visit the farm where Jenna works part-time, and spend a day making lumpia and walking near Waipio with her Hawaiian in-laws. It is everyday-gentle and lovely, and wonderful to be with Jenna, with whom I've had many capers over the years. She takes Sloane surfing (her first time) in a secret spot below the highway.

Bruce is restless, though. He wants to get out and do things (unspecific things, but *things*). He figures out local SIM cards for our phones and goes on early-morning grocery runs before the rest of us wake. Turner and I spend these days throwing the kids in the pool, walking through the Hilo farmers' market, reading back issues of *Vanity Fair* from a stack in the garage. We're doing Alexander's program at a lazy pace, no patterning, but in the late afternoons we deposit him over and over on the far side of the backyard and call to him from the lanai so he will hit his distance targets crawling back to us over the thick grass.

This holiday seems extra, unnecessary, cup-runneth-over-ish. But gift horse mouth-gazing we are not. In the evenings Jenna brings over homemade kombucha, and we grill local fish with her every night on the barbeque. Sloane gets to swim with the dolphins at a hotel pool on the Kona side, and we buy the DVD so she can show her friends. This is what our life used to be like, full of fabulous little adventures and family and privilege. But this week is just a fantasy, and we are hyperaware of how finite it is.

Standing on the edge of the pool, Dad looks at my faded bathing suit, its stretched-out straps. "You need a new swimsuit, girl! That thing's had the biscuit!"

Ha, yeah. I jump into the pool and wrassle with Sloane for the floaty noodle. There are no new swimsuits in my foreseeable future.

On our last night we return to a restaurant that hosted a big Bristowe family reunion dinner here in Hawaii more than two decades ago. The ceiling fans are the same, huge wicker blades on long, turning poles that capture Alexander's attention immediately. In 1990 my cousins and I spent our dinnertime scheming, trying to score booze to sneak back to the hotel. Our little cousin Samantha fell out of her chair and screamed like Axl Rose. Grandma Kay poked at her grilled fish with a fork: "They don't even take off the tinfoil at this place?" My uncles Alan and Leo needled each other while Bruce stressed out, trying to keep everyone happy.

Val looks down the table at us kids. She mouths at me: "You wait. You'll see." She makes a circle with her finger: *All of this family craziness?* She points and calls out, "This'll be you, someday. Good luck, kid!"

I could not have imagined.

43.

Remember the Specialized Services board interview we had in May? Alexander was approved, finally. Before England and the wedding, I began applying to various agencies that can coordinate the therapist hours funded by the panel.

There are only a dozen or so of these approved agencies in Calgary, and they all have waitlists of at least nine months or (far) longer. There's no coordination of the waitlists, so all families apply to all the agencies. And you're not allowed to start looking for an agency until you have your Specialized Services contract in hand. There are far fewer spots with these agencies than there are families with contracts, so most kids stay on waitlists for a year or more before they're even considered. This is how the conservative provincial government structured "early intervention" even when oil was nearly $95 a barrel, so don't be fooled by political rhetoric about any economic downturn being to blame.

The other option is that parents can put together a "private team." In this scenario, I go out, hire the approved therapists, pay them out of pocket, and then get (partially) reimbursed by the glacial FSCD reimbursement system about two months later. Since we are still stuck on the non-moving waitlists, I begin assembling a private team.

Communication will be Alexander's biggest challenge, long-term. He's now two and a half, and isn't walking yet, but I think he will walk perfectly fine—eventually. If he's like the kids I met in England, though, he might never talk and will probably always need help communicating.

So I start with the Alberta Speech-Language Association of Private Practitioners website and call a dozen of them one morning.

Most don't have room in their caseloads for us, but still make suggestions. One says, "This system is designed to be difficult to navigate
and hard to use. It's designed to make families give up and go away."
(That is quoted verbatim.)

Not me, though, right? I speak at length to three therapists who
have room for new clients. I outline our Institutes program and everything else we're doing at home. I explain that we'll centre the
Specialized Services team on the speech and language pathologist (the
SLP), since this will be Al's biggest challenge area. We arrange for
them to come to our house to meet Alexander, to determine if we'd
be a good fit for each other.

Only one of the therapists I speak with, one who doesn't have
room on her caseload, mentions money. She says, "Let me give you
the heads-up—Specialized Services funds Speech at $97.75 an hour,
but private SLPs actually charge $125 an hour."

So, uh, parents make up the difference?

"Most people arrange for the SLP to be at the house for, say,
thirty minutes, and then they have fifteen minutes of driving time, so
the hourly reimbursement pays the SLP's rate. People generally figure
something out."

So, but, wait—that means you charge for driving time?

"Oh, yes. We're compensated for driving."

At the same rate as being with a client in the home?

"It's standard that we charge for driving time, of course."

. . .

"Our driving time is time that we're not making money, otherwise."

Um, but everyone has to get to work, don't they?

"Sure—but before I had an office, when I had clients around the
city, I didn't charge for driving *to* my first client of the day and I
didn't charge for driving *home from* my last client of the day, because
that's the equivalent of driving to work. But between clients, yes,
I have to be compensated for that."

*Um, but . . . I've never heard of any driver on earth who gets paid
$125 per hour.*

"If I have to drive between clients, I can only take five clients per
day. If I'm in an office, I can see eight clients a day. I have to make
up that difference somehow."

She goes on to explain about overhead and insurance. Because she has a full caseload, it's not like she's talking about the actual money she would charge *me*, so there isn't conversational tension in this back and forth. But I get off the phone a bit queasy.

I'm not great at math, so maybe my numbers are a bit off. But an SLP who "works" an eight-hour day, including getting paid at $125 per hour to drive between clients, makes upward of $240,000 per year. Of course, you have to take into account taxes and insurance deductions, and, as that SLP on the phone explained, if you have an office there is overhead and insurance to think of.

But what does all this really mean?

It means that it is more cost-effective for the provincial system to create barriers to access for families with disabled children, in the form of arbitrary wait times, bureaucracy, panel meetings, reimbursement delays and on and on, even though in Specialized Services the SLPs are paid two and even three times as much as hospital SLPs and provide fewer hours of service to the community.

Why?

Because these multifaceted hurdles between families and Specialized Services weed out most of the parents trying to get help for their kids altogether, that's why. It's cheaper for the public purse (your taxpayer dollars and mine) to pay a speech pathologist three times their hospital hourly rate within the Specialized Services model, because the application process and all the barriers have eliminated so many children from the system before they get to this part.

The health-care system *could* pay three times as many SLPs to work in the (currently grotesquely oversubscribed, underfunded, badly managed) hospital-based system for the same cost. I pushed and shoved and bullied our way into Specialized Services mostly because it was murder to get any attention at the hospital (and the Institutes is focused on facilitated communication with the alphabet board, which Alexander still won't use).

So instead, let's pay the Specialized Services SLPs triple—and the occupational therapists too, no doubt, and the behaviourists, and the coordinator ($105 an hour to "coordinate," but the parent can't be paid to do this, nooooooo)—because for every Alexander who has parents who fight their way into Specialized Services, there are a dozen, a hundred, or more severely disabled kids' families who aren't getting *any services at all*.

. . . Because they're immigrants. Because they're single parents. Because they work full time or because they're unemployed. Because they are intimidated by the system. Because the inherent costs are too high. Because, in essence, the complications involved in getting to this point push those families out of the system.

And then, good news, taxpayers! . . . Ah, that's much cheaper. (For now. Wait until all these kids get older.)

It's fucking chilling.

Anyway, we need the Specialized Services team, so there's nothing to do but keep going.

Tonight is the interview with our first potential SLP. She arrives fifteen minutes late. She carries in two bags full of stuff and sets herself up on the kitchen floor. She pulls out flash cards and shows Alexander words starting with "B." Then "C."

She makes him use the sign for "more" in order to see more cards. She makes him give her eye contact. He is eating it up. This is going well. Last, she brings out a plastic Fisher-Price pig into which you put big plastic coins and it sings. Alexander is all over this. The therapist is a good fit.

Alexander starts getting tired and is obviously ready for evening patterning, and Sloane comes through the kitchen to get a snack. We start to stand up, and I thank her for her time. I'll be emailing her tomorrow morning with a yes, I think.

Then she starts digging in her bag. "So—I'll just get you to sign this invoice . . ."

Let me pause here. After that btw-we-charge-$125-to-drive-around-the-city SLP phone conversation last week, I began to get the feeling that therapists might expect to be paid for just showing up. I'd even warned Turner: *None of them have mentioned a cost for coming to the house for an interview. So if they attempt to hand me an invoice, it's going to get frosty in here pretty quick.*

"Oh good," said Turner.

Tonight in our kitchen, I play dumb. *An invoice for what?*

Her: "Well, it's standard that . . ."

I cut in. *This is a job interview.*

"Yes, but there's my time, and there's prep—"

Oh, of course. But this is a <u>job interview</u>. Absolutely, there's time and preparation involved. But I've never been paid for any job interview I've ever done.

She gets very angry, very quickly. "It is standard practice that—"

I interrupt again. *If you end up leading Alexander's team, we will follow all the protocols and standards. But we don't even have the funding until the team is in place. Right now we are talking to various people to see who's a good fit.*

I wait her out. Then add, *This is a job interview, and if you get the job, great.* She does stand to make at least $500 a month for four billable hours with Al.

She decides to leave gracefully, without a signature on her triplicate invoice, and good for her. But she does close the door pretty hard on the way out.

Though I am clearly an asshole on the inside, we've been told we're a dream family for people who work with disabled children. Our FSCD program officer said, on the record at our multidisciplinary team interview for Specialized Services, that we're in the 0.01 percent of families that follow through on everything.

So, frankly, I think that means we're worth something, too.

If you went into speech therapy because you wanted to actually help kids and help society and help make the world a better place etcetera . . . well, here we are. We're ready to work very hard. We're ready to let you lead us. In a world where many disabled children are left to be babysat by their various very-well-paid therapists, I think a family like us, that is *go hard or go home*, must be worth something, to someone.

And that's the someone we're looking for.

The candidate emails later that evening to say her schedule is full and she can't fit Alexander into her caseload. C'est la vie.

44.

I've been pondering the idea of sacrifice. We have a trip to The Institutes coming up, if I can get the required reporting done. The other day a woman who's been talking with us about fundraising suggested that we "should have to sacrifice something" in order to receive support to attend The Institutes as a whole family. Like, to bring Sloane and Gramma along.

Today is a beautiful day. It's 29 degrees Celsius, unusual for early October in Calgary. I went for a walk this morning, and we did great work with Alexander right up to his nap, including a whole sixty minutes of respiratory patterning. I love my son. I love the people we're working with now. I love our friends and neighbours who graciously volunteer their time to us. I am grateful for our house and our world.

But this comment has been going around and around in my head. It's the notion that philanthropy comes with a price, and requires an oblation, even symbolic, from its recipients. Gramma comes to provide child care while we are at the lectures, and to support us on the home front while we're in Philadelphia. Sloane comes because she is six years old, and has nowhere else to stay, and because we want her with us, and the Institutes strongly advise that the whole family come to revisits because we are a team and the program at home involves the whole family. Is it good to all be together? Yes. Does it make it more fun, more whole, more "us"? Yes. This woman's suggestion that something more should be sacrificed, that performative prostrations are expected, feels ugly. What, exactly, should we trade for this privilege of going together to Philadelphia?

Today is a good day. But if I am honest, I am sad this and every other day, for lots of reasons including this notion of sacrifice. I find a lot of joy in life, and I am a jokey, slapsticky type of person anyway. I try hard to remember my manners, and I look people in the eye, and I tell the truth most of the time. But often, even now (even now!), I wonder what happened to what I thought was my life. I find myself in reluctant conversations with something like God, still asking, *What am I supposed to learn from this? What do you want me to do with this?* I'm greeted with characteristic silence from the ceiling.

There are other little boys Alexander's age on our street, and when I see them, of course, I think about what might have been. Those other coming-up-on-three-year-olds are running now. They're riding tricycles, they're trying to cut their meat. They're explaining how they got hurt, and they're trying to put on their own Band-Aids. They say "Mama." I've heard them.

Today Turner left for his book tour. In the Before This time, I used to work on Turner's book promos and post-publication marketing. I'm not on this one. I can hear our fundraising acquaintance thinking, *Everyone with two kids has to make compromises about what's possible.*

A few years ago, at a Deakin Lectures dinner in Australia, I was introduced to a cluster of people as Turner's wife. Later in the evening, one of them asked me if I'd read his book. I said solemnly, *Oh, noooo. I can't read.*

It took three full beats before he realized I was fucking with him.

It was funny then, because I'd read that book front to back five times, been part of the copy-editing, helped with the tours. I was most certainly not-ever going to be just The Wife.

It's not funny now. Because Turner's book *The Leap* launches tomorrow, and I was there for the research and we talked through lots of the ideas and Turner told me what he was writing about each day, most days. But I'm not just not-part of this tour. I wasn't just not-part of the editing process. This time I haven't read the thing at all. The uncorrected galley has been sitting on my bedside table for three months, and every day I look at it and it just reminds me of being left behind.

I was finishing off Alexander's masking program at nine thirty tonight as I cleaned the kitchen. We didn't get to any of the ladder walking program, even though we were going-going-going all day.

In frightened moments, I wonder about ten years from now, twenty. Of course I do. You would too. I worry that we will have a difficult and dependent Alexander on our hands and no resources to support him; that Sloane will resent us and bolt; that the toll on my marriage will accumulate until we crack. And that, in the end, I will have accomplished nothing that is my own. That I'll only have hundreds of notebooks in which I chronicled in minute detail how I used every moment of every day for years and years, serving this boy.

Shortly before Turner decided I would go to England, I was confiding to a patterning volunteer that I was at the very edge of what I could handle. That I badly needed a break, a real push away from the house and the family and the program and all the worry and timers and logistics and stress. That I needed to just get some silence and have a chance to be by myself for awhile. It was a beautiful afternoon, the sun slanting through the trees. She said, "Ashley, should you really be asking people to support you if you can't handle what you're already doing?"

I was shocked, actually.

Everyone needs a holiday, even a weekend, sometimes. Everyone needs to have their own little look-at-what-I-dids, even if they're only scrapbooking or fishing or whatever. People who think Alexander isn't worth their time or energy or money because I don't have a smile on my face 24/7 just aren't talking to me.

My brother, John, left today for Australia. Moved, forever, with his two boys and his wife to the other side of the globe. He was so happy to get the fuck out of here, to shake off this wintery, unfriendly place and let it fall on the floor. He flung open the door and walked into the world. Barely a goodbye.

November.

Things are going sideways again. They always do at this time of year. It's the weather, and the darkness. I'm not made for these winter months, they eat me alive. I get sick over and over, bronchitis, then pneumonia. The only good thing this quarter is that we adore

Alexander's new aide, Jessica. She is keeping everything going, keeping the wheels on the road. We do the dishes ourselves. Jessica only works with Alexander. Church and state.

I am chest-rattlingly honk-coughing when I get to Philadelphia for our next check-in at The Institutes. I am here on my own because I couldn't get the reporting done, so Al couldn't come to the clinic. But they know we are still running the program, and we stay in touch with the staff, and Alexander's advocate Rosalind suggested I sit in on the next set of lectures to give me a boost. As before, when I'm on campus this week I feel centred. I am hopeful. I walk to and from my homestay through the wet streets and am able to breathe deep.

When I meet with Rosalind, I say, *We've begun putting Alexander to sleep in the respiratory patterning machine. He's tolerating it well.*

"Excellent, very good," she says.

I don't tell her that in September, after the Ridgeway and once Sloane was back in school, we'd decelerated the therapy program to five days a week. I know this is Not On. And we have never disclosed that we have aides working with Alexander, helping with the masking and other programming—we know that would get us booted out.

"Your only significant challenge is getting the reports in," Rosalind says. "You won't be able to remain in the Intensive Treatment Program without the reporting. We know the paperwork is a challenge, but the reporting is *very* necessary. You must measure and track Alexander's progress so we can appropriately respond with program changes. It's a crucial record. You are responsible for keeping excellent data on the sheets we provide. Do you need more reporting sheets?"

No, we have some at home. Thank you.

"Can you commit to having the quarterly reports in on time from now on?"

Yes. Absolutely. (We will never get them in on time.)

". . . Now, I need to talk to you about something. It's not something we say very often to parents here. But we are concerned about you." She pauses. "I think you're being too hard on yourself."

. . . Sorry?

"It's not about the program. Obviously you and Alexander will thrive on the program and it's the best thing for you both, and for your family. But we think you are taking on too much of the 'everything else.' Based on the emails I've received from you, and what you've told me on the phone and today, we are very concerned you are expecting too much from yourself. Be very cautious of wearing yourself out."

Turner repeats this story as a point of pride for months: "She's the first parent to be told 'Calm the hell down' by The Institutes!"

Still, even with Jessica carrying The Institutes load most days, there's still way-too-much to do. On-boarding the new Specialized Services team of conventional therapists, overseeing the various small renovations we're still doing on the basement floor, the living-room shelves, the kitchen counter. All the driving and child care and paperwork (and not just for The Institutes—every program has its own set of binders and files). I research therapy toys online, I read books about childhood vestibular fitness, I create learning materials. I am applying to get Alexander into yet another government program called PUF, for Program Unit Funding, which covers "kindergarten readiness." It has huge waitlists, but for different agencies than before. I read governmental policy, the legislation: same dance, different song. I'm still fielding periodic calls from old clients and people referred to me by past colleagues, and I still have to turn them down. Our car dies, and we trade in its husk for a vehicle that we'll spend years not paying off. Christmas is coming, and my pants still have holes.

My sister and our mother are going to my cousin Joshua's wedding near Toronto. We're invited but can't go. I can't think about it. I love Joshua and Toronto, and if I went to the wedding, I might slip out the back, get on the Lakeshore streetcar and never come home.

Ainsley calls me from the bathroom at the wedding reception. She says there's a card on every table with a photo of Alexander. The card reads: *In place of a gift for attending our wedding, we have donated in your names to Alexander's Fund.*

She says, "Did you know about this?"

No.

"They made a really amazing speech about the therapy program. How would they know about that if you didn't tell them?"

I don't know, Ains? Maybe from the blog?

"I cried, Ash. It was really beautiful."

I don't believe her about the cards. Can't. I get back to cleaning the kitchen. Turner's upstairs with the kids, doing teeth and jammies. I set out Alexander's word sets for tomorrow, straighten the couch cover, put the whiteboards back in their spot, rinse out the day's masks and put them in the drying rack, boil the kettle for bedtime tea.

Better not to think about it. Better not to wonder why Joshua would do that. Best to steer clear of my love for him and his brother, my little Thunder Bay cousins, now giant men living in the GTA. It makes me want to be part of their lives and have them in ours, learn each other as adults. Know their children. Laugh with their wives.

That's not possible, Ashley. Say thank you, wish them well and get back to the things in front of your face: driving Sloane to school, masking Alexander, keeping the paperwork current.

Two days later, in the midst of their honeymoon, Joshua and Courtney send an email asking for the Alexander's Fund bank account information. Turner handles it. I tell him not to tell me how much they are giving us.

That night, the dam breaks. I'm not made to not care. I cry for hours.

They've never even met our boy.

45.

I wake in the dark and the newest nosebleed has left trails across my cheek. In the bathroom mirror I look like a food-lineup brawler. In the morning, there's dried blood smeared across the back of my hand, from another nosebleed after I went back to sleep. Though I have weekends off the program now, the arid air and the cold winter and the still-worrying about Alexander have finally broken something physical in me, created a tangible fissure.

The Ridgeway and the Kleefstra meetup and the wedding did me so much good. I bought myself some breathing room. But by November you can't smell the earth, and it feels dead forever under there, under the snow, the green all snuffed out, a wasteland. And us, we're all husks, freezer-burning into open-mouthed conga lines of memento mori when the natural gas runs out for our furnaces.

Winter is always bad news for me.

That pedestrian bridge under the commuter train line—the rail's not that high. At night nobody's out there. That's where I'd go. Just hoist myself up, cold in the crotch as I slide over the metal. Then a quick drop to the water.

The water takes the breath out of you, cold like that. Off that bridge, in the winter, in the dark, even if I changed my mind, I wouldn't make it out of the river with all the coats and boots I'd wear, sogging me down. Fast to go numb, in that kind of cold.

Turner could tell the kids I was hit by a car. They'd always be careful crossing the road after that.

—

It's been weeks now of waking in the mornings to find crusted pools of blood on the pillow. We do laundry every day. I keep wet wipes in the car. I have to flee the Lycée lobby, hauling slowpokey Sloane by the arm, because I need to get somewhere quieter, private, to cope with my bloody nose. More and more of my days involve managing all the blood when these nosebleeds happen.

I can hear my heartbeat in my ears, *shussshhhing* under the earplugs. Another nosebleed has dripped on the pillow before I caught the flow with my hand. Dripped down the hall a bit too. I'll have to wipe the floor.

The next night, I'm standing in the bathroom with my camera, trying to capture one of these bloody Carrie prom faces I've been having, but the light is shit, all from above. Shadows under my nose like caverns. I should set up my photography strobes in here and leave them up, ready to go, so I can catch the spontaneous carnage dripping down my face onto my nightgown front. (I should, but don't.)

These days, my legs ache when I climb the stairs. The idea of jumping on the trampoline is painful—the thought hurts my head. But it can be done, and it would probably help. Just jump on the damn trampoline with your kid, Ashley. So I pull my legs into pants and my feet into boots and pull the pants and legs and boots across the deck and down to the yard and I jump with Sloane, us bundled in jackets, bouncing with snow chunks dancing around our feet. She screeches around the mat edges as I play the monster, chasing. But the bagpipe of sadness plays on and on in my head as I jump around with my gorgeous daughter, praying she can't hear the irritating drone, *wuhhhhhhhhhh*, the soundtrack of my life now.

Big smiles, everybody happy.

I get a referral to an ear, nose and throat specialist for the nosebleeds. There are twelve people in the waiting room, in a dingy half-basement office in Acadia. The walls are grey-green. The staff look mildewed.

The doctor barely looks up my nose. "Nothing should go in there. Do not pick anything out. You blow it too much. Stop bothering it."

I say, *I get nosebleeds every day*—

He cuts me off. "Stop touching it. Everyone who comes in here, I tell them, 'Don't put your fingers in there.'"

Okay, good advice. Got it. But my issue is not a nose-picking issue. *I have a definite sinus thing. I get a lot of sinus headaches here in Calgary.*

He is already done with me. "I can prescribe you a steroid spray. It will help keep your sinus passageways clear." He reaches for a pad on the shelf.

Wait, no, no. I've been on sinus sprays before, and they give me worse nosebleeds. (Years ago—the sinus thing has been longstanding, the price of living out West).

He flaps the pad back onto the shelf with a snap. "Well, what do you want? It can expand the capillaries, yes. But if you keep your fingers out of there, you will have no problems."

Nose-picking is obviously 99 percent of this guy's day. So I can't get his full attention. *Please, these nosebleeds are different—I get them in the middle of the night, in the shower, in the car. I'm not bringing them on. They're sudden. I hear a click inside my head, like a tap turns on. And they drip, a constant flow. It's a lot of blood each day.*

He is not listening. "Get a neti pot and use it in the morning and at nighttime. The salts you buy with the neti pot are better than just regular salt—buy the neti pot salts. You don't need to see me again."

Could it be stress? I'm kind of under a lot of pressure.

"—No." He scribbles something on my "chart," the single piece of paper in a file, with my name and health-care number on it. I'm pretty sure it'll go in the shredder at the end of the day, Duo-Tang clips and all.

But I am nothing if not obedient. I go buy a neti pot and I use it. I keep it in the kitchen, near the water purifier. I don't want Sloane or Turner having to watch me drain my nose into the sink where we wash our vegetables and dishes, so I hurry, and run the hot water as I go, to swirl everything down the drain.

It's gross. And the nosebleeds continue.

I see crosshatch patterns when I press on my eyes. Crisscross, crisscross. Is that normal?

Today I shat out something that looked like a jellyfish. Is that normal?

The base of my electric toothbrush smells like cat urine. Is that normal?

I look pregnant again, but I'm totally not. Is that normal?

I have split in two. Or in three, or five. One of the versions of me has a lovely Fun Mama voice. I can hear her good ideas and gentle, jokey words for the kids. I like that woman. I'm glad she has command of my throat. Because inside my head I am slamming the fridge door over and over until it breaks, flinging dirty dishes down the basement stairs, throwing the standing fan off the porch. Revelling again in rage and mayhem.

I stop recognizing myself in the mirror. I get up to pee in the night, and as I pass the bedroom mirror, I let out a yelp. *A stranger in my house? What the fuck!* But really, nobody would break in here. We're home all the time and there's nothing to steal.

When my heart slows, I try to look around the woman in the mirror. I must be there, off to the side, or behind her, surely. I'm at the wrong angle or something.

Then I understand. That woman in the mirror is the walking multiple personality disorder I've become: the jolly-up robot, the tyrant bitch, the underperforming overachiever, the snotty-sleeved mooch, the Nazgûl priestess, the clothes-rending stigmatic, the scary clown, the worn-out mare with a worm in her brain.

Easy, girl, easy.

Really, someone should put that old bag down.

Come December, I have a twitch in my chest. Under the ribs. Just there—*ping*.

Ping ping.

Then it goes away. My broken heart is acting up—I thought I'd fixed that in England, but it's back. I'm stress-chested, suffocating again, and on who-knows-what-this-time.

I'm probably just collapsing into the gravity of my missing soul.

I'm not occupying space, I'm not here, I'm invisible, I'm gone.

46.

Most of the time now, I pretend to myself that Val is dead. It is easier to mourn her. Kinder. This way I can miss her enormously without being resentful she's not here.

Years ago, before we had kids, we had a dog. Right before Sloane was born, it attacked Turner and ripped his bottom lip off. Turner needed surgery to repair the damage, and the dog was put down. We were traumatized.

Three weeks after the baby was born, I took her out to BC on the Greyhound to visit my mom. Val picked me up in Revelstoke and we drove down the wet, empty highway to Strawberry Hill.

Watching the forest whiz past the window, I said, *I am aware this will not sound like a sane question, but I have been so shaken by what happened with the dog. It's called into question the nature of reality in general. Do I know what I know? Can I trust the people I trust? You know?*

She nodded.

So I'm sorry, but I am compelled to ask: Would Nanny or Grampa hurt the baby? My maternal grandparents were still alive then, and lived on my mom's property. We'd see them in a few hours.

"What!" Val glanced at me. I was clearly serious. So she paused. Considered the question honestly.

"No."

Would Dad ever hurt the baby?

"No. Bruce would not."

Would Michael?

"Never."

It's terrible to think something might hurt Sloane, but everything in me now is about protecting this baby. It's ferocious.

"It is."

I don't know how we could have done things differently with the dog. I don't know why it happened.

"Think of it this way, dear. That dog did you a favour. She showed you what she was before the baby came." She put her hand on my leg. "It was a grace. A blessing. She was saying: 'This is who I am. Get rid of me before it's too late.'"

This was a different way to look at the attack, a gentler read that calmed the paranoia in my midsection.

Four years later, when I was six months pregnant with Alexander, with her father (my grandfather Alec) six weeks dead and Sloane a walking, talking child, Val screamed me off her property like a shrieking oracle.

She stood in front of me, slapping her chest, pointing at my pregnant belly, yelling, "Your priorities are all fucked up! You'll be sorry! This is a mistake!"

Her words punched, stabbed: "You should not be working! Your children are your responsibility! You cannot abandon your children to other people!" Pinpoint pupils in unseeing eyes. Slap, slap, goes her matam.

I got our things and packed Sloane into the car. Turner drove us home. I rocked in the seat all the way back to Calgary. I cried for eleven days.

When Alexander was different, was missing something, was diagnosed; when I fell through the darkness and wanted the river; when I pulled us to The Institutes and brought home a behemoth; when we stumbled and crawled alone—I wanted my mother to step into my emergency, shield me from its worst bites. I wanted her to hold my hand, literally hold it, and crouch by my side while I lay breaking on my kitchen floor. I wanted her to tell me I am brave and to say she is proud of me, and "Don't worry. I won't leave you." But she couldn't. I wanted something from far-too-long-ago. I wish I couldn't remember that safe harbour, because it was everything.

When you're keening for your mother, there's no acceptable

answer to *Why didn't you soften to meet the storm, couldn't you see it mauling me?* Any "reasons" are useless paper stairs—my foot falls through when I test if they can carry my weight.

Because she knew this was coming. She should have been prepared, could have been. She knew from long before that my life would slide off the road. That's the witchy side of our family. We know things, sometimes.

In August 2008 I'm standing at the bottom of her kitchen, beside the beer fridge. I've just peed on the stick and I've come up to her house to share the result. Val comes out of the bathroom. I see her in the closet mirror, reflected, shaking her hair.

Mum, I say.

"What," she says. My mother looks at me in the reflection, then rounds the corner by the coats, comes closer. Now she knows it's something, cocks her head. "What is it?"

I'm pregnant, I say. Turner and I had just discussed taking a break, waiting six months before trying again. But I had a feeling. So I peed on the stick, and there they were, two lines. I guess I'm happy, so let's do this, we're clicking up the roller coaster hill, off we go. Val is the first person I tell.

My mother's face collapses. She doesn't actually say, "Oh no, oh no," but I hear it. Her heart calls it out.

Instead, she says, "This is a mistake."

It's a tiny moment's decision: I pretend I don't understand. *No,* I say. *We've been trying for a few months. I just got the result. It's early—I'm three weeks, I think.*

Now she says it. "You'll be sorry."

Then, quickly after that: "Wait, wait, what am I saying—congratulations, dear."

She steps in and hugs me. She holds me, bony clavicle against my shoulder, and she's holding her breath, her hair across my nose and mouth. She smells like cigarettes and face cream.

I hear her say it again, into my head: *This is a mistake.*

This is a mistake? Like how she had more children after me— John and Ainsley—and I say they were "a mistake," joking that the twins should've been put in a sack and thrown in the creek?

Or it's a mistake for Sloane to have a sibling four years younger?

Or a mistake like an accident? I already said it's not an accident—we were trying for this child.

I'm not hearing her. I don't want to hear her. She's holding me hard and we're standing at the window and I can see the cats in the flower garden over her shoulder. She's stroking my back now, trying to be The Supportive Mum. But she's not breathing. She's not breathing—she knows something.

If she knows something, she should just say it. *Just say it so I will know, just share what you know so we can know it together.*

What aren't you saying?

. . . Really-are-you-really saying there is something wrong?

Are you saying this is A Mistake?

I breathe in to say all this, and she pulls away, pushes me to arms' length.

"You get back to your girl, now." She pats me on both arms, stiff, looking not into my eyes. "You go to her. I'll stay up here, I have some things to do . . . You don't have much time left now, just with Sloane! The countdown begins!" Her voice is all in the jolly character she does.

And now she's walking away. I'm still standing there. What the fuck just happened? Did she say what she said? Did she say what I heard? She says she loves being a grandmother, but she spends no time with my girl, does not seem to love it.

You'll be sorry—I'll be sorry? Why would you say something like that? To your own daughter? About your coming grandchild? In this moment I'm thirty-five years old. If I'm going to have any more children, it really should be now. It should have been sooner than this, already.

So that happened. And later, I needed her to be a penitent prophet. If she was going to know before it happened, at the very least I wanted us to face the collapse together. I get so much of my incremental discipline from my mother, my irreverence, my bossy high horse. But she says she has her own mountains to climb. I tried to win myself over, bring myself around, forgive and forget, get on with life in tandem with hers. As Alexander grew and I shrunk, I knew I was hurting myself to want solace from someone who wouldn't give it.

And it's been years since then. After the note she left about how the world breaks people, I had to keep on, and knew she wouldn't come. So I can't call her, don't write to her. There's too much to say, and she's the one who needs to say it. I think she thinks it's kinder to stay away.

It's easier to grieve her "death." Gone, she can't disappoint me. If she's dead, I can't possibly ask for too much.

For Christmas Turner gives me pre-inked stamps he's had made with Al's information carved into them so I can just ink, then stamp, the triplicate government forms. They will save me hours.

The card reads, "Romance is not dead."

47.

"You are not going to bleed out."

I don't believe him. I'm looking this paramedic right in the eye, blinking against my bloody tears.

"This happens a lot. We see this a lot. You are going to be okay."

We are at the airport departure gate, heading to my cousin Jessica's wedding in Puerto Vallarta. Bruce bought us last-minute tickets—we weren't going, now we're going. But the flight is boarding now, and my nose is bleeding and bleeding and I can't get it to stop, and what happens if I get on an airplane and the nosebleed won't stop? What if they have to land the plane somewhere in the US because it's a nosebleed emergency? Going to an American hospital would bankrupt us.

Sloane is here, holding her baba, eyes wide. I have her hand, but I keep dropping it to wipe my nose. She doesn't like mess, is weirded out by blood and boogers and vomit, so she wants to hold my hand but there's blood drying across my sleeve from where I wiped my eye. Turner rescues her, pulling her gently, a hand on one shoulder.

I can't help her. I'm locked in on the paramedic crouched in front of me. I have no sense of humour, scared like I've never been, searching his tone. Am I being mollified so I won't freak out in this public place? Is he worried enough to hurry enough? I don't think we are getting on this flight to Mexico.

"We see big nosebleeds all the time," he says.

With the bloody pile of paper towel against my face and the useless plastic nose clip, I can't speak. I'm trying to hold a huge fragile clot in my head and breathe around the blood dripping down the back of my throat. But my expression blares: *You do not see* *nosebleeds <u>like this</u> all the time.* Sure, nosebleeds. But this is a gusher, a disaster.

I finally choke out, *Like <u>this</u>?*

Paramedics must be taught the psychology of trauma. They handle domestic violence scenes, drunk idiots who've smashed their hands on beer bottles, bad sports injuries, motorcycle accidents. They must do a whole semester on how to handle people in all sorts of situations. . . . A semester at least, right?

I'm thinking at this guy, *Are you telling me the truth? Or is it time to just cough and lose the clot, is it time to let go and just lie down and bleed?*

Because it's really just you and me in the world right now, buddy—though, yes, there are a lot of people here in the international departures wing, gawking. After four hours of bleeding I have lost so much blood that I'm dizzy. For sure, I can't stand.

You're my guy right now, it's just you and me. So tell me the truth, right fucking now.

I say none of this, but he answers anyway. "Okay, yeah no, actually, this one's big. But I mean this: *You are going to be okay.* This is a big nosebleed, yes. It's serious, yes, and you've lost a lot of blood. But you are okay, and you are going to be okay. *You are not going to die today.*"

The guy never blinks. Even if he is lying, I believe him.

Good job, dude. Fucking thank you.

I can hear a woman over my shoulder, talking to Sloane, asking her questions to distract her, getting her to answer. "Grade one? What's your teacher's name? . . . Sorry, sweetie, I didn't hear you, what's your teacher's name?"

I can't see her face, that woman. By her voice she is older. She knows how to talk to children, is probably a teacher or a grandmother. I can't thank her. But she knows what she's doing. That's everyday bravery, taking action, getting involved. It doesn't take much. Thank you, too, lady.

Hours and hours later, I'm in bed, back at home, and get a ping from Sean Nazerali after I posted about what happened on Facebook. He says, "Up enjoying some quiet time?"

I write back:

Insomnia. Despite stiff upper lip & jokey spin on FB, I was scared today. I lost a lot of blood and was badly shaken by the whole thing. Waiting for the paramedics, I could hear my eustachian tubes filling with blood, glub-glub-glub. It felt like I was drowning inside my head. The look on Turner's face when my tears went bloody was something I hope never to see again. Sloane was afraid & I was unable to reassure her.

Bleeding out my eyes = one of my best tricks so far, eh? Still heading to Mexico for the wedding if I'm cleared by the ENT tomorrow. I'm weak but okay, now just thinkitty-thinking it through. Feeling my mortality, wondering if that suffocation & loss of control is what the moments before death will feel like. Cheerful stuff like that.

x A

We make it down to Mexico in the nick of time. There is a kind of bandage in my nose that is holding the cauterized clot in place. If it falls out, I have to find a Mexican hospital. And that's not happening, because I am the replacement matron of honour (my cousin's best friend can't make it). I hold a ceremony for Jessica on the beach with the other women here for the wedding, and I give a funny speech at the reception dinner. I know my role here and I play it well.

Later, looking at the photos, I realize the bridesmaid's dress I chose makes me look pregnant. I call Jessica.

Good christ, why didn't anyone tell me?

"We thought you might be," she says. "You weren't drinking . . ."

Jess! NO! I had a sinus hemorrhage two days before the wedding! I was not allowed to drink!

The hotel is beautiful, all high ceilings and good staff, stylish and comfortable. It is a big family moment on the Mexican coast, one of far too few in this new life. My younger cousins, being fabulous grown-up versions of themselves, chase Sloane into the ocean. We Bristowes all poke each other with forks at the buffet and run down the hotel hallways together.

As I walk above Alexander, doing his crawling distances and masking along the resort walkways, my auntie Anne, mother of the bride and a no-bullshit dame, comes chortling up behind me. "You are so fucking strong, Ash," she says. "Why the hell did this have to happen to you? Jesus christ. But you're doing it—I am so proud of you."

Thank you, Auntie.

I scoop up Al and we go join the other relatives in the shade, to gossip about the family members who couldn't make it down here for the party.

But at night I stare at the ceiling and I can't breathe.

Turner is now deeply worried about me. We have arrived at a let's-do-whatever-the-fuck-needs-doing-because-Ashley-being-a-tense-snarky-asshole-all-the-time-is-getting-really-old stage. Now he is asleep beside me, warm to the touch from the sun. The half-curtains separating the room into two parts are moving slightly: Alexander is awake, silent, pulling on the fabric from the other side. I roll over. There's nothing to be done but to keep going.

Everything is shitty and I hate everything. Nothing is shitty and I should just buck up.

A suite in Puerto Vallarta at an all-inclusive in January can't fix it.

But why can't it even make it better?

After the wedding, we head to a surf beach rental with the kids for a week. At night there, while I'm staring at the ceiling, my brain is going a thousand kilometres an hour.

If I put the kids' stuff in the silver hardback, then we can use the green zippered bags for Al's program equipment and our books, but not too many books in one bag, because then they get heavy and we don't want to get dinged at the airport for extra weight fees.

I can't sleep and I can't sleep and I can't sleep, and I am packing our luggage in sixteen different combinations in my head. We don't fly home for days yet, but I can't help it. Round and round. I'm not in control of my mind anymore.

I don't want all the books in a carry-on, though. I've tried that, and you lug it onto the plane and it's stupid heavy.

Turner shifts in bed, snoring lightly now. I sit up, facing the closet.

What if we get something when we go to Tequila in a few days, like a special mescal. We can bring some home for people, gifts. People like booze. I'll need to use the silver hardback for bottles, that's the best one to protect stuff in transit.

Something flap-lands in the tree outside. Bats crinkling around in the mango branches. *Is it even mango season here? Must be, Bruce said they're fruit bats. But mango season is later in India . . .*

Okay, okay, lie down. Go to sleep, for chrissakes.

Need to get up early before the heat, to take the kids to the beach. Sloane'll be up by six thirty; she's still on Calgary time.

Okay. So, hafta make sure Turner's good wool jacket goes in the black suitcase. If the booze explodes on the way home, it'll ruin that jacket. . . . Fuck, I might forget. . . . K, wait, I'll make a note.

I pull out my phone, open the Notes app and type: *Packing— Turner's wool jacket *NOT* in silver hardback.*

Lie back down.

A motorbike blares in the distance, accelerating up the town road. Eye roll in the darkness. *Why would you drive so loudly at night? People are fucking sleeping.*

Rooster starts crowing on the lot across the street. It shuts up after one crow. Thank god.

But the packing (sitting back up, bamboo bed frame squeaking): *Eight days until we leave. I'll forget what I planned and might put shit in the wrong places. We need less stuff. Less stuff overall. All the stuff, we should burn it. Out back on the lawn, when we get home. A January bonfire, a pyre on the snow, burn up all the clothes and books and stuff.*

Turner flips over, opens his eyes. "Jesus christ, Ash. Go to sleep. Just lie down."

I lie down. He pats me, wrong hand over shoulder, pat-pat, there-you-go.

"Close your eyes. Just shhh. Go to sleep. It'll all be there in the morning."

I lie there with my eyes open. The ceiling is blue. I don't know if it's white and looks blue in the dark, or if it's actually painted blue. I turn on my reading headlamp and look up: inconclusive. Everything bleaches out in LED glare. *I'll figure it out in the morning, see if it's blue. Make a note? Nah, I'll remember.*

We have a thin knitted sheet over us—it's not so hot that the nights aren't cool here. You'd get cold if you slept naked. Ocean's a bit too cold too. Not walk-right-in warm. *Costa Rica is better for the ocean. I'd rather be there, but can't go because Peggy's at Dad's place with her kids and grandkids.*

I tilt my head back, look at the dirty window hinges. *I wouldn't want to own this house. Too far from the beach. But it's cool in the daytime, masking Alexander inside during the heat was good. And the new literacy work is going well. I don't know if he's fucking learning anything, but he looks at the cards. He likes it.*

Sloane says something in French in her sleep, across the hall. The geckos out on the porch ceiling trill as the wind shakes the leaves outside. I sit up again.

I can put the masks in the black suitcase, in those big front pockets so they're easy to access. Won't mask him on the plane. Don't want some do-gooder asshole interfering, thinking we're asphyxiating him.

So, okay: my stuff in the silver hardback, then T's in the black one, with the kids' stuff in the green zips . . .

It is eleven thirty. We have been in bed for two hours, and it has been dark for five. Everyone, everywhere, is asleep except me. And my brain goes around and around and around.

I'd like to know what you'd do if you felt like you were being suffocated. If you were anxious all the time. In this scenario, all your worries are valid—each item is real, part of your life, and worthy of worry. But not *this* much worry. Not *all* the time.

As an adult, you're allowed to drink. You can drink as much as you want, really. You probably shouldn't tell people how much you actually drink, because it's a lot more than you "should" drink, but so long as you don't drive a car or endanger your children, you can drink as often as you like. It's a free country and nobody's stopping you.

. . . Unless you live with someone like me, who sometimes drinks a lot but worries about *your* drinking if you drink a lot. Thinks about it and monitors it, quietly, like background surveillance, but then I eventually talk to you about it. And I try to be rational and supportive and truth-telling-ish about it all and we're not on the same page and we just go away not agreeing to disagree but the drinking cools off for awhile before slowly creeping up again eventually. Turner knows what I mean. So then I'm the fucking Stasi in the house, except I also want you to have a good time and have a drink now and again, and I want to drink sometimes myself, in part because drinking is fun and in part because, as I've repeatedly mentioned, I'm being suffocated all the time. Like being crushed, the hug after you want the person to let go—way after that—once you're losing your breath and getting mad but they keep going, as a joke and an aggression, those guys at university who thought it was funny to immobilize us in hugs because they were so much bigger and could prove they were strong by holding you hostage in the loud bar and they put on that "ha ha ha" look so no one would suspect your head was mashed into their shoulder, neck back, looking up and can't find the eye of anyone in the crowd who will help.

Like that, without the weird sexual threat. The anvil on my chest. That.

Drinking loosens that suffocation and I forget about it for awhile. But I also wake up at four in the morning with a headache and the dread. Then the worries crowd in—Arab Spring trying to gain traction in Syria but al-Assad isn't stepping down and oh fuck it's going to be a bloodbath; if the Lycée doesn't give Sloane that scholarship we will put tuition on the credit card but is there room?; the cat's licence is expired and I keep getting notices and ignoring them—I worry about all the things, all at the same time.

Shut up shut up shut up. Let me sleep, let me live my stupid tiny rabbit-warren life full of timers going off and midden cupboards stuffed with educational crap. With a few compatriots, companions, my favourite cousins, I could make this okay, I think. It could be a classical education, a Waldorf sort of house, homeschooling, CBC on a little radio in the kitchen, we could get a dog and I could take the kids to the river on walks — but the being-crushed is so debilitating, it chases away the me who loves my kids, it makes me into a horrible cave bear with Turner, lashing out, *Fuck you, you're free, your work your career your penis frees you from this.* I can't get anywhere toward the willow-branched cob oven outdoor faery homeschool life while I can't think and I can't breathe.

People say, "You've accomplished so much. You should be proud." I am not. This formless, not baseless, but-c'mon-haven't-we-accepted-that-he's-defective-and-your-life-is-different-now-Ashley-let's-get-on-with-things inescapable anxiety has been with me, growing, every day since he was born. It is huge. But I need to move the fuck on. We need to move the fuck on.

What will it take?

48.

Turner and I walk past the shady Mexican pharmacies for four days before I have the nerve to go into one and ask. I've never seen actual Valium in real life before, but it's right there at the counter. It isn't cheap. I buy the smallest blister pack they have: ten 10-milligram pills, at $5 a pill.

As we walk away, I'm clutching my expensive little bag of drugs, and Turner laughs. "Makes drinkin' look cheap!" I've done my share of drinking and, cheap or not, it isn't helping anymore. I'm on to mother's little helper.

I wish it didn't sound so plaintive, but the word for what I am now is "weary." Just utterly. I just can't anymore with the brain-blather and constant pointless worry. I want to focus only on what is important, right now, do that important thing and move on to the next important thing. I am a list-maker, but now the lists give me anxiety. *Have I listed everything? Can I do everything on the list? Where will the money come from for number three? Do I have to do this by myself?*

I still talk a good game for government meetings and on the phone, but behind closed doors I cannot get my shit together whatsoever anymore. My responsibilities natter-whisper in my ears all the time, each a bouncing karaoke ball going *me~me~me.* . . . And then come the tentacles to wrap my chest and push it closed. Even though in photographs this life is clearly awesome, I hate everything now.

So that night, after much worry about addiction and pharmaceutical interventions (maybe I should give in and pay for yoga?), I take a quarter pill.

The Valium works.

Within twenty minutes I'm able to think clearly for the first time in years. One thought at a time, start to finish, before a new one begins. Holy shit.

And then I sleep through the night, nine hours.

The next day, I see my children anew. They are remarkable, twinkling miracles. I jump in the waves with Sloane and land up on the beach towel alongside Alexander, all wet and exhilarated and right-down-to-my-wishbone happy. My boy looks at me with his face full of love. This is my life, like tongue on hard palette: unquestionably known, mine, yes. I remember this. I breathe all the way in, the oxygen going down down into all my alveoli.

Turner looks up from his book to check on me, and I laugh out loud: glorious man, that's mine own husband.

He raises his eyebrows at me: ("We okay over there, madam diazepam?")

. . . Yes. Finally yes.

But underneath the relief there is a sharp horror:

. . . *Oh my god. Where have I been?*

PART
FOUR

Let me not pray to be sheltered from dangers but to
    be fearless in facing them.
Let me not beg for the stilling of my pain but for
    the heart to conquer it.
Let me not look for allies in life's battlefield but to
    my own strength.
Let me not crave in anxious fear to be saved but
    hope for the patience to win my freedom.
Grant me that I may not be a coward, feeling your
    mercy in my success alone;
but let me find the grasp of your hand in my
    failure.

RABINDRANATH TAGORE, 1916

49.

We have been home from Mexico for three days. The rest of our holiday was fabulous. I slept through, every night. We drove across country to Guadalajara, past volcanoes and agave fields; the kids rode horses in Tequila; we ate churros at the side of the road. We abandoned the broken playpen we'd lugged all the way down there for Al, howling with laughter—why are we using this piece of shit, all crooked angles and gibbled railing?

So the only thing we've found in the last two and a half years that has made me feel normal has been a wildly addictive benzo-from-Mexico-slash-depressant.

Turner: "That in and of itself doesn't say anything, except that . . ."

But oh my god, Turner! I have done all the things! Massage! Running! Walking across England! Counselling . . . and I feel the most like myself right now, when I've got all sorts of leftover Valium running through my system!

"I don't think that's necessarily the only thing that's happening."

Okay, sure. I just had two weeks of vitamin D and I'm finally pulling together the non-profit mandate documents for Alexander's Fund—

"You're seeing a world that seems manageable to you fall into place for the first time in two years."

But I got a sudden, actual, real boost. With the Valium I got to pull my brain together and have a holiday from the anxiety.

"Every other thing you've done has involved people wanting too much from you when you had too little to give. We couldn't give you enough time away, there wasn't enough money to buy the things or the help for it to be enough . . ."

I tried all the things, Turner! I did meditation! I got up early! I drank lots of water! I white-knuckled it, I was faking it until I could make it. But I was DYING inside. The anxiety had entered this crazy self-perpetuating spiral. There was nothing causing it anymore. It was just this constant sputter of angst and distress, and I couldn't get away. Of course I don't want to be "on" anything. But—

"You took dramatic action while we were in Mexico. So okay, you've taken the dramatic action, and you came home and talked to a doctor, and now there's a next step: here's what you do."

The doctor told me three times, "You did the right thing coming in"—in such a tone as I was like, Do I sound that crazy?

"Well, no, but when you tell the story, he's probably like, 'Okay, over-the-counter benzos from Mexico are bad, but you've found something that works, and that's good.' He probably wants to positively reinforce that you should have tried pharmaceutical intervention months ago. Maybe years ago. Hence the antidepressants he's prescribed now."

I sigh. *I tried to get help, years ago. There were no doctors then.*

"It's okay—there's no point regretting anything that's happened. You are where you are. You feel pretty centred right now; you might still need a bit of a—"

But I'm sad that the Valium is gone, you know?

"Sure, any drug has a comedown."

No no no. I'm not coming "down." I feel like . . . what if the antianxiety drugs the doctor prescribed—I have the prescriptions in my wallet—what if they don't calm me enough . . . or . . . whatever enough? The tiny dose of Valium each day was perfect. I didn't feel high. I felt like I'd ripped off an iron maiden I'd been locked inside for years. I felt re-reborn into ME.

"If what he's given you doesn't work, then you go on to the next chapter and the next chapter. I mean, these things are . . . fluid."

Wait, I need to say this: in Mexico I got given the gift of "Here's you without all that worry and panic," and I am very reluctant to give that up.

"Hmmnnn."

Not because it felt so great to be on the Valium. Valium feels like half a drink, without the loss of inhibition. My judgment was not impaired.

Turner nods.

But being able to mute all that crazed brain-spin, and to discover that I'm still here on the other side of all this, after these years, it was a shock to come back to myself. I had forgotten myself. . . . I'm grateful! Thunderously! So I really want it to <u>work</u>*, whatever the next thing is. Because the Valium is gone now and it's obviously not a long-term solution in any case.*

"Well, people who battle serious depression their whole lives, this is something they deal with, they constantly cycle through things—

And I also worry about how much more YOU have in you— Like, are you okay? I finally have the brain space to think about how to take care of <u>you</u> *for the first time in . . . a long time! You're dealing with all this, too, and there's been no room for you to have any reaction of your own. What if I go on something else and I end up . . . slightly-different-crazy, or truly tipping-point suicidal, and then you have to walk me through that fucking* <u>next</u> *thing because I'm on some fuckin' Paxil or Prozac or something that hits me wrong . . . that happens, you know!*

"Yeah, but it's not about reaching some absolute limit. When you were freaking out every day and every day and every day, I could feel—not like 'Oh, I'm gonna have to leave,' but there were certainly periods where I was thinking, 'Well, if this is indefinite, this is going to take some serious recalibration of—'"

I bark-laugh.

"'—things.'"

"I'm gonna stop loving her and then it'll be <u>really</u> *hard."*

"It was not so much that, but we had to find a way back to some kind of equilibrium. Because our natural baseline is solid, easy. And through it all, with Alexander and just being parents and the house and the family stuff, we're still really respectful of each other and all that. And we can be in the same room together ninety-nine times out of a hundred—and I think that's where a lot of marriages really break down. Like, people probably realize, 'Actually, I don't even really want to be around you, anymore.' You know? Not in a hostile way, but 'This is just too much.' —Well, I think marriages must break down a thousand different ways, but . . . you know."

Yeah. I never wanted to leave you.

"No, and I never wanted to leave you, but I—"

I wanted to leave this. But I wanted to take you with me.

"When I felt like that at all"—the doorbell rings—"it was more like 'I am sick of dealing with this,' not 'I don't want to do this anymore.'"

Yeah.

Turner goes to see who's at the door.

I call after him, *Good talk!*

I am now armed with a non-Valium and temporary (emphasized by the doctor) prescription for the antianxiety drugs lorazepam (quick-acting, a rescue for panic) and clonazepam (longer-acting, a gentler ride). I'm supposed to start an SSRI; I have the prescription filled and I carry the little bottle with me. But I have been afraid to begin the antidepressants.

You must, by now, be worn the eff out with the relentless return of my woes. I'm sure you're thinking, *Okay, seriously? Just take the goddamn drugs, Ashley.*

And, yes. The Valium vacation put so much into perspective.

Yes, I must keep going with Alexander.

And I must protect our daughter and provide her with a happy, sane Mama.

And I've been wearing Turner out. I can't let this take my marriage.

That is what is important: us, the children, our family. Peace.

I write an email to Turner as he sleeps next to me.

So I took the first antidepressant. I had it in front of me,
right on the bedside table, for hours before I could glunk it
down the hatch. I swallowed it when I was finally
exhausted, right before turning off the light. The doctor

said for the first few weeks it would wake me up or make
me tired. And here I am, awake again at 3 a.m. I guess I'm
the type it wakes up.

Tomorrow I'll take it again, and I'll keep taking it, and
we'll work at going forward.

I love you the most.

Thank you, Turner.

x A

Turner's reply, emailed the next day from upstairs in his office.

Was sort of taking personal inventory and thought, you
know, the only thing I'm actively troubled about is your
mental health. I don't mean that to sound like pressure or
guilt, it just struck me that we need you to start getting
whatever you need to feel centred day to day, that your
life's going in the right direction. And I think we have the
room and energy in our lives for it now. It's been a long
road and we're all in it together.

Love you too.

love T

DAY 1 OF CITALOPRAM

I don't seem drugged. . . . Will I even notice if I outwardly change?

DAY 2

Strange ringing in ears, a rushing. Got afraid. Went to bed early
with Sloane and, reading to her, gradually came back to myself.

DAY 3

What has been, these past few years, can't go on.

Text conversation that night:

GRAHAM: What ho?

ME: Started the SSRIS a few days ago, now I'm nauseous

GRAHAM: Huh—do you suspect them?

ME: Yes, but I can't live being clutched by the throat with talons every day

The Valium woke me out of the nightmare, but it's addictive, not an everyday tool

So, onward, I accept that

GRAHAM: It can take a week or so to get used to, but worth persevering

You only have to look at me to see how well-adjusted SSRIs can help one to be

Ho ho

ME: Carried Day 1's pill around with me for almost a week before putting it down the hatch

It's causing insomnia, I'm exhausted

Does that go away?

GRAHAM: I never slept that well anyway, so I can't judge

But you get used to them. Give it 2-3 weeks

ME: Hehhhhhh okay

GRAHAM: Honest

If this SSRI turns out not to be right for you, get something else

Find the right thing

Be sure

ME: I fear the "right thing" might be tons of lorazepam

And giving in to being a total asshole all the time

Flaming poo bags on many porches

GRAHAM: LOL

That may be, but get what you need pharmaceutically

Stick with it all

ME: Grrr

GRAHAM: It'll be fine

ME: Keep telling me, keep telling me

GRAHAM: I will

G'night

DAY 4

Feel good. No nausea. Didn't need antianxiety meds today.

DAY 5

Spinny from lack of sleep. Long night awake. Tight in my chest by noon, needing the anxiety meds. Went spirally and can't drive.

WEEK 2

Everything feels turned down. Dampened. I speak quietly. But not very much. Few whims. Breathing well. I need things to look forward to or years will slip by a medicated calm. . . . Though that might not be so bad.

EARLY MARCH

Last night I dreamed I was swimming at night with Sloane. There were humpback whales in the water below us and ahead. I could see their huge shadows. I wasn't afraid.

MID-MARCH

GRAHAM: How you do?
ME: Oh I'm waaaaayyyyyy better
Drugs make things ALLLLLL better
GRAHAM: Glad to hear it
ME: Have you seen Almost Famous?
GRAHAM: Yes
ME: Billy Crudup is on this suburban roof, on acid
he yells, "I'M ON DRUGS!" and all the kids cheer
and the Cameron Crowe kid says, "Uh, try something more quotable for the magazine?"
so he tries but it sucks but then he grins and yells again, "I'M ON DRUGS!!"
And all the kids cheer
Then he jumps into the pool from the roof
I feel like that
GRAHAM: . . . Wow
Doesn't do that for me
But hey YMMV
ME: I'm SO fucking relieved

GRAHAM: Now THAT I understand

ME: Really it's that things have settled out

Equilibrium found

It's not euphoric

Except in the OKAY, FINALLY! LET'S GET SOME SHIT

DONE!! department

GRAHAM: Thing is, meds help you get on an even keel

Once you can stand up, you can start to fend for yourself

Which is what it's all about

ME: Yes

Though I seem to be having the weight gain side effect

A bummer, but mostly I don't care, because:

OKAY! FINALLY! LET'S GET SOME SHIT DONE!!

I'm drinking not at all and not missing it, which is awesome

GRAHAM: Good, well done

ME: Clearly I was using it for anxiety alleviation

Like a tool. Not good

GRAHAM: Anxiety is a real fucker

ME: Oh damn, must go—therapist here for Al

GRAHAM: OKAY. Love you loads

ME: I'M ON DRUGS!!!!

GRAHAM: ME TOO!

50.

They've only just begun to work with Alexander, but these high-paid Specialized Services therapists are underestimating him enormously. They've got years of experience and they think they know, but somehow they really don't. Every time they come, I have to ask them to set their bars higher, *please*, much higher.

Today is our first all-team quarterly meeting. Going around the table, each therapist and the Specialized Services program aide, Angie, are giving updates. The behaviourist reports that Alexander can't identify an egg.

What?

She explains that, in an identifier trial, he doesn't correctly point to the plastic egg three times in a row, in three session tests, over three consecutive days.

I say, *This protocol asks him to point to the egg correctly twenty-seven times in a row? Of course he doesn't do that. Al knows what an egg is. He eats them every morning.*

Them: "Well, we don't know for sure that *he* knows, unless he can do the trial correctly."

Alexander uses the ASL *sign for "egg." He asks us for them. He definitely understands the concept of "egg."*

"We can't say with certainty that the child has the concept." She turns to the aide. "Let's bring down the difficulty, go from three options down to two options for a few weeks, and probe whether that improves his accuracy."

But he still has to point at the egg twenty-seven times? In a row? No, no, no. *Come on! He's <u>bored</u>!*

Everything goes quiet for a few solid beats. We've only been working with this team for three months. All four of these women are suddenly thinking, "It is *not* working out with this family . . ."

But then the behaviourist says, "Ummmm . . . so what would you suggest?"

I lean in, earnest, glad to say it. *Go the other way. Go faster. Show him more. Demand* more *of him. The Institutes program we run is about making sure he never gets bored. I'm not surprised he won't point to the egg over and over and over. I'm sure by this point he's sick of pointing at the plastic egg. When you underestimate him, he loses motivation to keep going. Would you point at an egg twenty-seven times?*

Of course they wouldn't. They hate me today, but this meeting is a breakthrough anyway. The team adjusts their approach, I suspect initially to prove me wrong. But he excels at the higher-speed trials and the team is surprised, and they say so. They change their protocols with all their therapy tasks. It is a gradual process that takes us years to nudge along, but this meeting is the real starting point of breaking through in the conventional therapy world.

Meanwhile, in the mornings, while Alexander works with the Specialized Services aide, I rake the side yard, fixing the slope so spring rains don't keep flooding the basement. I'm very slow. I have to stop regularly to rest. I resent having to keep on fighting even when I win.

But the drugs help and my chest is loose and I can sleep at night. It's progress.

51.

We are in Toronto for the 2012 National Business Book Awards. Turner's book *The Leap* is one of three nominees. We are put up at the Ritz-Carlton, and in the hotel elevator, I recognize the tall guy who just got on with his friend.

Hey, I say.

He turns, glances. "Hey."

I have a smile for him. It's good to be in Ontario. I love Toronto. Smells right.

You look familiar. Do we know each other?

Him, sure: "No."

You never know, maybe. I don't live here anymore, but I used to, ten years ago? Or maybe from Queen's?

Him: "I don't live here."

I hear it in his voice: *Oh, you're American.*

He looks at me, questioning. I shrug.

The friend smirks. Tall guy stays neutral.

Now I see. This has happened a million times. He looks familiar to a lot of people. Strangers talk to him every day in elevators. *Oh. You're famous, right? You look familiar to everyone? You must get asked all the time.*

Him, amused: "Yeah."

I say to his friend, *So it happens all the time? And you get ignored?*

Friend: "Pretty much."

Sorry about that. Nice though, eh? Ritz-Carlton?

"Yeah . . ." They pull out their phones. They're done talking.

We reach the penthouse floor; its lounge has little sandwiches and art books and fruited water. They remain in the elevator. As I hit the hallway, I look over my shoulder. *You coming?*

"We have to go back for something."

I'm ah-very-good embarrassed: *K. See you, famous guy. And friend guy.*

No reply, and the elevator doors close. Whatever. I make for the little sandwiches.

The next morning I walk up Spadina through the grey Ontario morning, breathing the spring wind. I buy a $15 fascinator to wear to the awards thing, and some Taiwanese candy to take home for Sloane.

In the lobby of the banquet area we find and chat with a friend-of-friends. We end up at weddings and launches with her every year, and now she's at these awards somehow, a genuine smile in the crowd. Peter Mansbridge patters past, trailing hangers-on, getting ready to host the show. The room is full of PR people and media and others, craning their necks and not sipping the champagne. It's eleven thirty, a luncheon event, a weekday.

We're seated at a table with Turner's old agent Sam Hiyate, fellow nominee Conrad Black, sporting a small, orangey Band-Aid on his forehead, and the guy who ends up winning.* The $30,000 prize would've gone to extremely good use in our skinflinty house. Our takeaway joy has to be the bread rolls with actual butter. On Alexander's nutritional program we have not eaten wheat or dairy for years. We rediscover that bread and butter is glorious and decide everyone should know. We both tell Twitter.

The press are all here to gawk at Lord Black, with a few students and principled scribblers deigning to interview the actual winning author. After lunch in a quiet moment, I give Mr. Black greetings from a mutual friend, and manage to genuinely surprise this unflappable man. He hasn't heard her name in decades; it's beyond unexpected that we would have someone in common. He nods once. "And you give her greetings from me."

---

* Bruce Philp, for his book *Consumer Republic: Using Brands to Get What You Want, Make Corporations Behave, and Maybe Even Save the World*

Afterward Turner and I linger to chat with Sam and a familiar woman from The Word On The Street, watching the sad sycophancy of Canadian media chasing Conrad Black across the room, with Mansbridge fawning alongside. Eventually we wander out, leaving our name tags on an abandoned black-draped table near the door.

There is no next stage for a national nomination thing, no runner-up money. This is as second-hand glam as it gets in Canadian Books: a night amidst gold-legged furniture (don't touch the mini-bar) and a double set of curtains over a view of the CBC headquarters. We nap off the bread and in the evening walk ourselves up to Swatow for dinner, stepping around the sidewalk grocer boxes and breathing in the street smells as tiny electric charges ping in my chest: *Don't leave tomorrow. This is home. Don't go.*

If we moved back to Toronto, we could do a regular dinner with Turner's aunts, they could be part of Sloane's everyday world as she grows up. We have dear old friends here, all missed and loved and ready to throw us into regular rotation if we moved back to town. If we bought a place near the Grange (possible, here in 2012), the hospitals are just a big block over for appointments and meetings, and a doctor friend will be here from Australia next year for his fellowship at SickKids. The Nazeralis are a quick drive up the 400 on weekends and holidays.

Thrilling in this image, I hear maples shake-dancing in the wind above and streetcars calling in the distance. I could revive my stuttery Urdu with the Pakistani taxi drivers. And I might be able to pull off a few photo shoots a year, enough to stay connected, enough to place some solid work and just keep going.

Before we booked the flights, I (reluctantly) agreed this trip would be just in-and-out. We have to get back to Alexander's program, to the Calgary therapists, to the brittle morning drives to Sloane's school, to still-bare-treed Alberta when Ontario is already green and glowing. Of course I wanted to stay a few days, to see our people and rest my heart. But there are no extra free nights at the Ritz. And we're getting to an age where Turner feels awkward asking to stay overnight at friends' places. (Not me. No shame. People are welcome at my house anytime for any amount of time, so I have no problem requesting sleepovers at theirs.) We didn't tell anyone we were coming.

But the fizz in my chest is pulling, nagging, whining. *Don't go.
This is life, this is home. Stay.*

The next morning we catch the early flight to Calgary. I snuffle-
cry against the window for the first half hour as Turner rubs my
shoulder rhythmically, back-forth, back-forth, scrolling through the
social media he loaded before boarding.

The drugs don't make me completely numb.

Rules for Having a Disabled Child

1. Be grateful. For everything, including but not limited to: the
child themselves, God's gift of choosing you to be the parent of this
miracle, and any and all "help" received, which includes a) asking
how you are, b) feeling sorry that this has happened and c) thinking
of you even if they don't get in touch.

2. Take care of the child yourself, but also have a job or inheri-
tance that pays enough that you don't have to ask for any money
from the government, your parents, or friends and strangers in the
form of fundraisers. (If you must raise money, make sure it involves
booze.)

3. Don't be sad. It makes you a bummer to be around.

4. Don't be angry. Nobody likes angry people.

5. Don't be articulate about the situation. You'll make everyone
uncomfortable.

6. Don't have any other life complications. Make sure your
marriage, other children, family relationships, friendships, finances,
accommodations and career are all unmentionably copacetic.

7. Do not get upset when people suddenly unfriend you on
Facebook and vanish forever.

8. Follow all advice, and seek out advice from lots of people,
but also take all advice with a grain of salt.

9. Keep track of every medical visit, every doctor, every specialist, request forms you don't know about, fill everything out in triplicate by the end of each month and mail it to the right department,
when the government messes up the reimbursements make sure you
have forensic accounting to prove they "owe" you even thousands

of dollars from last year and don't get mad, stay on top of appointments, always arrive on time and don't be irritated when the specialist comes in late (even very, very late, even nearly 3 hours late): refer to points #1 and #4.

10. Become an expert on your child's condition, and have the capacity to envision what will be required before it's necessary, and arrange to get your child on all the inevitable waitlists, and provide documentation including the full text of firewalled academic studies as they come out.

11. Already have what you need. You cannot now reap what you've sown to this point in life. You are plowing all new furrows for yourself, and responsible for all other duties as required.

The Druids fought the Romans by yelling. Here were people not at all blind to the damage a sword could do. Yet they chose to face encroaching armies by screaming at them. They screamed not in protest, but in *defiance*. (Apparently it was completely terrifying.) And against soldiers with spears and swords, the Druids sometimes won. When I am yelling NO on Alexander's behalf, I sometimes think of the Druids. Because sometimes we win only because I say NOOOOOO, loud and long.

I think I am frightening, too, because there is obvious justice within my NOs. Trying to cut services to a severely delayed child is wrong. The bureaucrats we encounter are foot soldiers enforcing policy and rules. I think they probably want to be good. But so many people are casual cowards. When I say NO it points at their collusion with everyday injustice. They resent that I demand they put themselves in my place and wonder, "What would I want, if it was me?" They don't want to think about that. They resent the reminder that it can happen to anyone. That you don't earn your success while others earn their sorrows. So much is down to luck and the choices of other people, beyond your control.

Turner says, "I'm not sure if it's partly a result of you being a child actor and being bullied for years, or because you had cancer at eighteen and beat it, or that you've lived overseas. . . It's probably a combination of all of it, plus being the oldest child. You have a confidence, a sureness about you that comes across—not as aggression or arrogance, necessarily, but you're someone who knows exactly what they think about certain things.

"You're not immoveable and you adapt and change your mind and you're willing to listen to other people and consider what they say carefully. But I've watched people react emotionally to your certainty. In what are intellectual conversations when they think *they* should be the authority, but find you've clearly thought through everything they could say and are way beyond it now; that you're working on things at a level they haven't gotten to, they react defensively. Loss of control makes a lot of people small and ugly. And there's no question that you being a woman plays into it. People defer to *me* in those conversations. And I'm like, 'Talk to *her*.' I can walk into a room and just own it, as a man. People give it to me. But they fight *you* for it, even though you would do a way better job."

Hehhhh. *People like to test themselves against me. I am a whetstone.*

"That's an apt metaphor," Turner says. "I think you're right. People suck."

People do suck. But we need them anyway.

(You do, too.)

52.

Most people at a remove from special-needs children don't know how to talk to people like me. You don't want to say something that will hurt us, or set us off, or "cause a problem." So here's a primer of topics that are fair game:

- Your kids.
- Your kids' school(s).
- Your kids' sports.
- Your kids' Halloween costumes.
- Your kids' latest exploits.
- Funny things your kids said or did.

These are all good. Really. So long as you listen to the answers when we offer them ("Oh hey, coincidence, Alexander was Yoda last year, too!").

But if you're concerned that people like me will be made secretly jealous by these kid-related topics, how about:

- Your spouse.
- Your pets.
- The book/movie you recently enjoyed or hated.
- Furniture design.
- Dentistry fuckups.
- Weird Australian slang.
- Your car. Your first car. Your worst car.
- The strip mall-ification of Canadian cities.
- Politics.
- Religion.

I really don't care about some slight you experienced at the hands of the service industry, but I'll listen the first few times you start in on that stuff. If you've got nothing else, sure, fall back on those complaints. Everyone loves to gripe.

Some topics, however, are not okay.

And with that, let me segue here to That Time I Did a Bad Thing—conversationally, I mean. It's February, and we are at the Banff Springs Hotel. We are having a celebratory brunch for John Johnston, who has received his landed immigrant status in Canada.

(I'll say in my defence that it was a trying drive up here, with the kids, from Calgary. And that I am very aware that the Springs' brunch buffet is $40 per person, even though I won't be the one paying for the beautiful food going into my stupid mouth, which is good because if I'd had to pay, we couldn't've come, even though I love JJ and want to celebrate him and his landed immigrant status. Of course I do. But Turner has been on a writer's retreat at Berton House in Dawson City, Yukon, for two months, and he has another month to go, and yes, I said—insisted—he should go, that I could handle it. But we're still broke, and Sloane fought me on the boots she should wear to Banff for sledding later, and today I am at the end of my rope.)

I am seated at the far end of the table, surrounded by some of Sara's relatives, who are discussing good buys on the stock market. I try never to look Plainly Bored. But they've been quite awhile on this one thing. We could've been talking about Hagar Shipley or canola varietals or training dogs—anything other than money. Then they move on to mutual fund ROIs. I feed Alexander and drink coffee and sit there listening to the ambient affluence with truly nothing to add. Sloane is way at the other end of the table with Sara's kids, joking and having a fine old time.

I've been to the Banff Springs lots over the years; Val claims I was conceived here on a ski holiday my parents took in January 1973. This restaurant used to be the Rob Roy Room, a bloody-roast-beast dark-curtained dining room our parents would bring us to for practice with cutlery settings and French onion soup. I always make a point to run my hand over the huge carved beaver newel that overlooks the sunken dining floor. I feel at home here. It's not that.

Now Sara's uncle or cousin is telling us all about his son's new pension. Proud, pointing. The son whose pension being discussed is across the table, nodding, smiling. Younger than me by a bit, little kids on his other side. The uncle says, "Yep, great benefits at this job, his take-home is about doubled, with the perks, eh?" The cousin guy with the new pension nods more.

I drink water, push a lemon Danish into my face. Chew.

I am the only person who hasn't spoken yet. I should have taken Al to the toilet, gone to the stairs to pet the beaver newel. Or shoved my way into the kitchen and put my hand down on the pancake griddle. Anything. Because eventually, unavoidably, and of course, they now look at me.

I am right there, obviously not a relative—John's friend or something? Must be. The polite next step inevitably comes: "And what's *your* line of work?" They all turn.

And I sit up straight: "Oh, me?"

I take care of my son [gesturing at Alexander]. *He's disabled and there's a lot of bureaucracy around making sure he gets therapies. No pay, though.*

. . . Oh no. I'm just going to say it all, aren't I.

I used to work, but that's over. If I was working with someone else's child with my qualifications—I have a master's—I'd make $77 an hour to coordinate therapies, or more if I was still a photographer, but I'm working with my own disabled kid, so there's nothing. My husband works, but it's sort of only three-quarters of the time because of the therapies, and he's a journalist and journalism has kind of collapsed as a thing over the last decade.

I continue piling scrambled eggs into Al's mouth and keep talking.

We fundraise to keep our son's program going. Because if you pull one parent out of the workforce and you double all the costs in the household? There's kind of a predictable result. We're going into massive debt, obviously, so we do these fundraisers and we started a non-profit society to help with that stuff, but there's just not enough money in the system because it's a closed loop. We feel weird asking people to help us, and then when we sometimes do ask, some people say no, so I get really wrapped up in this sort of terrified timidity, and that doesn't help us raise money either.

That's enough. They get it. Please stop, Ashley.

But to answer your question, I don't "work." I mean, obviously, I work all day, but I'm not paid. I'll never have a pension. And RRSPS—you were saying your employer contributes to yours? Yeah, me—no employer. So no contributions. I'm thirty-eight years old and I think I have . . . $11,000 in RRSPS? And that's mostly from when I worked as a teenager. Ha! Haven't been able to contribute since 2003. And pensions . . . when I worked at the government, before kids, they took deductions off my paycheque, but I'll never make enough to even get the Canada Pension Plan, I don't think.

Okay, fine, go ahead and scorch the earth. Might as well.

So yeah . . . pensions and benefits, it's like hearing about a fantasy world. It's like yachting around BVI—I'll never go there. The Alberta government keeps trying to cut off the funding to his programs, so we have to fight that *every year. There's a lot of logistics. We could never pay out of pocket for what speech and occupational therapy costs—it's bananas. I have no income at all. Anyway, hearing you talk about retirement, I'm like yeaaaahhhhhh—that'll never happen for me. Ha! Never!*

I finally stop, take a sip of water.

They all look slapped.

After a few beats a (more) polite (than I deserve) female relative asks me a few follow-up questions, but I physically wave her off. All-together-now we accept that I've bombed this whole end of the table. As one, they turn to face the other way and began injecting comments into conversations at the opposite end.

I shovel sliced pineapple toward Alexander and sit there miserable, like the shitty asshole I am, because I am a shitty asshole. Drugs don't fix shitty assholery, as it turns out.

"Just because they're true doesn't mean you should say some things," Jana would tell me. But I don't think Jana gets jealous and petty, and I definitely don't think she wants to burn the world down. She's a better person overall than I will ever be, but she does give good advice.

I just don't follow it.

I complain throughout this book about being trapped at home, but I still seem to travel a lot, right? This week, mid October of 2012, I pack up Alexander and Sloane and fly to San Antonio, Texas, to attend the first North American Kleefstra syndrome family meet-up.

My thumb hurts in the joint where it meets my hand. I've been thinking it's the stress of this gathering, collecting in that tiny spot. It was hard to grab a pen and sign my name on the customs declaration. Perhaps my thumb is trying to stop me from writing all this down. In the hotel at night, Al folds the corner of a few pages of my book and gives a long, quiet "aaaaAAhh." He wants my attention but doesn't know how to ask for it. I imagine him thinking, *I know She doesn't want me bending book pages. That's the rule in our house. I'll try that and maybe She'll notice and make me stop.* I do.

I am wrung out from discovering the ins and outs of all these families, these other North American Kleefstra kids, from the stories about fights with doctors over G-tubes and seizure meds and constipation remedies and funding assistance. I'm chilled by the spectre of one Kleefstra child whose parents keep him physically restrained because he has an unpredictable temper. (He is eight years old, and they say he can tear a bath towel in half.)

This morning I had a worry-vision of Alexander, grown up big and unpredictable, his eyes too far apart, teeth splayed. "Mama, Mama," he says in a low voice, this big Lennie of a man. He is half-shaved because he fought me off that morning, and is trying to put his head under my shirt to play "in the tent." He's thirty-four years old and I'm seventy, and my feet are hamburger, all purple veins and cracked edges. I can't run anymore because I didn't run enough, while I could.

The potential of these visions tastes sad when I fully wake. They have the tang of rainwater caught in the glass you left outside overnight, the thin saliva when you're nearly done crying, too tired of yourself to go on. These are old worries, regurgitating with new force for the last time, hopefully. *Keep at the program, Ashley.* It's what staves off these dark visions that lurk, waiting, whenever I let up.

Today I'm bloated from eating weird Texas hotel food, and worn down by Alexander screaming earlier over the rock in his shoe and Sloane being maddening, not wanting to talk to the other siblings-of-Kleefstra-kids who obviously want to be her friend. I pushed Sloane into the corner and snarled in her face this afternoon. Afterward I was wrapped in a kind of euphoria. A horrible release—this way to the dark side. I apologized a bit, but not enough. A few minutes later I could hear Sloane making-it-better for Al in the other room, doing the hand puppet saying, "Henneh! Henneh! Kiss! . . . Oh, dissss-GUS-ting!"

She made all the right voices, untainted and undiminished by my assholery. A big sister. Protecting him. God, I love her. *Do better, Ashley.*

We Kleefstra families exist in similar but separated universes, managing or not, each on our own. Some of these families live with horrible situations. Divorces with ugly support battles. Some kids' eyes go in different directions; one girl's jaw is skewed to one side so her mouth doesn't close properly. There are complex wheelchairs and many children have had multiple heart surgeries. We've seen complications Alexander doesn't exhibit that obviously take years off those other children's mothers' lives.

It's hard to situate our family's future inside this mashup of strangers. The parents are everything from sugar glider breeders to military personnel; there's a cattle rancher, a lapsed Amish family, teachers, a dude who does agricultural machinery maintenance, a design engineer at Nike. These forty-two families are a true cross-section of the population, white people and Latinx and Black and Asian, and even a woman who came over from Ireland. I meet two other Kleefstra families from Calgary, here in Texas.

I explain, casually at lunch tables and more boldly in boardroom meetings, how Alexander's Institutes program works, our successes with this approach. I recommend that everyone read the *What To Do* book. Many of the mothers already know my views from posts in our online Facebook groups. Nobody wants to hear more than the basics of what we do for Alexander. It sounds complicated, I know. (Fuck yes, do I know.) But there are children here it could help. After a few tries and some rolled eyes, I get the picture: *Please, shut your mouth.* (I'll keep on telling them about it in the years to come, online and at these sorts of get-togethers, and share that I didn't believe it myself, that it's incremental and impossible, and that it works. Because I'm a stubborn asshole that way.)

In the breakfast room I watch the Kleefstra babies sucking on bottles full of milk and think, *No . . . no dairy, don't . . .* But we are here to join the family. I drag Sloane around and make her shake other parents' hands. I do love hearing the different accents, feeling out each new family's groove. It's only later, back in the room with my kids, when I am sloshing around in upendedness, that I am all weird and wondering wtf all over again.

These American families really don't want to know how we've cut to the chase of helping Alexander. Call it a cultural difference. Their children are somehow blessings just as they are. Most of them think the main problem is the list of identified symptoms their children show, like being unable to poop, getting fevers or having absence seizures. I ask around and learn that none of these children can read. None of the parents are teaching them. There are, of course, nuances to each family's situation that I don't understand because we are all still strangers to each other. So much is not shared, I'm sure. I show Alexander his vocab flash cards at breakfast anyway, half-defiant, trying to be an approachable example if other moms want to ask what I'm doing, and half-working our rosary of Institutes interventions to keep myself calm.

It's evening again, and now I am slumped on the bed here in Texas, watching *The Walking Dead*, thinking about the other families, thinking about us. Does Al seem like a zombie sometimes? When I say, *Go to the door and get your shoes*, he starts opening and closing kitchen drawers, looking at the ceiling, touching his hair. But put a hand on his shoulder, steer him a little, nudge him toward the door with, *Al. Go to the door and get your shoes.*

"Door. Dor-dor-dor. Hmm. . . . Dor. . . . Dor."

And off he goes.

Now he's in the shower and I perch on the bathroom counter to think. He's been in there so long the bathroom is melty, the walls sweating. Bless all hotel water boilers, everywhere. I hear the Angry Birds theme song playing outside the bathroom door, where Sloane is camped out with the iPad. I peek around the shower curtain at my soggy little boy, still baby-like though he is now three and a half years old.

You want out?

He doesn't look up at me, but clearly says, "Ah": *yes*. Then he keeps splashing.

You want out? If you want out, stand up.

"Out-out-out." He makes the hand sign for "out." Then returns to splash-flapping his hands in the water, staring at the drips running down the side of the tub.

Al. If you want to get out, stand up.

"Mama." (Yes, he can say it now.)

Stand up. C'mon. He doesn't move.

I turn his shoulder the smallest bit, reach and gently place his left hand on the edge of the tub.

And it's like a switch flips to "on." He can suddenly do the rest, both hands go up, he pushes himself to standing, turns, brings a foot up to the tub ledge for leverage, reaches for me.

There's some kind of thought-action barrier in his brain. A problem with initiating. What part of the brain does the starting-of-things-you-want-to-do? That flash of action, spurred by desire? That's a real something, and all these Kleefstra kids have a problem with it.

Medicine will identify it someday, name it, know what part of the brain or which gene is responsible, might be able to fix it. Right now, these kids are here in this world but not of our world. When I ask other families if they've noticed this initiation delay, they act like I'm asking about Igbo verb tenses or the molar mass of manganese: not their department. I think they just think their kids aren't paying attention. I drop it.

Now I wrap Alexander in the hotel towel and put another over his head. *Are you the Obi-Wan Kenobi baby?*

"Mama."

Hello, lovey love.

"Love." We are smiling, nearly nose to nose.

"MAAAAM!" At the sound of my conversation with Alexander, Sloane has realized she's bored with the iPad.

I call, *Yes, lovey? Let me get Alexander out. We can talk in a sec.*

I rub a hole in the steam of the mirror. A year ago the mirror was frightening. I was breaking, and I looked like it. Now I'm okay with the dark rings under my eyes, the lines coming in around my mouth, and even the jowls. After all the aches and sleeplessness, the years of stress-drinking and now tamping down the panic with antidepressants and Ativan, I'm older and I look older, and I do not mind. We outlasted the years of fever visions and self-harm dreams and super-strength despair. I have earned this face. That is me, in there.

And that dimple at the back of my knee makes me smile—*I'm finally fat*. My family always said I was, but now I really am. Small price. I wedge Alexander into the corner of the bathroom countertop and pull all my curls, shiny in the Texas bathroom humidity, up into a messy ponytail at the top of my head. Great hair, so there.

Although I hate all things a lot of the time, I do finally believe we will escape the hell. That the keeping on and The Institutes' program will continue to save us. That the Specialized Services speech therapy will help him learn to talk, really talk. All of it together, going on day after day, will keep us going.

From Texas we are returning home to an election campaign. Turner's putting his principles into action and is running for office, which is why he didn't come to San Antonio with us. He's out door-knocking today in Calgary, bundled up in the photos, the weather turning toward winter again. But tonight I will take the kids on a drive through the San Antonio suburbs with the windows down, ignoring the health insurance and malpractice law billboards, breathing in the warm air. Then I'll get email addresses for those two Calgary families with Kleefstra kids.

Tomorrow we go home. I don't want to, and I have moments of slippage where I worry what the future holds for Alexander, but I'm not actually afraid, anymore.

53.

INT. KITCHEN—NIGHT

Counter is strewn with EDUCATIONAL MATERIALS (math dots, large word cards, intelligence bits), a plastic MASK, a COLD PACK.

ASHLEY leans on the counter in front of a LAPTOP, typing an email to Jenna. We see the screen:

> ASHLEY (EMAIL)
> *Hey JennaLem—this acupuncture college in Hilo! <Link>*
> *Also we got dehydrated banana snacks yesterday*
> *and I thought of youuuuuuu & Sharkey's farm.*

Ashley hits "send" and closes the computer.

Pulling out, we see the kitchen is a disaster, many POTS with things cooking and cooling, and CAT FOOD DISH tipped on the floor, with dry food scattered.

Sinead O'Connor's reggae album plays in the background: track 11, "Untold Stories."

Ashley goes to turn off elements, puts lids on things, wipes counter—closing up shop for nighttime.

We hear a voice calling from upstairs, eight-year-old SLOANE.

SLOANE (O.S.)
MAAAAAM!

ASHLEY
(calm, yelling because of the distance)
WHAAAT!

SLOANE
Just wondering where you are!

ASHLEY
I'll be right there!

Ashley gathers onto a TRAY: HALF AN APPLE, a dish of
OLIVES, 2 TEACUPS and a full TEAPOT, a CLUB SODA
BOTTLE and her IPHONE. She turns off the music and picks
up the tray.

POV Outside kitchen window: Ashley walks away from the
crazy-full sink. She hits the light switch at the kitchen doorway. Darkness.

INT. BATHROOM—NIGHT

Shower is running, kids inside. We hear splashing and children-in-
bath noises. Mirror is half-fogged and the room is a little bit
steamy: the shower has only been running a short while.

Ashley is sitting on the toilet, looking at her phone. Then she looks
up, notices the BATHMAT still on the tub edge.

ASHLEY
Sloooooooane. Get that mat off there! Seriously! It goes on the
floor!

Sloane's hand slops the bathmat down to the floor, goes back
behind the curtain. The mat is half-soaked.

Ashley looks back at her phone.

On her phone screen: she is texting her cousin TANYA.

    ASHLEY (TEXT)
How was the Italy accelerator?

    TANYA (TEXT)
Awesome. Might be going back in June if the data supports more work

    ASHLEY (TEXT)
Do you feel ACCELERATED?

    TANYA (TEXT)
DEFINITELY

    ASHLEY (TEXT)
I woulda got dizzy, me

Ashley looks up, then around for the TOILET PAPER.

    ASHLEY
Sloane . . .? Where's the toilet paper?

Sloane pulls back the shower curtain. We see a little girl standing inside, with a smirk on her face, and the half-obscured head of a second child sitting in the tub below.

    SLOANE
Heh? Al pushed it into the bathtub, and, y'know, things happen.

Sloane flings a soggy roll of toilet paper out of the bathtub. It hits the floor at Ashley's feet. It is ruined.

ASHLEY
Don't put the toilet paper roll on the bath edge, k? Put it on this wire shelf on the other side, here.

SLOANE
Okayyyyy.

INT. BATHROOM—LATER

Shower sounds continue. Mirror is now fully fogged and the room is very steamy: it's obvious the shower has been going on for a long time.

Ashley is standing naked, clothes at feet, bra and one sock still on. She is looking at her phone.

On her screen, an email from Turner:

TURNER (EMAIL)
Sloane can come to Whitehorse on the 21st. I rented a car, so we'll drive up to Dawson and have wheels.

Sloane emerges from the still-running shower shiny wet, dripping, standing on the wide tub edge. She looks pleased with herself.

Ashley wants to finish reading the email, nudges Sloane back toward the shower.

ASHLEY
. . . No. I don't want you out here. Go back in.

SLOANE
I'm done.

ASHLEY
(looking at phone, wants more time)
Go back in and brush your teeth in there.

> SLOANE
> (not having it)
> I want to brush my teeth *out here*. I have to *floss*.

Ashley gives up, puts the phone on the bathroom counter.

> ASHLEY
> Fine. Fine.

INT. BATHROOM—LATER STILL

Inside shower, naked Ashley is bent over four-year-old ALEXANDER, one hand on his wet head, other hand holding TOOTHBRUSH and brushing his teeth. Alexander stands with his mouth open, compliant, looking up at her.

We see Alexander's MEDICALERT BRACELET on his wrist.

> ASHLEY
> (singing Raffi song in time to the toothbrushing)
> Iiiiiiiiii . . . wake up in the morning
> at a quarter to one,
> and I still don't know what to do for fun,
> Soooooooooooo . . .
> I brush my teeth.
> Ch-ch-ch-ch-ch-ch-ch-ch-ch-ch

INT. MASTER BEDROOM—NIGHT

Queen bed has four large PILLOWS and a fluffy white DUVET.
A warm-spectrum bedside lamp is glowing. The scene is cozy and comfortable.

Sloane sits in bed, hair snaky and wild, naked from the waist up, snuggled under the covers, below. The now-empty kitchen tray is beside her, on the bed.

Teapot, cups, and dish of olives are on the bedside table. Sloane takes a bite of the apple half. Chewing, she opens the club soda and takes a big swig from the mouth of the bottle. She is also holding a PENCIL and looking at a CLIPBOARD in her lap.

Sloane screws on the bottle top and, without looking, puts it on the bedside table, concentrating on the clipboard. She is the picture of nimble childhood ease.

INT. BATHROOM—NIGHT

Shower is off, curtain open. Bathroom fan running, low.

Alexander stands on the tub edge, being rubbed dry by Ashley. They play a game with a TOWEL: Peek! Then Ashley rubs Alexander's hair. Then peek again, rubbing head again.

> ASHLEY
> Peek! *Bonjour, monsieur!*

> ALEXANDER
> *Boh-jouuu!*

We hear Sloane calling from down the hall.

> SLOANE (O.S.)
> MAAAAM!

> ASHLEY
> We're coming, Sloane! . . . Just! Wait!
> (to Alexander)
> Ready?

> ALEXANDER
> Ah!

INT. HALLWAY—NIGHT

Ashley is drag-carrying a towel-wrapped Alexander, their discarded clothes bunched up under her other arm, a HAIRBRUSH in her teeth.

One of Ashley's boobs is uncovered and flops in time to her steps. Very glamorous.

An orange and white Siamese cat, LOKI, walks past, going the other direction, and howls.

>   LOKI
> *Reeeehhhhhhhhhhh*

>   ASHLEY
> Shut up, Loki.

INT. MASTER BEDROOM—NIGHT

Ashley places Alexander on bed, naked, in towel. She then goes to move FOLDED CLOTHES from the changing tabletop and puts them away in drawers. She is clearing a spot for Alexander.

>   ALEXANDER
> Me me me!

>   SLOANE
> Mam? You know that book we're making? I found a name for it.

Ashley looks over. Sloane turns the clipboard around. The page reads *Quest for the Moon!* with a half-filled storyboard below.

>   ASHLEY
> That is great!
> (throwing hairbrush at Sloane)
> Here, brush your hair.

Ashley puts Alexander on the change table.

> ASHLEY
> Rubs?

> ALEXANDER
> UH. . . . Back, back, back.

Alexander turns over.

> ASHLEY
> K.

Ashley gets MASSAGE OIL out of drawer, squirts it on Alexander's back, rubs it around.

> ASHLEY
> (singing)
> Sacha's gettin his baaa-aack rubbed.
> Baaa-aack rubbed. Buuu-uuum rubbed . . .
> Sacha's getting his le-egs rubbed
> Before he goes to behhhhhhd . . .

INT. MASTER BEDROOM—LATER

Alexander is now in pyjamas, Ashley and Sloane are wearing nightgowns.

> ASHLEY
> K, Al, say "good night, Sloane"!

> ALEXANDER
> Soney.

> SLOANE
> Wait! I want him to walk on my back!

ASHLEY
No no, he doesn't like it.

SLOANE
Let's try again. Maybe he will.

ASHLEY
Okay.

Sloane is arranging herself prone on the bed. Ashley lifts
Alexander above Sloane, but he pulls his legs up. He starts to
whine, then yelp.

ASHLEY
Sloane, look at him. Look.

SLOANE
(face down)
Come on, Al! Walk on my back!

Alexander is squealing. He doesn't want to walk on Sloane's
back.

ASHLEY
Okay. He won't. Good night, Sloane!

Sloane flips to a sitting position.

SLOANE
I want to HOLD HIM!

ASHLEY
No . . .

SLOANE
(arms out, reaching, dramatic)
The BOBBY! Gimme the bobby!

    ASHLEY
. . . Fine. OKAY, yes. Yes. Here.

Ashley hands Alexander to Sloane. Sloane squooshes his
face. Alexander begins wailing.

Ashley does not want to interfere in the sibling "love."
She straightens the change table blanket, grabs damp
towels from the bedroom floor and throws them out to
the hallway.

Sloane has her face right in Alexander's face.

    SLOANE
Moogoo-moogoo!

Alexander's protests tip toward real crying.

    ASHLEY
Okay, that's enough. Gimme him.
C'mere, Al. Good night, Sloane!

Ashley scoops up Alexander and he stops crying. Alexander
gets down from Ashley's arms, walks unsteadily toward the
door. Ashley steers him by the head.

    ASHLEY
Sloane, say good night to Al.

    SLOANE
Good night-ee, little bobby!

    ASHLEY
(to Sloane)
Brush your hair, love.

INT. KIDS' BEDROOM—NIGHT

There is a tallboy SHELF stuffed full of books beside an IKEA
BUNK BED. The bottom bunk has boy covers and two BLUE
STUFFED HIPPOS. A modern glider ROCKING CHAIR is in the
middle of the room.

>   ALEXANDER
> Bed. Bed-ah. Bed-ah.

Alexander heads directly for the bottom bunk.

>   ASHLEY
> Hey, come back here. Get in your machine.

>   ALEXANDER
> Scheen.

>   ASHLEY
> Ma-*chine*.

>   ALEXANDER
> Ma ma ma.

>   ASHLEY
> (pointing to her mouth, emphasizing the syllables)
> Maaa-*chine*. Maaa-*chine*.

>   ALEXANDER
> (looks lovingly at Ashley)
> Scheen scheen.
> (beat)
> Mama.

>   ASHLEY
> Only one "chine," love.

Ashley lays out a fabric JACKET with long Velcro fastener
strips and cords attached. Alexander lies down on the
jacket and Ashley helps him put his arms into the jacket
holes. Alexander then lies face down, compliant. Ashley
sings as she folds up the jacket sides, putting the Velcro
ties in place.

    ASHLEY
(singing)
I love the mountains, I love the rolling hills . . .

Sloane suddenly arrives, hair obviously unbrushed. She climbs
over Ashley and Alexander, around the rocking chair.

    SLOANE
Comin' through! Gotta find some books!

Sloane goes to the bookshelves. Ashley is still putting ties in
place.

    ASHLEY
(singing)
I love the flowers, I love the daffodils . . .

    ALEXANDER
(face down, muffled)
Love! Love!

    ASHLEY
(singing, sliding Velcro ties)
I love the fireflies, when all the lights are low . . .
(to Sloane)
Sloane, we're getting out of here in a sec. Pick something and
let's go. Go brush your hair.

Sloane is perusing a bookshelf.

SLOANE
Hmmm . . .

Ashley pats Alexander one-two and he knows the jacket is
done up. Alexander belly-drags himself over to the bed, the
cords that attach the jacket to the RESPIRATORY
PATTERNING MACHINE trailing behind him.

Ashley goes to a box at the foot of the bunk bed and flips a
switch. We hear the respiratory patterning machine pump
begin to hiss rhythmically, squeezing and releasing. It is loud.

Ashley looks over at Alexander but speaks to Sloane, louder now.

ASHLEY
How about a Babar? Bottom shelf.

ALEXANDER
Book. Book.

ASHLEY
Not you, Al. You had the rub, it's bedtime. You got your hippos?

Ashley puts the stuffed hippos near Alexander's head.
Alexander reaches for one, pulls it closer.

Sloane chooses a book and nearly leaves, but turns back.

SLOANE
Mama, we pick up the kitten on Saturday, right?

ASHLEY
Yes, love. Hundredth time. New kitten, Saturday. Okay? . . .
Get out of here!

Sloane leaves. Ashley pulls Alexander's covers up.

> ASHLEY
> Okay, Al. Gooooood niiiiiight.

> ALEXANDER
> Love. Lovey.

> ASHLEY
> I love you, my love.

> ALEXANDER
> Love.

> SLOANE (O.S.)
> MAAAMAAA!

> ASHLEY
> (to Sloane, over shoulder, projecting very loud, calm)
> I. AM. COMING.
> (leaning into the bed, kissing Alexander on the head)
> Good night.

> ALEXANDER
> Mama.

Ashley turns off the light. We pull back to precede her out of the room. She steps out into . . .

INT. HALLWAY—CONTINUOUS

Ashley pulls the bedroom door shut. She stumbles, then kicks the damp towels farther down the hallway toward the bathroom.

Ashley gives a huge SIGH. Not unhappy, just: "parenthood."

Loki appears, walks pointedly around the towels.

LOKI
Reeehhhhhhh

ASHLEY
I know. . . . C'mon to bed.

54.

We all fail, over and over. At the end there's no great triumph other than the cobbled pile of life you've built and earned. Before Alexander came to me, I failed people, and I've failed people throughout the period covered in this book, and since, and I will continue to do so.

People will continue to fail me, too, and they'll fail you. The act of living is just putting your will on display, one foot in front of the other. Of course, there are starburst moments and scenes that only want for a swelling violin score. But life is about the long game: deciding what you believe in, tattooing it on the palm of your hand and slapping yourself in the face with it every time you're tempted to slip. It's the only way to earn your peace.

Tara Nazerali said, "You're painting your way across a room."

That's it, that's life, for all of us. Every day you get up and you put a coat of paint on the wall. Each layer is infinitesimally thin, imperceptible. But month after month, and year over year, the layers build up. Slowly slowly, you move yourself to the other side of the room.

All we have are stories now.

And so, big exhale—I can't believe it (it's a trick, it's a trick, somehow they'll take it away)—Al is going to kindergarten. With kids nearly-his-age (we held him back a year). With regular kids.

I took him there, to the school. I want to end the book by saying he went up the stairs by himself, turned and waved, and went through the door into the rest of his life.

But it didn't go like that.

We walked together in through the side door and used the kinder-garten stairwell, stopping at the hooks outside the classroom. There were a lot of other children, and Alexander ignored them. I got his jacket off and the teacher brought him inside. I sat at the back of the class and the aide helped him with the potty four times that first morning. I was sure they'd think, *Oh god, is this how it's going to be every day?*

But they were okay. It was okay. The morning passed quickly. Another child fell, and two cried. Alexander understood circle time and sat quietly. He knew what to do for most things, but kept repeat-ing, "Go home, go home, all done." We hung out with some neigh-bour families after school was finished and let Al go down the playground slide, over and over.

Then we walked home. He was hungry, and we were both tired. The afternoon therapy program began at one o'clock, so he had time for lunch and some reading. I needed to go to bed and decompress. I lay there wondering if the morning was a success or a "meh," or what. Didn't come to any conclusions.

Life with a disabled child is not very romantic or specifically uplifting. All parenthood is a long road with—you hope—a boring "ending." And taking everyday care of a special-needs kid doesn't end, it's just a forevermore world of mystery and worry and vulner-ability. But the stories you tell yourself, the ways you find to frame the narrative, stave off the black dog.

With Alexander's entry into school, I'm coming to the end of an incarceration. This is the place past which I couldn't see.

If you think all the worry wasn't warranted, this book wasn't for you. Sorry to bury the lede like that. Or maybe you're a narcissist dickhead—consider that. It's one thing to focus your life on a deep understanding of coffee or craft beer or the golf courses of Scottsdale. It's quite another thing to hear a call for help and say, "I hear my name, but surely they didn't mean me." Do better. I mean it.

So to it: they said he might never walk, and would certainly never speak. But he can, and he can even read, and the world has a (flawed, but safe) place for him to go for a few hours a day. For now. And on that first day of kindergarten, Alexander walked up the stairs all by himself, turned and smiled and waved at us, and then he went through the door.

EPILOGUE

Mexico, 2014. Day trip to Colima, to visit some kind of market. We're driving cross-country, straight toward the volcano. Little wisps of smoke are puffing out the top. Later in the day it will burp hard, and we'll stop at the side of the highway to take photos. The locals will laugh at the gringos pointing at their familiar caldera.

We enter Colima in the afternoon, but it's one of those narrow-streeted towns with no signage and high courtyard walls, doors opening right onto the road, tiny children hugging the sides as cars pass, and dogs lying in the strips of shade, inches from passing wheels.

It's way past lunchtime. The car occupants (we) are hypoglycemic, and the air conditioning isn't working, so all the windows are open. Everyone is getting quieter and quieter.

Turner rolls down and down this road. Now there are longer spaces between gates and trees, and no toddlers on the verges, and we realize we are heading out of town.

We should turn around.

"Yeah."

The road is very narrow, and sandy on one shoulder, and we're worried the wheels might get caught. A ten-point turn commences, and the manual steering creaks. The hangry judgey thoughts get louder and louder. Turner suggested this drive, this town, this market, and he drove, and we can't find the market and, what the fuck, this is his fault.

Then, into the angry silence of the car, Alexander blurts, "Ha! Dada made a mistake!"

Bruce is sitting between the kids in the back seat. He is floored. "Did you hear that?"

Yes, Dad.

"No—did you hear what Alexander said? He said, 'Dada made a mistake.' That's *totally appropriate* to the situation!"

Of course. He knows.

My dad, mouthing silently to himself: "*Wow.*" I am watching him in the makeup mirror.

Within minutes we find the actual square, the actual market. Another car is leaving, so we luck out on parking and all leap from the car. Bruce says, "I'm taking Al," and marches away with our little boy.

Later, I see them, far away across the market crowd, sitting together at an outdoor restaurant. My dad is leaning across the table, talking to Alexander animatedly, pointedly. Telling him things.

Alexander is watching his face, delightedly: "GRAM-pa!"

At last.

POSTSCRIPT

I completed the manuscript of this book while locked down in the initial pandemic quarantine of 2020. The irony of finishing a book about being trapped in my house while being trapped in my house did not go unfelt. And I'll admit some schadenfreude; everyone has just had a little taste of the toxic impacts of intense isolation. I feel seen.

It is now August 2020. Alexander, eleven years old, is down at the river with Turner, throwing rocks—something he does every day, for several hours a day, in spring, summer and fall. Al can definitely throw farther than you can from a seated position (like, surprisingly far). He can read most of what's put in front of him, especially the travel journal we keep together. He loves Björk, ceiling fans and swimming in the ocean—especially in big, unpredictable surf. Until the pandemic, he attended the local English-language public school with his peers, supported in the classroom by an aide. He still receives Specialized Services, and we still—nine years and counting—work with the same fabulous therapists, who unfortunately appear here only in the scene where I push back about Alexander identifying an egg twenty-seven times in a row.

We still run Alexander's Institutes program every day, at a much-decelerated pace. Including and especially the nutritional program diet of no wheat, soy, dairy, corn or sugar, and with leafy greens in every meal. When we were at another Institutes revisit several years ago, I told Charlotte (the staff person who was insistent that we never feed him ricotta), "Tell new program parents that the diet is *easy* after only five years!"

I maintain a chronicle of Alexander's adventures and issues surrounding special-needs children and parenting on Facebook. It's called "Alexander's Friends." Check us out.

Sloane is now fifteen, a pitcher for the Alberta provincial baseball team and an avid boulderer (a type of rock climbing). She is also a newly learner's-permitted driver, currently out practising her highway gear-shifting technique with Grampa Bruce. She is a fabulous writer, plays the drums, and is involved in social justice issues, not least as a special-needs advocate among her peers.

My husband, (Chris) Turner, has put out three books since the end of the time period covered here:

• *The War on Science: Muzzled Scientists and Wilful Blindness in Stephen Harper's Canada* (about the Conservative government's defunding of science research and rejection of evidence-based policy, Greystone Books, 2013).

• *How to Breathe Underwater: Field Reports from an Age of Radical Change* (a collection of his award-winning magazine work and other essays, edited by Jeet Heer, Biblioasis, 2014; winner of the City of Calgary W.O. Mitchell Book Prize).

• *The Patch: The People, Pipelines, and Politics of the Oil Sands* (a journalistic primer and comprehensive review of the how and why of Alberta's role in the global energy economy, Simon & Schuster, 2017, and winner of the 2018 National Business Book Award: whoo!).

If you don't already follow Turner on Twitter, you should: @theturner. He's a fricken delight.

My Own Blood was supposed to be published in early 2020. It wasn't the pandemic that derailed its original timeline. In January 2019, in the midst of the last draft, I was simultaneously diagnosed with both kidney cancer and heart failure (the latter a long-term impact of the radiation I received in 1991 as treatment for Hodgkin's lymphoma). The scene where I describe "falling through the cowl" in the bathroom and being unable to get up—I didn't know it then, but that was an actual heart episode. I experienced this kind of blackout many more times throughout November and December of 2018, the blackouts accelerating in frequency and intensity until I was finally admitted to hospital. In the end I lost a kidney and gained a pace-maker, and the book schedule got pushed out a full year, to 2021.

This book is the story of what happened to me as the parent of a disabled kid, who I became inside that pressure cooker. So much more happened than could fit in this book, ridiculous injustices and bureaucratic cruelty and sudden shocks that jolted us hard. In 2017, I was diagnosed with PTSD caused by some of the events described in this book and other, related, experiences. (Recently I've found EMDR/ART therapy and strongly recommend it to anyone with unresolved trauma.) Being overwhelmed by despair and suicidal thoughts is not uncommon among people with disabled kids. Frankly, I'm surprised more parents of special-needs children don't abandon their families or kill themselves. Legal drugs are indeed a tool and may be a huge support to you. Don't dismiss them out of hand.

So much of the worst of my mental-health lows could, however, have been alleviated by a form of basic household financial support provided to parents with a severely disabled child. It's impossible to keep your head together when you can't afford to pay your power bill. I still worry about other parents, especially folks who speak English as a second language, new Canadians, and BIPOC people, who face huge struggles in wrangling the system. We are extraordinarily lucky that my father, Bruce, has supported us through the worst times. Without his love and generosity, we would certainly have lost our house and our marriage may not have survived. Most people do not have this kind of emergency saviour in their lives. The role of govern-ment is irreplaceable for most families with a disabled child, and dis-investment in support programs is devastating for real people like us.

Stress is a killer. Remember the naturopath who treated my knees with the magic machine after Alexander's diagnosis? She said the kidneys are the seat of fear. I was terrified, every day, for years. It is not surprising that this eventually resulted in cancer. Studies show that social support and increased availability of services for special-needs children create far better parental mental and physical health outcomes. I hope I am in the last generation of parents who are so isolated; since the normalization of everyday texting, and the rise of curated social media to provide robust online communities, life has become much less lonely for so many of us. But Canada—and the world generally—needs to get a fucking grip on the fact that we are failing our most vulnerable, and the stress of that cannot be dealt with politically as an anti–Field of Dreams (where if you ignore it, it will go away). We are here and we need *federal* policy to address the rights and needs of both disabled and elderly Canadians, and to prioritize the integration and wellbeing of these populations through interventions in housing, city planning, schooling and recreation. Not province by province. At the national level. Immediately. (I have a master's in Planning, and I'm available for consulting.)

This book never mentions (until right here) that when Alexander was born, my mother, Valerie, was grappling with the recent loss of her parents, who had lived with her until just before they died. She and Michael had been neck-deep in their needs for nearly a decade, overseeing my grandparents' complicated health conditions while enduring their intense personalities and related drama. The scene where Val screams me off her property took place a month after her father, Alec, passed away (our son is named after this grandfather, predeceased a year earlier by my grandmother Gloria). That February, Sloane and Turner and I were visiting my mother (along with my cousin Jana, and her mother, Aunt Bonnie, who was executrix to my grandparents' "estate") to assist with the multifaceted bureaucratic and practical matters people leave behind after they're gone. Val was unpacking decades of unresolved anger with her parents right when I began to need her the most. Though I was well into my thirties, I wanted and needed my mother, badly. In the moments (unrecorded here, but there were some) when I was a rational human being, I was, of course, aware that Val was worn the fuck out, done with the thought of being a caregiver of any kind to anyone.

But children are selfish and never grow out of needing their parents' undivided attention. I am no exception. She couldn't and didn't want to be, but I wanted my mom with me in the trenches anyway. It was an impossible and destructive impasse. This story has moments that make my mother look very bad indeed (Bruce is redeemed by his obvious generosity and sheer persistence despite his own terror, and my dickhead siblings know I love them), but this is an incomplete rendering of my mother. She is a strong, stubborn, hilarious, wise and complicated human being. Much of my parenting of Sloane, and particularly of Alexander, comes directly from Val's playbook. She may have stayed away even if she hadn't had a decade of caregiving prior to Alexander's arrival, but that recent history didn't help. I can't imagine she'll love how she's portrayed herein, but we both know these things happened. Although her prophesies tore us apart, I thought about them daily. On some plane, Val perhaps sacrificed our relationship to help save her grandson.

Women bear the disproportionate burden of managing external and internal pressures on the family unit. Right now we are seeing twenty years of gains in workforce participation disappear into the maw of the Covid-19 pandemic. As a feminist and a mother, I am especially horrified by the deliberately destructive provincial government (under Premier Jason Kenney) that's dismantling the social safety net in Alberta—drastically undermining the school system, privatizing health care, and defunding social supports specifically for special-needs children and adults. Alexander does not have a properly secure future in Alberta or anywhere we could move to. Shame on "leaders" who sacrifice our priceless social safety net for political gain, and fie upon the people who elect politicians and parties that abandon and prey on the powerless.

Our financial situation is still not great. We cannot afford to maximize Alexander's RDSPs. Many of our bills still have to be handled in a strategic order. (People, pay freelancers on time!) My pants usually don't have holes now, but we still live very close to the edge. What will happen if/when Turner and I can no longer care for Alexander? What if Sloane predeceases Al? I think about these questions every day. Every parent of a special-needs child thinks about these things every day.

There are almost no residential placements for special-needs adults in this country, anymore. Most special-needs "group homes" house only two to four people, "supported" by aides who come in periodically. The residents have limited interaction with the community, which means they spend a lot of time alone. I want instead for Alexander to be surrounded by a huge community of people who are both like him and neurotypical. The L'Arche model and communities based on the philosophies of Rudolf Steiner seem to be good ways forward. (Another excellent model has been, at various times in its history, the St. Amant Centre in Winnipeg, MB. Originally a residential hospital for Down syndrome children, this facility has a school, a pool, farm, guest huts where residents had sleepovers with their families, a post office, canteen, and many wonderful public-facing programs that brought the community inside and outside the centre together.) Sadly, political impotence, real estate prices and systemic bias against disabled people prevent enough of these kinds of communities from being established or properly supported in most of urban Canada. Those that exist have twenty-year waitlists. You read that number right.

The true solution is a wide-scale embrace of radical hospitality in our society. Reinvestment in and humane expansion of our social safety net: it's *time*, hosers. No one should be without clean water or fucking homeless in this country, even temporarily, and even metaphorically.

At the micro scale, your time and energy and open mind can change the world for a disabled child and their family. Stop pretending everyone is on a level playing field. Neuro-diverse and chronically ill people are all around you. Disabled kids and their families are isolated. Be brave. It costs you nothing. Be the parent who encourages your child to invite my kid to birthday parties. Say hi on the street when you zoom past. Speak up and support us and our kids at school council. Make an effort. The personal is political. It means everything to us.

THE THANKINGS YOUSE

If Chris Turner and I hadn't done this together, it wouldn't have been done. Turner held me aloft (for years, and over and over) as the flood-waters rose and swirled and retreated and flooded again. This test of character was an ass-kicking. When prolonged crisis steals your mate and renders them unrecognizable, keeping on with no end in sight is a noble choice. Turner, there's never thanking you enough for every-thing you are, including being a much better and kinder person than me (and loving me anyway). You believed this book would happen long before I did. Thank you, my best love.

Sloane, thank you for coming first, and for being my wise teacher and my darling lovey girl.

Thank you, Alexander, for your grateful soul and hard work. I remember the feel of your little bum under my hand, through my skin, in my belly. You chose me and I choose you.

Thanking my mother-in-law Margo Turner (née McConnell) of Antigonish, Nova Scotia. For loving Alexander all the more for his challenges, and for unconditionally pledging your life to our kids. You are an anchor for these children. For swooping in time after time, when I've been suddenly sick, and during the 2012 by-election cam-paign, and whenever our lives got too complicated and expensive to properly function without help. Thank you for carrying us and keep-ing everything going. "Aw, it was nothing!" you always say. But it's everything.

Thank you very, very much to my agent, Hilary McMahon, who was a genuine believer from the start. Your gentle hand, professional grace, and quick laugh were everything I never knew I could earn.

Thank you to Anne Collins, my editor, who championed this book at Random House Canada, and Penguin Random House Canada. It's been a gift to know you and work together. A gigantic thank you for everything.

Thanking Jana Johnson and Jay Way, my children's guardians and our beloved cousins, for being exactly who you are. You were with us at the very start of this new world and at our sides every step from far away. I've never had to censor what I am with you.

Thanking Gillian Deacon, whose girlfriendship changed my world. Your warmth was so singular in those dark early days.

Thanking Gillian Irving, who came before us and lighted our way to the Institutes. We couldn't have done it without you. You said it would be okay, and you were right.

Nicole Schön and Kevin Cunningham—you crazy kids are irreplaceable. The perogies-making parties and fireside potlucks and open back doors were everything.

My dear cousins Jessica Bristowe, Tanya Roussy, and Jenna Roussy held my hand (virtually and really) through many of the shittiest bits. Thank you for these many years going around the sun together.

Thanking Garry Black, whose stalwart friendship and viper wit was much appreciated. Your legacy here remains an everyday treasure. And thank you, Alli Sinclair, for walking in the damp alongside me and being someone I knew I could tell. We miss you both every day.

Thanking Meike Wielebski, whose early support and continued work on Alexander's behalf is matchless. You are a dazzling, fabulous friend, my only German, fellow truthteller. In my next life I will be taller and more chic so we can match, I promise. I love you.

Thanking Moonira Rampuri, who gave us loving maps through the maze. Your nazar hung on Alexander's incubator in those early hours and has kept him safe since. I will always fight on your team.

Thanking Sara Simpson, without whom I would have burned my house down. You are a lioness and a sister. You and I both know so much more happened than could be set down here. I remember it all.

Thanking Naheed Nenshi, for asking me to do the campaign portrait for your amazing 2010 run for mayor, my last gig before the quicksand closed over my head. You gave me a tiny part in something that got bigger than all of us and ricocheted across the years.

Thanking John Johnston, whose lovely baritone was a touching discovery in the early days of Alexander's patterning program. Your steady friendship has been a gift for three decades.

Thanking Margaret Drummond, Alexander's godmother. I love you, love you. And thanking Steven Drummond, Alexander's godfather. You are so game. Come over anytime.

Thanking Angad Singh Chowdhry, Tara Chowdhry, and Neelam Mansingh. You sat on my shoulder and whispered in my ear, making the years of isolation much less lonely.

Thanking Kelsey Thoms, who stepped into the chaos and helped make it work. The electrical panel scene was the only one of many bananas moments you witnessed. We are so grateful you were with us that first year of the program.

Thanking Lisa Adams, my children's self-appointed fairy godmother, whose regular Tuesday-night phone calls from Australia were pivotal. You brought loyalty to my life and anchored the presence of god when neither felt familiar.

Thanking Becky Rock and Terry Rock, stalwart friends and neighbours. I think a lot more went on in the background than we know. You've been in our corner since we first put out the call. Thank you.

Thank you to Greg Compton, Jules Fisher, Christine Gibson, Janet Tapper and Ania Wojciechowski—friends and doctors who stepped up and encouraged me to take my own health firmly in hand, and who followed my progress with gentle enquiries and no-bullshit reminders.

Many, many thanks and much love to Jessica Sawatzky, who entered our world with an open mind and a glowing, willing heart. There are no words sufficient for the consistent joy you brought our boy. You are always welcome in my home.

Thank you, Sharon Monkman, who came every week without fail, with a smile on your face and stories and laughs. Thank you for living your son's love and your own, and bringing them through my door.

Thanking Chlöe Atkins, Aruna Mitra, Callum Atkins-Mitra, and Zephyr Atkins-Mitra. We were so lucky to have found you at last. Your insight and love buoyed us and felt like home. Thank you for choosing us, too.

Thank you Allison Lockhart, Alexander's "Zin-Zin." You are with us every day in Alexander's drawings and swimming and love of windshield wipers. Your devotion to Al was a gift to us all.

Graham Smart, your visits and wisdom made me feel utterly normal and hugely blessed when blessings and normalcy were in terribly short supply. Thank you for everything you are.

Thank you to Alicia Carvajal for showing up and showing up and showing up. Thank you for knowing when to break character—you always say the right thing, especially when the chips were down. Maraming maraming salamat po, ikaw ay hindi kapani-paniwala.

Thank you, Carla Bellamy. You are one of a kind, grace under pressure. Thank you for coming to Philly and helping make it feel like an adventure. We cherish you. Part of this book was compiled in your Harlem apartment. Thank you so much for that gift of time and solitude.

Thank you, Amanda Delong and Mark Raheja. You kept coming, and made a point of it. *Hello, what's really going on, tell us.* Over and over. That shit counts. Big time.

Thank you, Morgan Corbière, for the many pummellings and safe dark tunnels. Your friendship was such a sanctuary in the darkest years. You are a brother through the looking glass.

Thank you to Shannon Lenstra, boss lady and bestie, who saw my situation in all its complexities and decided, "Ladies gotta stick together." Your cackle makes the world better. Thank you for slinging your arm through mine.

Thank you, Nita Pronovost. You gave me the key to the door.

Sheila Nazerali and Cherry Robinson, Tara Nazerali and Sean Nazerali. Thank you for always being the people I wanted to tell. You will recognize in parts of this story those long, long emails I wrote to you, trying to figure it all out for myself. You have been my companions in a huge world for decades, the best of friends, my chosen family. Thank you. So, so much, and even more.

Thank you to Valerie Bristowe and Michael Garvey, for the offers of assistance and household items, and the sewing of requested costumes and hassock covers, the painting of mirrors, the socks and birthday packages, gardening guidance, and for the little table we have used in Alexander's programming since the first. You reached out many times when I could not respond. I think we broke each others' hearts. I know you were thinking of us the whole time. I am very sorry we could not have you with us on this journey.

And finally, enormous thanks to my father, Bruce Bristowe. You nailgunned stability onto our shambolic post-Alexander domestic lives, bringing furniture and wine and trips and takeout and unrequested advice that shored up our edges over and over like sandbags in a years-long hurricane. Dad, you came even when you were afraid, and you came even when you didn't believe. That's courage, and love. Thank you.

It's impossible to properly acknowledge the hilariously hardcore, irreplaceable Institutes for the Achievement of Human Potential in Philadelphia. They were our unshakeable light in the darkness. If you have or know a child with special needs, the groundbreaking work of the Institutes and now, Doman International, can help them. Thank you to the staff and directors of IAHP, especially Janet Doman, and Alexander's advocate, now with Doman International, Rosalind Klein Doman.

Running an Institutes program is a huge, life-altering undertaking that forces you to mine your community for more help than you think you can possibly muster. We couldn't have done it without dozens upon dozens of volunteers, a few of whom came every week, and many who helped just once. Every single time was important. Thank you.

Patterners & Programming

Christina Bahry
Sean Bristowe
Lindsay Bumanis
Juliet Burgess
Maggie Carter
Dana Corkey
Claire Cummings
Lina diGregorio
Ian Drummond
Margaret Drummond
Stephen Drummond

Zoe Ferguson
Paul Haavardsrud and
    Allison Mader
Serene Ho
Heather Jaques
Jana Johnson
Fong Ku
Tracey Loston
Cheri Macaulay
Heather Maitland
Jan Markley

James May   Graham Smart
Sandra McIntyre   Marlene Smith
Sharon Monkman   Janet Tapper
Trina Nestibo   Kelsey Thoms
Moonira Rampuri   Mary Troicuk
Brad Roulston   John Turner (Jr.)
Jessica Sawatzky   John Turner (Sr.)
Sara Simpson   Margo Turner
Abigail Speltz   Jay Way

Many people are paid to get involved in your life when you have a disabled child.

Alexander's Therapists and the Home Team(s) 2009–2020:
Alicia Carvajal   Melanie Gushnowski of
Jessica Sawatzky   Brilliant Beginnings
Kelsey Thoms   Trish Lawrie
Catherine Mercer   Allison Lockhart
Achievements Unlimited   Angie Maeots
Jenn Beattie-Lutyk   Andrea Satviet
Erin Diana   Kelty Wattie of Calgary Youth
                                    Physiotherapy

Family Supports for Children with Disabilities (FSCD):
Ashley Cooper   Diane Anderson
Jacalyn Dickson   Annette Titsing

Thanking Alexander's various medical team members, in particular Dr. Thiru Govender (Pediatrics) and Dr. Micheil Innes (Genetics).

Thanking the medical staff and particularly the nurses of Calgary's Rockyview Hospital NICU, where Alexander lived and breathed (with much support) for the first two weeks of his life on the outside.

Thanking Dr. Ken Sato, family friend, for the ninja quip in the ultrasound suite. Very well timed.

Grudging thanks also go to the now-defunct Infant Team at the Alberta Children's Hospital in Calgary who, in 2009 and 2010, were still trying and mostly failing—due to management-designed understaffing, budget restrictions, and exploding caseloads—to deliver essential services to families with disabled children in southern Alberta.

Having a child with disabilities is expensive.

Thank you, Calgary's Charitable Foundation for the Family, and Dean Koeller, for providing the charitable umbrella under which Alexander's non-profit society rests. We established this non-profit society, Alexander's Fund, to provide a framework for and due diligence around fundraising on behalf of Alexander's therapies and family supports. If you would like to donate funds toward Alexander's programming, we'd gladly accept them in exchange for a charitable tax receipt thanks to this singular organization.

Alexander's Fund Past and Present Board of Directors:

Meike Wielebski	Judith Heidbuurt
Terry Rock	Jana Lait
Becky Rock	Julia Berry Melnyk
Dana Corkey	Chris Wharton
Zoe Ferguson	

Alexander's Philly Kitchen Party Fundraiser:

Natalie Bach	Garth Kennedy
Bev Bruce	Grant Kennedy
Trevor Day	Marsh & Donna Kennedy
Chris Demeanor	Lorrie Matheson
Donovan Deschner	Britney McKinnon
Gillian Dickie	John Rutherford
Hillhurst Sunnyside	Mark Sadlier-Brown
Community Association	Jenny Saarinen
Maryanne Campbell and In Gear	Chris Wharton
Mark Hopkins	

Thank you to the Masonic Lodge of Calgary, for honouring Past Grand Master Alec Horbow of Shuniah Lodge (Thunder Bay, ON) with help for his granddaughter in my hour of need.

The Canada Council for the Arts funded a large visual arts project I had underway when Alexander was born, providing me with the opportunity to create a last set of work prior to Al's diagnosis, along with many incredible memories, which sustained me through some of the darkest days described here.

This book was completed thanks to the generous financial support of the Banff Centre, Ms. Haidenger-Bains and the Patricia Clifford Scholarship Fund, the Alberta Foundation for the Arts, the Woodcock Fund of the Writers' Trust of Canada, the Calgary Arts Development Authority, numerous JRB Starving Artists' Bursaries, and the insight and vision of Shannon Lenstra of Kon-strux Developments in Calgary.

I strongly recommend Pema Chödrön's perfect book *When Things Fall Apart*, a compassionate and essential buoy for anyone whose life is smashed by sudden crisis. Thanking Patton Oswalt, whose bit, "The Sad Boy," helped me finally consider anti-depressant medication, which saved my marriage and, probably, my life. And thank you to Maria Bamford, whose bit with "I want a cup of boiling hot water . . . with ice, and I don't want the ice to get all tiny. Okay . . ." makes this weird and often horrible world bearable.

Thanks also to those who saw us through, inspired us, and cheered us on:

Our neighbours of
   10A Street NW
Caroline Adderson
Natalie Bach
Jennifer Banks-Doll
Susan Barth
Jennifer Bascom
Bill and Debbie Bennett
Vera Bennett
Patricia Bravo
Caitlind r.c. Brown
Ian Brown
Juliet Burgess
Jowita Bydlowska
Joni Carroll
Pratap Chahal
@chonnymo
Jodi Christensen

Nancy Close
Gregoire DPdL Compton
Jim Conley
Ian Connacher
Karen Connelly
Sandrine Darcel
Kate Dimbleby Howe
Marc Doll
Anthony Ewen
Druh Farrell
Greg Frankson
David Friese
John Frosst & Andrew Frosst
Janice Galloway
Wayne Garrett
Dale Genge
Björk Guðmundsdóttir
Sheila Heti

Karen Hines

Greg Hollingshead

Joshua and Courtney Horbow

Stephen Hunt

Cheryl Johnson

Jonathan Kane of the Naked
  Leaf, Calgary, AB

Sarah Kapoor

Tasleem Kassam, ND

Daniel Kirk

Landmark Worldwide

Kiese Laymon

Dan Libman

Nancy Loranger

Claire Lording

Cory Mack

Alexis Bahry Mackenzie

Bruce Manning

Anne Kowalewski Mason

Lee Mason

Matt Masters

Mate and Zsuzsa Matolsci

Elizabeth May

Colin McAdam

Mary Elizabeth McConnell

Sandra McIntyre

Ashley Mitchell

Sean Monkman

Deanne Mudd

Patty Nowlin and the staff of
  Sunnyside Natural Market,
  Calgary AB

Adora Nwofor

Natalie Odd

Peter Rishaug

Keitha Robert

Leor Rotchild

Brad Roulston

Devyani Saltzman

Lauren Simms

Julie Ann Simpson

Brian Singh

Natalie Sit

Amy Shaw

Lane Shordee

Jared Shore

Jessie Steinberg

@theevilp

Todd Tarantino

Jenn Thompson

Terry Thoms

Cathy Thornton

Dagmar Timmer

Pépé Traça

John Turner (Sr.)

John Turner (Jr.)

Mario Vaira

Elizabeth Wakely

Maggie Weaver

Anne Yourt

Melissa Zulli

And finally, the kids who light up Al's world. Thank you Tarn, Betsy, Nikolai, Laura and Emerson, Kai and Bo, Zephyr and Callum, Ian and Alex, Astrid and Annika, Jake and Max, Carrick, Thorsten, Liam, Azeez and Zaid and Abdul, Patrick, and Kaiden.

ASHLEY BRISTOWE has been a radio producer, development planner, and a portrait and editorial photographer whose work has appeared around the world in print and online, from *The Globe and Mail* to *Raygun* to the *South China Morning Post*. In the 1980s she was the child star of ACCESS TV's *Harriet's Magic Hats*. She lives in Calgary with her family.